Stranger in Their Midst

Stranger in Their Midst

Pierre L. van den Berghe

UNIVERSITY PRESS OF COLORADO

Copyright ©1989 by the University Press of Colorado
Niwot, CO 80544
Printed in the United States of America
All Rights Reserved
First Edition

The University Press of Colorado is a cooperative publishing enterprise supported, in part, by Adams State College, Colorado State University, Fort Lewis College, Mesa State College, Metropolitan State College, University of Colorado, University of Northern Colorado, University of Southern Colorado, and Western State College.

The paper used in this publication meets the minimum requirements of the American National Standard for Information Sciences—Permanence of Paper for Printed Library Materials. ANSI Z39.48–1984

Library of Congress Cataloging-in-Publication Data

Van den Berghe, Pierre L.
  Stranger in their midst.

  1. Van den Berghe, Pierre L.   2. Ethnologists — Zaire — Biography.   3. Ethnologists — United States — Biography.
I. Title.
GN21.V36A3   1989   301'.092 [B]   89-14732
ISBN 0-87081-202-5 (alk. paper)

To my mother, Denise Caullery, who started it all; to my wife, Irmgard Niehuis, who bore it all; and to my sons Eric, Oliver, and Marc, my half-shares into the future.

CONTENTS

Acknowledgments — ix

Preface — xi

1. Kith and Kin — 1
2. Growing Up in War and Peace — 24
3. A Colonial Interlude — 60
4. The Farm — 85
5. Reluctant Soldiering — 100
6. The Left Bank — 125
7. The Yard — 137
8. Apartheid — 153
9. Scrambling Up the Academic Ladder — 180
10. Africa Again: Kenya and Nigeria — 201
11. Back in Seattle — 231
12. Los Caminos del Inca — 248
13. Academic Wanderings — 272
14. Some Musings on Human Behavior — 289

ACKNOWLEDGMENTS

Autobiography is, in a sense, protracted acknowledgment, so I can be brief here. My main debt goes to the members of my family who have had to put up with me. As several of them are wont to remind me, I am not easy to live with. But I want to thank specifically those who read portions of the manuscript in draft form. From their many comments and corrections, I discovered how fallible human memory is. They include, besides my immediate family (whose main contribution was to try to keep me honest), several persons whose names appear in these pages and a few others besides: Heribert and Kogila Adam, Nick Colby, Harvey Dyck, Ulf Hannerz, Hilda and Leo Kuper, Richard La Piere, Jacques Maquet, Ben Orlove, Naomi Pascal, George Primov, Ramón Ruiz, and George and Louise Spindler. As a confirmed materialist, I should acknowledge the all-important contribution of my typist, Matt Fenner. In my entire career, I never encountered anyone who combined such skill, intelligence, and good cheer in converting my unsightly scribblings into a beautiful typescript. At the University Press of Colorado, Luther Wilson wisely encouraged me to tone down some of my broadsides, and Alice Levine did an elegant, sensitive job of editing my prose, and purging it of superfluous italics, quotation marks, and capitalizations. And, of course, the bucolic setting of the Center for Advanced Study in the Behavioral Sciences at Stanford made my task an exercise in hedonism as well as narcissism.

PREFACE

Autobiography requires even more of an apology than most other books. The personal motivation for writing one is obvious enough and goes to the root of the human condition. Having evolved a large self-conscious brain, we are cursed with the certainty of death. Finding that prospect disagreeable, we strive to achieve two forms of survival beyond the confines of our perishable carnal envelope. The first we share with all life forms: we strive to survive and reproduce biologically or, as evolutionary biologists put it, to "maximize our fitness." Because we are partially conscious animals, our reproductive drive is at least in part a matter of deliberate choice, and our modern technology of contraception has recently widened the scope and reliability of that choice. Yet, quite clearly, the linkage between reproduction and consciousness in our species is a fluke, a by-product of developing a one-and-a-half liter thinking machine in the last couple of million years of hominid evolution. Most life forms manage to reproduce quite well without consciousness. Indeed, as Richard Dawkins so eloquently put it in *The Selfish Gene* (1976), the diploid organism is an ephemeral assemblage of genes. In sexually reproducing species such as ours, the individual organism cannot even be said, in any strict sense, to reproduce *itself*. The gene is the replicating unit, and the organism is merely a carnal vector programmed to play its constituent genes' game of self-replication. We are mere gene-survival machines, and, with each descending generation, our "true self"—our genome—becomes diluted by one-half through sexual reproduction.

Reproduction, highly satisfying though it still is for most of us is thus a very imperfect answer to the quest for immortality. Not only do we fail to pass on to our descendants our individual consciousness of self; our very genome becomes inexorably watered down from the little half-selves we call our children to our little quarter-selves (our grandchildren), and so on, down the generational pipeline. This is better than nothing, but hardly a total answer to our existential Angst.

The second path in our quest for immortality, or, perhaps better, our rejection of mortality is, of course, survival in the consciousness of others through what anthropologists call culture. In the broadest sense, all of human language and culture constitutes a projection of self onto others, from the most limited, trivial, and ephemeral to the most widespread and enduring. The problem with this potentially almost limitless expansion of self is that the consciousness of others is a scarce commodity, entry into which is fiercely competed for. The result is a highly pyramidal distribution of "expanded selfhood." The overwhelming majority of us only survive in the memory of a few score of intimates and then only for three or four decades after our death. Only a few thousand individuals survive the test of a million memories for a century. Each of us parasitizes, in a sense, the consciousness of others, but vastly different numbers of others and for greatly variable lengths of time. Immortality is highly relative! Of the two types of immortality, the biological is relatively democratic (especially for females), while the cultural is highly elitist.

Perhaps the most presumptuous of all cultural products is autobiography, an insistent invitation to others to focus their attention on oneself, with amusement as the principal lure. The risk is substantial, of course: typically, far fewer people are interested than the author thinks. Vanity is not an easily marketable commodity: the supply invariably exceeds the demand.

There are several things that make one interesting, but they all boil down to fame or notoriety. These, in turn, are achieved either directly by being at the giving or receiving end of important or unusual events or vicariously by associating with famous or notorious people. My claims to any of these are quite unprepossessing. I am far too powerless to write a *Mein Kampf*. I derive a certain perverse intellectual pleasure from outraging people (*épater le bourgeois,* as the French say), sometimes including, unhappily, members of my family; but I am no match for Xaviera Hollander or Elizabeth Taylor. I have never been the Prince of Wales' valet or Brigitte Bardot's lover. To be sure, I have met my share of famous or prominent people, but not long or intimately enough to sustain an interesting flow of gossip or anecdotes. I have had my share of interesting and unusual experiences, but nothing fascinatingly horrible has happened to me, so, even if I had the talent, I could not produce a *Gulag Archipelago* or a *Cancer Ward*.

So what have I to offer and to whom? Such small measure of notoriety as I have achieved has been almost entirely confined to the academic community, principally in the social sciences, and most specifically in sociology and anthropology. Obviously, this is where my audience lurks. My claim to the attention of social science colleagues is two-fold. First, the circumstances of my life have exposed me to an unusually rich variety of cultural and political settings that should have an intrinsic interest to a number of social scientists. Second, I flatter myself to believe that my view of the world, though a composite of many very old ideas, has a modicum of both originality and validity. In the aggregate, adding book sale figures, and making an allowance for journal and library readership, and for the resale of secondhand textbooks, I have intruded on the consciousness of perhaps 200,000 to 300,000 people through my writings. To be sure, the great majority of them were captive students whose choice of reading matter was imposed on them by my colleagues, but a perusal of annotated secondhand copies of my books in university bookstores indicates that a proportion of the students derived some enjoyment and perhaps even enlightenment from our mental encounter.

Quite immodestly but not totally unrealistically then, I believe that a few thousand people out of some 4.5 billion are interested in what I have to say about human behavior in the variety of cultures I encountered. Perhaps a few hundred are even interested enough in what I think to want to know how I came to my idiosyncratic vision of the world, however perverse, wrong-headed, or preposterous it might seem to them. This autobiography thus falls into the most presumptuous sub-genre of all, the "intellectual" autobiography. In a nutshell, I shall attempt to throw some light on how my life experiences shaped my perspective as a social scientist or to achieve what some of my "critical theory" friends term the unity of theory and praxis.

No doubt, I shall fail. Everyone does. For what more elusive task can there be than to objectify the subjective; to render explicit and visible the multitude of influences to which one has been subjected; to achieve, in short, the Socratic injunction of self-knowledge? The reasons the endeavor is doomed lie, I believe, very deep in our evolutionary history. First, we are equipped with a brain (or a mind, as most of my colleagues would prefer to say) that, prodigiously complex and clever though it is, evolved to understand and monitor its environment, *not* to understand itself. The human mind is its own ultimate black box. Second, the brain, as suggested by Edward O. Wilson, Robert Trivers, and other evolutionary theorists, evolved to serve the selfish interests of its carriers, and an important part of that self-serving character is a susceptibility to self-delusion and mystification. Consciously or unconsciously, we seek to deceive others in the pursuit of self-interest, and the ultimate form of deceit is self-deceit. This work is no exception.

Nonetheless, there is no harm in trying to elevate one's level of self-consciousness and stripping social reality of its thick incrustations of myth, ideology, religion, and other self-serving delusions under which we hide the material (and biological) basis of life. The above remarks obviously imply a set of epistemological and substantive premises to which I came in the course of my intellectual development and which I shall try to make more explicit in my chronological account.

A few comments on my approach to autobiography seem appropriate here. I do not think of myself as terribly interesting, but I have lived through very interesting events in a wide range of situations and places. As a social scientist, I claim a degree of special expertise in analyzing these events and situations, and skill in extracting from them some vision of the human condition. Yet I am enough of a "reflexive" social scientist to believe in the unity of theory and praxis.

Please excuse the jargon. What I mean is that I do not believe that I am out to discover an objective reality "out there." There is an important material and biological basis to our existence; so important, in fact, that only fools can deny it. But it is also true that we interpret and thereby modify the social matrix that shapes us. We are both object and subject of the social process that encompasses our existence.

Some social scientists claim an ability to objectify the social world and to remove themselves from it in order to analyze it. There is nothing wrong with a search for detachment and objectivity as a *method* of approaching "reality," but as a statement of achievement, objectivity is an illusion, an ever elusive ideal. I prefer to see myself as an integral part of the reality I study and a part that has been inevitably shaped by the whole. Even as a methodology, I do not believe that a relentless search for dispassionate objectivity is the royal road to "truth." Rather, I believe that reality is best approached through a dialectically alternating immersion into, and detachment from, the reality one studies.

This is the life story of an anthropologist who has been profoundly shaped by his experiences and who seeks to understand both the world and himself through this process of interaction. This statement is, of course, a pretentiously stated truism. We are all the end products of the interaction between our genes and our environment. But often the process is obscured. I shall do my best to bring it into the open. This I seek to do in at least two ways. First, I try to take nothing for granted in the social world around me, least of all the verbal statements that people make about it. Second, I endeavor to apply to my own behavior the same standards of skepticism and cynicism as I attribute to others.

The account to follow deliberately interweaves three levels of reality: personal anecdotes and involvement, ethnographic description, and sociological analysis. I have always seen the three as inextricably intertwined. In a sense, this book is a spatially disjointed ethnographic monograph, with my life history as the thread of continuity. In each situation, I alternate and interweave my role as participant and as observer. Being an anthropologist means, at the limit, being "in the field" all the time, but never "going native." One participates, not to immerse oneself

PREFACE

in the ambient flow of social consciousness, for that is the antithesis of ethnography. One participates to test one's observations. One plunges as deeply as one can or dares into the social situation, in order to alienate oneself from it.

Autobiography for an anthropologist means being one's own principal informant, being simultaneously the native and the ethnographer. This approach raises two questions. First, how long have I been a self-conscious observer and analyst of my own existence? To some extent, no doubt, I shall project retroactively into the events of my early life a critical position that I only developed long after the facts. This is certainly true of my early childhood, but I think I can truly say that my critical, cynical self began to emerge from the chrysalis of naiveté around age 12, certainly long before I became a social scientist. Where a discrepancy between my old and my newer self exists, I do my best to bring it out.

Second, there is the question of language, a particularly acute one in this case, because I have lived my life in four principal languages: French, English, German, and Spanish, in rough order of chronology and importance. Ideally, I should have liked to write the first chapters of this book in French, the language in which I lived them. The realities of the publishing world constrained me to use a single language, and I opted for English, my principal working language as an anthropologist, if only because it reaches the widest audience.

Like all ethnographic accounts, this one is strewn with native words. When these are drawn from languages other than English, I italicize them. When drawn from non-standard, English dialects, I use quotation marks to set off divergent or obsolete usage. To sanitize my account so as not to offend the sensibilities of my readership would mean gagging my natives, and no anthropologist would want to do that! Thus, for instance, feminists might be offended by references to "girls," meaning young adult women, in the 1950s or 1960s, but that is what young adult women were called by natives of both sexes then. Any other term would be anachronistic in that context. Similarly, my accounts of sexual relationships and mating systems in various settings are written from a male perspective because I was a male participant in male-dominated groups. To pretend that I was a sexless hermaphrodite would be neither honest nor accurate. I hope I have made it clear throughout that the opinions of the natives are not necessarily my own and that this participant-observer keeps his tongue firmly planted in cheek. No doubt, I will offend many; but if I did not, it would indicate that I did not have anything worth saying.

Perhaps I should explain why I decided to write an autobiography at

PREFACE

what might seem like a somewhat premature time. At 51, with two-thirds to three-quarters of my life behind me, I am at what is euphemistically described as one's "prime." I may be at or close to the peak of my career and what material and psychic rewards it has to offer. But, while not yet senile, I am clearly well beyond both my intellectual and physical prime, which, in our species, is best put from age 18 to 25. The trouble with people at their true prime is that they have not lived long enough to be very interesting. However, there is also a powerful argument for not waiting until one's dotage to write an account of one's life. Wines mellow with age; brains unfortunately soften. Social scientists have been able to hide that fact because they pursue a craft that only requires a modicum of intellect, but mathematicians and "hard" scientists are well aware of it.

The immediate catalyst for writing was a request by my colleague Bennett Berger that I contribute a chapter-length statement for his edited collection of autobiographies by sociologists. After complying, I was left with an unfulfilled urge to indulge at greater length. At this point, an invitation by the Center for Advanced Study in the Behavioral Sciences to spend a year at their Stanford "think motel" afforded me the "leisure of the theory class."

As I look through the glass wall of my study this late summer of 1984, my gaze falls, through a largely defoliated California oak, on that unwitting architectural approximation to a circumcised phallus with its bright red glans, irreverently known to generations of Stanford students as "Hoover's last erection." The Hoover Tower has long housed that other local think tank, one supposedly devoted to the study of "war, revolution, and peace," but, in fact, primarily dedicated to the prevention of revolution. On the eve of Reagan's reelection, Herbert Hoover's aims seem to have been crowned with domestic success, but to have met dismal failure elsewhere.

Thirty-four years—half a lifetime and a momentous historical epoch—have elapsed since I first came to Stanford (from the then Belgian Congo) to begin my undergraduate studies. In 1950, the United States was the uncontested center of a hegemonic empire, the only incontrovertible victor of World War II. Golden California was still a largely unspoiled paradise, radiant with the healthy animal hedonism of the 1950s. San Francisco was a clean, dynamic city with just enough cultural patina to claim some urbanity, and it showed as yet few of the signs of urban squalor and decay. Stanford—the "Farm," as it was affectionately known to its students—was an idyllic country club for the golden youth of the West Coast plutocracy. (It already claimed to be the "Harvard of the West," but it was to take another fifteen or twenty years for its achievements to catch up with its pretensions.)

PREFACE

On the whole, the Stanford of 1950 did not seem a bad place for an eagerly curious lad of 17 to start his adult life. Except for Hoover's tireless petrified tumescence, much has changed in the interim; but the Center for Advanced Study appears to be an apposite locale for the aging professor into which the young lad has grown to reflect upon that life.

Stranger in Their Midst

CHAPTER 1

Kith and Kin

Like most people, I have no real memory of any event that occurred before the second half of my second year of age, and even then such recollections as I have remain nebulous until age 4 or so, belonging to that twilight zone where one cannot be sure whether one actually remembers an event or merely an early account by a relative or other adult witness. Considering what we know about the potent determination of early childhood experiences this infant amnesia puts sobering limits on the extent of our consciousness. We clearly do many things for reasons that almost totally elude our consciousness.

One of my earliest childhood memories is a disagreeable one. I remember being spoon-fed—indeed, force-fed—a cornmeal pudding by my paternal grandmother. Besides the half-dozen spoonfuls that were insistently pressed to my mouth beyond the point of satiety, the most unpleasant part of this social ritual was my grandmother's use of the spoon to scoop up from my lower lip and chin whatever I contrived to expel from my mouth. To forestall this irritating maneuver, I would sometimes expectorate explosively, a ploy that would generally give me a three- or four-hour reprieve until my next ordeal. I can still feel the rather thin edge of my baby silver spoon irritating my lower lip!

This was only one-half of my predicament. The other end of my digestive system was being simultaneously abused. Indeed, the site of these sittings was a torture instrument known as a high chair, cunningly devised for the restraint of infants and, thus, the convenience of adults. (In many ways, it closely resembled the restraint chairs, used in primate research centers, which animal rights advocates would like to ban.) All hope of escape was effectively thwarted by the combination of a nasty wooden tablet with a bruising edge and a leather shoulder harness. But the really diabolical part of the contrivance was an egg-shaped hole in the seat, beneath which a small enamel chamber pot was slipped. For hours on end, my naked posterior chafed against the wood of the chair, a sensation that still lingers in my flesh. Because I was of the male sex, the apparatus was only partly effective. The final refinement—urine deflectors, which robbed male infants of their last vestige of retaliatory power—had not yet been invented.

If I dwell on these mundane details it is not to provide ammunition to my psychoanalytically inclined colleagues who will profess to predict my subsequent behavior from these traumatic beginnings, but rather to stress how early I learned the lesson of inequality, a topic that was to become a central concern of my scholarly career.

These feeding-cum-toilet-training séances, repeated three or four times a day, were also an early lesson in paternalism. Far from being a sadist, my grandmother positively doted on me. She equated obesity in infants with health, and, for the next decade of my life, every vacation spent with my paternal grandparents was converted into a fattening contest. Success was daily measured by my grandfather on a remarkably accurate potato scale, every 100 grams added to the counterweight being hailed as a victory over the forces of malnutrition and insurance against future illness. All this discomfort was imposed on me *for my own good,* it was claimed, no doubt in total honesty. Squeamish visitors to primate research centers, disturbed at the sight of baboons trembling in bare-toothed fury in their restraint chairs, are also blithely reassured by the staff that these contrivances are really quite humane and comfortable. One of my favorite fantasies has always been to see adults (and primatologists) trade places with their charges. In any case, I think that by age 2 or 3 I was already a rebel. Indeed, practically every 2-year-old is a rebel, throwing tantrums at the discovery of his impotence. By age 4 or 5, domestication has set in—adults call it "good manners," and social scientists "socialization"—and the rebelliousness is repressed, but the discovery of inequality around age 2 is one of the great existential crises. At least, it was for me.

I am running somewhat ahead of my story, but I introduced the obvious starting point for the story of a social scientist, namely his class and cultural origins. At the risk of providing ammunition to my critics on the left, I must confess to a good measure of privilege. I was born to parents who belonged to the *haute bourgeoisie* of two of the richest countries in the world, and to make matters worse, I was born a colonial. On January 30, 1933, I was born to a French mother and a Belgian father in the "European" (i.e., "for whites only") hospital of Elisabethville, Katanga Province of the Belgian Congo (in contemporary parlance, Lubumbashi, Shaba Province of Zaïre). Racial apartheid—another major theme of my professional life—thus intruded itself on the first day of my life. Presumably by coincidence, this was also the day when a little Austrian lance corporal and aquarellist manqué became reich chancellor in Berlin.

My father, Louis (born in Ghent, October 29, 1906; died in Johannesburg, January 3, 1979), then a 26-year-old tropical parasitologist, was doing post-doctoral research on malaria in the Congo, which explains the appearance of this white baby in a black world. Three years before, he had married Denise Caullery (born in Paris, June 23, 1907), a few months his junior, the daughter of Maurice Caullery, an eminent French zoologist. The relevance of this biological ancestry will become apparent later. Only the first ten months of my childhood were spent in the Congo, after which my parents returned with me to Belgium.

I can recapture glimpses of that early Congolese infancy through my parents' photo albums, where I appear in various poses surrounded by much of the paraphernalia of colonialism: wearing my father's pith helmet; sitting on a leopard skin next to my father's rifle; being pushed in a pram by a black servant; being attended to by a white nun (the very one whose life was described in *A Nun's Story* and made into a rather good film starring Audrey Hepburn); sitting on the fender of my parents' Model-T Ford, parked next to a tent. My first house, a flat-roofed, whitewashed bungalow with a wide verandah and its standardized government-issue "modern" furniture, was the typical abode assigned to the junior ranks of the higher civil service, my father's niche in the colonial pyramid.

That first year in Africa was also very nearly my last. I nearly died of a heat stroke in the train that was taking my parents and me from Lubumbashi to Beira, prior to embarcation on the *Trieste* back to Belgium via Suez. A few snapshots attest to that journey: I do a balancing act on the promenade deck of the ship, and make my debut as a tourist in my mother's arms, on top of a camel in front of the Pyramids of Gizeh.

My next appearance in the photo album, proudly assembled and cutely annotated by my father, is as a toddler clad in a white rabbit fur coat against the chill of my first Belgian winter. I was to spend much of the next two years with my paternal grandparents in Ghent, while my parents travelled in the United States on another one of my father's post-doctoral grants. Throughout the next fourteen years of my life, many of my school vacations were also spent in Ghent, and the social world of

My African origins in 1933, with my father's colonial paraphernalia. Taken in what was then Elisabethville, Katanga, Belgian Congo, now Lubumbashi, Shaba, Zaïre.

my grandparents during the late 1930s and early 1940s remains vividly inscribed in my memory. My grandfather, Samuel van den Berghe, a strikingly handsome and tall (1.85 m) man was born in 1868 and died 91 years later. Except for his last years, which were plagued by a succession of small strokes that left him partially paralyzed and with impaired speech, he enjoyed robust health and good fortune. My grandmother, Berthe van den Neucker, was a few months his senior. She was quite short, rather stooped in her old age, and distinctly plain in physical appearance; she cut a poor figure next to my grandfather. Iron-willed and highly intelligent in a rational, calculating manner, she was clearly the boss at home, notwithstanding my grandfather's occasional coleric outbursts, which she tactfully ignored. Until her final illness, an intestinal cancer, which carried her off in 1944, at age 77, she too was in good health and suffered only one major tragedy, the death at age 10 of her second child, my father's older brother Pierre, after whom I was named. My grandparents had three children, of whom my father was the youngest and only surviving son. His elder sister, Marie, born in 1899, eight years before my father, married a civil engineer, Paul Mouson, but left no issue. Thus, I have no first cousins on my paternal side. My aunt died, robust at 74, run over by a tram in Brussels.

My paternal grandparents epitomized the Catholic upper-bourgeoisie of a large Belgian town. Ghent had a population of some 200,000 and, while a bustling provincial capital with a glorious medieval past, had little of the thriving vitality of the great harbor of Antwerp, or the urbane cosmopolitanism of Brussels. The historical heyday of Ghent lies in the late middle ages, from the thirteenth to the mid-fifteenth century, when, along with Bruges, Ypres, and other Flemish towns, it rivalled the northern Italian cities. Monuments to its past glory still adorn the city center: the majestic town hall, the castle of the Counts of Flanders, several gothic churches, and opulent guild houses. But in the twentieth century, Ghent had become distinctly provincial and "backward." Until the late 1940s, for example, the private automobile was a bourgeois privilege, and the streets were liberally sprinkled with horse manure left by the delivery vans of sundry tradesmen. Milk, bread, beer, furniture, and wedding and mourning parties were being regularly conveyed by horse-drawn carriages.

Many houses (including my grandparents') were still unconnected to city sewage. The telephone, running water, electricity, the radio, the flush toilet, the motorcar were relative novelties, having made their first widespread appearance after World War I, and having reached only the middle classes by the 1930s. While Brussels was already much more "modern," Ghent still bore many marks of a prior era. Ghent was a resplendently archaic city ruled by a proudly reactionary bourgeoisie. While it never had its Thomas Mann to evoke its social world, the Lübeck of *Buddenbrooks* is a fairly good facsimile of the Ghent of my childhood.

To my grandparents, Ghent was the hub of the universe. Brussels, a mere 60 kilometers away, was reluctantly visited after my parents settled there in 1935; but it was an alien, unfamiliar, untrusted world to my grandparents, especially my grandmother. My grandmother was in fact only one generation removed from the land. Her father, Pierre van den Neucker, was a physician—a general practitioner in the small town of Harelbeke, near Kortrijk (Courtrai)—but he began his medical studies rather late, at age 30, and was himself the son and heir of a rich farmer. For all his wealth (he owned several farms and was a landlord as well as an operating farmer), my great-great grandfather was distinctly a peasant, and traces of his rusticity could be seen in my grandmother. As an only child (or so everyone believed), my grandmother had had a very substantial dowry and later inheritance, and she received a young lady's education, which is to say that she learned French, reading, arithmetic, embroidery, and piano playing at a nuns' boarding school. Nonetheless, her mother tongue was clearly Flemish; her written French was not flawless, and her spoken French was Flemish-accented, all blemishes for a member of the Flemish bourgeoisie in that period.

I qualified the statement that she was an only child, for, in fact, she was not, but that discovery was only made at her burial. When her family crypt was opened, my father noted a mysterious extra coffin. Neither his father nor his sister could enlighten him and only the old family cook, my grandmother's contemporary, confidante and servant of fifty years was in on the dark family secret. My grandmother had had an idiot brother who was given to the care of a convent where he died in his thirties, forgotten to the world, but reunited with his family in death. The main reason for such secrecy was that a mentally retarded sibling would have seriously jeopardized my grandmother's marital prospects, notwithstanding her large dowry. So much so that, even after nearly a half-century of marriage, she never told her husband. Indeed, my grandmother, strong-willed and independent as she was, engaged in numerous little conspiracies of silence with her maids, her children, and even her grandchildren against my grandfather.

My paternal grandfather was a physician, general practitioner, and fanatical homeopath, like his own father, his father-in-law, and his junior brother. Thus, the entire family exuded not only a medical atmosphere, but a sectarian one, characteristic of members of small dissident minorities under siege. Like all Belgian homeopathic physicians, my grandfather had undergone "proper" medical training at the University of Ghent and was thus a "legitimate" physician, but he felt the victim, with his fellow homeopaths, of a vast repressive conspiracy of "allopaths" who dominated "official" medicine.

His proudest boast was that, unlike his allopathic colleagues, he had never killed a patient because homeopathic pharmacology (largely a catalog of toxins diluted well beyond the point of harmlessness) merely aided nature in steering the patient toward recovery. Cure was to be achieved through drugs that produced in the healthy the same symptoms as did the disease in the sick, but diluted something like one part to the quintillion. Imagine, for instance, a cure for alcoholism based on the thrice-daily administration of six droplets of a mixture of a bottle of wine and the contents of the Caspian Sea. I am sure the cure would achieve total sobriety if kept up for a couple of months. Later in the course of my anthropological studies I was to learn that homeopathy was a form of sympathetic magic, but as a child I was treated to my first exposures to both sectarian partisanship and intellectual dispute.

At the slightest provocation, my grandfather would launch into tirades against the nefarious machinations of allopaths, citing some egregious cases of "medical murder." His outbursts were all the more vigorous as many other members of the family, including my father, my maternal grandfather and my Uncle Paul, regarded homeopathy with considerable skepticism. My maternal grandfather took the most extreme view of treating it as a dangerous quackery, hinting that my paternal grandfather had killed his own son by opposing an appendectomy. My father more tactfully suggested that the best medicine was neither allopathic nor homeopathic, but a synthesis of everything that produced good empirical results. My uncle mischievously teased my grandfather by suggesting that the success of homeopathy was largely attributable to the placebo effect and the skillful application of psychotherapy to mildly hysterical (and predominantly female) patients.

In any case, these disquisitions were among my first lessons on the behavior of beleaguered minorities, on the intrusion of passion into the ostensible domain of science, and on the thinness of the line separating reason from unreason. As a young child, I sided with my paternal grandfather, whose passion and missionary conviction carried the day with me. Later, my maternal grandfather's worldly cynicism and cool positivist rationality gained the upper hand in my world view.

My paternal grandfather exhibited none of the rusticity of my grandmother. His family had acquired urban bourgeois status at least two or three generations before him, and, though he was fluently bilingual in Flemish and French, French was clearly the dominant home language of his parents. His father was a fashionable physician to the upper bourgeoisie of Ghent, while his father-in-law was a small-town general practitioner ministering to a clientele of peasants and small tradesmen. Money talked in the end. My grandmother's large dowry and "prospects" (of an inheritance, that is) saved the marriage from being viewed as a *mésalliance*.

Soon, however, a serious family rift developed, which was to last almost as long as my grandfather's life and which neatly epitomized the conflicts of the bourgeois world. My grandfather came from a brood of six; he had one younger brother and four sisters. Only two other siblings married, one sister, Louise, to Hubert van Houtte, a distinguished historian at the University of Ghent. She became the mother of Jean van Houtte, my father's first cousin and life-long rival, who in the late 1940s and early 1950s, was to become Belgium's finance minister and, briefly, prime minister. The three celibate siblings formed a joint household led by my great-uncle Fernand, also, almost inevitably, a homeopathic physician.

My great-grandfather had foreseen the unwisdom of settling both of his sons as rival heirs to his medical clientele in the same city. He, therefore, set up my grandfather, after his internship, into a comfortable home and practice in the larger medical pastures of Brussels, with the understanding that my grandfather would leave his junior brother to inherit his father's practice in Ghent. To my grandmother, Brussels was at the end of the world, almost a two hours' train ride from her parents. She, therefore, maneuvered my grandfather into returning to Ghent, thereby breaking the family pact. My grandfather and great-uncle (who, by the way, was just finishing his medical studies) thus became direct rivals for their father's practice. In compensation, my great-grandfather tried to reestablish the balance by disfavoring my grandfather in his will, and the solid rock was laid for a half-century of family discord.

Until a few years before their deaths, when they became belatedly reconciled, the two enemy brothers managed to live about 1 kilometer from one another without exchanging a word. Their quarrel was proverbial in the bourgeoisie of Ghent, but the external appearance of civility was maintained in public. There were two principal points of contact between them. One was the common homeopathic pharmacist (and cousin) to whom both their clienteles had to turn to get their prescriptions filled. The pharmacy was thus the principal conveyor belt of news between my grandfather and his celibate siblings. The other principal overlap in their lives was their common barber, where they would occasionally meet and curtly nod to each other while silently awaiting a turn in the chair.

The barbershop incidentally is another vivid childhood memory of

My father's father's father, Adolphe van den Berghe, his wife and six children, Ghent, circa 1883. To his left stands my paternal grandfather, Samuel. All three males in the picture were homeopathic physicians. The youngest daughter gave birth to my father's cousin and school rival, Jean van Houtte, who became Prime Minister of Belgium after World War II.

mine, a setting of both mild physical torture and psychological vexation. My grandfather escorted me there with great regularity. He dictated his tonsorial tastes to the barber, who, well aware of which side his bread was buttered on, inevitably inflicted on me what I thought was a hideously short haircut. Adding injury to insult, he also used a hand-operated clipper, which painfully pulled my hair. When I protested, he countered that it was I who moved too much. The truth, no doubt, lay somewhere in between, but the disparity of power allowed little compromise. My favorite retaliation was to grab a bottle of cologne and spray it on the large mirror. This spectacle of prankish machismo amused my grandfather and was thus reluctantly tolerated by the barber, who, of course, knew that he could always "get" me in the end.

Relations with my grandfather's married sisters were better, although the rivalry between my father and his cousin Jean van Houtte was intense. Both attended the same elite French-medium Jesuit college, Sainte Barbe, and both headed the respective sections of their class (as they were nearly exact contemporaries). At stake was a gold medal awarded to the rare student who, in his six years of secondary school, managed to end each year the first of his class. The rub was that, because of attrition under that fiercely competitive system, my father and his cousin, who hitherto had been safely separated in parallel sections where each could be the *primus,* were suddenly thrust into direct competition. Only one of them could get the gold medal, and it was Jean van Houtte who got it; my father finished second. From then on, their careers diverged, my father entering medical research and his cousin law, university teaching, and politics. Both were successful, but Jean van Houtte's meteoric rise in the conservative Christian Social Party (Christian Democrats) led him to the post of prime minister, numerous academic honors, directorships of SABENA and other firms, and eventually a title of baron. Though their achievements were scarcely comparable, his cousin's worldly success rankled my father. My father, always a maverick, looked down somewhat on his cousin as a plodding, conventional, conservative type. Clearly, both were highly gifted individuals. Both were greatly favored by a common background of class privilege, but my father probably questioned the basis of that privilege more than his cousin who was more content to accept its bounty.

The class structure that produced the two rival cousins was indeed a highly pyramidal society, ruled by convention, snobbery, and inherited inequality of wealth, rank, and educational opportunity. The ruling bourgeoisie of Ghent and, indeed, by extension, of Belgium, was divided into two rival camps, along religious lines. The Catholic camp, associated with the Social Christian Party, opposed the anti-clerical camp, which was linked with the Liberal Party and Free Masonry. Both shared the same conservative conviction that the political and economic kingdom was rightfully theirs. Nevertheless, the religious cleavage also created a social rift within the bourgeoisie.

KITH AND KIN

My grandparents belonged to the Catholic camp and spoke of the Free Masons as dangerous, devious people with whom one best avoided all social contact. Contact between the children of the two camps was largely averted through attendance in separate school systems, both state-supported, but one officially Catholic and the other officially non-denominational. The religious minorities of Belgium—Protestants and Jews mostly—were too small to have any political weight and thus had to accommodate themselves to the "lay" schools. Even at the university level, the cleavage still survives today in the rival traditions of Louvain (or Leuven, in Flemish), the Catholic university, and Brussels, the Liberal, anti-clerical university.

To my grandparents, religion as such was not much of an issue. Both were firm Catholics (even though they exhibited most of the bourgeois values associated by Max Weber with the "Protestant ethic"), but more so out of social convention than out of deeply felt religious conviction. One was simply born a Catholic and died one, routinely going through the rites of passage of baptism, first communion, confirmation, marriage, and death. One went through Catholic schools, joined the Catholic branch of youth organizations like the Boy Scouts, voted Social Christian, read the Catholic newspapers—lived, in short, from the cradle to the grave in the womb of the Church. As this was a world wherein no other competing faith had to be dealt with, there was little need to argue belief or theology. Protestants were seen as mostly foreigners: English, Dutch, Germans. Jews were a somewhat mistrusted, alien, supranational community with local representatives, but generally outside one's social circle. My grandparents were certainly mildly anti-Semitic, as were most members of their social world, but no more so than they were anti-Free Mason, anti-German, or anti-Protestant.

Being a Catholic, then, meant, more than anything, membership in a community, indeed in the only social community that transcended class. Church was the only non-utilitarian context where one met one's social inferiors, although reserved chairs in the front rows insured a good measure of social segregation even in the face of the Almighty. It was only in later childhood, around the age of 11 or 12 that I was exposed to religious controversy and started to question my beliefs and upbringing, largely through the influence of my maternal grandfather, an anti-clerical atheist in the nineteenth-century positivist tradition.

The paternal side of my family was unquestioningly Catholic, and old family albums attest to numerous contributions to the clergy. A number of stern, pompous, and joyless celibates of both sexes (attired in clerical garb) stare at me from yellowed photographs. A legendary figure was my grandmother's uncle who went to Ireland to found or revive a religious order. As a child, I accepted the definition of his role as that of a "missionary," and only later did I begin to question the need of the Irish for Catholic missionaries! In any case, as the Congo was the only other context in which I ever heard of missionaries, I lumped Ireland and the Congo into a global colonial category of benighted savages in dire need of salvation. Neo-Marxist theorists of internal colonialism would currently attest to the validity of this outlook.

The subject of missions recalls a few episodes of my childhood. One was the collection of aluminum foil and old postal stamps "for the missions." I always wondered what Congolese children did with little balls of foil paper or with cancelled stamps, but it made me feel good to help the little black children among whom I was born. The other was an ingenious collection box, found on the counters of many shops. A grinning black boy sat on top of a collection box labelled *Pour les missions*. When you inserted a coin in the slot, the head of the boy nodded in thanks. This sight was so irresistible that, one day, I quickly grabbed a 20-franc silver coin—a substantial sum at the time—out of my grandmother's purse to make a contribution to the enticing box as well as to play a mischievous prank on my grandmother. This was one of the few occasions when my doting grandmother scolded me. Charity was all well and good, but it began at home. My grandmother, a great one for "amoral familism," was fiercely protective of her brood in the best "Jewish mother" tradition; but she was highly mistrustful of the outside world.

No account of the social world of my paternal grandparents would be complete without reference to the "language problem" of Belgium. My early experience not only of bilingualism, but of *invidious* bilingualism, was certainly formative in steering my subsequent professional interests. Belgium, like the 90 percent or so of the world's states that are "nations" only by a convenient misnomer, is, in fact, multi-national and suffers from a chronic language problem. The Belgian situation, however, has a number of unique, or at least unusual, features.

The principal line of conflict in Belgium has been not so much between Flemings and Walloons, two conventional ethnic communities living within fairly sharply drawn geographical boundaries. There is indeed a linguistic frontier running from east to west, just south of Brussels, that separates rather clearly the bulk of ethnic Flemings (who speak dialects of Dutch) from ethnic Walloons (who are French-speaking). Much of the bitterness of the language question, however, was due to the overlap of language with social class. Starting with the hegemony of the Grand Duchy of Burgundy (to which Flanders belonged in the fourteenth and fifteenth centuries), the aristocracy and later the bourgeoisie of Flanders became increasingly francophone. Much like the ruling classes of pre-revolutionary Russia, upper-class Flemings used French more and more as a "prestige language," while remaining for the most part fluently bilingual. Thus, language, specifically one's degree of fluency in French, became an invidious mark of social status in Flanders. Since World War II, this situation has been largely attenuated if not reversed, but during my childhood, it was still very much in evidence. The bourgeoisie of Flanders spoke French among themselves, both at home and in public, and, during the nineteenth century, French was virtually the exclusive language of the political and economic elite.

My grandparents' household was a neat microcosm of this situation, of which I became aware at quite an early age. Flemish (or, officially, Dutch) was the language of menials, *les gens du peuple* as the phrase went. *Les gens bien* all spoke French, sent their children to French medium schools, and looked down condescendingly on Flemish as a colorful peasant dialect, appropriate perhaps for the telling of off-color jokes, but hardly a vehicle for cultural and intellectual intercourse.

The physical layout of my grandparents' home in Ghent was a spatial microcosm of the wider situation, a linguistic "Upstairs, Downstairs," if I may borrow the title of the brilliant BBC series on the British class structure. Built on four levels, their house epitomized an upper-bourgeois dwelling. A large entrance door allowed the access of horse carriages (and later automobiles) to a back court, the carriage house, the stalls for the two horses, the hay loft, and a small attic room for the coachman (who slept immediately above the horses, better to minister to their needs). The house proper had four spacious floors, of which the basement and the upper story were largely the domain of the cook and the chambermaid. The main floor housed the public reception rooms: my grandfather's consulting rooms, the parlor, and the formal dining room. The first floor up consisted of the family bedrooms and an informal family boudoir.

As domestics were recruited from the Flemish peasantry and working class, they spoke principally Flemish, although long-term association with the bourgeoisie gave the servant class a better command of French than the rest of the Flemish "common people," that is, peasants, farm and factory workers, craftsmen, and small tradesmen.

The coachman disappeared from my grandparents' household when the Germans requisitioned the horses during World War I. After the war, my grandfather reluctantly bought a custom-made Panhard automobile, though he continued lovingly to saddle-soap his horse harnesses for another forty years. The cook and the chambermaid, however, remained permanent fixtures of the house, lifelong family retainers, paternalistically treated and unchanging. The cook was my grandmother's contemporary, who grew old with her and had the good taste to wait until my grandmother's demise in 1944 to retire and die shortly thereafter, her life's mission fulfilled. The chambermaid, some fifteen years my senior, was hired as a girl of 14 and was retired around age 50 after my grandfather's death in 1959 finally dissolved the household. Lifelong celibacy was an unspoken condition of employment (although, in the old days, marriages between a coachman and a cook were encouraged, provided they remained childless). The younger maid committed the faux pas of having an illegitimate child by a German officer whom my grandparents were forced to billet during World War II; the maid was discreetly sent away when her pregnancy became obvious and returned to family service after giving her child away for adoption.

Materially, the maids were, no doubt, better housed, clad, and fed than they would have been in their families of origin, and my grandparents were certainly humane exemplars of their class. Indeed, my grandmother and the cook had an intimate, almost conspiratorial relationship, though the chambermaid was clearly everybody's underling, including the cook's. Yet my grandparents, like almost all members of their class, took it completely for granted that they should deprive their servants of nearly all privacy and freedom, allowing them an hour on Sunday morning to attend early mass, their Sunday afternoon, perhaps two or three annual visits of two or three days' duration each to their families and an occasional day off for marriages and burials of close kin.

But I digress from the language question. My grandparents spoke French exclusively to each other, to family members, and to their class equals. Both were fluently bilingual, and Flemish could even be said to be my grandmother's first language, or at least her emotive language. She particularly relished telling scatological jokes (her favorites) in Flemish, claiming that the earthy flavor was irrevocably lost in French translation. To the maids, my grandparents spoke principally Flemish, as they did to their tenant farmers (some of them distant kinsmen of my grandmother), and to the tradesmen, deliverymen, craftsmen, and working class patients of my grandfather's. The linguistic domains were coterminous with class boundaries.

The socio-linguistic segregation was reflected in the use of space within the house. When tenant farmers, for example, came to pay their annual rent, they were received by my grandparents, but they ate in the kitchen with the maids, unless they were kinsmen. My grandfather's clientele was also carefully sorted socio-linguistically. There was a rather Spartan, working-class waiting room to which proletarian and rustic patients were led by the maid, while the bourgeois patients waited in the family parlor. My grandfather even had separate consulting rooms: a plush study lined with leather-bound medical volumes and adorned with a plaster bust of Samuel Hahnemann, the founder of homeopathy; and a small, bare office decorated only with a photograph of his favorite horse, Harlequin. (The association of the lower orders with the equine world was undoubtedly unconscious but nonetheless suggestive.)

This segregation called, of course, for rapid social judgment on the part of the maid who opened the door and, inevitably, there were marginal cases. Social ambiguity was resolved, however, through an ingenious device common in bourgeois houses and appropriately called an *espion* ("spy"). This device, a mirror outside a window, was tilted so as to give a reflection of the caller at the front door. When the bell rang, the maid rushed to the mirror, made a judgment of status, quickly consulted with my grandmother in ambiguous cases, and then opened the door and steered the visitor to the appropriate waiting room—to the Flemish or the French microcosm.

The social universe of my maternal grandparents was also that of the *haute bourgeoisie,* but nonetheless quite different from that of my paternal grandparents. My mother's parents were Parisian and, though less wealthy than my father's, were much more worldly and cosmopolitan. Physically, my maternal grandparents were as mismatched as my paternal ones, but in the opposite direction. Indeed, I always felt that, had my grandparents switched spouses, a much more harmonious outcome would have resulted. (This conclusion is, I think, well corroborated in a family picture taken at the baptism of my brother, Christian.) My maternal grandmother, Sabine Hubert (1881–1968), was a slender, tall, elegant aristocrat with high cheekbones, a finely chiseled aquiline nose, and a grace of movement that commanded immediate attention. She was thirteen years younger than my grandfather, but a good half head taller, at least in her high heels and feathered hats.

My grandfather, Maurice Caullery (1868–1958), was rather short, totally bald by his thirties, and had a rather pudgy face dominated by a bulbous nose and elephantine ears. His most attractive features were his eyes, which radiated intelligence; but, otherwise, he cut a comic contrast to his wife. His total indifference to sartorial elegance added to the contrast. Conventionally but sloppily dressed in baggy, unpressed suits sprinkled with cigarette ashes, his necktie askance and his pockets bulging with papers, cigarette packs, and matches, one could scarcely imagine a better caricature of the academic.

He also satisfied the stereotype of absentmindedness. One of the favorite family anecdotes is of his coming home one evening and mentioning to my grandmother that he had met in the street a strikingly hand-

With both sets of grandparents at my brother Christian's baptism, Brussels, 1938. Adults from left to right are: my maternal grandparents, my mother holding my brother, my father's older sister, Marie-Louise, and my paternal grandparents.

some woman whose face looked very familiar, but whom he could not place. Not so coincidentally, my grandmother had found it odd that my grandfather had ceremoniously tipped his hat to her, as if to a stranger. Lost in his thoughts, he had not consciously recognized his own wife!

Another anecdote gives a measure of my grandfather's character. He was a prolific author of more than a score of books, most of which had modest sales. There was one best-seller among them, however; it was a book he had quite innocently entitled *Les problèmes de la sexualité* (1913). He never could understand why it sold so much better than the others. There must have been a lot of disappointed readers, because my grandfather, a specialist in marine invertebrates, dealt mostly with the sexual antics of zooplankton.

Nor was the mismatch between my grandparents limited to physical appearance and sartorial concern. My grandmother's moderate intelligence was no match for my grandfather's brilliance. Like nearly all women of her class and generation, she received a superficial education, not even passing her *bachot* (secondary school completion examination); but she was artistically sensitive (an uncle of hers was a distin-

KITH AND KIN

My maternal grandparents, Maurice and Sabine Caullery, with their four children. From left to right: my father, Louis; my grandfather; Michel; Francine; Solange; my grandmother; and my mother, Denise. Photo taken in 1934, at Wimereux, France, the site of the marine biology station my grandfather directed, and where my parents first met.

guished painter). My grandfather, a brilliant graduate of the prestigious Ecole Normale Supérieure, was to become a professor of zoology at the Sorbonne, the director of a marine biology station, the president of the French Academy of Sciences, and a foreign fellow of the British Royal Society. Artistically, however, he was an unabashed philistine. Music to him was an expensive noise, and I suspected he was very nearly tone-deaf. Painting he regarded as a frivolous venture, and his color blindness (which, as a sex-linked recessive gene, I inherited from him) was the butt of numerous family jokes. As for poetry and fiction, he considered these forms of communication to be squanderous wastes of paper.

My grandmother was an eager socialite, attending all the free concerts, painting exhibits, weddings, official receptions, and state funerals to which her status as wife of a member of the Academy entitled her. My grandfather was openly contemptuous of such a waste of time in the company of his intellectual inferiors. Finally, religion also separated them. My grandmother was a conventional practicing Catholic, unconcerned about theological issues, but enjoying the pageantry of the Church as an essential ingredient of her social whirl. My grandfather, in the tradition of the Ecole Normale Supérieure where he was a student, was a nineteenth-century positivist and materialist, an anti-clerical, and an atheist. He refused to marry in the Church, and my grandmother had their children baptized without his prior knowledge and consent.

Notwithstanding all these differences, their marriage lasted nearly a half-century, produced four handsome children (in chronological order, Solange, Michel, my mother Denise, and Francine), and was relatively free of discord. They seemed to have reached a modus vivendi where each lived in his or her sphere, meeting at meals. Immediately after dessert, my grandfather would withdraw to his smoke-filled study, the only place in their five-room Parisian apartment where my grandmother would tolerate his pestilential Gauloises.

By social background, my mother's parents were somewhat alike. Both were of aristocratic ancestry—my grandfather from the provincial nobility of the French part of Flanders, in the town of Bergues; my grandmother from the Parisian court nobility. My grandmother was much more of a social snob than my grandfather, and she treated me to many stories of her colorful ancestors. These included a painter and traitor to his class whose sympathy for the Paris Commune of 1871 nearly got him executed; a cavalry general who took part in the French intervention in support of Emperor Maximilian in Mexico; and a set of nine brothers who went to Saint Domingue (Haiti) to run a sugar plantation and who were all killed the same day in the slave revolt of 1791. Much of her family fortune was dissipated by the nineteenth century, leaving her only with a couple of farms.

My grandfather was generally contemptuous of all forms of ascribed status and, as an intellectual heir to the French Revolution, of the pretensions of the aristocracy. In fact, his family had long stopped using its nobility title. His father, an army officer, was cashiered on half pay with the modest rank of captain during the long peace of 1870–1914. He died when my grandfather was 18 years old and left his widow and two children in strained economic circumstances. This experience left my grandfather with a parsimonious disposition, not because he loved money but because he reluctantly recognized it as a passport to security and freedom. He despised wealth and ostentation, being extremely frugal in all respects but for his intemperate smoking. For instance, he always had two pairs of shoes in current use, one with worn soles to be used in dry weather and another in good shape for rainy days. Before deciding which to put on, he would look at the sky and tap his barometer.

Despite his contempt of all social distinctions except those based on merit and intelligence (for he certainly was an *intellectual* snob), my grandfather seriously claimed to have been a descendant of Charlemagne. Considering the fifty-odd intervening generations, each exposed to uncertainty of paternity, the claim is highly dubious at best. More credible is the kinship with Joris de Caullery, a student of Rembrandt, whose magnificent portrait by his master, dated 1632, now adorns the De Young Museum of San Francisco. There I saw him on a recent visit, staring at me across three and a half centuries of time and 12,000 kilometers of space, with my grandfather's sparkling eyes and bulbous nose! Perhaps he was also staring at the disappearance of his line. When my Uncle Michel died without male issue a few years ago, the name of Caullery ceased to have a living carrier.

Both of my maternal grandparents had a single junior sibling of the opposite sex. My grandmother's brother, Roland Hubert, was a vain, rather stupid, self-centered spendthrift with a supercilious aristocratic manner; the family felt he never amounted to anything and my grandfather treated him with disdainful silence. My grandfather's sister, Adrienne, very much resembled her brother in character, intelligence, and physique. Both enjoyed robust health and died around age 90, my great-aunt of a gangrenous leg and my grandfather when he decided that he had lived long enough. He went to bed, started refusing solid foods and let himself die slowly and peacefully, in his own sweet time. Adrienne married Félix Mesnil, also a distinguished biologist and my grandfather's closest professional friend and collaborator until his death in the 1930s. The process of cementing professional ties through marriage was repeated at the next generation, this time with a disastrous first-cousin marriage. My eldest aunt, Solange, became infatuated with Adrienne's second son, named Maurice after my grandfather. Both fathers, as geneticists, were well aware of the risks of inbreeding and did their best to prevent the union, but the 17-year-old Solange was very headstrong, as indeed she remains to this day. The couple had two mentally unstable children who were stricken with progressive blindness and took some thirty years to die; the unhappy situation led to the divorce of their parents. Both Solange and Maurice happily remarried, but Solange was past childbearing age and has no surviving children.

My other maternal aunt, Francine, much the youngest of the four Caullery children, also remained childless through a stormy marriage to Vadime Elisséeff. Vadime, a brilliant son of Russian émigrés (Serge Elisséeff was Harvard's prominent Sinologist), was a Japanologist, art historian, and curator of the Cernuski Museum in Paris. In the end, Vadime divorced Francine to marry one of his students, with whom he had several children.

My Uncle Michel, two years Solange's junior, became an engineer, married into the bourgeoisie of Lyon, and raised three daughters, all junior to me and my only first cousins on either side: Martine, Solange, and Danielle. All three are happily married and have produced a brood with whom I have only been able to maintain sporadic contact.

My grandfather, the pure intellectual, was one of the pivotal figures in my development, and I am told by all who knew him that I resemble him in character (and perhaps approach him in intellect), though the physical resemblance is more with my mother, who in turn took after my grandmother. My grandfather, like many people of superior intelligence, found human contacts difficult, including those with his own children. He set exacting standards for others and, almost inevitably, grew irritated at their failure to meet his expectations. He quickly reached peremptory judgments of people, the most frequent of which was: *C'est un imbécile.* Such was his estimation of nearly all politicians (for whom he also frequently added the epithet of bandit) and most of his students and colleagues. He had a handful of brilliant post-graduate students who exerted much influence on mid-twentieth-century French biology, but the mass of his undergraduates were terrified of him. (*Cette vache de Caullery* was a common student summation of him.) Of friends, he had none, except for his co-author and brother-in-law Félix Mesnil.

His children, too, alas, failed to meet his expectations of brilliance, and their "failure" created some distance and coolness between him and them. All were, to be sure, of above-average intelligence, but none became an intellectual. Three of them were female, and intellectualism was not expected of women of their generation, even in the bourgeoisie. Only Francine, the youngest, received some university education. My grandfather's big disappointment was his son, Michel, who clearly lacked his father's intellectual panache. He completed respectable engineering studies, but not from a *grande école* like Polytechnique or Centrale, and had a routine career in industry.

Luckily for me, by the time he had become a grandparent, my grandfather (whom I called by the more formal *grand père,* reserving the more familiar *bon papa* for my paternal grandfather) had mellowed somewhat, and we had an excellent (and, for me, a most formative) relationship. Even with me, however, he could ill conceal his impatience at my failure to comprehend instantaneously algebra at age 11, or to read Xenophon fluently in the original after six or eight weeks of summer tuition. He could still recite by heart entire pages of the *Iliad* sixty years after he had read them. Besides his routine baggage of classical languages, Latin and Greek, he had a good command of English and German, although he spoke both with an abominably thick French accent.

His ears, though pendulous, were seemingly immune to all nuances of sound.

The social world of my maternal grandparents was less familiar to me than that of my paternal ones. This was partly because it was a much bigger and more complex world and thus a more difficult one to grasp. Ghent was a village compared to Paris, Belgium a *petit pays* (in the words of my maternal grandparents) compared to the *grande nation* of France. Also, Ghent was a mere 60 kilometers from Brussels, the site of my youth, and Paris a good 250, a substantial distance in those days of cobblestoned, tree-lined, narrow highways. Moreover, the war years restricted travel severely. Thus, I got to see my father's parents weekly, my mother's once or twice a year.

My maternal grandparents were certainly bourgeois, but they belonged to the intellectual bourgeoisie, rather than the moneyed one. They lived in a nice second floor, five-room flat, spacious by Parisian standards, but not luxurious, in the not-very-fashionable 15th *arrondissement,* on Boulevard Pasteur. The turn-of-the-century apartment house reflected France's class hierarchy. A concierge in a tiny loge screened visitors. The building had carpeted front stairs winding around a creeping elevator encased in a wrought-iron cage. Narrow, ill-lit dingy back stairs led to the *chambres de bonnes* (maids' rooms) on the seventh floor, under the roof. There was no lift to reach the proletarian seventh floor, and the plumbing facilities there were also rudimentary: one cold water tap in the narrow hallway and a single flush toilet common to some twenty small rooms. The flats below all had hot and cold running water and a full bath per apartment, of course. To each flat were assigned two maids' rooms, the standard complement of domestics for a bourgeois establishment in turn-of-the-century Paris.

By the 1930s, and certainly after World War II, the evolution of class relations had rendered that elaborate social ecology of class apartheid obsolete. Bourgeois households, by and large, no longer had live-in servants. My grandparents, like countless others, now had a *femme de journée* who came two or three days a week, was paid by the hour, and was even called Madame, rather than by the more familiar first name appellation used with live-in servants. The *chambres de bonnes* were transformed into *chambres d'étudiants,* giving growing children, visiting nephews and nieces from the provinces, and indeed the whole budding intelligentsia that converged on Paris for their studies, a convenient, if Spartan, abode. Many of the ideas and babies of the post-war generation were conceived in the *chambres de bonnes,* now upgraded to nurseries of the intelligentsia.

In Belgium, incidentally, this entire social evolution was delayed by at least a generation. There, most of the upper bourgeoisie live in spacious houses rather than flats, and live-in servants (now drawn principally from the semi-periphery of Europe—Portugal, Spain, Southern Italy) linger on to this day. This is a good example of how a simple ecological factor, like availability of space, can affect the tenor of class relations.

Besides their Parisian apartment, I associate my grandparents with two other locales, only one of which survived World War II. The first was the Marine Biology Station of Wimereux (near Boulogne, on the Channel coast of northern France), which my grandfather directed and which fell victim to the construction of the "Atlantic Wall," Nazi Germany's vain attempt to repel the Allied landings of 1944. Wimereux was really the first seed of my beginnings since this is where my parents met. My father visited there as a post-graduate student and fell in love with my mother, Denise. There was some reluctance on the part of both sets of parents to the engagement and then to the marriage in 1930. My father's parents rather hoped that their son's bride would bring in a more substantial dowry. My mother's parents looked down their noses at my father's, regarding them as somewhat ostentatious provincials, speaking French with a comical and vulgar Belgian accent (the butt of countless jokes in France, where Belgians play the dim-witted role of Poles in the Polish jokes of the U.S. repertoire of ethnic "humor"). But love triumphed, at least for a while.

The other setting associated with my grandparents is some 150 years old and survives to this day. Now known as La Colonie, it is a small estate in the Forest of Rambouillet, some 60 kilometers from Paris. It was originally established as a *phalanstère* to implement the ideas of Charles Fourier, an early nineteenth-century utopian socialist and inspired crackpot. The *phalanstère* was to be an agricultural and handicraft settlement whose members would live in common under the single roof of a long building, where they would sleep in individual family rooms but eat in a common dining hall and produce in common for a common economy. (The contemporary *kibbutz* is, in fact, much like a reinvented *phalanstère,* except that it worked better in the Zionist fervor of Palestine than in the bourgeois France of Louis Philippe's monarchy.)

To make a long story short, the utopia rapidly failed as a unit of production and became transformed into a cheap vacation colony for a small but very select group of intellectuals, professionals, and artists of rather conservative disposition but of liberal ideas. La Colonie became a literary and intellectual *salon*-in-the-woods, retaining of its socialist ideals only the ritual of the meals taken at the long common table.

My grandparents were members, and so is my mother. Through La Colonie, numerous ties of friendship, enmity, and marriage (the three not being mutually exclusive) were established within a small but influential circle of the Parisian intellectual bourgeoisie. For example, the Bruckers, an Alsatian family, have known the Caullerys for three generations, and in the third generation, my younger sister Gwendoline, after spending most of her life in the Congo, California, and Peru, returned to France to marry Alain Brucker, the nephew of one of my mother's childhood friends. As for me, I remember spending several summers there as a child with my grandparents. Subsequent visits as an adult provided one of the few fixed anchors in a world of flux. The spirit of Fourier is long gone, but his bricks remain, an ironic monument to the failure of social reform, but a delightful oasis for a jet-lagging, peripatetic professor. La Colonie was also the setting of my first Greek lessons under the stern aegis of my grandfather and, much more enjoyably, of my first exposure to natural history under his inspired guidance.

Much as kibbutzim now increasingly hire Arabs to do the dirty work, La Colonie now employs a couple to cook the *colons'* food and to keep up the grounds. The cook, it happens, is a Polish Jew and an Auschwitz survivor. One morning, as I went to the kitchen to fetch my steaming bowl of *café au lait*—part of the breakfast ritual—I saw the purple, six-digit tattoo on her forearm. *Café au lait* never tasted so bad. It was a stark reminder that civilization always precariously trembles on the abyss of barbarism. The worst of it all is that, after a century of organized social science, we still have little idea of what pushes us into the abyss. Tyranny has no nationality, no sex, no color. It temporarily assumes certain historical disguises, but ultimately tyranny is Man (by which I mean, alas, both sexes). We have seen the enemy and he is us.

CHAPTER 2

Growing Up in War and Peace

World War II neatly brackets the middle of my pre-adult life: I was 6 when it started, 12 when it ended. Though I was too young to be an active participant in it, I was old enough to retain vivid, precise, indelible recollections of it. The last months of it are even recorded in a "War Diary of a Twelve Year Old Child," my first book, as yet unpublished, written at my father's suggestion.

My grandparents called World War I, the Great War. They were right, but only for twenty years. The Second was to dwarf the First. It was about twice as extensive in geographical area and three times as lethal. It produced a charnel of some fifty million corpses, give or take a few million, roughly the total population of France. These figures do not even include the twenty or more millions butchered in the Stalin purges, which, for the sake of historical accuracy, rightfully belong in the same great wave of barbarism. At least three-fourths of these deaths were deliberately inflicted on non-combatants—mostly women, children, and the elderly—by methods such as the Nazi and Soviet concentration camps; massive executions, starvation, and forced marches of prisoners by the Japanese, the Germans, and the Soviets; terror bombing by the *Luftwaffe,* the Royal Air Force, and the U.S. Air Force; mass executions of civilian hostages and systematic destructions of entire towns by the Soviets, the Germans, and the Japanese; and, not to be outdone, the first use of the atomic bomb against strictly civilian targets by the United States.

GROWING UP IN WAR AND PEACE

Unlike my wife, Irmgard, who experienced the same events from the German side of the fence and who copes with them by repressing any memory of them and refusing to read or view any documents relating to World War II, I have become increasingly obsessed over the years with a need to understand the causes of this massive orgy of wanton killing. Films and books about the war, and especially its purest distillation of barbarism—the Nazi concentration camp, exert a morbid fascination on me. Most terrifying is that the more I look for the special role of perverted sadists, for the special extraordinary pressures of danger or greed, for the unique cultural or ideological features of a particular society or political party, the more I simply encounter a universal potentiality of human nature. My dear friend, Leo Kuper, in his masterly studies of revolution and genocide (*The Pity of it All,* 1977; and *Genocide,* 1981), comes, I fear, to the same conclusion, though he cannot bring himself to articulate it as explicitly as I have.

There are, of course, many ways to try escaping such a pessimistic view. The main one is historicism or exceptionalism: pleading unique, exceptional circumstances, such as extreme stress, danger, terror, revenge, blind fanaticism, temporary insanity, and so on. As a general explanation, historicism, by definition, must fail. There are, to be sure, exceptional events and unique cultural phenomena (for instance, the suicidal behavior of Japanese soldiers in the face of capture). But how can one explain that two of the world's most exquisite civilizations—Germany and Japan—were capable of producing such unspeakable horrors? How could an ordinary haberdasher from Independence, Missouri, pull the atomic trigger? Truman's reaction to the "success" of Hiroshima was unabashed delight. So was that of the pilot of the *Enola Gay* who dropped the bomb on August 6, 1945. He even had the bad taste to take a repeat "nostalgia" flight over Hiroshima to recapture that glorious moment. Tens of millions of Americans entered the era of possible planetary annihilation with a huge feeling of relief that the war was over and of pride in Yankee ingenuity. Only a terrified Robert Oppenheimer quoted to himself from the *Bhagavad Gita:* "I have become death, the destroyer of worlds." Truman, Eichmann, what's the difference? They all meet in the banality of evil, as Hannah Arendt so well put it, in the routinization of genocide, in the bureaucratization of violent death.

I am afraid I can produce examples from my own direct experiences and acquaintances. Take a distant cousin and exact contemporary of mine who shall remain unnamed. The son of a lawyer, he received a good bourgeois education, but enlisted in the Belgian paratrooper battalion that fought on the American side during the Korean War. That made him a patriotic anti-communist, and he came back a war hero, much decorated for bravery under fire. So far so good. Then, bored by civilian life in Belgium, he went to the Congo and became a plantation overseer. Applying his wartime skills as a crack marksman, he invented a new method to stimulate the productivity of his workers. He shot laggards in the legs with a 22-caliber rifle. This was judged a bit too drastic, even by Belgian colonial standards, and he received a light jail sentence, but it did not disgrace him in colonial society. His real opportunity came at the time of Congolese independence. He found his true vocation by becoming chief of police to Moise Tshombe during the brief Katanga secession. Finally, he met an untimely and, no doubt, disagreeable end at the hands of his Congolese captors.

I played with that boy who, but for his age and historical accidents, could very well have sat in the glass cage in Eichmann's place. To be sure, as a child he was already a gun nut and relished shooting birds with his air gun. But so, I am ashamed to confess, did I. There, but for the grace of God . . .

Or take my father's laboratory assistant in Antwerp. World War II made him a resistance hero. Without telling my father, he had converted my father's lab into an underground arsenal, in the full knowledge that my father's other assistant, a beautiful Russian émigrée, was being hotly courted by a German officer. A slight lapse in his sense of social responsibility, one might say. Only a few years later did I discover that he was a psychopathic killer. With great relish he related to me what his favorite wartime assignment had been. The underground discovered that a number of prostitutes in Antwerp's brothels were at the source of denunciations to the Gestapo. He was dispatched as a willing avenging angel and bragged of having slit the throats of about twenty women in the act of love. Knowing him, he probably exaggerated by half, but still . . .

Exhibit C: Another assistant of my father in the Congo, a brilliant self-taught entomologist who discovered some 3,000 new species of insects, was a very charming and warm individual who took me on several bug-hunting trips. We became as good friends as a thirty-year age difference allowed. What puzzled me about him was how such an intelligent and scientifically inclined man could be such a crude racist, believing against evidence that blacks were stupid and childish. This was to be expected, said my father, because he came from a humble social background, savored the power that his white skin now gave him, and was compensating for his sense of social inferiority. He had an only son, then aged about 5 or 6, who was a bit of a lout and enjoyed bullying my 3-year-old sister. Some years later, I visited the father. Naturally, I asked him about his son. Oh, he said, picking up from his desk a portrait of a cocky, smiling, khaki-clad youth, had I not heard? He had been killed as a white mercenary in the Congo. At the peak of embarrassment, I condoled, but his face suddenly lit in a satisfied smirk: "Yes, very sad," he said, "but he took quite a few niggers with him." Hate, it seems, conquers everything, even fatherly love.

Exceptional circumstances? Exceptional men? I wish I could believe that. Having found myself on the winning side of World War II, and too young to have taken an active part in it, I was spared the feeling of guilt of many Germans, for instance, who are but a few years my seniors. But I was also not given an opportunity to test how I would behave under duress or threat. I am relieved to say that all the members of my immediate family did behave, if not heroically, at least decently. But that is not to say that I would have acquitted myself as well in their place.

There is one more episode over which I pondered a great deal. Shortly before the war, there arrived in Brussels a gentle, brilliant, charming Hungarian Jew, Dr. Blitzstein, who had a prescience of impending events and thought he had found a safe haven in Belgium. Like my father, he was a physician, specializing in tropical medicine. My father, by then a securely established professor of tropical medicine in Antwerp, took an instant liking for him and did his best to find him employment. A frequent visitor to our home, he was loved by all of us. When the Nazi order for Jews to register and wear the Star of David armband came, my father urged Dr. Blitzstein to go into hiding, and we offered him shelter for a few weeks. Soon, however, the German authorities threatened to billet officers in an empty bedroom of our large house. Obviously, a new hiding place had to be found for Dr. Blitzstein. It was provided by friends of my parents who hid him in their attic for some two and a half years. My story has a sad end, alas. Dr. Blitzstein survived the war, married a Belgian woman, found a job in the Congolese medical service, and, shortly after arrival, contracted an incurable tropical eye disease which, he knew, would lead to total blindness. So as not to become a burden to his wife, he put a bullet through his head after writing her a tenderly apologetic suicide note.

The point of my story is: would I, in my father's place, have jeopardized my life and that of my family by sheltering a Jew? I will never know, of course. Would I, as a 10- or 11-year-old child then, have denounced him to the Gestapo under torture or threat? Almost certainly yes, I fear. Could I, under the right circumstances, time, and place, have joined the Gestapo or the SS? Quite possibly.

Anyway, these and many other encounters with tyranny turned me into a rebel and an anarchist who always sought to avoid both responsibility over, and subordination to, others. Academia is not a bad refuge from both sides of the power equation. If I could only do away with examinations, how gladly I would do so.

Let me backtrack to pre-war Brussels, where my parents settled in 1935, in a spacious four-story house, 52 Rue de Turin, near the fashionable Avenue Louise. There we stayed until the family's departure for the Congo in 1948. Brussels, thus, was the main setting of my childhood, although, since the death in 1973 of my last close Belgian relative—my father's sister Marie, I now feel much more at home in France than in Belgium.

Those four or five years before the war were, in retrospect, quite happy ones. By 1937, my father had secured an excellent job, a chair at the Institute for Tropical Medicine at Antwerp, a short forty-minute commute by train from Brussels. A chair at age 31 was quite an accomplishment, by the way. The institute was both a research setting with well-equipped labs and a teaching institution to train physicians and nurses about to depart for the Congo. (The film, *A Nun's Story*, puts it well.)

My father, whose specialty was malaria, did his best research in those years. I remember his lab quite well and spent quite a few hours over his microscopes, heating and blowing glass tubes over gas burners, visiting the experimental rats, guinea pigs, rabbits, and monkeys, and even a forlorn chimp that my father, to my intense wonderment, would engage in a hooting "conversation." Most distressing was the shaved rabbit used to feed the *Anopheles* mosquitoes necessary to my father's research. I greatly admired my father's abnegation when he himself, in the interests of science, would occasionally stretch his naked forearm under the mosquito netting to feed his hungry insect brood.

Those were also the years when my parents were happy with each other and gave birth to their second child, my brother Christian, born in 1938. We lived in an elegant house, tastefully furnished, and in a grand style that exceeded my father's modest academic income, but which was cheerfully subsidized by my paternal grandparents. A resident couple of Flemish domestics helped my mother keep house, though, in truth, the husband had outside employment as an electrician and my mother did much household work, alongside our cook-maid. The physical layout of our house was much like that of my grandparents in Ghent, though on a somewhat grander and much more modern scale. The plumbing was much more lavish: we had three bathrooms to my grandparents' (rarely used) one. The house was, in fact, so vast that about one-third of the rooms went almost totally unused.

My parents made a handsome, radiantly happy couple. My mother inherited aristocratic grace and beauty from her mother, as well as her artistic sensibility. She was a gifted aquarellist in her youth, though she stopped painting in the last thirty years or so. Her education stopped at the *lycée* (the French high school; that is, about the equivalent of two years of American college), but she is well read and knowledgeable in Western painting, sculpture, and architecture; she contributed much to my appreciation of the visual arts. Unlike her older sister Solange, she is anxious, self-effacing and soft-spoken, and she easily lets herself be taken advantage of. She raised her three children with gentle discipline, closely following our school progress, and inculcating into us the virtues associated with Weber's Protestant ethic: thrift, foresight, deferred gratification, sexual puritanism, excellence, competition, internally generated discipline, self-assigned goals and deadlines, work before pleasure. Though she is by tradition a lifelong practicing Catholic, I always kidded her that she was at heart a Calvinist, or at least a Jansenist. It is clearly from her that I learned what I might call the methodology of success.

My father (who died of intestinal cancer in Johannesburg in 1979, at age 72) was an extremely complex figure with whom I had a stormy relationship, which began in adulation, turned to bitter conflict in adolescence, and ended, alas, in something like quiet indifference. Gifted both intellectually and artistically, his talents and his foibles were of quite large dimensions. He had been spoiled rotten by his mother who, almost literally, worshipped him, regarded him as her gift to humanity, and clearly preferred him to both her husband and her daughter Marie (who was 8 years older than my father). That adulation, reinforced by facile school success, turned my father into an intensely self-centered, egotistical, vain person, very nearly convinced that he was a Renaissance genius in practically all fields: architecture, interior decoration, drawing, music, administration, science. In his chosen field of science, he made moderately important contributions to tropical parasitology during the ten years or so when he actually did research. After that, however, he got bored with science, became an administrator of research and gave vent to his unbridled dilettantism.

Over the years, he became increasingly mentally unbalanced, withdrawn into himself, and erratic and extreme in his likes and dislikes; but he always retained the qualities of charm and brio necessary to seduce and manipulate people to his ends. Most of his human relationships went, with increasing tempo as he grew older, from a phase of intense liking to utter rejection. My mother attributes the beginning of his "difficult" phase to a traumatic automobile accident, which, in 1939, mashed his knee and left one leg about 5 centimeters shorter than the other. As he was a vain man, who was very conscious of his physical appearance and spent a fortune on his clothes, this accident was, no doubt, a tremendous blow to his self-esteem. This is indeed the time when he started to engage in a long series of extramarital affairs and to become an increasingly philandering husband and episodic father. His involvement with us began to fluctuate sharply between brief spells of intense concern and increasingly lengthy periods of absence and neglect.

I got to know several of his mistresses well, for he often brought them home with him, and, on the whole, he had an excellent taste in women. I, too, was fascinated and infatuated with several of his choices, especially his gorgeous Russian lab assistant, one of the first of the lot. Both physically and mentally, my father was a very seductive person. Tall and slender, with piercing blue eyes, he had a natural, slightly effeminate grace. He was an excellent dancer and dressed fastidiously. He must have had five to ten times as many clothes as my mother, his bedroom closet brimming with hundreds of ties and a minimum of 50 to 60 suits. He was, incidentally, also an inveterate collector of a disparate array of objects besides clothes: pipes, old maps—you name it; he started a new obsessive hobby every couple of years. Although I took from him a strong liking for art collecting, I always rejected his sartorial exuberance, and, like my maternal grandfather, I am nearly totally unconcerned about clothes.

Despite my highly ambivalent relationship with my father, I clearly acquired a good deal from him and, perhaps at least as much, in reaction *against* him. Next to my maternal grandfather, he was probably the most formative figure of my youth. I admired his many gifts. To a child, even his amateurish efforts in drawing and piano playing, for instance, seemed brilliant. A polished speaker and elegant stylist, he gave me a sensitive appreciation of both the spoken and the written word. An effortless polyglot who spoke fluent French and Dutch, very nearly flawless English, tolerable Swahili, and a few phrases in a smattering of other languages, he motivated me strongly to emulate him in this domain. Mostly, he helped me make the use of language my favorite intellectual game.

I was also seduced by his amiable cynicism, his religious agnosticism, his independence and originality of thought, his iconoclastic approach to political ideology, and, perhaps most of all, his intellectual elitism combined with a refreshing absence of class, ethnic, or racial prejudice. Intellectually, he rebelled against the stifling conventions, conservatism, and provincialism of his parents and his milieu, and quickly became a cosmopolite. He complied with his father's wish that he become a physician, but rejected homeopathy and, indeed, mere medical practice, to enter teaching and research. Religion to him was an amusing set of conventions for the masses, but not to be taken seriously. He was no militant anti-clerical because the issue was not important enough to him to fight over, and he sent me to Catholic schools because he thought the Jesuits gave one the best education, but he willingly signed me phony medical excuses to exempt me from morning mass attendance. My own distaste for convention and skepticism of all types of orthodoxy has thus a dual ancestry, both in my father and in my maternal grandfather.

Two other adult family members lived in Brussels in the lovely residential suburb of Uccle, my Aunt Marie (whom I called Tante Mimi) and her husband, Paul Mouson. My aunt, an accomplished pianist trained at the Paris Conservatoire, taught me much I know of classical music, although efforts to make me a performing pianist failed dismally after some two years of painful weekly lessons. I remember that, one day, out of frustration, I furiously scratched with my nails the beautiful polished lid of our Pleyel. Still, she did manage to make me an avid listener. Her musical tastes, while fairly eclectic (in the Western classical tradition, that is), leant in the direction of those of her Conservatoire teachers: Ravel, César Franck, Debussy, Saint Saens, while mine evolved increasingly with age toward the Baroque and Roccoco eras. But I spent many hours listening to her playing. I remember her amused shock when in my youthful enthusiasm for my recent discovery of Vivaldi, I asserted that Vivaldi was at least the equal of Bach since the latter cribbed so much from the former. Now I have learned that giants sometimes perch on the shoulders of dwarfs.

In addition to her musical accomplishments, my aunt was also an engrossing storyteller. Her endless tales of a mythical cat, Raminagrobis, enthralled my younger years. Its supposed abode was a hole in the hedge of my aunt's garden, but my investigations were always frustrated, thereby adding mystery to the elusive feline. Like most women of her class and generation, my aunt was badly educated in a nuns' boarding school; but she was a receptive listener, and she had the good sense never to speak on topics of which she was ignorant. Others thought her dull-witted because she was often nearly silent, but I never heard her say anything stupid. This, in itself, is, I think, proof of considerable intelligence. I wish more of my colleagues in academia took after her.

Temperamentally very different from my mother, the two of them never hit it off, especially when she refused to be disloyal to her philandering brother. Like her mother, she had a fierce sense of "amoral familism." Kin always came first. She disapproved of my father's behavior, being a prim, conservative, and very conventional Catholic and a sexual prude; but she would never say so.

My Uncle Paul, a civil engineer by training, hailed from Namur and was the lone Walloon in my Belgian family. But he went to university in Ghent (where he met my aunt), made the effort to learn the "inferior" language, and became quite fluent in Dutch, a rare feat for Walloons. He came from a relatively impecunious petty bourgeois family, which my grandparents never let him forget. They put pressure on him to start making money, and this led him to abandon engineering, a trade he loved, and to join his senior brother in a fashionable Brussels furrier business owned by the wealthy family of his brother's wife. His knowledge of languages (he spoke very passable English, German, and Spanish) made him the natural purchasing agent for the firm, and, thus, he travelled frequently to London, Moscow, Montreal, New York, and other world centers of the fur trade. Perhaps because many of his business associates were Jews, he developed a marvelous self-deprecating sense of humor, which I found most engaging. One of his favorite witticisms when people asked him his profession was to reply that he was an *ingénieur en poil* ("hair engineer"). My aunt, whose sense of bourgeois propriety overshadowed her sense of humor, was always embarrassed when he said it in public.

What I most appreciated in him was his human warmth. He and my aunt remained involuntarily childless, an additional burden on him vis-à-vis my grandparents who naturally assumed that no daughter of theirs could be infertile. I thus became their favorite nephew, if only because I was the oldest. During my stormy adolescence and conflicts with my father, my uncle became practically an adoptive father to me. To avoid the tension of my parents' home, I sometimes spent several days with them, much to the mutual relief of my father and myself.

My uncle's main contribution to my education was his tutoring in algebra and trigonometry (never my favorite subjects, though I held my own quite tolerably in geometry), and his appreciation of the old Flemish and Dutch masters. He especially introduced me to the great Dutch museums in Haarlem, the Hague, and Amsterdam, not to mention the ones closer to home. To this day, the Flemish "primitives" (what a silly label!) and the Dutch masters of the seventeenth century have remained my favorites.

The pleasant world of Brussels in the late 1930s was brutally shattered by the outbreak of war. All four of my grandparents had seen it coming, from a general pessimism born out of experience. It was axiomatic to them that a nationalist Germany would seek revenge for the defeat of 1918. My maternal grandfather, though he had spent a year of postgraduate work making the rounds of the great German universities and much admired the German scientific world, was also an ardent French nationalist. Far from thinking that the terms of the Versailles Treaty were so harsh as to have driven Germany into the arms of Hitler, he thought they had been too lenient. The Versailles Treaty, he believed, should have provided for a permanent French occupation of the west bank of the Rhine, France's natural frontier. He clairvoyantly saw the absence of French intervention after Hitler's remilitarization of the Rhineland and the Munich agreement for the disasters they soon proved to be.

My paternal grandparents' views were equally Germanophobic, though somewhat more prosaic. My grandfather never forgave the *boches* for having stolen his horses during World War I. (He had kept the never-redeemed promissory note of the German commissary to fuel his resentment.) My grandmother, like the proverbial ant of the La Fontaine fable, had stocked food against the prospect of war ever since 1918. She even had a large, hidden larder built into her house and stocked it with non-perishable foods. The world might collapse around her, but her family would not go hungry! Everyone made fun of her excessive providence, but, in the end, everyone was grateful to her for keeping us in sugar, flour, rice, and such through much of the war.

There was also little doubt, in my paternal grandparents' opinion, that the next war was to be much like the first. Belgium would again be the path of the German attack against France, and four or five years of German occupation would follow until the eventual victory of the French, British, and American allies. It turned out that, as far as Belgium was concerned, their scenario was amazingly accurate. For France, it was far too optimistic.

For us, "real" war only began with the German invasion of the Low Countries and France on May 10, 1940. From September 1939 to May 1940, we went through the *drôle de guerre* ("phony war"), when all was quiet on the Western front. My father, a first lieutenant of the reserve in the Belgian army's medical corps, was mobilized. He had his tailor make him two elegant new uniforms, which he wore on and off on sporadic duty, but his military career was abruptly cut short when he became a casualty in a military car crash. The steering of his staff car failed, and he smashed into a military truck. He was propelled out of the car, his left knee was shattered, and he spent the next several months in a military hospital. Had he not been a physician, the surgeons would have taken the easy course of amputation, but my father, after seeing his x-rays, demanded to have his leg put in traction. He was in agony for weeks, sedated by morphine shots, but he kept his leg. It was shortened and stiffened, but still quite serviceable.

My first memory of the no-longer-phony war was being shaken out of a deep sleep by our maid. I looked at my bedside clock. At age 7, I was

GROWING UP IN WAR AND PEACE

With my parents, Louis and Denise, and brother, Christian, in 1940. My father in Belgian army uniform is recuperating from a car crash during the "Phony War." Brussels, spring, 1940.

very proud of my newly acquired skill of telling time! It was 5 A.M. on May 10, 1940, a good two hours before my appointed time to get ready for school, and it was still pitch dark. I asked her whether she had taken leave of her senses to wake me up so early, and, indeed, she nearly had for fear. The hum of the *Luftwaffe* bombers and soon the muffled noise of distant explosions answered my question. The war was really on this time. Compared to the terror bombing of Rotterdam four days later, Brussels was left virtually unscathed. Nevertheless, as an object lesson, it was quite sufficient to send us packing and to begin what we later called the Exodus.

Within two hours, we crammed our black 1938 Chevrolet sedan with valuables and clothes and left for Ghent for a family council with my grandparents. Conveniently, we left our house in the care of Bertha and Frédéric, our faithful servants. My father had just been discharged from the hospital but not from the army. Thus, he was still in uniform, but he could only hobble on crutches. My brother, Christian, was a few days short of his second birthday.

It only took us a few days to realize that the *Wehrmacht* would make a clean sweep through Belgium, as it had in 1918. My grandparents said they were too old to move. But we should wait out the end of the war with my mother's family in France, after the French army would stabilize the front somewhere along the Marne and the Somme rivers. My other grandparents' weekend retreat in La Colonie, near Rambouillet, was our next stop, but it proved much more temporary than anticipated. After Dunkirk and the capitulation of the Belgian army (which my Parisian grandfather thought an act of treachery by King Léopold III), it was clear that the Germans could not be stopped before the Loire. So, like what was left of the French government, we left Paris in the direction of Bordeaux. My French grandparents and a colleague of my father in Antwerp joined us there.

By then, the roads had become nearly completely clogged with French troops still moving north, defeated Belgian and French stragglers fleeing south, and vast hordes of Belgian and northern French civilians escaping in panic. The fortunate bourgeois had cars (often with a mattress on the roof, as a desultory protection against strafing), while peasants and workers fled in horsecarts, push carts, baby carriages, and on foot. (The masterly French film, *Les Jeux Interdits,* recaptures the atmosphere beautifully.) We were strafed by German planes two or three times, but I do not recall any casualties. Whenever planes appeared, we assumed they were German, we jumped out of the car, and we dispersed in the roadside ditches and hedges. The flow of traffic on most north-south roads was reduced to 5 or 10 kilometers an hour, and disabled ve-

With a caravan of Belgian refugees fleeing in front of the *Wehrmacht,* southern France, June 1940. Our car, my brother and I in the left foreground.

hicles were simply pushed off to the sides. At night, we slept in the car, or with luck in a farmer's hay loft. To a 7-year-old, all of this was very exciting, like a premature school vacation.

To add to the confusion, we had to pass through military checkpoints that had been set up every few kilometers to check papers and unmask the famous "fifth column" of German paratroopers behind the lines. My father, with his tall Nordic physique and his broken leg, was a prime candidate for suspicion. He was, in many French *gendarmes'* minds, a German paratrooper who had broken his leg in a jump and was disguised as a Belgian officer. After a half-hour palaver, we usually managed to convince the sergeant or lieutenant in charge of the guard detail that a German paratrooper would have been unlikely to take his wife and two children along on his lark, and we were let go.

Stage by stage, we advanced and reached another temporary stop in the village of Talence, not far from Bordeaux. Soon, the Loire was breached, and it was clear that the Germans would only stop at the Pyrenees. Meanwhile, my Uncle Michel, a reserve captain in the French artillery, joined us. He had been separated from his unit and was dressed in a pale blue uniform of World War I vintage. I still see him desultorily cleaning his little 7.65-mm officer's pistol and remarking that this dainty toy was hardly appropriate to stop Hitler's Panzers.

What to do? My father had academic connections in the United States and decided that we should try to cross the Spanish border, another 300 kilometers to the south. We procured visas at the Spanish consulate in Bordeaux and resumed our southward journey to Hendaye, the French border station. There, the roads were so clogged that we were given the option either to enter Spain but only on foot or to return to Bordeaux in our car. With my father on crutches and my brother a toddler suffering from diarrhea, the choice was clear. We turned back to reenter Bordeaux at about the same time as the first armored columns of the *Wehrmacht*. At that stage, Mussolini deemed it safe enough to attack the Côte d'Azur and establish his token occupation zone in France. The game was over.

My first glance of the victorious enemy impressed me immensely. After the hordes of dishevelled stragglers, the sight of an impeccably dressed *Panzergrenadier* column rumbling through the nearly deserted streets of Bordeaux in their spanking-clean lorries, half-tracks, and motorcycles made it clear why they had won. Or, at least, so it seemed. In fact, the equipment of the Allies (planes aside) was not appreciably inferior to that of the *Wehrmacht*. But the French dispersed their armor, while the Germans thrust it all in the spearhead. Most of the German army and supplies throughout the war moved in a combination of trains and horsecarts, much as in World War I. Only the Americans and British fought an entirely motorized war. But we only began to *see* the German horsecarts in the retreat of 1944. The French debacle was a defeat of organization, not of technology.

For both the Germans and the Japanese, World War II, especially after the attacks on the Soviet Union and the United States, was an insane gamble that could only be lost. That, however, only became obvious after Stalingrad. In 1940, the world, as we knew it, had collapsed. The future was dark indeed.

The next step was obviously to return to Brussels, a task much easier than anticipated. With Teutonic *Gründlichkeit* ("thoroughness"), the *Feldgendarmerie* ("military police"), on its best behavior, cleared the roads of debris, courteously directed traffic, and distributed gasoline coupons, eager to have the population go home and production return to normal within the briefest possible delay. Indeed, the first year of the Nazi occupation, though humiliating, was better than expected. Food, though rationed, was still in adequate supply. Open persecution of Jews had not yet started. The military governor of Belgium and northern France, General Alexander Freiherr von Falkenhausen, was, everything considered, a decent sort. He held the dual distinction of having been arrested by the Gestapo in 1944 for complicity in the July plot to assassinate Hitler, and condemned by the Belgians in 1951 for executing hostages. He was, in short, a Junker, not a Nazi. He made attempts to secure the cooperation of the Belgian population and especially courted the Flemings, who in Nazi ideology were racially closer to the Herrenvolk than the effete, degenerate Walloons. One ploy to exploit Belgian ethnic conflicts and divide the conquered was to release Flemish prisoners of war before the Walloons.

The German labor draft of young men to work in German factories had not yet started. More than anything else, the labor draft was the major factor that escalated opposition to the Nazis and fed the ranks of the underground. The Résistance was not so much a wave of patriotic fervor against the oppressor, as the response of hundreds of thousands of young men who hid from the German labor draft. Thus, lofty historical events are often best explained as the sum of thousands of inglorious little acts of self-preservation. In France, the best organized underground was that of the Communist Party, and it, of course, only became active after the June 1941 Nazi invasion of the Fatherland of the Proletariat. Before that, since Hitler and Stalin were allies and partners in the rape of Poland, the Communist Party undertook nothing against the occupiers.

The real hardships only began to escalate, in rapid crescendo, in the second half of 1941. Food and other essentials became scarcer and scarcer, and existing stocks were increasingly siphoned off to Germany. The machinery for the Holocaust was set in motion. Concentration camps proliferated; one, I remember, near Malines, was within sight of the main Antwerp-Brussels highway. We did not directly see the inmates, but a watchtower and a long stretch of electrified fence were clearly visible, a bare 200 or 300 meters from the bicycle path we travelled.

The labor draft and the underground snowballed in direct correlation with each other. As the underground became more active, German reprisals mounted, the principal form of which was the shooting of ten hostages for every German killed. In an attempt to deprive the occupied countries of their leadership, prominent people, especially academics and intellectuals, were choice hostages. Thus, my maternal grandfather was arrested as a hostage, notwithstanding the fact that he was in his seventies, though he was released after a few days. A favorite spot for hostage executions was a prison in Brussels. I remember hearing gunshots as I passed by in the streetcar. Indeed, the Germans made no effort to conceal their reprisals. Quite the opposite: they almost daily distributed large yellow posters publicizing the latest edicts of the *Kommandantur* ("military government") and the names of their victims.

None of the members of my family were actively involved in the Résistance, although, like the vast majority of the population, we were in full sympathy and provided help and shelter whenever needed. My father probably had the closest brush with danger, through his lab assistant, the enthusiastic whore-killer, who used my father's lab as an arsenal. My father one day discovered that his glassware cabinets were now housing pistols and hand grenades. What made the discovery even more unsettling was that it took place while a German officer was visiting. The German, a physician and tropical specialist like my father, was courting (and later married) my father's other lab assistant and former mistress. He was a delightful, cultured man, and, twelve or thirteen years later, I visited him and his wife (on whom I, too, had a boyhood crush) in Germany. Ironically, *I* was then occupying *his* country as an American GI!

Among the masses of the population, ourselves included, opposition took more prosaic forms. The general attitude toward the occupier was one of stone-faced silence. Whenever troops marched in the streets, for example, I could not help but watch, but my mother or grandmother always pulled me away and ostentatiously turned their faces away from the Germans. Military parades, typically accompanied by loud bands, singing soldiers, and the strutting horses of the officers, marched through virtually empty streets. We were forced to billet a couple of officers through most of the war, but I had firm instructions not to "fraternize" with them, despite tempting offers of chocolate and sweets, and the maids were instructed to exchange only a curt nod with them when they opened the door. Incidentally, most of them behaved with impeccable courtesy, and I remember it as a painful experience not to be allowed to respond to their obvious overtures of friendship and human warmth. (There is a beautiful short novel, entitled *Le Silence de la Mer,* on the subject by a French Résistance writer, using the *nom de guerre* of Vercors. It deals with a German officer, a musician in civilian life, billeted with an old man and his niece. Unable to break through the wall of silence, he tries to reach the young woman by playing Bach preludes on the family harmonium. In the end, Nazi barbarism defeats his search for a common ground of humanism.)

We also engaged in countless little symbolic acts of passive resistance and defiance. Despite the rising tide of brutal repression, the increasing visibility of the Gestapo in their ubiquitous, black, front-wheel-drive Citroens, the frequent stopping of streetcars and frisking of passengers by the *Feldgendarmerie,* the curfews, the hostage executions, we were not really cowed. To be sure, it was always with a shiver that I passed by the Brussels Gestapo headquarters, a ten-story building on Avenue Louise, on my way to school by streetcar. And I remember it as one of the happiest days of the war when a courageous and skillful RAF fighter pilot put a well-aimed cannon round into every floor of the building. The next morning, on my way to school, the streetcar was slowed by a stream of ambulances and scurrying SS troops clearing the wounded and the debris. An unforgettable sight!

A common form of defiance was the telling of anti-German jokes (such as: "The typical Aryan is blond like Hitler, thin like Goering, and tall like Goebbels") and the use of derogatory epithets in reference to the Germans (like the old World War I term, *boche,* and the newer *doryphore,* a potato beetle, in reference to the Germans parasitizing our food supply). As school children we also tried to peer through the light at the lines of our textbooks that German censorship had blacked out. (They dealt mostly with World War I in our history manuals.)

The bravest among my older classmates engaged in the sport of either cutting off the silver tassel hanging from the short ceremonial dagger worn by German officers or burning cigarette holes in their beautiful greatcoats. Either could be fairly easily accomplished on the crowded standing platforms of Brussels streetcars. The Germans, however, quickly put an end to the sport by reserving for themselves one-half of a wagon on the two-wagon trams. These lost opportunities were compensated by a greater freedom to make derogatory remarks about the Germans. A shiver of sheer terror sticks in my mind, however. One day, as I was telling my classmates the latest anti-*boche* joke, a Gestapo agent in civvies tapped my shoulder to tell me he was going to arrest my father. The point, nevertheless, was that we never felt so cowed that we feared making openly anti-German remarks in public.

Perhaps the deepest and longest-lasting effect of the war was that it acted as a social leveller. Much as the Colt was the proverbial equalizer of the American West, so was World War II for Europe. Some of its effects only became obvious after the war, for example, the demise of the colonial empires of all the victorious powers (except, ironically, the Soviet Union, whose empire expanded, thanks, in part, to the naiveté of Roosevelt at Yalta). Even during the war, however, it was obvious that patriotic solidarity against the enemy transcended class lines. But, to an extent still not sufficiently recognized, it was in the little mundane aspects of daily life that the war irreversibly changed the structure of European class relations, sweeping away many residues of a lingering nineteenth century and transforming Western Europe into a modern open-class society.

Let me elaborate from personal vignettes. Shortage of transportation forced people into closer class promiscuity. Absence of gasoline, except for the German military, rendered the bourgeois private car instantaneously useless. We kept ours hidden in our garage throughout the war, hoping that it would escape requisitioning by the Germans, as, indeed, it did. But the luxury of car travel became a memory, starkly replaced by the reality of always overcrowded streetcars and trains. I cannot remember taking a trip during the war without being squashed from all sides, usually in a standing position, and mostly by odorous, sweaty people whom our social circumstances would have enabled us to avoid before the war.

The female members of my family were particularly affected by this enforced promiscuity. My mother, my aunts, my grandmothers bitterly resented having their nostrils continuously assaulted by offensive odors, their ears violated by crude language, their flesh pressed by their social inferiors; but they had to put up with it or stay at home. My Aunt Francine, then a very attractive young woman in her twenties, was especially incensed at having her bottom regularly pinched in the crowded Paris subway, a form of male aggression then quite common in French working-class culture. My Aunt Marie would rather walk several kilometers than take the tram. (She always hated trams, dear soul, and, by a terrible irony, as she was stepping out of a taxi, she was killed by one in 1973.)

Yet, we all had to use trains and streetcars if we wanted to see our relatives, go to work and school (in my case, four times a day, because we came home for lunch), and even get food. At fairly regular monthly intervals, for instance, we took a 30-kilometer trip to the farm of one of my grandmother's distant cousins in Voorde, near the market town of Ninove. This meant an hour on a slow tram, followed by another hour in a horsecart. (The latter portion of the trip was, of course, great sport.) The tram journey was something else, especially the return trip in the evening. The main purpose of the expedition was foraging for scarce food (principally eggs, butter, cheese, and meat), that was unavailable through our ration tickets. When we arrived at the farm, around noon, we would be treated to what seemed like a Lucullan meal with two meat courses. The tables were literally being turned on the urban bourgeoisie! Now mere peasants ate much better than the newly starved urbanites. The meal was worth the trip by itself, but we would also buy from our rural kinsmen one or two kilos of butter, salted pork, eggs, cheese, and similar otherwise unattainable luxuries, at "friendly" prices, that is, much below the urban black-market prices.

The problem was getting the foodstuffs back to Brussels and past the cordon of police inspectors who ruthlessly confiscated this contraband on the trams. Women's skirts were the principal hiding places, but the effect of the heat and the overcrowding on the produce was devastating.

(The plastic bag had not been invented yet.) Not infrequently, before we made it home, my mother had butter dripping down her legs, not to mention the involuntary beginnings of a premature omelette.

It is true that the well-to-do could convert their assets into food purchased on a thriving black market, and stories were rampant of pianos, Oriental rugs, silverware, and other luxuries moving from the cities to the rustic dwellings of the newly affluent peasants. Sugar, flour, meat, and butter, in particular, fetched astronomical prices in the latter war years, when shortages had become quite acute. By 1943 or 1944 our ration tickets would get us little more than unspeakably adulterated bread, half-rotten potatoes, rutabaga (a peculiarly Teutonic turnip that found little favor with us), mouldy or shrunken apples, a little skimmed milk if there were children in the household, a few hundred grams of bony meat and margarine a month, an occasional sour herring, all this supplemented by what few vegetables, chickens, and eggs your backyard would produce (assuming you were lucky enough to have a garden).

Nevertheless, food rationing too was a social equalizer. Like most equalizers in history, it was a *downward* equalizer. Practically everyone was eating worse than before the war, but the bourgeoisie was eating *much* worse, despite their black-market purchases. Only a tiny elite of war profiteers who collaborated with the Germans had unimpeded access to caviar, *paté de foie gras,* champagne, and other pre-war delicacies. Thus, eating well became politically suspect. A florid, overweight appearance was distinctly in bad taste and exposed you not only to envy but to dark allegations of misdeeds. My paternal grandparents who, thanks to their peasant connections and my grandmother's foresight, managed to keep an enviably laden table through much of the war warned me not to tell anyone what we had for lunch or dinner. Of course, I already knew better than to flaunt my relative good fortune. *Ostentation* of wealth—the mainstay of the pre-war bourgeoisie—was thus even more severely reduced than the substance of it.

Queueing was another novel and democratizing phenomenon. One queued not only for food, but for all necessities and superfluities of life: soap, toilet paper, hair brushes, tobacco, pencils, textiles, shoes, whatever. Indeed, queues became their own attractants: one often joined one without being very sure of what one was queueing for. If a queue had formed, by definition, it was worth queueing for. The queue was probably the war's most lasting contribution to democracy. As hapless denizens of the regions east of the Iron Curtain well know, the queue has become a permanent fixture of life in the workers' and peasants' Utopias. No other democratic institution survived communism, . . . but for the resilient queue.

The war-time queue was the democratic outdoor *salon* of the whole population. Even bourgeois women now spent time queueing, which they previously would have squandered reading novels, playing bridge, or drinking tea in each others' homes. Even men (and children) who, before the war, would never have gone shopping were now sent out by their wives (and mothers) to hold places in queues. Queues, being slow and tedious affairs, fostered conversation, from social bantering to the exchange of news (or, more frequently, rumors). And conversation inevitably crossed class lines, more than ever before. One's queue neighbor was unlikely to be of the same social class. As newspapers could no longer be believed, the queue also became the most important news agency (next to the clandestinely listened to BBC). Even if 90 percent of what one gleaned turned out to be unfounded rumor, one could still piece together a much better picture of events than from the Nazi-controlled press or radio. And if one had missed the last BBC newscast, the queue was the place to catch up on it, with optimistic embellishments. In fact, as shortages became worse, the news, in uplifting quid pro quo, was improving. El Alamein, Stalingrad, Monte Cassino, Normandy—what joyful morale boosters these names were and how well they made up for the absence of soap and toilet paper.

Shortage of textiles had a peculiarly levelling effect. To be sure, a well-stocked bourgeois wardrobe could survive four or five years of war better than a meager proletarian one. Still, shirts became frayed, sleeves lustrous with rubbing, boys' pant seats patched (often with clashingly unmatched material, as I remember). More than anything, the disappearance of silk stockings—that ultimate feminine badge of high status—was a strong blow for democracy. One could pace the streets without them and not lose face. Quite the opposite: now, only *cocottes* of German officers sported them. Perhaps the demise of the silk stocking was also the first blow for the liberation of women from other forms of uncomfortable body containment that were soon to join the silk stocking on the roster of feminist anathema: corsets, high heels, bras, the lot.

Finally, the shortage of fuel also played its role in the spread of social equality. Not only did it immobilize a whole fleet of bourgeois automobiles, it also made central heating (still a bourgeois privilege then) a suddenly useless anachronism. Our rations of a couple of hundred kilos of coal a year barely sufficed to keep the kitchen oven and perhaps one additional little stove going through four or five months of chill. In great houses and in hovels alike, social life shrunk to a small circle around the kitchen stove or perhaps a small family common room.

In our house, and in that of my grandparents in Ghent, it positively revolutionized our life-style. The upstairs-downstairs apartheid of master and servant became instantaneously obsolete. We now spent our waking hours in the heated basement, our family in a converted dining-sitting room heated by a small coal stove and our servants next door in the kitchen. At night, we all retired, hot-water bottle in hand, to our unheated bedrooms. Downward material equality was very nearly achieved, at least during the winter months. The majestic first floor with its marble entrance hall, its stately staircase, its antique furniture, grand piano and Persian rugs had become a museum to a past epoch, a mausoleum to the pre-war bourgeoisie. When I look at the family album where the image of these elegant rooms is preserved, I am looking at a showcase of the past, not quite ready for the Louvre perhaps, but quite at home in, say, New York's Metropolitan Museum. Yet, I am looking only forty years into the past.

There is a little postscript to this story. Some ten or twelve years ago, as I was taking a nostalgic walk through my old Brussels neighborhood, the Moroccan flag was flying from our old home. It had become the Moroccan Consulate General and host to a vast proletarian population of "guest workers" from that country. As it was a public building, I entered. My old house was now a somewhat run-down shell, but it still showed traces of its former elegance. My father's study had become the passport office, and the parlor a waiting room. Where the nineteenth-century portrait of a French ancestor had hung above the Italian marble fireplace, there now hung the photograph of King Hassan. The corner showcases, formerly displaying Persian miniatures and Berber jewelry, were empty. The plush green leather armchairs and the red-leather, Chinese wedding chest had given room to flimsy folding chairs and a little table with a few travel brochures. My parents' privileged friends had been replaced by shabbily dressed Moroccan men who had come from the sunny Atlas to drizzly Belgium to give their families a chance to escape the vicious circle of Third World poverty.

I cannot conceal that I felt sad; but I also knew that the house was now put to better use than it had during my occupancy. A clerk at a typewriter courteously asked me, in impeccable French, whether he could help me. I could barely believe myself when I told him I once lived there. *"Faites comme chez vous"* ("Make yourself at home"), he said affably. I no longer could.

My Brussels years, bracketed by the war, were also those of my primary and much of my secondary education, and since I spent about one-third of my waking hours in classrooms during these years, no account of this period would be complete without a description of the kind of schooling I received. Belgium then had (and, to my knowledge, still has) a twelve-year school system, divided into six years of primary school

GROWING UP IN WAR AND PEACE

In our Brussels living room, 1946. My sister, Gwendoline, has just appeared on the scene. Now the waiting room of the Moroccan Consulate.

and six of secondary school. The entire system was divided into eight institutional cubicles. There were French-medium schools, where Dutch was taught as a second language, and Dutch-medium schools with French as a second language. Each of these systems was subdivided into Catholic and lay schools, all state-supported. As most of these schools were sex-segregated as well, the total number of niches in the Belgian educational columbary was thus eight.

It was pre-ordained which of the niches I would fill: birth made me not only male, but Catholic and francophone. French was even more exclusively my mother tongue than was the case for most members of my class, since my mother was French. She never saw any need to learn a language that was of no social value to her and that her French upbringing had taught her to regard as peripheral to the center of world civilization: her birthplace, Paris. My father was still fluently bilingual in French and Dutch, but never spoke Dutch at home, though he lectured in both French and Dutch. Dutch was always a foreign language to me; once I spoke it well enough to muddle through both written and oral examinations. But I never seriously tried to master it, and I have only retained a reading knowledge of it.

At age 5, I entered a neighborhood Catholic boys' school, a stern establishment of the Frères des Ecoles Chrétiennes. It was close enough to home that I could walk to it in about fifteen minutes. My mother or the maid escorted me for much of the first year, but I soon resented this veiled aspersion against my capacity to find my way home. My first grade was spent in an educational daze. I barely understood my teacher, a Fleming who spoke such a heavily accented French that I thought he was speaking an exotic language. Perhaps he was a missionary from the Congo, I thought.

The teacher was a stern disciplinarian, insisting that we sit silently unless called on, upright on a wooden bench built in defiance of a boy's anatomy, with arms crossed. The index finger of the right hand was to be raised to ask permission to speak. We were to stand in unison whenever he or another teacher entered the room. Otherwise, we were to remain seated until the school bell, followed by his own permission, released us. We were forced to write with our right hands. (I still do although I am clearly left-handed, one of my many minority-group memberships. When I spontaneously offered my left hand to adults, I was told to give my *belle main,* despite the fact that I failed to see an esthetic difference between my two upper appendages. I also resented the often-stated assumption that, because I was left-handed, I was clumsy.)

Discipline in class was maintained by a nasty little wooden instrument, known as "the signal," and held by the teacher. It produced a sharp clap. Held within 10 centimeters of one's ear, it was an effective remedy against somnolence. Punishment took the form of a sharp rap on the fingers with a ruler (though only a couple of the more rambunctious working class boys fell victim to that particular form of barbarism). Rewards were awarded in the shape of a weekly distribution of medals to be proudly worn on the left lapel of one's shirt or coat. (Those tended to go almost exclusively to "well behaved," that is, middle-class, boys.)

Even outside the classroom, we were marched in mock-military drills. We assembled in silent columns of twos, by class, in a big hall. From there, we were taken to the courtyard for boisterous ten-minute breaks, to the gym for more quasi-military calisthenics, or to the classrooms for another two hours of enforced immobility. Michel Foucault, in his masterly book, *Surveiller et Punir,* gives a very good account of this particular brand of Goffmanesque total institution. My first grade was merely a foretaste of twelve years of systematic frustration inflicted in the name of discipline.

Of my classmates, only two stick in my memory. One, a loutish bully, was the son of a neighborhood butcher. His expertise at playing marbles commanded my admiration. He made a clean sweep of all the marbles of those foolish enough to challenge him. I admiringly watched him from the sidelines, reserving my precious few marbles for weaker opponents. Thirty years later, I saw him at the counter of his father's butchershop, which he inherited—an entire destiny played out within a 500-meter radius! The other was a very good-looking, well behaved little bourgeois boy of whom the teacher instantaneously approved and who, much to my envy, spent most of the year with one or two medals pinned to his lapel. I lost sight of him, but he had all the makings of a successful politician in the Christian Social Party. We shared one thing, however, namely the unwanted attentions of the school director, an obvious pederast who, two or three times a week, would call one of us in his office, stroke our hair or cheek, and tell us what nice little boys we were and how much he liked us.

I told my father, who did not seem overly scandalized. Pederasty in the Catholic clergy seemed an accepted fact of life (as witnessed by much French literature where the theme appears, though usually in veiled form, for example, in the works of Peyrefitte, Montherlant, Gide, and others). Anyway, the director stopped calling me in, but he continued in office, I suppose to his happy retirement. "Let the children come to me, and do not hinder them; for to such belongs the Kingdom of Heaven."

Luckily, my second to fifth grades were a notable improvement over the first. I really liked two of my teachers, who, behind the institutional facade of rigor, let a real *Mensch* peer through. Unlike my obtuse, sadistic first grade teacher, they were also good pedagogues, and I quickly reached the very top of my class. My bourgeois good manners no doubt contributed to the recognition of my intellectual merits, but I was now firmly ensconced in my impregnable position as teacher's pet, destined for great things. On the liability side, this did not endear me to my classmates, but, somehow, even then, I seemed to care little for popularity. Popularity, my maternal grandfather told me, was the chimera of fools. It was worth noting. What counted was self-respect. I soon came to agree with him.

Well-adapted to my school world though I became after the shock of the first year, I never stopped to question that world or, indeed, all the other worlds I encountered thereafter. I was especially intolerant of authority and skeptical of opinions that did not conform to my experiences. In short, below the high-achieving, well-behaved little boy, there already lurked a rebel.

The rebel first came out when I transferred from my neighborhood primary school to the prestigious Jesuit Collège Saint Michel. My primary school was common to all social classes. Saint Michel was the bastion of Brussels' upper bourgeoisie, one of a handful of elite secondary schools in Belgium, with rigorous intellectual as well as social standards of selection. In theory, there was no *social* selection, but the very fact that the school was francophone already excluded half of Belgium's population. It was a boys' school thereby excluding another half of the remaining half. Finally, even among francophone boys, its academic standards were so demanding and its competition so stiff that few not born to the advantages of the middle class could hope to succeed. (In defense of the system, however, the gifted few who overcame the handicaps of a lowly birth were pampered and groomed for a high level of performance that a more lax, American-style system could never produce. I would certainly choose to be a Belgian or French factory worker's son rather than a ghetto black proletarian in the United States.)

Like most Belgian secondary schools, Saint Michel was further internally stratified into a "classical" curriculum and a "modern" one. The former stressed Latin (six years), Greek (five years) and letters (composition, literature, rhetoric in French and Dutch), with a lesser emphasis on mathematics, history, and geography. We had a mere six years of algebra, five of geometry and two of trigonometry. The modern curriculum, by contrast, offered no Latin or Greek, substituting two modern languages (usually English and German) and more math (to include analytical geometry and calculus). The classical curriculum opened the doors of all university faculties; the modern curriculum only those of engineering faculties. Clearly to be in *modernes* was second rate. That is where you went if you flunked out of the classics, though a few went straight there by choice.

My first year at Saint Michel was dominated by the comical figure of my teacher, a septuagenarian recalled to active teaching by the war, who excited his charges' hilarity by still wearing a tailed coat. (He was a lay teacher, not a Jesuit.) In many ways, he was a carbon copy of his counterpart in *The Blue Angel,* and, like him, he had to cope with forty beastly little monsters, though probably not with a Marlene Dietrich. He considered me his chief tormentor. Two idiosyncrasies of mine drove him to distraction: one was to climb steps two by two, a feat that he could no longer emulate, and the other was what he considered to be a perpetual sarcastic smile. Partly because I excited his ire, and partly because it took me some time to adjust to the faster pace of Saint Michel, I dropped from my customary first place to seventh, if I remember rightly.

The next school year, 1944–1945, was the last of the war and full of excitement: the Normandy landings in June, the liberation of Paris in August just before the end of the vacation, that of Brussels in September after classes had begun, the anxious moments of the Battle of the Bulge around Christmas, and lastly the Rhine crossing and the final Allied victory in May. Compared to Holland, which suffered a frightful famine during that winter, we were extremely fortunate, though food was still scarce and monotonous. I remember a diet of pickled herrings (abundant in the North Sea after four years of little fishing) and imported American powdered milk and maize flour, which Belgian bakers were not trained to transform into edible bread.

The liberation of Brussels by British and Canadian troops was an exhilarating experience. Brussels was spared any fighting. We gleefully saw the withdrawing hordes of the *Wehrmacht* and the SS flee, not in trucks and tanks as they had come, but in dilapidated stolen civilian cars, in horsecarts and on foot. I can still see, through the cracks of closed shutters, the last motorcyclists of the rearguard withdrawing along Avenue Louise and shooting a few machine-gun rounds to keep people indoors. Some civilians, eager to display prematurely the welcoming Allied flags lovingly sewn at home from available rags, were actually shot by the fleeing Germans, but otherwise the city was intact.

The reception of the first British columns was delirious. Within minutes, the shuttered facades opened up, Allied flags appeared in every window, and the crowds embraced the Tommies, showering them with flowers and kisses. Every tank became a moving float overladen with ecstatic damsels. There was competition to offer the troops the hospitality of one's home. Almost every day, my father landed a couple of British,

Canadian, and later American officers and soldiers, who, in turn, showered us with cigarettes, chocolate, chewing gum (my first exposure to that then peculiarly American habit), and K-rations (great delicacies to us; oh, the joys of discovering Spam!). Among schoolboys of my age, the rage was the wearing of Allied insignia: divisional shoulder patches (the Screaming Eagle of the 101st was in hot demand), chevrons of rank, anything. My coat was a kaleidoscope: on the left sleeve I was a British corporal, on my lapel a U.S. captain, on my right arm a member of the Middlesex Regiment (that patch was a great hit, with its hermaphroditic implications). My campaign ribbons stretched from Sicily to Normandy. Even my little brother, Christian, was the envy of the first grade, thanks to our parents' hospitality and our shameless demands on our poor visitors, who entered our house lieutenants or majors but left rankless.

The months of late 1944 also had their ugly side. An armed rabble of competing underground groups (many of dubious accomplishments and belated formation) was scrambling to fill the political void and was quick to exact vengeance against both collaborators and private foes. Luckily, the Allied military government was quick to install the safely conservative, London-based, Belgian government-in-exile and to restore a semblance of order by disarming the *maquisards* ("underground fighters"). Equally luckily, the Communist Party was not nearly as strong in Belgium as in France where it came close to plunging the country into civil war. Nonetheless, hundreds—perhaps thousands—of people were mysteriously killed. Cases of arson and looting abounded. Girls accused of having consorted with the enemy had their heads shaved and were paraded through jeering crowds.

Our circle of acquaintances was not spared: our dentist's son was mysteriously shot in front of his house, for no apparent reason; a young man we knew was shot dead at night, seemingly for no other reason than that he was a salesman for Pfaff, a German sewing machine firm. He had held that job before the war and kept it during the war, which entitled him to a few liters of gasoline. That privilege was probably his death warrant. Finally, the farm in Voorde where we went on our foraging forays was set alight because the fiancé of one of the daughters had been foolish enough to enlist in the Flemish legion that fought on the German side on the Russian front. (He never came back.)

By 1945, things had returned to normal, and the era of private vengeance and kangaroo courts was over, much to everyone's relief. Ninety percent of all Belgians had been neither heroes nor traitors, but ordinary folks trying to make the best of a difficult situation. They were now quite ready to forget and get on with their lives.

There was, however, one important political sequel of the war that would not go away, namely the *crise monarchique* as it was known. King Léopold III came under much fire, both within and outside of Belgium, for his role during the war. Unlike his father, Albert I, who became the "soldier king" by fighting at the head of his troops throughout World War I, Léopold surrendered his army to the Germans after eighteen days. Unlike his colleague, the Dutch Queen, who went to London to head a government in exile, Léopold spent the war in his Laeken palace on the outskirts of Brussels, supposedly a German war prisoner but in a conspicuously gilded cage. Furthermore, he had the bad taste to remarry during that time—to a commoner at that. To make matters worse, the new wife of Léopold had to compete in public affection with the ghost of the vastly popular Queen Astrid, killed before the war in an automobile accident—the sports car was recklessly driven by the very same Léopold. Obviously, Léopold was not the most astute politician.

What made the monarchical crisis so grave is that it split the country largely, though not entirely, along ethnic lines. Support for Léopold came mostly from the Flemish north; opposition centered overwhelmingly in the Walloon south. It also split my family. My maternal grandfather regarded Léopold as a traitor, and my father, the eternal maverick, was also an anti-monarchist. I sided with them. The rest of my paternal family was strongly royalist, especially my Aunt Marie who, after Léopold's abdication, rushed to stock up on postage stamps. For many years thereafter, she used old Léopold stamps as a symbol of loyalty. In the end, a referendum was held. Léopold won, but by such a slender margin that he was wisely advised to abdicate in favor of his son, Baudoin, then still a boy, under the regency of Léopold's popular brother, Charles.

The main reason, incidentally, my Aunt Marie was such an ardent royalist was that she was on the jury of the prestigious musical competition, the Concours Reine Elisabeth, sponsored by the Queen Mother, Albert's widow. This gave her access to the court, which she craved, and an entrée into the nobility. Her main mental feat was the instant production of the exact genealogical relationship between any two members of Europe's reigning houses (and quite a few deposed ones as well). Her royal politics were, thus, intimately intertwined with her social life, her musical avocation, and her intellectual hobby. Royalism was, in short, her raison d'être, quite beyond the scope of rational discourse. She never debated the issue with me, but she was pained by my state of *lèse-majesté*, which, with the callousness of youth, I would not let her forget.

To get back to my studies: in my first year of secondary school, I managed to recapture the first place in my class, despite all the excitement. I also had an excellent teacher, who made us thrive on competition. He divided the class into two sections, each led by a captain and two lieutenants (who were the six best students in a class of forty or so). As *primus,* I was the captain of the A team, a heady position! Our teacher pitted us daily against each other in television-style contests: he would demand to know, for example, the second person singular of the subjunctive imperfect of an irregular Latin verb, and the first camp to have the right answer would score a point.

The next year, 1945–1946, I had a mediocre teacher whom I scarcely remember, and I slipped a few places in performance—down to fifth, if I recall. This year also marked the beginning of my open intellectual revolt against Jesuit brainwashing. I proclaimed myself an atheist and a communist, displaying a little red flag on the lapel of my coat. My parents had already caused some scandal a few months before, by displaying in their windows a Soviet flag alongside that of the other Allies. In our bourgeois street, there were many American, British, French, and Belgian flags, but ours was the only red flag. Needless to say, my rebellious views also caused scandal at Saint Michel, but my father never suggested that I recant. Indeed, he rather supported me in my dissidence, amused to find the same independence of thought as he had shown.

The beginning of my puberty and active interest in girls also occurred during the year following the war's end. Given the one-sex environment of a Jesuit college, the absence of sisters (my sister, Gwendoline, was just born in 1945), and the presence of rather sexually puritanical grandparents and mother, I had much to learn. My father took me into his study and gave me a rather lengthy and systematic clinical lecture, illustrated by his old medical books. I had already furtively peeped into them, but to little avail. The cross section of an ovary, or a thousandfold magnification of a follicle or a blastula does not teach a 13-year-old much about sexuality. I had also furtively read some of the great classics of erotic literature: Brantôme, Boccaccio, La Fontaine (his *Contes,* not his *Fables*), Balzac, Voltaire, and Rabelais; but these left me puzzled. Either the language was archaic, or they took more knowledge for granted than I possessed.

My father's clinical explanations helped, but practical experience was still several years off. At this stage, my sexual adventures consisted largely of exchanging dirty jokes with classmates, ogling schoolgirls on streetcars on the way to and from school, commenting on their appearance, and following them home from a distance. I also vividly recollect watching a rather alluring and much older girl undress in a house across the street from my bedroom window. She always turned off the light too early for my taste.

Incidentally, the reading list I just mentioned testifies to my rebelliousness. All these books were on the infamous *Index Librorum Prohibitorum* of the Catholic Church, as were indeed a good two-thirds of the world's great literature. For Catholic consumption, the Church produced painstakingly expurgated versions of the classics, not excluding the Bible itself. Most of Shakespeare, for instance, was considered bawdy and subversive. *Macbeth* and *King Lear* escaped fairly unscathed because they dealt with such healthy impulses as murder, ingratitude, greed, ambition, and treachery. But *Hamlet, Othello,* and *Romeo and Juliet,* where love raised its ugly head, were ruthlessly slashed. The Jesuits' library was, indeed, a sorry rump of world literature, devastated by a horde of frustrated celibates who did not want anyone else, least of all their students, to have fun.

For my next two years, I was blessed with a great pedagogue and a warm human being as my principal teacher, Father Bribosia. Unlike most teachers, he addressed his pupils in the familiar *tu* and used our first names. From others, we might have resented the familiarity. (The transition from *tu* to *vous* normally marked promotion from primary to secondary school.) From him, we accepted it as a mark of concern and affection. Father Bribosia was a short, rotund bon vivant who, unlike many of his sour colleagues, had a healthy touch of hedonism. He winked at our foibles, bent the rules of discipline, encouraged intellectual inquiry and skepticism (within limits in the religious sphere, of course, but even there he was a liberal), and showed unwavering good humor. Whereas we mercilessly hazed and ridiculed some of the other teachers, Father Bribosia so won our affection and respect that he never had to punish any of us, an extraordinary achievement in retrospect. Luckily, he was promoted with me into the next class, so I had him for two years in a row.

Without doubt, he was a major influence in my life. Of my teachers, he was the first to transform the deliberately dry school subjects from drudgery to joy. For example, we had been reading Julius Caesar and Xenophon with dedicated concern for ablatives and subjunctives, but no one had ever bothered to explain to us what a bunch of crazy Greeks were doing running up and down Asia Minor or who on earth the first centurion of the second cohort might be. In a flash, Father Bribosia made the classics come to life by explaining the role of Greek mercenaries in the Persian Empire and the organization of a Roman legion.

In addition to teaching the classics and history, Father Bribosia also taught us French, and it was he who guided my first faltering steps on the long road to a competent, disciplined use of the written word. By age 17, at the end of high school, I had become a tolerable stylist, and what is more, I had learned to *enjoy* writing. It would still take quite a few more years before I had anything worthwhile to say, but the mechanics of the skill were firmly in place.

Not only did Father Bribosia stimulate my mind, fully sensing that I was destined to be a dissident; he also provided me with crucial moral support. I was now fully engulfed in the Sturm und Drang of adolescence, and my relations with my father had turned to sharp hostility. My father resented my sudden assertion of independence and strong-headedness. I bitterly resented his self-indulgence, his philandering, and his increasingly abusive and insulting treatment of my mother. This bitter rift was never really healed, although, after a few years of hating him, my dominant emotion toward him turned to that very worst of human relationships: indifference. Hate is, after all, still a form of caring. We still saw each other at irregular intervals when he visited the United States, or I his place of retirement near Nairobi, or we met, almost by chance, in Belgium. But we had become strangers to one another. When he died of cancer in Johannesburg in 1979, we had not seen each other for eleven years. A few months before, he had written from Nairobi that he was dying. I replied from Seattle that we should try to arrange a last meeting, as too much had been left unsaid between us. He did not answer, and that was our last exchange.

Father Bribosia, in whom I confided about our family situation, listened patiently and sympathetically, and though, concretely, he could do nothing, he gave me tremendous comfort. So did my Uncle Paul, who, from that time, became a surrogate father to me. My mother, isolated from her family, sought an ally in me, a role that I played willingly enough. But I needed to get away occasionally from the tensions of home and the erratic rages of my father. More than ever, he was becoming seriously unhinged, was losing all sense of balance, and was turning into a withdrawn, moody egotist, a hypochondriac and a megalomaniac. Conversation had become impossible, as he turned all attempts into soliloquies, occasionally brilliant but increasingly rambling. I really needed the cheerful balance and sanity of a Father Bribosia at that stage!

Two other teachers stick in my mind. Though they played a negligible role in my education, their position in the school revealed a good deal about our educational and social system. Both were lay teachers unprotected by the charisma of the cloth, and both taught what we regarded as secondary and lower-status subjects: Dutch and mathematics. Father Bribosia, a Walloon with minimal command of Dutch and a Latinist with little regard for math, unwittingly reinforced these prejudices. Both teachers were the prime targets of that institutional characteristic of all repressive schools. We called it *chahutage,* roughly "to create a premeditated commotion." Alas, no single word in English captures the rich connotations of *chahutage*. Saint Michel, like other *boîtes* (roughly, "joint" in the prisoner's slang), had a cherished tradition of *chahutage*. Epic instances of it were transmitted from student generation to generation, and it was our ambition to concoct a prank that, through either its scope or its inventiveness, would live on in the oral tradition. This was not easy; everything had already been tried, but we nevertheless spent hours of our break times plotting new pranks.

There were definite rules to the game. Violence or destruction of any sort was taboo. The object was to disrupt teaching and humiliate or embarrass the teachers or, better yet, college authorities like the hated prefect of discipline, a reincarnation of Torquemada, the Grand Inquisitor, and the source of all official punishment. The prank had to remain anonymous, so that the instigator could not be singled out for punishment. Snitching was the ultimate crime; it led to ostracism and weeks of the "silent treatment." Certain teachers, like our beloved father Bribosia, were out of bounds. Others were naturals, inevitably those who resorted to official punishment a lot, though it was not always clear which was cause and which was effect.

Occasionally, a technological innovation offered an opportunity for a truly novel trick. Thus, our class was the first to make innovative use of that great gift from the transatlantic barbarians; chewing gum. We used it to jam the keyhole to our classroom, creating a good hour's commotion and exciting the gratifying fury of the prefect of discipline.

The Jesuits, as intellectuals, did not believe in crude physical punishment. Instead, they honed the searing art of mental torture. Lateness called for forced appearance a half-hour earlier the following morning. The punishment slip had to be returned with a parental signature. *Chahutage,* slackness, and other serious shortcomings were punishable by special Sunday morning sessions spent copying, in neat cursive, two, three, or four hundred times, a motto directly related to one's infraction. (Thus, in later years in the Congo, my brother was made to write two hundred times, in punishment for alleged laziness, the inspiring motto: "As I am white, I must work, otherwise I am a white nigger.") Punishment came in multiples of two hours, to be purged on Sunday morning from ten to twelve. Thus, a relatively minor infraction called for a single spoiled Sunday, more serious ones for up to a month of ruined weekends. (Note the cunning timing, smack in the middle of our free time that only began on Saturday noon. This had the desired effect of inconveniencing the parents as well and eliciting from them additional opprobrium.)

The risks of *chahutage* were thus substantial. Still, the game was irresistible, especially with such tempting targets as our math and Dutch teachers. The former was a totally humorless, insecure person who, in addition, had the misfortune of speaking in an effeminate falsetto. We went for the jugular. One of our pranks, well-rehearsed, was to pretend that his fly was unbuttoned (zippers were rare as yet) and to orchestrate a smooth crescendo of "oh's" ending in the whole class standing in unison pointing to the core of his questionable manhood. The effect was devastating. He reddened like a beet, not daring to look down. Instead, he withdrew behind his desk, raised his briefcase for additional screening, and remained incapacitated for the rest of the hour.

The Dutch teacher was a different case altogether. There was no question of his virility, for he was a strapping man of almost brutish appearance. But he was the school's social pariah, as a Fleming of rustic origins who spoke a heavily accented French. Our favorite sport was to imitate his accent, but we did so with diabolical cleverness: in class, we would, to his despair, exaggerate our French accent when speaking Dutch and imitate his Flemish accent when speaking French. The outcome produced involuntary squeals of laughter, which the teacher never really seemed to understand, so he ended up punishing, not the merciless imitator but the hapless victim of the laughing fit. Thus, he opened himself up to indignant charges of unfairness with the prefect of discipline, an aristocratic francophone, who undermined the Dutch teacher's last shreds of authority by occasionally reducing the punishment, say from four hours to two.

A few remarks about the Jesuit intellectual perspective are apposite here, for it marked me for life. Whenever my wife, for example, is losing an argument, she accuses me, not inaccurately, of being Jesuitical, or "Catholic," which to her (a Lutheran) is the same thing. By that she means that, even though she is hard-put to specify which mental trick of casuistry I used to twist reality my way, my argument is specious. (She is especially impatient of one of my favorite ploys, the reductio ad absurdum.) Jesuit casuistry is marked by nearly all the same characteristics as two other great Western intellectual traditions: the Talmudic and the communist. That is why I have always gotten along so well with both Jewish and communist intellectuals. However few opinions the Jesuits and I may have shared, their method of argument was so seductive a game as to overshadow the substance. This was also the end product of my Jesuit education: I emphatically rejected the substance of the teachings, but I retained the powerful method.

Basically, the method is the antithesis of science. Instead of modifying a theory to fit the facts, it consists in twisting the world to fit an a priori intellectual construction. Honed primarily in the defense of the intellectually untenable, namely the Faith (whether it be Catholic, Jewish, or Communist), where the very untenability of the doctrine requires prodigiously agile mental convolutions, it is applied to the whole of the empirical world as well. It becomes an all-encompassing, self-contained method of approaching reality, of fighting the unbeliever, of running one's life, in short, a thoroughly consistent Weltanschauung. Once the method is mastered, it can be applied with equal effect to all logico-deductive philosophical systems. What a great weapon!

Applied to pedagogy it led to a very peculiar way of approaching subjects, especially the teaching of languages. The latter were taught not with the aim of speaking them or even of writing them for purposes of communication. We never even *attempted* to converse or communicate in Latin or Greek. Indeed, the very superiority of the dead languages over the live ones was that even the *temptation* to communicate in dead languages did not exist because there was no one to communicate with.

Languages were taught in the most anti-natural and, therefore, traumatic way conceivable. The pedagogy also incorporated the unspoken premise that, like medicine or jogging, learning had to taste or feel bad in order to be effective. To learn a language naturally, say through the Berlitz method, was to become a talking parrot in a second language, not to become a self-conscious analyst of that language, the sole aim of the Jesuit method. One learned a language through its syntax in order to analyze it, that is, to dissect it into its smallest logical (or pseudo-logical) components. The deader the language, the duller the exercise, the more complex and full of exceptions the grammar, the better that language was in training one's mind. Hence the unquestioned superiority of dead languages over usable, live ones.

This view of learning made, of course, for an exceedingly dull school experience. Even potentially lively subjects like history and geography were eviscerated to yield their maximum quota of formative boredom. History was reduced to a mental exercise in memorizing dates. A table of random numbers would have done just as well. Geography was not a window on the world but a list of place names to be memorized in sequence. Rivers were especially useful for that purpose because they were organized in hierarchies of tributaries, sub-tributaries, and so on, from source to estuary. There was a rich multitude of possible errors in recitation. Literature, especially poetry, served the same purpose: it was to be recited by heart to train the memory rather than understood or related to one's experience.

I have drawn somewhat of a caricature, of course (one of the favorite tricks of the Jesuits in attacking their foes' ideas, and one that I now take special delight in turning against them). The mental torture was sometimes relieved by the likes of Father Bribosia who quietly sabotaged or at least mitigated the system. There was an occasional teacher of geography who had actually travelled and could communicate a personal vision of the world (slides did not exist yet). Occasionally, a history teacher really understood the social forces at work in the period he dealt with. But those were exceptions, indeed *subverters* of the system. Yet, and this is no mean admission, the Jesuit system worked remarkably well—for those who survived it. It trained first-class intellectuals and very frequently rebels who became formidable opponents. Clearly, I owe them much of what I am.

One final aspect of my life during these post-war years remains to be dealt with, if only because it provided such a stark counterpoint from Jesuit studies. Between the ages of 12 and 15, I was an enthusiastic Boy Scout. Like almost every large organization in Belgium, the Boy Scout movement was split along religious lines: there were Catholic and "lay" scouts. By tradition, and also because it had its den closest to home, I joined a Catholic troop. Our Sundays were spent taking long walks and playing war-like games in the Forêt de Soignes, the large patch of woods near Brussels. Once a year, during the summer, we would spend a week or so camping, usually in the hilly Ardennes.

Being a scout meant principally enjoying the companionship of boys in a setting other than school and the freedom of the outdoors. Of course, *le scoutisme*, as we called it, had a brand of discipline of its own—the stupidest of all, based as it was on the military ideology of its founder, Lord Baden-Powell, an aristocratic nitwit more famous for his homosexual dalliance than for his military prowess. His main claim to fame was to have held Mafeking against a ragtag Boer army during the Anglo-Boer War of 1899–1902, and this event was said, in Boy Scout mythology, to have been the inspiration for the movement. Later, as a student of South African history, I was to learn that, during the siege of Mafeking, Baden-Powell helped the British soldiers under his command survive by starving the black civilian population. But at the time, that racist saber-rattler was my unlikely hero.

Another contribution of my experience as a scout was that it put me in continued contact with working-class boys. Saint Michel was a largely bourgeois milieu, but my scout troop was mostly proletarian. This made me feel self-righteous in my newly embraced communist ideology, but I was highly critical of the religious rituals of the troop, such as attendance at mass and prayers. These, I attributed to false consciousness, suggesting to my more intelligent mates that they read the forbidden *Communist Manifesto*.

By age 15, I had outgrown scouting, and my attendance became more and more sporadic. I was about to enter a new chapter of my life. I was fully grown, hairy-legged, and I even had a soupçon of downy moustache. My voice had shifted from boy soprano to tenor, and I had just graduated into long pants. (Boys in Europe then wore short pants until adolescence, even in the dead of winter.) I thought myself a man and resented any unfamiliar adult using the familiar *tu* in addressing me. To prove that manliness, I secretly smoked my first cigarettes and thereby started a stupid habit that I only shook at age 29. In mitigation, I must say that both my parents were light smokers, as were nearly all their friends. Smoking, especially long, aromatic British or Turkish cigarettes at the end of an ivory filter, was definitely the smart thing to do. The skeptic should see *Casablanca* again and count Humphrey Bogart's cigarettes.

The year was 1948. France and Belgium had recuperated from the war, though the "economic miracle" was still a decade into the future. Germany was still devastated, and Britain's recovery was halting. What was later to be called the Third World was on the move, though we barely noticed. The communists were on the threshold of success in China. The Soviets were completing their digestion of Eastern Europe. The Cold War was simmering to a slow boil. The State of Israel had just been created, insuring several decades of Middle East turmoil. Indonesia and the Indian subcontinent just had or were on the verge of overthrowing the yoke of colonialism and launching their very own orgies of nationalist genocide. Indochina was just beginning a thirty-year war of independence, eventually to defeat both France and the United States.

This was the context in which we left for the Belgian Congo. Africa still seemed quiescent enough. There, it seemed that colonialism would last forever or, at the very least, to the end of the millennium. In 1947, my father had founded, with Belgian government support, a multidisciplinary research organism, which he baptized Institut pour la Recherche Scientifique en Afrique Centrale (IRSAC for short). In inspiration, it was similar to the Institut Français d'Afrique Noire (IFAN), but, through my father's clairvoyance, it did not have to find a new label at independence in 1960. (A less imaginative and more conventional man would have called it something like Institut Royal de Recherche Scientifique au Congo Belge.)

My father had preceded us in the Congo by a few months, and we followed him in June 1948—my mother, my 10-year-old brother, Christian, my 3-year-old sister, Gwendoline, and myself.

CHAPTER 3

A Colonial Interlude

The Belgian boat that took us in a leisurely three weeks, from Antwerp to Lobito in Angola, was a World War II Liberty ship, the *Tervaete*. Outfitted as a troop transport, it was made only marginally more comfortable for civilian use. A rich residue of vivid impressions remains from the trip. Except for two Channel crossings during a brief trip to London and Cambridge with my father in 1947, this was my first sea voyage, or more accurately, the first one I remembered. At age 10 or so, I had a brief romance with the sea, dreaming of becoming a sailor, but, alas, a visit to the ophthalmologist dashed my hopes. I was discovered to be color-blind. I resigned myself to remain a landlubber, but the sea retained its lure.

After a duly stormy passage through the Bay of Biscay, we entered calmer waters. The weather became balmier by the day. Flying fishes started dispersing before the bow of the ship, heralding the approaching tropics. Soon, we stopped in Santa Cruz de Tenerife for a day's reprieve from our confined quarters. The Canaries to me had meant little yellow birds that sang prettily. Now those little balls of musical sunshine suddenly exploded in the exuberant splendor of sub-tropical isles. It was as if *Robinson Crusoe, Treasure Island, The Mutiny on the Bounty,* and Captain Cook had all come to life in a kaleidoscope of colors, a bouquet of exotic fragrances, which insistently overwhelmed all the senses. To make the illusion more complete, the gleaming white silhouette of a four-masted square-rigger—the Spanish navy's training ship—was docked at Tenerife for our arrival. Where had I been all my life? I was enchanted. For the rest of my life, the lush tropics have remained my vision of paradise.

The ship's company also offered much of interest to my inquisitive adolescent mind. We lived in very cramped quarters. The bow of the ship, below deck, was a male dormitory where we slept in three-tiered bunks. The stern, the female reserve, was marginally less crowded. The superstructure had been converted into a few cabins for the officers and a passably comfortable lounge and dining hall. The crew was sharply divided into Belgian officers and sailors (only the former ate with the passengers) and a Congolese staff of mess attendants and cabin stewards. The passengers, some 80 to 100, were also divided into two groups, although that division was less visible and only emerged after a couple of days at sea. Except for a British missionary family, all were Belgians; but some were returning colonials with years of African experience, mostly civil servants and missionaries, and others (*les bleus*—"rookies"—as the "old Africa hands" quickly dubbed them) were going to Africa for the first time. My Congolese birth put me in a marginal category. It spared me the traditional salt-water dunking at the crossing of the Equator, but, of course, my colonial experience was quite limited.

A fascinating process of what sociologists call "anticipatory socialization" took place on board; it was one that later helped me understand race relations better. The *bleus* were on the defensive; furthermore, they were full of uncertainty and anxiety on the threshold of an adventuresome change of life. The European image of the Dark Continent was not one to allay fears. How was one to react and adjust to this land of untamed cannibals, blood-sucking insects, creeping jungles, and slithering snakes?

Indeed, an entire Belgian industry—that of colonial outfitters—thrived on this image and on these fears. We, too, paid a visit to the best-stocked of these colonial emporiums and left for the Congo with more than 100 metal trunks (all padlocked against allegedly thieving natives). These trunks were crammed with all the impedimenta (the word was never so appropriate) deemed essential to survival in the *brousse* ("bush"). Besides the obvious items, such as the pith helmets and what later came to be called "safari suits," there were such stand-bys as kerosene stoves and lanterns, tents, mosquito nets, water filters, and a complement of firearms including, as a bare minimum, a revolver for close-quarter self-protection, a double-barrelled 12-gauge shotgun for small game, and a high-powered rifle for big game. The trunks themselves were a marvel of mercantile ingenuity. There were *malles-chapeaux* for hats; *malles-fusils,* long enough to accommodate rifles;

and that ultimate masterpiece of sybaritic colonialism, the *malle-tub,* an oval-shaped contraption, the contents of which were exchanged for the body of its proprietor after the lion hunt.

The water-filter, a heavy cylinder made of thick pottery, is also worth a brief comment, for it, too, represented an extraordinary bit of colonial nonsense. The usual practice of colonials was to boil the water first, which was sensible enough, but then to pour the hot water directly into the filter, to be mixed with the tepid water within. The filter itself was cleaned (usually with unboiled water) about once a fortnight, and, in the interim, provided a marvellously cozy environment for bacteria to proliferate in. We sensibly boiled our water but did not filter it.

But I digress. Back on board the *Tervaete,* the *bleus* were eagerly pumping information from the old hands, who, naturally were only too glad to establish their superiority by obliging. It would never have occurred to anyone, by the way, to ask any of the Congolese on board what their country was like. The result of this process of "education" was a crash course in colonialism. At the outset of the trip, the behavior of the rookies was most markedly divergent from that of the old hands in the treatment of the Congolese catering staff. Most of the new colonials had had virtually no prior contact with blacks and initially treated them quite courteously. Indeed, in the uncertainty created by the novelty of the encounter, some even treated the black servants more politely than they would have treated white servants.

The old hands, for their part, treated the blacks with their customary colonial arrogance and discourtesy in the case of civil servants, and paternalistic condescension in the case of missionaries. They also made amused remarks concerning the behavior of the rookies. When the newcomers would get to know the blacks better, they would change their tune, they said. Blacks, said the missionaries, were a childish, ignorant, but good-natured lot. If you dealt with them gently but firmly, it was really surprising what you could get out of them.

The civil servants had a more "realistic" view. This "idealistic" view of blacks was all very well if you simply expected them to go to mass, but it was not practical. Blacks were a stupid, lying, thieving lot. All they understood was force. Give them an inch and they'll take a foot. They were always on the look-out to cheat, steal, and deceive you. For instance, you always had to mark in pencil the level of the alcohol in your whiskey bottles after you took a drink and to keep all cabinets locked, otherwise they would shamelessly strip you of everything. Kindness, they mistook for weakness. You had to make clear to them who was master. The worst natives were the educated ones. Those *singes savants* ("trained monkeys") actually believed they were as good as whites. It

A COLONIAL INTERLUDE

took us 2,000 years to become civilized, and they were expecting to be so in 20. Such cheek!

To demonstrate to the rookies the proper treatment of Africans, the old hands would be on their best colonial behavior. They would never say "please" or "thank you"; they would either ignore the presence of a servant or insult him by calling him *macaque* (a favorite Belgian colonial epithet for blacks); instead of asking for a fresh drink, they would snap their fingers, point to an empty glass, and shout imprecations at the stewards if the glass was not refilled within ten seconds or if it was refilled with the wrong drink.

A handful of the more liberal and better-educated newcomers remained skeptical that this was the best formula for carrying the white man's burden, but the vast majority modified their behavior with alacrity, if only to demonstrate how quick they were at getting to know the natives. By the end of the three-weeks' journey, the behavioral and linguistic boundary separating the two groups had all but vanished. The *Tervaete* had just graduated a freshly baked class of racists, even before arrival in Africa. Yes, indeed, the newcomers *had* changed their tune.

Although I was not aware of the implication of that experience at the time—indeed I was myself too much part of the process to understand it—later that episode helped me realize what nonsense the psychoanalytic view of prejudice was. Prejudice is not a deeply rooted phenomenon lost in the remotest corners of the sub-conscious as the result of dimly remembered childhood frustrations. Rather, it is the ideological product of a structure of privilege and inequality. It serves material interests and can easily be acquired and shed to suit the circumstances. The very same people who quickly learned to call Africans *macaques* equally quickly shed the habit a few years later, after independence.

On arrival in Lobito, we transferred from ship to rail, to cross half a continent. In three days, we arrived in my birthplace, Elisabethville (now, Lubumbashi). Our vintage train was hot and dusty. The wood-burning locomotive was constantly spewing incandescent ashes and made it imperative to keep the windows shut. At night it trailed a glowing veil of sparks. I thought we would be crossing jungle, but most of the landscape was a flat, semi-desertic shrub-land. Decades of travel by our wood-burning locomotive had cut a 200-kilometer-wide swath of semi-desert out of the African savannah, a visible demonstration of the *mission civilisatrice*. Cattle had finished the job through overgrazing—we saw the same lanky, lyre-horned beasts found on 4,000-year-old Egyptian bas-reliefs and which my enthusiastic young brother, Christian, first mistook for buffaloes. The buffaloes had, alas, long vanished, as had the other big game. Indeed, the story went that, at one time, the locomotives had to be mounted with a machine gun to prevent impulsive rhinoceroses from derailing their iron rivals.

The last leg of our trip took four days. By a combination of dusty road and lake steamer, we arrived at our final destination, Bukavu, the capital of Kivu Province, on the southern shore of gorgeous, high-altitude Lake Kivu (a kind of African Lake Tahoe). There, I was to spend the next two years and to finish my secondary schooling at the Jesuit Collège Notre Dame de la Victoire.

While crossing Angola, the old hands gave us a quick lesson on the differences between Belgian and Portuguese colonialism. The Portuguese had a special way with the natives. Their way worked for them because they were really half-natives themselves. It operated on the principle of screwing them and kicking them in the butt. As a result, Angola was full of uppity mulattoes and *assimilados*. No wonder blacks were losing their respect for such poor examples of Europeans who did not know how to keep their distance. But you had to give it to the Portuguese; they had their fun in Africa.

Belgians also had their fun in Africa, of course, but they were a bit more hypocritical about it. Almost every white bachelor in the Congo, I was soon to discover, cohabited with one (or more) strikingly elegant and attractive Congolese girl, euphemistically known in colonial society as a *ménagère* ("housekeeper"). My father, who could not help noticing my admiring and concupiscent glances—indeed, I had never seen such gracile, erotic femininity—sternly warned me that these girls all had gonorrhea, syphilis, yaws, or some other infectious tropical disease. He gladly produced photographic plates from his medical collection to illustrate the consequences of interracial promiscuity. I can still vividly recall plates of patients with scrotum enlarged to the size of a large pumpkin or pudenda devoured by hideous, suppurating sores. Quite an object lesson for a horny 15-year-old!

In his defense, I must say that my father practiced what he preached, confining his amorous ventures to the light end of the color spectrum. Not that he was a racist, mind you; he was one of the least racist people I have known; but he was, after all, a tropical parasitologist well up on his epidemiology. Anyway, for two years I had to live with the constant tease of these voluptuous tropical seductresses, tantalizingly undulating their hips when I came across them on my way to and from school. Always my father's medical plates rudely interrupted my fantasies.

The main difference between the Portuguese and the Belgians was that the former kept their African mistresses "up front" and frequently recognized their children by them, while the Belgians kept them in the backyard servants' quarters when European guests arrived and, more often than not, deserted their illegitimate offspring. Even the male Catholic clergy were not immune to the charms of their female parishioners, except for the 20 percent or so who preferred little boys. But they were even more discreet about it. You could always tell whether you were in a Catholic or in a Protestant mission, it was said, by the number of mulattoes around it. Protestant missionaries were mostly married and had few African bastards.

If I seem overindulgent in stressing the sexual side of my African initiation, it is because Africa for me first brought sexuality into the open. This may sound like an extraordinary statement, but I had been raised in a very puritanical, sex-segregated, and repressed society, in which sex, unlike children, should be *neither* seen nor heard, except reluctantly, in clinical terms. All of a sudden, I discovered a society where eroticism was flaunted. If I had felt like paraphrasing Claude Lévi-Strauss, I would have titled this book *Sexy Tropics*. *Tristes Tropiques* always seemed to me an incongruous juxtaposition of words. The tropics, especially the African and Afro-Brazilian tropics, have always had a powerful aphrodisiacal effect on me, although it took quite a few years to erase the dampening effect of my father's clinical photographs.

Belgian colonial society has, alas, never been systematically studied. Unlike its French and British counterparts, it produced little literature, besides a little polemical pamphleteering against the atrocities of Léopold II's agents around the turn of the century and some pompous, self-serving apologetics of the *mission civilisatrice* by ex-governors general. There are no documents about the Congo to match *Kim, A Passage to India, The Raj Quartet,* and other literary masterpieces spawned by British India. Conrad's *Heart of Darkness* comes closest, but says little about colonialism. Most anthropologists studied "unspoiled natives," oblivious to their colonial context. The works of Monica Wilson, Max Gluckman, Hilda Kuper, Clyde Mitchell, and Philip Mayer in English, and of Georges Balandier in French are the main pre-1960 exceptions to this anthropological blindness to African colonialism. In a sense, this was almost inevitable. Anthropology could not study colonialism. It was part of it.

In any case, colonial society is a prime example of a society that *did,* in fact, vanish before the anthropologists got to study it. And it is a pity. I, for one, certainly learned a good deal from it as a social scientist, although this only became clear long after the fact. Here I can merely attempt a reconstruction, a pale archeological shadow of colonialism, dredged up from the deep stratigraphy of my memory.

It was Georges Balandier who best and earliest captured the nature of the "colonial situation" in print, and my encounter with him in Paris in 1956 was a flash of revelation in helping me organize my experience. As he put it in his 1963 classic, *Sociologie Actuelle de l'Afrique Noire,* the colonial situation is a *cas privilégié* for understanding the nature of relations of production and of power, precisely because colonial society rests on naked coercion, on unabashed privilege, on blatant exploitation. The ideological superstructures of legitimation are so transparent as to expose with great clarity the structure and mechanisms of domination and exploitation. (*Exposer les rouages du système,* "to expose the clockworks of the system," was how Balandier put it.)

Later, I was to find that South Africa had the same properties and that is, in part, why I picked South Africa as my first major field work site. From there, having come into contact with Leo and Hilda Kuper, and later Max Gluckman and Michael G. Smith, I espoused the model of the plural society. But more of that later.

It was perhaps the saving grace of colonialism that it made no bones about resting on coercion. To be sure, colonialism developed a thin veneer of ideological justification: paternalism, indirect rule, the civilizing mission, the white man's burden. But hardly anyone took that claptrap seriously, certainly not the colonial subjects (except, perhaps, very briefly, in the 1930s, a tiny Westernized elite in "francophone" West Africa). Even the colonizers themselves had contempt for the ideological apologists of the system (much as today, in South Africa, the pragmatists of white supremacy despise the proponents of "enlightened" apartheid). The system, in short, stood naked for inspection, if one only cared to look. The pity is that so few social scientists did look.

An immediate problem presents itself in my retrospective account of colonialism. My account is now inevitably couched in the language of a trained social scientist, whereas my experiences were those of a naive adolescent who, furthermore was a direct participant in the system. I must first attempt to reconstruct my own perspective then, trying not to embellish it with a wisdom and perspicacity acquired only much later. In many respects, I adopted many of the typical colonial attitudes, manners, and habits, and I must, in all honesty, say that I enjoyed the unearned privileges that my light pigmentation gave me. I did not actively *question* the political legitimacy of colonialism. I simply enjoyed the pleasant existence that the system afforded me.

At the same time, however, I did not unquestioningly *accept* the system either. From the start, it was obvious to me that colonialism was based on naked coercion and resulted in exploitation. Examples were simply too glaring to ignore. Although the two situations—that of German occupation in Belgium and Belgian occupation of the Congo—were sufficiently different on the surface to hide the numerous similarities, I clearly perceived that I was now on the other side of a political fence. I was on the winning side for a change, and it was far more pleasant than to be on the losing one. Even then, I saw the colonial situation as a set of political and economic relations, not as an ethical issue that needed a legitimating ideology.

Indeed, the ideological façade of colonialism never convinced me. First, it was too transparently self-serving; second, it was overwhelmingly rejected as "too idealistic" by the vast majority of colonials themselves; third, it was premised on a view of Africans that simply did not fit the reality I observed. Africans never looked childish, or stupid, or depraved to me. They were, of course, unknowledgeable about many technical aspects of our civilization, as I was of theirs. But that was no proof of stupidity. Their resistance to colonialism used similar methods to those I had known as a loser, during the war, and to those I was then applying in my frequent tugs of war with adult authority at home or in school. The supposed moral depravity (pilferage, sullenness, "ingratitude," work shirking, and so on) attributed to Africans was clearly a cunning, rational defense against tyranny and a proof of intelligent pursuit of self-interest. The *absence* of those traits would have been a proof of stupidity, not their presence.

I should, however, not give myself too much credit for perspicaciousness. To be sure, I was already growing into a fairly cynical young man, but I totally failed to see the fragility of the colonial system. I perceived it as well-nigh eternal. The contemporary events of Indonesia, India, and Indochina had, I think, practically no impact on our own colonial vision. The more intelligent among us argued that Asia was a totally different kettle of fish. It represented old, advanced civilizations with long traditions of statehood. Africa was "primitive" and supposedly incapable of self-rule for a long time to come.

Also, my attitudes were not typical because I belonged to a very special microcosm of colonial society. Many of my closest adult associates were on the staff of my father's institute, IRSAC, and were scientists, technicians, and other highly educated and intelligent individuals. Some of them were trained social scientists, like Daniel Biebuyck, Jean Hiernaux, and Jacques Maquet. Indeed, Maquet was the first anthropologist I saw in the field and the first person able to communicate to me the intellectual excitement of trying to understand an exotic culture from the inside, of penetrating the barrier of relations of power erected by colonialism to appreciate the richness and complexity of another civilization. At that time Maquet was studying the neighboring Tuzi kingdom of Rwanda; that work was later to be published as his masterly *The*

Premise of Inequality in Ruanda (1961). More than anything, Maquet impressed on me that such a study was only possible on a basis of mutual respect between the ethnographer and his informants. What also impressed me about Maquet is that he extended this respect to me, treating me as an adult and patiently answering my questions without a trace of condescension. I can truly say that he was my first professional "role model" (a phrase I detest), though I had not the remotest idea then that I would become an anthropologist.

Besides Maquet, my father's friendship with the Mwami (King) of Rwanda, Mutara IV, also made a tremendous impact on my respectful vision of Africa. The tall, slender, elegant, refined, astute figure of the king impressed me enormously, as did the gentle, dignified, aristocratic grace with which he received my father and me in his palace. A good 2.10 meters tall, he jokingly accepted my father's 1.92 meters as qualifying him for the status of honorary Tuzi, but my 1.78 meters was clearly below par.

Mutara also reminds me of one of the most acutely embarrassing episodes of my life. The Mwami was an enthusiastic hunter, as was every self-respecting Tuzi aristocrat. As I was describing to him how my carbine tended to shoot to the left, I unthinkingly demonstrated by pointing to the nearest convenient object, a photograph over the king's fireplace. I can still hear him interrupt me in his most suave and fluent French: *"Vous tirez sur mon père."* ("You are shooting at my father.") I felt the rush of blood to my face, mumbled an apology, and shut up for the rest of the meeting. I was very lucky of course. Had I been a Tuzi and he, his father, I probably would not have survived the episode! Summary executions for *lèse-majesté* were the order of the day in the "interlacustrine kingdoms," as anthropologists call these central African societies of Rwanda, Burundi, and Uganda.

I should also add that both of my parents were remarkably free of racism, though for very different reasons. My mother, a gentle, charitable person very seldom says anything negative about anyone. But I also have irrefutable positive proof of her total lack of racism in old letters to her parents, written in 1933, in which she explicitly mentions how all the Africans she encountered failed to conform to the European stereotypes of them. My father, on the other hand, was an extremely arrogant person and a thorough intellectual snob, but he had instant affinity and sympathy for other superior and unconventional people, and he had an uncanny ability to recognize merit quite irrespective of gender, class, or race. He encouraged talent in whomever he encountered it, except, ironically, in his own sons where a perverse sense of rivalry interfered with his judgment. By then, in any case, our relationship had deteriorated beyond repair.

Most of my two years in the Congo were spent in school, finishing my secondary studies at the Jesuit college. This was the best secondary school in the entire Kivu Province, and it was, like all colonial institutions, rigidly segregated along racial lines. Both students and teachers were Europeans, although, like the rest of colonial society, the school grounds swarmed with adult African servants (gardeners, cooks, cleaners) whom we called "boys." It was axiomatic that a white person did no physical work of any sort. When pupils boarding at the school came back from their vacation, for example, they would hire African boys to carry their suitcases the 100 or 200 meters from their parents' car to their room. (Some twenty years later, I was to find that the same behavior had lingered in independent Nigeria: when black Nigerian university students came back to school, they too hired "small boys" to avoid the stigma of physical labor, however trivial. The transition from colonialism to neo-colonialism was indeed smooth in most of Africa.)

In all fairness to the Jesuits, their racial attitudes were, on the whole, slightly more liberal than those of most other colonials, though much overladen with paternalism. One episode gives both the measure and the limits of that liberalism, as well as provides a telling vignette of colonial society. Bukavu had a complex educational system, as schools were segregated on three dimensions: sex, religion, and race. Mercifully, the Dutch-French cleavage vanished in the Congo. All the schools were French-medium, much to the displeasure of Flemish nationalists who would have dearly loved to extend Belgian language conflicts to the Congo Basin. Still, schools were either Catholic or lay, for boys or for girls, for Europeans or for Africans.

But what of the "mulattoes"? Until then, they had gone to the African schools. All of them were children of Congolese mothers and European fathers. Many of them had been deserted by their fathers and raised as Africans by their mothers, speaking little or no French. A few, however, had been officially recognized by their fathers, spoke fluent French, and were, by law, Belgian citizens (as distinct from the Congolese who were Belgian *subjects,* but not citizens).

The Portuguese had an official category of *assimilados* who had technically the same legal rights as white Portuguese nationals (which, under Salazar, meant precious few rights). The Belgians had a revealing term to describe westernized Africans—*évolué*—but it was a term of contempt and derision, and no special rights went with it.

The Jesuits thought, however, that it was unfair to expect westernized mulattoes recognized by their fathers to attend inferior African schools. (It goes without saying that both the standards and the facilities of the

African schools were vastly inferior to those of the European schools.) Thus, they decided cautiously to admit a handful of mulattoes (into a school of about 400 white students) during my years in Bukavu. Even this dribble of tokenism raised a storm of protest among parents and pupils, who saw this event as the first hole in the dike of colonialism. It is to the Jesuits' credit that they held their ground, simply riding out the storm in the racial teacup.

Most of my teachers, save one, were unmemorable. To Father De Wolf, my principal teacher in my last year of high school, however, I owe a considerable intellectual debt. An erudite classicist with a razor-sharp Cartesian mind, and a superb stylist, he helped me perfect my writing skills, and what is more, taught me logic. Unlike Father Bribosia with whom I had a warm relationship, I did not like Father De Wolf, but I respected him. I think our feelings were mutual. He resented my atheism and my snotty radicalism, but he nevertheless helped sharpen a critical brain, even in the knowledge that I was going to use it against what he stood for. He was a great believer in the Socratic method (we were simultaneously reading, in the original, Plato's *Dialogues*) and our classroom exchanges turned into intellectual jousts in which he did not hesitate to cut me down to size when I needed it, which was often. He was ruthless, but always fair.

He had, however, an Achilles heel: his sexual prudery. As we were studying the French Impressionists, I was to make a half-hour report. I deliberately chose Renoir because he offered the widest array of seductive nudes, which I intended to show my classmates to illustrate my talk. I could see Father De Wolf visibly reddening and squirming in his chair during my presentation. (I was watching him out of the corner of my eye, as he was sitting next to me.) My plan was working. At the critical moment, I read a direct quotation from Renoir: "If it had not been for tits and ass, I would not have become a painter." As planned, Father De Wolf totally lost his cool, became beet-red, told me to shut up, and dismissed the class. I became a class hero.

My other memorable triumph was equally unfair, but it was aimed at a more deserving target, a pompous and rather stupid math teacher. It was the bane of my Jesuit education that I had not a single decent mathematics teacher and thus always remained rather obtuse in that subject. The Jesuits looked down on mathematics, always let low-status laymen teach the subject, and seemed deliberately to pick mediocrities as math teachers so as to vindicate their low opinion of the subject. My last math teacher was indeed a sorry example of mediocrity, compounded by a towering inferiority complex and a short temper. At the slightest provocation, as when a student was not able to answer a question, he would make cutting, sarcastic remarks. Naturally, I could not resist needling him. My favorite ploy was to pretend inattention by looking out of the window, thereby inviting him to snap a question at me. I would relish his discomfiture when I would smilingly and off-handedly give him the correct answer. One day, I made him lose his self-control altogether. In a rage, he called me *infâme individu* and ordered me out of the classroom. I went straight to the director, complained of having been publicly insulted for no good reason, and demanded that the teacher apologize to me. I never expected that my request would be honored, but the director called the teacher into his office and made him privately apologize to me. The teacher tried his best to fail me in the oral examination at the end of the year, but there were three examiners present to ensure fairness. Our feud had become notorious, so he was reduced to impotence. I performed passably well, though far from brilliantly.

I graduated third in a small class of twelve. Two weak subjects (Greek and algebra), my cheek, and my aggressive anti-clericalism cost me quite a few points. I soon lost sight of all my classmates, save one, Etienne van de Walle, a fellow iconoclast, who, like me, emigrated to the United States where he became a distinguished historical demographer at the University of Pennsylvania. The odds against the two of us becoming American social scientists after graduating from a small, provincial, Congolese high school were long indeed! Father De Wolf, I think Etienne would agree, had a lot to do with our success.

Vacations and weekends were spent travelling a great deal in the eastern Congo, in Rwanda and Burundi (then Belgian U.N. Trusteeship territories), and as far as Uganda and Kenya. Travelling was the best way to understand the colonial system. The first and most obvious feature of it was how thinly spread the European presence in Africa was. In the late 1940s, the white population in the Congo was approximately 50,000. At its peak, just before independence in 1960, it reached about 80,000. The size of the Congolese population was, quite literally, every *administrateur territorial*'s guess. There was never a proper census. Every adult man had to pay a "head tax," about the equivalent in cash of two months' wages for an unskilled laborer, for the privilege of being alive. Every local colonial official was charged with collecting that tax. He then applied an arbitrary multiplier to the number of head-tax payers to arrive at a guesstimate of his district's population. Because the Congolese were as good as anyone in evading taxes, the baseline figure was invariably an underestimate. But this was seldom corrected, since no *administrateur* wanted to admit that he was inefficient at collecting taxes. The more statistically inclined might ask the first ten or twenty women in a village how many children they had and use the mean as the basis of their multiplier, but most trusted their much vaunted knowledge of the natives to arrive at a figure. Twelve to fifteen million Congolese would have been the best possible guess, not including another three to four million in Rwanda and Burundi.

Of the whites, the majority were dependents, that is wives and children of civil servants, army officers, planters, traders, mining technicians, and Protestant missionaries. That left about 20,000 men to rule over a population nearly 1,000 times as large, spread over a difficult, inaccessible terrain 82 times the size of Belgium. Even those figures give a distorted picture. At least 90 percent of the whites lived in urban centers, principally in Léopoldville (now Kinshasa) in the other five provincial capitals, and in a handful of mining towns. Bukavu, the capital of Kivu Province, for instance, had about 3,000 whites. The rest of the vast province had a few hundred scattered planters, missionaries, and civil servants; and Kivu, a high-altitude region with a delightful climate, was exceptional, being regarded as the "white highlands" of the Congo. Other provinces, like Equateur, had virtually no rural whites.

Nor was the Congo an unusual case of European colonialism. Only a handful of European colonies in Africa and Asia had a white population exceeding 1 percent of the total. The African exceptions were South Africa (20 percent white), Southern Rhodesia (5 percent), and Algeria (10 percent). How could so few rule so many? There are several important components to the answer, and, although I shall use the Congo as my example, my remarks can be applied, mutatis mutandi, to much of the rest of colonial Africa.

First, the Congo was very "thinly" governed. Vast stretches of rain forest were barely penetrated, much less effectively administered. Districts the size of half of Belgium were ruled by an *administrateur territorial,* two or three lower-ranking *agents territoriaux,* and perhaps in some cases a white agricultural agent and medical officer. There might be one or two mission stations in the district, each with a half-dozen whites. With luck there might be a small mission hospital with a medical missionary and two or three white nuns-nurses. In total, some 20 or 25 Europeans were spread over 10,000 to 20,000 square kilometers. They would be backed up by a small detachment from the hated Force Publique, some 15 to 20 black soldiers under the command of a black sergeant.

How did this skeletal staff of Europeans affect the African population? Naturally, Western technology (in medicine, mining, agriculture, transportation, and weaponry) gave the actions of the few whites a tremendous multiplier effect. Some regions, like Katanga with its copper mines, were profoundly affected and intensively exploited. A few regions, such as Kivu, suffered appreciable land expropriation for the benefit of white coffee or tea planters. Other areas were disrupted by the forced collection or cultivation of cash crops (rubber in the early days, later principally cotton), and this often had catastrophic ecological consequences. Preventive medicine, especially vaccination of school children in the mission stations, launched Africa on its population explosion with its sequel of ecological catastrophes: human and bovine overpopulation, overgrazing, deforestation, rain and wind erosion, desertification. In the aggregate, and over time, the impact was obviously enormous. But the effect of the European presence was very *unequally* felt: some areas were devastated, others barely touched.

One must not overstate the extent to which the Congo was actually governed. In many places, government was largely limited to annual tax collection; an occasional promenade of the administrator through his domain; the maintenance of a couple of dirt roads and flimsy bridges; the adjudication of a few disputes; and the arrest of a few criminals or troublesome characters.

Second, colonialism was invariably based on a system of what the British called "indirect rule." In effect, colonialism was a system in which Africans were made to cooperate in their own subjection in exchange for a measure of local autonomy. The Belgians, French, and Portuguese deluded themselves that they were practicing "direct rule" in contrast to the British, but, in fact, there was precious little difference between "direct" and "indirect" rule. Almost everywhere, local African villages largely ran their own affairs at the grassroot level and were left to their own devices most of the time. This is not to say that Europeans did not frequently try to interfere, naming and deposing "chiefs" or creating chiefs where none had existed before. But the leading principle of native administration was that it should be *cheap,* under no circumstances costing more than the taxes collected. The basic modus vivendi was: keep quiet and pay your head tax, and we will leave you alone. The village "chief" was sometimes a traditional authority, as in the centralized pre-colonial kingdoms of Rwanda and Burundi, but very often he was little more than an unpaid tax collector and go-between. He was given a brass plaque of office by the administrator, but could be summarily deposed if he proved troublesome. Very often, he received little respect from the population who saw him as an opportunist and an errand-boy of the whites.

The administrator was in theory a link in a bureaucratic structure, under the direct authority of the provincial governor and the governor general in Léopoldville, but distance and isolation made the control of the center very tenuous. In fact, the administrator was ruling a quasi-private domain, but as he was rotated every couple of years, he seldom had time to develop a deep knowledge or a real interest in his charges. He almost never learned the local language, though he often had a smattering of the regional lingua franca, such as Lingala or Kiswahili. He was supposed to be a jack of all trades, in charge of health, agriculture, road maintenance, tax collection, and, most of all, peacekeeping. His success was measured by the absence of trouble. Trouble meant having to send in troops from the provincial capital and that was expensive. A good administrator was one whose reports to the provincial governor were short and free of problems.

To achieve that state of administrative Nirvana, one had to rely on pliable, accommodating, "reasonable" village chiefs, and these, in turn, were only forthcoming if one made one's presence as light as was consistent with tax collecting and other demands of the central government (such as forced cultivation of cash crops, or corvée labor, for porterage). In short, a light hand could do wonders for one's administrative advancement. Leaving the natives alone was the winning formula.

The principal flag-showing exercise was a periodic *tournée d'inspection* (duly noted in the periodic written reports), a ceremonial tour of the estate, often combined with tax collecting. The administrator, carried in a bamboo sedan-chair, preceded by a flag-carrying corporal, a bugler, and five or six soldiers, and followed by twenty or thirty bearers carrying his guns, his tent, his *malle-tub,* and his provision of Johnny Walker, would meander from village to village, chat with his chiefs, and shoot game for sport on the way.

At his headquarters, the administrator mainly prepared his reports, organized emergency work parties to repair bridges after flash floods, adjudicated disputes (but only those voluntarily brought to him by plaintiffs), and passed sentence on minor offenders. (More serious cases went up to professional judges in the provincial capital.) Administrators were on the whole reasonably well-educated, well-meaning, uncorrupt, decent chaps. They were mostly plodding career bureaucrats whose main occupational hazards were boredom and alcohol. (In the British colonial service, district commissioners were often "Oxbridge" graduates and some of them warded off boredom by becoming anthropologists; but Belgian standards of recruitment were a bit less demanding.) A marvellous pictorial introduction to colonialism, incidentally, is the brilliant French film, *Noir et Blanc en Couleur.* The French system was quite similar to the Belgian one.

Third, the colonial system was sustained by a reasonably efficient transportation network. In retrospect, this was probably the most remarkable achievement of Belgian colonialism in the Congo. The complex and fragile system of river and road transport broke down almost immediately after independence, with the result that Zaïre is even more tenuously governed now than the Congo was in Belgian days. The government controls Kinshasa and environs and the provincial capitals. The only effective means of transportation left is by air, using imported technology and personnel, but ground transport has broken down and with it control over the "bush."

In the bad old days, the Belgians maintained a fleet of wood-burning stern-wheelers on the navigable stretches of river, no mean achievement in rivers with constantly shifting sand banks. These, in turn, were interconnected by rail links plied by wood-burning steam locomotives pulling rickety cars on narrow gauge. Where river and rail gave out, 4-meter-wide dirt roads took over. These had to be kept in daily repair against tropical rains. A veritable army of *cantonniers* insured that never-ending task: every 5 kilometers or so, a small camp of two or three grass huts housed a half-dozen men responsible for their stretch of road. The more onerous tasks, such as rebuilding bridges, were performed by corvées of prisoners in striped suits under the guard of Force Publique soldiers. Some of the prisoners were simply serving time for two months in lieu of their annual head tax. They were unchained. The real convicts were chained.

Finally, at the end of the transportation system was human porterage. Tse-tse fly infestation prevented mule or donkey transport in most of the Congo. Any white colonial had the privilege of recruiting porters, at the set rate of 5 francs (then about 10 cents U.S.) a day. This was also the rate at which the annual head tax (equal to two months' work) was computed, and porterage in the more remote regions was the main source of the cash necessary to pay the tax. Thus, the head tax had the intended consequence of providing a steady supply of bearers. The load was officially limited to 20 kilograms per man, and the distribution of inevitably uneven loads between porters was always the subject of considerable arguments between carriers.

Often, men were unwilling to do such strenuous work for such low pay, especially early in the tax year, and labor was impressed by coercion. The favorite ploy was to wait for a market day in the neighboring village and then to encircle the marketplace with a small contingent of soldiers obligingly loaned by the administrator, and force the young men into service. This method was often self-defeating, however, as the reluctant carriers would desert at the first opportunity, typically during the first night on the road, leaving one stranded in the bush with a ton of baggage. There, as in many other cases, colonial tyranny was tempered by effective means of passive resistance.

On the whole, however, if one considers the combined obstacles of a difficult topography and a reluctant population, Belgian logistics were remarkably efficient. To be sure, it took a couple of months for the 200-liter petrol drums to make their way from Matadi, to Léopoldville, to Stanleyville, to Bukavu, for example, and occasionally gasoline was a bit short for a fortnight, but the miracle was that the goods arrived at all. Clearly, the system rested on a great deal of direct and indirect coercion, the principal one being the obligation to pay the annual head tax. The head tax was probably the most effective single invention of colonialism, not so much as a source of revenue, but as a method of forcing Africans into the cash economy.

Fourth, colonialism was a system of economic exploitation. Where there were resources to be extracted, powerful interests, such as the monopolistic mining companies, conspired to make it work. That, in turn, meant principally using the coercive machinery of the colonial state to provide capitalists with a cheap, docile labor force. Such was, as we just saw, the principal aim of the head tax. Of course, colonialism was also a system of production; however, a purely economic analysis of it leaves much unsaid. Vast stretches of Africa were poor and devoid of exploitable resources; yet, there too, colonialism was present, if only minimally.

Colonialism was *both* a political and an economic system, and I have always argued for the priority and primacy of politics over economics in *most* historical situations. This, I would argue, was certainly true in Africa. The assertion of European territorial claims was largely a pre-emptive political game between the European powers. Economic considerations were generally secondary (though not in South Africa after the discovery of the Witwatersrand gold deposits), and territories were eagerly grabbed or claimed without any idea of whether they would pay off. Many never did, and when they did they often benefitted, not the system as a whole, but a few economic interests who let the colonial state carry the "overhead," that is principally the logistics of transport and the apparatus of repression.

Fifth, the most extraordinary element of the colonial system was missionary zeal. What an astonishing idea that one should spend one's entire life trying (often with extremely limited success) to change other people's thinking. Yet thousands of missionaries did just that, sometimes at considerable risk to their health, and generally for very meager material rewards. True, their psychic rewards were often enormous, power being not the least of these. Missionaries often behaved as insufferably priggish, conceited, self-righteous despots. They *knew* they were right and could scarcely disguise their impatience at the natives who were so benighted as not to accept the gift of grace when it was offered them on a platter.

The study of missionary action is another missed opportunity for social science (and one that also fits very poorly in a simple Marxist model). It is often said, with considerable truth, that missionaries were agents of colonialism and precursors of crasser economic and political interests. It is quite true that missionaries were an integral part of colonial society. They certainly accepted, indeed they helped develop and disseminate, the ideology of paternalism that underlay colonialism. Seldom did they accept Africans as fully equal human beings, and that is their most damning indictment. Even lionized philanthropists and Nobel Peace Prize winners like Albert Schweitzer were petty paternalist tyrants and even reveal themselves as racists when you examine closely their actions and writings.

By and large, missionary action in Africa (and I mean here the Christian missions, in the full knowledge that Islam also had a vast but radically different and often much more effective influence) was a comedy of errors based on a "working misunderstanding." Concretely, the missionaries offered Western medicine and education. The value of the former took little time to make itself obvious. Health was well worth a mass. As for Western education, its value was not so much intrinsic, for a lot of it was totally irrelevant to African experience. Africans, like all other people, had an educational system of their own, which served their traditional needs much better. But it soon became obvious that what the missionaries called civilization and education was the royal road to all but the most menial jobs in the colonial economy and to the few positions of power and security to which Africans could accede. Later, it also turned out to be the key that opened the political kingdom. The political class that inherited the mantle of colonialism and quickly appropriated the state apparatus for its own gain, becoming what Stanislav Andreski aptly called a "kleptocracy," was largely made up of "mission boys."

If getting a regular salary as a postal clerk, for example (this was Patrice Lumumba's job before he became prime minister), meant having a little water sprinkled over one's forehead, listening to a priest's Latin mumbo-jumbo, and doing all the funny things expected of a mission boy, so be it. Numerous were the boys in the Congo who even entered Catholic seminaries without the slightest intention of entering the clergy. The very idea of celibacy, for one, is simply grotesque in African cultures. But the seminary was the *only* post-secondary education available to the Congolese before independence.

The missionaries, then, were a crucial factor in the colonial equation. Not only did they effectively "open up" vast areas and implant a European presence on the ground, but they almost singlehandedly trained the entire class of African petty collaborators of colonialism, without whom the system would either not have functioned or would, at any rate, have become vastly more expensive. Had they not existed, the *évolués* (as they were sneeringly referred to) would have had to be replaced by much more expensive Belgians. Literally tens of thousands of petty but essential positions in government, transportation, the army, commerce, and mining were filled by literate Congolese trained in mission schools. Indeed, there were hardly any schools at all for Africans, besides the mission schools. The missions provided the colonial state with an unending supply of very eager, bright, and hungry boys (hardly any girls were educated) willing and able to be the flunkeys of colonialism. That was the best to which they could aspire: to become a clerk in business or government, a lorry driver, a "messenger boy," a postal employee, a sergeant in the Force Publique (General Mobutu's former job).

Sixth, the Congo was not a nation, but a patchwork of some 200 or 300 ethnic groups speaking mutually unintelligible languages. The Belgians did not have to divide in order to rule. The divisions were already there. To make matters better (for the Belgians), even the political boundaries were drawn in total disregard of language and ethnicity. It is true that, in some areas, such as those occupied by the Kongo, the Tuzi, the Zande, the Kuba, and the Lunda, to name but a few, there had been centralized kingdoms incorporating hundreds of thousands of people for several centuries before the colonial era. But these kingdoms were mutually hostile and were easily conquered with European firearms. In fact, once conquered, these kingdoms were often more easily ruled than the smaller, stateless societies, because they already had a political machinery of control in place. All the Belgians had to do was to utilize the traditional authorities under a system of indirect rule.

Lastly, there was the big stick, the Force Publique. A force of about 10,000 Congolese soldiers and non-commissioned officers (up to the rank of first sergeant major), commanded by a lily-white officer corps, the Force Publique was cordially hated by the Congolese and admired by the Europeans. Dressed in short-panted khaki uniforms and a fez (the fez was a widespread symbol of servility in Belgian colonialism, being also a great favorite for the servant staff of hotels and restaurants), they were always much in evidence in the provincial capitals, which all had garrisons of several hundred soldiers. But even remote outposts had small detachments, always under direct European control. The Europeans and their *askari* (Kiswahili for "soldiers") had a nearly total monopoly of firearms. Even as few as 20 single-shot, bolt-action rifles—the basic Force Publique weapon in the 1940s—went a long way against tens of thousands of civilians armed with bows, spears, machetes, and a few ancient muzzle-loading hunting guns.

But it was not weaponry alone that made the Force Publique the feared machine it was. Belgian policy was to post soldiers as far away from home as possible to insure that they had no ties to the civilian population, other than fear and hostility. Local civilian revolts were ruthlessly suppressed by simply unleashing the Force Publique on a rampage of looting, raping, and killing. Conversely, when local units of the Force Publique mutinied, a constant danger and a not uncommon occurrence, they could rely on no civilian support. Troops from other ethnic groups would be brought in to pursue the mutineers into the bush, where they quickly split up into small groups. The rebels who had been terrorizing and stealing from civilians were gladly turned in to the loyal troops and were generally shot immediately on capture to avoid embarrassing trials.

In 1950, the year I left Africa, colonialism still seemed unshakeable. Yet, next door, in Kenya, the first rumblings of independence were already to be heard. To these events, too, I was an early witness. In the summer of 1949, my father decided that it was time I learned English. He sent me to spend a few weeks with a British colleague of his, a Dr. Worthington, who had a farm in Limuru, near Nairobi. (An added attraction was that he had three daughters, the eldest of whom was my age.) In any case, this was my first sustained exposure to spoken English, though I had acquired a rudimentary reading knowledge, paging through *Life* magazine, the *National Geographic,* and such.

As I arrived, I found a much more tense and anxious political atmosphere among the British settlers than prevailed among the cockily self-confident Belgians. For one thing, India and Pakistan had recently received their independence, and the presence in East Africa of a large East Indian colony was a constant reminder to the British that the same could happen in Africa. Indeed, I remember that the Asian community quietly celebrated the anniversary of their motherland's independence while I visited Nairobi. For another, whites were all excited about a mysterious new movement cropping up, which they called Mau Mau. The name stuck, at least in British historiography, although it did not have any meaning in any African language and was not an African term. Though the British did not know it, the curtain had just been raised on the Kenya War of Independence. Kenya, like the Congo, was no nation, but a conglomerate of what the Europeans conveniently called "tribes." What are called "tribes" in Africa are Africa's real nations, while the multi-national states are nations only by the fiat of the United Nations (itself a double misnomer; the organization should call itself the Squabbling States).

Of these dormant nations of Kenya, the largest (numbering over a million) and most centrally located (surrounding the capital of Nairobi) was awakening to political consciousness. They were the Kikuyu, among whom an educated elite of schoolteachers were beginning to spread notions of self-determination. A radical wing of the incipient nationalist movement took to the hills of Mt. Kenya and the Aberdares and began a long guerrilla campaign directed both against the white settlers and against the collaborationist petty bourgeoisie among the Kikuyu. Some 12,000 people were killed, all but a few score of them black. Most victims were Kikuyu who were either assassinated by the guerrillas to discourage collaboration with the British or killed by the British in their brutal (and, in the end, militarily successful) counter-insurgency campaign.

During the so-called Mau Mau Emergency, the British refined many of the techniques of modern counter-insurgency later used by themselves in Malaysia and still later adopted with great alacrity by the United States in Vietnam: "model villages," later restyled "strategic hamlets," for instance, were a British invention. To deny the guerrilleros civilian support, the whole civilian Kikuyu population of entire districts was forcibly removed to barbed wire enclosures, which they were only allowed to leave during daylight hours. Actually the British had done much the same with Afrikaner women and children during the Boer War of 1899–1902 in South Africa. There they labelled their invention "concentration camp," but, unfortunately, the term had acquired a bad name in the interim, so a new label had to be found. "Model villages" sounded jolly nice. The United States developed its own concentration camps during World War II, calling them "relocation camps," but the basic idea was the same: the preventive incarceration without judicial process of any kind of entire civilian populations—men, women, and children—on the theory that their ethnicity alone makes them unreliable.

The entire British campaign of repression was quite brilliantly executed, and it worked, laying to rest the myth that a guerrilla movement cannot be defeated if it has broad civilian support. Mau Mau *was* defeated in Kenya. How? Largely through a cunning combination of brutal repression, massive detention, torture and brainwashing of tens of thousands of suspects, and a clever counter-propaganda war.

The chief anti-guerrilla ideologue and propagandist of the Kenya War of Independence was the distinguished human paleontologist, the late Dr. Louis Leakey, who can be credited for inventing and legitimating the great Mau Mau myth. Leakey had long cultivated his reputation for "knowing the natives." He spoke fluent Kikuyu, a rare achievement among white settlers who, for the most part, spoke a Kiswahili pidgin (jocularly known as Ki-settler) with Africans. When the guerrilla movement started, he was a natural source of "information" about the Kikuyu for the colonial government. Leakey was only too glad to provide a most convenient version of the events in his two books, *Mau Mau and the Kikuyu,* 1952, and *Defeating Mau Mau,* 1954. Far from being a modern war of liberation, said Leakey, the Mau Mau movement was an evil secret society, a throw-back to atavistic savagery, which coerced its recruits by forcing them to utter unspeakable oaths and to break every traditional taboo in Kikuyu society. Thereafter, said Leakey, the recruits had, in effect, burned their bridges to decent Kikuyu society and fell under the nefarious spell of Mau Mau.

The aim of the government should, therefore, be to make Mau Mau suspects undergo a process of "de-oathing" to reincorporate them into Kikuyu society. This was an early version of "deprogramming," "brainwashing," "political re-education," and similar practices later adopted by both sides in the Vietnam War and even applied domestically in the United States to members of religious "sects." In any case, the British set up concentration camps (in addition to their somewhat more benign "model villages"), rounded up tens of thousands of suspects (essentially all poor, young Kikuyu men who could not get a European to vouchsafe for their reliability), tortured and terrorized the "detainees" into denouncing each other, sorted them into hard- and soft-core, and then "reprogrammed" the hard-core.

But that was not all. An evil genius had to be found behind this atavistic savagery (the Kikuyus', that is). Jomo Kenyatta was the perfect candidate. A highly educated Kikuyu with a master's degree in anthropology from the London School of Economics, he was a moderate, bourgeois nationalist, active in the Kikuyu teachers' association, but totally uninvolved in, and, indeed, unsympathetic to the more radical guerrilla movement. He had, however, a singular advantage over the real leaders of the guerrilleros: he could easily be caught as he had not gone underground. The British set up a kangaroo court, condemned him on the basis of perjured testimony by Crown witnesses, and clamped him in jail, as a "leader unto darkness and death," in the words of the governor general.

By 1954, the guerrilla movement was crushed. A few years later, the British started negotiating to operate a smooth transfer of power into "responsible" hands, and whom should they turn to, but Jomo Kenyatta. Like other moderate nationalist leaders, such as Kwame Nkrumah and Julius Nyerere, he was trotted out of jail to become his country's first prime minister and then president. When I was to meet him in Nairobi in 1967, the "leader unto darkness and death" had become reincarnated as the epitome of responsible, moderate statesmanship, the darling of the white community, and the architect of the Kenya brand of pro-capitalist neo-colonialism. While he wallowed in luxury and corruption in State House, I also met some of the aging veterans of the War of Independence. They were paupers languishing in the ghastly Nairobi slum of Mathari Valley, neatly tucked away from tourist sight. The fruits of independence were not for them, because they were not "educated."

Needless to say, I developed the above views concerning the "emergency" many years after the fact. In 1949, I accepted Leakey's vision of Kenya. Indeed, Leakey was very much a liberal on the political spectrum of British settlers. So was my host, Dr. Edgar Worthington, an eminent biologist. I saw him and his family as charming, sensible people defending a civilized (and most pleasant) way of life against a bunch of crazed extremists bent on turning the clock back to savagery. So we slept close to our guns, behind wire-meshed windows, wondering how long the "emergency" would last. The construction of security fences was becoming a booming business, but otherwise life on the white highlands of Kenya went on largely undisturbed.

The Worthingtons, typical British upper-middle-class professionals, organized their lives around books and horses. Farming was a mere avocation, something to amuse oneself with, all the real work being done, of course, by Africans. In the daytime, I would accompany the girls on long horseback rides or attend jumping shows. In the evenings, I would practice my English, reading and conversing with them. A weekly shopping trip would take us to Nairobi, a bustling commercial town full of the well-stocked stores of ingratiating Asian traders. As soon as we entered a shop, the trader would instantaneously ignore his many African customers and scurry about us, asking us what was our pleasure. All this I did not question at the time. It was just part and parcel of the colonial scene.

The Worthingtons were far too well educated to be crude racists. They had much the same liberal attitudes as my parents. They believed that blacks were just as bright as whites on the average; they were just backward and uncivilized, but they could easily be trained in a few years. As for the Asians, they were very clever indeed, perhaps a little crooked and underhanded, but handy to have around and so very polite. They were really just as cultured as we were, as their ancient civilization proved, although it was often difficult to penetrate their mentality.

Dr. Worthington was intelligent enough to foresee that his pleasant life as a gentleman-farmer-cum-scientist on the White Highlands was coming to an end. It turned out that he was unduly pessimistic. After Kenya became independent in 1963, the colonial life-style of the British, upper-class, horse set remained almost totally unchanged. One no longer called domestics "boys," and one even bothered to learn their last names now. But, except for a few such niceties of etiquette, and the presence of more black faces in high places and in the bars and hotels of Nairobi, the neo-colonialism of President Kenyatta clearly showed its colonial parentage.

This was the world to which my father retired, after the debacle of Congolese independence in 1960. He bought a little farm in Karen (named after Karen Blixen, author of *Out of Africa*, and on the very site of her farm) and spent the remaining two decades of his life raising horses. There, I was to see him for the last time in 1968, when I returned to Kenya for a year's stay. Ten years later, in January 1979, he died in Johannesburg, where he was being treated for terminal cancer. His ashes are buried in his Karen garden, in the central African soil that had become his.

For me, 1950 marked the end of my African interlude. I had graduated from high school. The Congo then had no university. It was time to move on. But where? The most common choice of young Belgians going on to higher education was to attend one of the four Belgian universities. The next most common alternative was to go to South Africa. But my father, who naturally assumed that he was in the best position to make an informed decision about where I should go, was not a conventional person. He was always much at ease in the English-speaking world, and, through a visiting professorship at Tulane, he had a number of American academic connections. He thought the United States would be a good place for me. He liked the climate and setting of California, and Stanford was, he believed, the best university in the region. So Stanford it was to be. I had never heard of the place!

My last long Congolese journey took me, my parents, my brother, Christian (aged 12 then), and my baby sister, Gwendoline (aged 5), first by road to Stanleyville (now Kisangani) via the Mbuti ("Pygmies") of the Ituri, then by a slow side-wheeler down the Congo River to Léopoldville (Kinshasa) and Brazzaville, then by train to Matadi, and finally by slow mixed-cargo ship to Newport News, Virginia. It is easy to forget how recent mass air travel is. That trip took us six weeks, time enough to see and experience a lot more than the modern jet plane permits. That was the last I saw of the Congo, though, happily, not of Africa.

A COLONIAL INTERLUDE

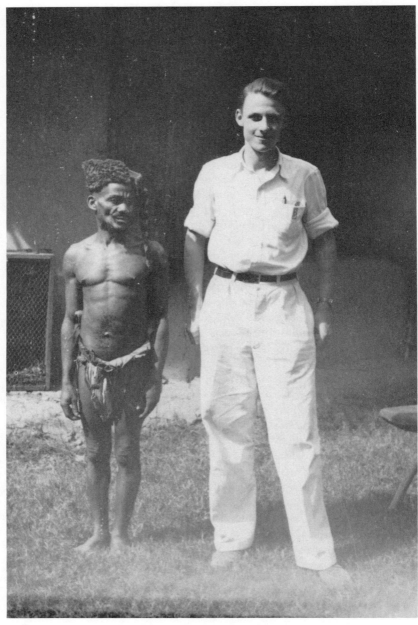

With a Mbuti ("Pygmy") in the Ituri Forest, Epulu, Zaïre (then Belgian Congo), 1950, just before departing Africa for Stanford University.

CHAPTER 4

The Farm

This chapter, which opens my adult life, has the special advantage of being written in situ. Telescoping over thirty years of life spent on five continents, I find myself once more on the setting of my young adulthood. Though I have done much besides sleeping in the interim, I have been far and long enough away from Stanford to experience a Rip Van Winkle effect. The sleepy "Farm" of yesteryear is now a bustling major university. It certainly was nothing of the sort in my undergraduate days, though its pretensions to greatness were not lacking even then. The difference is that now these pretensions have to be taken seriously.

Before arriving in Stanford, we spent several weeks travelling across the United States by car, first along the East Coast with stops in Washington, New York, and Boston, and then across the continent via the Southwest. To say that I was bombarded with novel experiences during these few weeks would be an understatement. It was a time of intense learning. I knew that in a few weeks' time I would start my studies in one of the country's leading universities, yet I had had something like two or three months of exposure to its language. I had to learn fast if I was to cope.

Besides language, there was this overwhelming Brave New World of wealth, waste, and triumphant technology to deal with, something quite unmatched in my prior experience. The Europe whence I came was still lagging far behind the United States in standard of living, in levels of energy consumption, in scope of modern technology. And, of course, I was not coming straight from Europe, but from the heart of the Dark Continent. My recent trip by steamer down the Congo River put me in the nineteenth-century world of Joseph Conrad and Mark Twain. Suddenly, I was thrust into the civilization of the skyscraper, the freeway, and the supermarket.

Perhaps, I should stress here that I felt in no sense like a pioneer in the New World. In many ways, the United States was already familiar to me. As the world's hegemonic power in 1950, it cast a shadow that even reached the Congo (which produced, incidentally, the uranium used in the first U.S. atomic weapons). Besides, two generations of my family had had American connections. My paternal grandfather undertook a tour of homeopathic hospitals and medical schools in the eastern United States in the 1890s. My maternal grandfather made an extended visit to leading American universities in 1916 and published a book in 1917 on *Les universités et la vie scientifique aux Etats Unis*. My father won post-doctoral fellowships to Harvard, Berkeley, and other American universities in 1935 and, in later years, held a visiting professorship in tropical medicine at Tulane. The United States was hardly terra incognita, yet such knowledge as I had of it was merely a yardstick against which to measure my experiences.

In New York, I was at the very nub of that society, and I was dazzled by the size, the pace, and the intensity of the place. I suppose the main effect it had on me was awe at how such a society reduced the scale of man. From the top of Rockefeller Center, even automobiles looked like columns of army ants on the march. People shrunk into near invisibility. The first large American city I saw before New York was Washington, D.C., and the capital did not have that effect on me. I knew that I was at the very core of the greatest concentration of power the world had ever seen, and I was vastly impressed with the riches of the National Gallery and the Smithsonian, but Washington was still a world I knew and understood. Its physical plant had all the symmetry, logic and elegance of an eighteenth-century mind—and a French one at that! Washington is a kind of Versailles for the people. The great palace is the Congress, and the White House is like its Petit Trianon. Monticello and Mount Vernon also looked very familiar: they were colonial plantations established by gentlemen farmers living off the work of blacks. This was not very different from the Congo I knew.

But New York was something else. I was never able to recapture the awe of that first visit. Unlike most other great cities that have "grown" on me over the years, New York has "shrunk." I like the city less and less on each successive visit. The only feature that reconciles me with its existence is the Metropolitan Museum. Its inhumanity has remained, but my awe of it has vanished. To me New York is now merely a reluctant stop—when I need to talk to my publishers—on the way to Europe. Increasingly, even the publishers avoid it!

Boston (then still a low-rise city) and Cambridge were again more like Europe, and I immediately took to them, especially to the Harvard yard, which in a few years was to become my abode, and to the old Boston of the Commons, Beacon Hill, and Faneuil Hall. I was also astonished to discover that seemingly half of the French Impressionists had emigrated to Washington, New York, and Boston. I felt it was a bit unfair that money could bring about a country's cultural despoliation, but if French museums were too obtuse to recognize greatness in time, they only had themselves to blame.

Then came the crossing of the Great Plains, a dreadful experience of unrelieved boredom. The unremitting monotony of the landscape was reinforced by the most amazing cultural uniformity and unspeakable ugliness I had ever experienced. Accustomed to a world, both in Europe and Africa, where, every 100 kilometers or so, one encountered a new language, a new architecture and a new style of dress, the middle of the North American continent seemed like a 3,000-kilometer strip of service stations, automobile dealerships, supermarkets, and roadside restaurants and motels. Almost everywhere else I have travelled, I still have vivid memories of where I ate and slept. For example, Calcutta, Addis Ababa, Cuzco, Guadalajara, Rome, Lagos, and Beirut all conjure a distinct bundle of images, sounds, and smells quite unlike any other.

By contrast, my American trips merge into one composite reminiscent of the description of many gases in my high school chemistry textbook: odorless, colorless, and tasteless. The only blotch of recollection that emerges from that grim canvas of flat homogeneity is Chicago, thanks to its great museums, the Art Institute (with another flock of Impressionists), and the Field. The rest of the Middle West, to this date, blends into a single picture made up of cornfields and grain elevators interspersed with interchangeable cities that left so little impression that I am not even sure whether I have ever been in them. Duluth blends into Des Moines, Milwaukee into Minneapolis. Was I ever in Cincinnati? Or was it Cleveland?

A quick spin through the Southwest, Grand Canyon, and Death Valley took us from the ridiculous to the sublime. Ever since that first trip to the West, there was no question that, of all places in North America, the Pacific Coast was where I wanted to live. There at least nature was grand enough to ward off for a while the most concerted attempts to deface it.

So we finally came to Stanford, called the "Farm" because it was built on the estate of the nineteenth-century railway robber baron, Senator Leland Stanford. He and his widow bought their share of immortality by returning a share of his ill-gotten gains to establish a bucolic liberal arts and engineering college. The campus still sports a renovated old barn that now houses a branch of the Wells Fargo Bank and sundry boutiques, and the senator's racing stables (he was a great fancier of trotter races), where the better-heeled undergraduates can still board their horses. Next to the lavishly renovated stables, a decrepit little shack, worthy of the worst *barriadas* of Mexico City, houses a family of Chicano caretakers. Apparently, the social order has not changed much since the senator's days.

My father, in anticipation of divorce (in 1954), bought my mother a little house (for $13,000, if I remember rightly) in the unfashionable hills of Belmont. There he dumped her along with my young sister, Gwendoline, and he returned to the Congo with my brother, Christian. Christian was to finish another five years of high school in the Congo before joining his mother and sister in California and then follow, in my footsteps, as a Stanford undergraduate.

This long separation from my brother contributed to a strained relationship between us. We both became academics (he as a teacher of French language and literature at the University of Santa Clara, after he earned a Stanford Ph.D.). But there the resemblance ends. We are about as different from one another as two persons of similar background and heredity can be. So are our wives, which did not help any rapprochement. Our tastes, temperaments, physiques, and opinions are antithetical. Physically, he resembles his father, and I my mother. He is thin and balding; I turn to hairy corpulence. He is conventional, conformist, and accommodating; I am iconoclastic, categorical, and abrasive. He likes pets; I only enjoy animals in *their* natural habitat, not in mine. He is a practicing Catholic; I am an anti-clerical and an atheist. His civism and respect for state authority clashes with my anarchism. His conservative politics preclude discussions of any social issue. I thrive on vigorous, open intellectual debate; he shies away from disagreement and controversy.

For the next three years, I was to commute between the Stanford campus, where I boarded during the week, and Belmont where I spent most weekends and vacations with my mother and sister. In contrast to my strained relationship with Christian, I developed a warm, quasi-paternal tie to Gwendoline. In our father's absence, the twelve years' difference between us was magnified into a generation, yet there is much less of an intellectual and emotional gap between us than between my brother and me. I was a father figure to her, and there was some tension when I tried to wean her from what I saw as the nefarious influence of American teenage culture. We had some animated discussions on the respective merits of Mozart and Elvis Presley, for example. But we are very alike in character and intellect, and we get along famously.

I flatter myself that I exerted a considerable influence on her intellectual development, and, despite strong competition for her attentions from her age peers, she became a well-educated person. She followed my suggestion to go to Berkeley rather than Stanford (in the mid-sixties, Berkeley was still much the livelier and more intellectually oriented university, at least at the undergraduate level), and she graduated with honors in anthropology. She then went on to a Sorbonne doctorate, also in anthropology, under my old professor, Roger Bastide. Her field work experiences in Chiapas, Mexico, and Lima, Peru, also closely paralleled some of my career trajectory. Thus, our warm personal relationship is reinforced by an equally close intellectual and professional one. I suppose I am enough of an intellectual that I find it difficult to maintain a close relationship that does not have an important intellectual dimension. This is at least as true of my relations with women as with men. I never could find a stupid woman attractive, but I find the combination of brains and beauty irresistibly seductive.

Let me try to recapture my reactions to Stanford in the early 1950s. Stanford brought me my first breath of adult freedom, a permanent and welcome break from paternal authority, my first relatively unimpeded access to the opposite sex, and an extremely pleasant physical environment. The climate was just barely cooler than that of the central African highlands. The then semi-rural setting of the campus gave it a relaxed country-club atmosphere more conducive to hedonistic than intellectual pursuits. In short, Stanford was a closer approximation to the Garden of Eden than anything I have known before or after.

By one crucial test, however, Stanford failed me. It did not give me a good education. Partly, this was my fault. I did not take maximum advantage of what Stanford had to offer, even then, when it was still a long way from being a first-rate university. But the main culprits were the strongly anti-intellectual orientation of the undergraduate population and the mediocrity of much of the faculty. I am convinced that I would have gotten a better (and cheaper) education at Berkeley.

Initially, I approached my studies with considerable trepidation. My English was still very halting. I understood and read it passably enough, but I spoke and wrote it so badly, I thought, as to handicap me seriously in university-level courses. My first big academic surprise came in a freshman composition class. I was competing against native speakers of the language. What chance did I have? It turned out that I got a B+ (long before the days of grade inflation). I quickly discovered that my writing and analytical skills in French, and my Latin, Greek, and French vocabulary were largely transferable to English and that I was, in fact, writing better English than most native speakers. I only had to learn the finer points of idiomatic usage.

My freshman Western Civilization class was a joke, a superficial promenade through three millennia of history at the rate of a couple of centuries a week. The course attempted to cover in a few weeks what I had done in six years of high school, and our assigned readings consisted overwhelmingly of brief translated snippets of works I had already read in their entirety and often in the original language.

The next shock came around the first mid-term examination. There I had my first contact with the multiple-choice question. It was traumatic. I knew quite a bit more about the course material than was expected of me, and "excess" knowledge, for most multiple-choice questions, was crippling. In many cases, I could with ease construct a very plausible argument around more than one of the four or five alternatives. Yet the test was devised to leave approximately five seconds' reflection time per question. The object of the game was not to find *the* right answer, for obviously there was no such thing, but to try to guess what my teacher might think was the right answer. I had long been told that a little knowledge was a dangerous thing. I was now discovering that too much knowledge was even worse.

The essay part of the Western Civilization exam was equally stupefying. We were invited to cover centuries of major developments in the whole of Europe in twenty or thirty minutes. One mind-boggling example sticks in my memory. The question went something as follows: "Discuss the social and political effects of the changes in military technology between the breakdown of the Roman Empire and the Late Renaissance." A little over a millennium in thirty minutes! The expected answer, I found out later from my TA, was very simple really: firearms made body armor, cavalry, and castles obsolete and led to the centralization of power in the monarchy at the expense of the nobility. If this was the expected level of answer, I countered, then three minutes were perfectly adequate to the task; therefore, I had assumed much more was expected. My TA replied that, instead of showing off my erudition, I should stick to a clear and straight line of argument. My answer, though rich in content, was diffuse and lacked a central theme. History, I was told, had central themes, something like one or two for each period. Never mind the details. I had committed the fatal flaw, for instance, of getting "sidetracked" on the role of galleys versus sailing vessels in the Mediterranean versus the Atlantic. This was clearly a wrong tack to take when my TA only knew a galley as a small kitchen on his father's yacht. The professor probably knew better, but he could not be bothered to read the 375 essays in his class. Anyway, my performance was still good for a B+, probably my modal grade at Stanford.

Luckily, not all courses were so dismal. I went to see the dean of students to convince him that I was wasting my time in most of the freshman classes, and he quickly agreed that my Belgian secondary school education was worth a year of transfer credits in foreign languages, history, and art. By going to summer school and taking an extra course every quarter, I completed my B.A. degree in two calendar years and graduated in 1952, technically in political science, but actually with the equivalent of a double major in sociology as well.

A few of my courses were excellent. The introductory biology sequence filled a gaping hole in my secondary education, and I still remember vividly our shark, frog, and cat dissections, our experiments in *Drosophila* genetics, and some brilliant lectures in evolutionary theory. Quinn McNemar's statistics courses proved to me for the first time that mathematics could be made exciting. Most of my political science courses were unmemorable, but they forced me to read some classics I might otherwise have missed: Hobbes, Hume, J. S. Mill, Locke, *The Federalist* papers. (The French ones, Montesquieu, Rousseau, Voltaire, were already part of my high school baggage.) I do, however, remember Graham Stuart's course on U.S. foreign policy in Latin America. A couple of economics courses helped me fathom the mysteries of a market economy.

In sociology and anthropology (then still a joint department), I faced a very mixed bag, and unfortunately the department was then so small that I had to take practically everyone's courses to accumulate the requisite 40 units for a major. Of the anthropologists, two made a lasting contribution, Felix Keesing (who was close to the end of his teaching career) and George Spindler (who was just beginning his and who helped me draw on my Congo experience to develop my interest in non-Western societies). When I was still a senior, Spindler flatteringly invited me to join his graduate seminar, and I remember reporting on the Tuzi, a most superficial rehash of the little I had learned from Maquet.

Unfortunately, there was only one good sociology teacher, Richard T. La Piere. His acerbic wit, sound common sense, and contempt for obfuscating jargon appealed greatly to me. I particularly relished his devastating attacks against Freud, in an age when psychoanalytic nonsense was rampant in American social science. It was to be another thirty years before the term "psychobabble" was coined, but it was La Piere who made it clear to me that psychoanalysis was the ancestral psychobabble in Western intellectual history, surviving as a sect in the total absence of any demonstrable relationship to the real world. I also liked his critique of Durkheim and of all those who would reify social structure as something more than interacting individuals. In this case, however, he did not totally convince me, nor dissuade me from going on to study under Talcott Parsons at Harvard. La Piere also poked delightful fun at Parsons, but it took me another ten years to see that that particular emperor had no clothes. When I had the great pleasure of meeting again with La Piere a couple of years before his death, he was an amazingly vigorous and undiminished 85 years old. He was amused to learn from me that Parsons was enjoying a revival. His comment was pure vintage La Piere: "How clever Parsons has been at concealing how dumb he really was!"

Everyone else on the sociology staff at Stanford was unfortunately an unmitigated disaster. I shall refrain from mentioning names. One was an insufferably dull old fogy whose central, nay sole, interest in life was U.S. Social Security legislation. I simply had to take ten excruciating units of Social Security to qualify for my double major. Another was a pretentious young assistant professor, with a freshly baked Ivy League Ph.D., so deeply imbued with his sense of self-importance that he was totally impervious to humor, wit, or intellectual playfulness. We got along very badly, but, again, I was forced to take three of his courses toward my quota of forty units. He gave me straight Cs in all three, the only Cs of my Stanford career. In Stanford's defense, he did not get tenure.

There was more to my Stanford existence than lectures and labs. Stanford lived up to its reputation of being one of the country's leading playgrounds. "Intellectual" students were distinctly a beleaguered and ridiculed minority, accounting for perhaps 20 percent of the total. Made up in good part of Jews from Los Angeles and New York, impecunious foreign students, and children of faculty members, the intellectuals were pitied as repressed, introverted bookworms who never dated, never got drunk, did not join fraternities, were inept at sports—in short, were missing out on all the essential activities of college life.

At the other extreme were the fraternity boys. (Stanford then had a carefully limited number of female students, but no sororities.) They were proudly, loudly, joyously anti-intellectual. A grade above a C in any course demanded an apology to their brothers. Drunkenness every weekend was de rigueur. They were for the most part the spoiled brats of the West Coast plutocracy. They cluttered the campus with their convertibles and engaged in a frantic round of dating and social life, centering around football games and the drunken orgies connected with post-game parties. Not all "Greeks" were athletes, but nearly all athletes were

Greeks. The fraternities vied with each other to attract football and basketball stars, but even the "minor" sports—swimming, track, and others—carried some prestige. Inebriation, rowdiness, anti-intellectualism, sexual braggadocio, and athletic prowess were their main criteria of masculinity. (The word machismo had not crossed the Rio Grande yet.)

In between these two extremes were the 50 or 60 percent of the men who lived in dormitories. Only a small number of students were commuters then. Commuting was strongly discouraged, as it cut you off from the "real" life of the campus, that is, its social life. This middle ground was also shared by most "coeds," since they had no sororities to turn to. A small minority of men (myself included) belonged to a half-dozen or so "eating clubs." My main reason for joining was to gain some relief from dismal institutional food in the dormitory dining halls. But the idea of the eating club was to provide a watered-down (and cheaper) version of fraternities, offering the congeniality of a small group without the distracting rowdiness. You ate in your club, but slept in a nearby dormitory. The eating club was the organization to join if you felt moderately sociable and studious at the same time, and it seemed a reasonable compromise to me.

Social life was, of course, dominated by relations between the sexes. The Stanford of the 1950s probably represented the most frustrating sexual environment imaginable and the one most conducive to a non-stop "war between the sexes," best epitomized by the MM and BB films. Women were supposed to be alluring but to remain virgins until marriage. "Heavy petting" short of intercourse was considered the normal outcome of a series of expensive dining and movie dates, to be financed exclusively by the young man. A set of wheels was another prerequisite for these activities, in part because public transportation was then virtually non-existent, in part because rigidly sex-segregated dormitories with draconian "parietal" rules precluded alternative venues and mostly because the motorcar itself provided the cramped setting for sexual gymnastics. The 1950s created a generation of sexual contortionists.

However, Stanford managed to improve on this design by creating that most anomalous of all ethnographic curiosities: a polyandrous society. Stanford prided itself in having been one of the early leaders in "co-education," but with reservations. It abided by the rampant paternalism of all American colleges, acting in loco parentis to supervise and police the private lives of its students. It blatantly discriminated against female students who were subjected to curfews and other rules not applicable to men. The dean of women saw herself as the "keeper of the chastity belt." In all this, Stanford merely followed standard collegiate practice.

The additional Stanford twist was the sexual quota system. On Mrs. Stanford's theory that a few women had a restraining influence on the rowdiness of male students, but that too many of them would divert the university's function of educating men, Stanford had first a ceiling of 500 women and then, until 1973, a 20 percent quota on female admissions. This slanted four-to-one sex ratio created a number of problems, not the least of which was the multitude of sex-starved men battering the doors of the girls' (sorry, that is what young women were called in those benighted days) dormitories. Some women thrived on these competitive courtship displays, but many suffered from an overload of unwanted attentions. Also, the quick circulation of women among frustrated suitors made for a rich and sometimes vicious flow of sexual gossip. Women were categorized into pigs, prudes, prick-teasers, and easy lays. Dating success was measured by the ability to move a student from the third category to the fourth. The first two classes were to be shunned altogether.

Not only did polyandry escalate verbal aggression in the war of the sexes. It added insult to injury (for the men) by creating a situation in which women were, on the average, intellectually superior to the men. Stanford was supposed to be academically selective for both sexes, but the effect of that selectivity on the males was often dubious. For one thing, there were all those beefy athletes who had obviously been chosen on criteria other than intellect. They had no female counterparts, because inter-collegiate athletics were than a virtually all-male preserve. For another, since a woman had only one-fourth the probability of a man of being admitted, the women were indeed appreciably brighter than the men. The male defense against female superiority was to define bright women as either pigs or prudes. Many women were well aware that a visible show of intellect could wreck their social life. They kept their mouths shut in the classroom for fear of being stigmatized as intellectuals, and a number even deflated their grade-point average to the puzzlement of college authorities who wondered why women underachieved. They were doing only *marginally* better than men when, according to their college entrance test scores, they should have done *much* better.

My own social life at Stanford was largely limited to the small community of foreign students, principally French-speaking Europeans. My American contemporaries with whom I shared dormitory rooms (first in Encina Hall, now home of the Economics Department, then in Toyon and Stern) and my meals in my eating club (El Cuadro), struck me as being rather immature and uninteresting, except for a couple of intellectual Jews. I attended three or four football games, but more as an ethnographic experience than out of an intrinsic interest in the game and its attendant social life.

Most of the foreign students with whom I associated were graduate students and thus a bit older than I was. My amatory incursions included some Americans, but I quickly tired of the standard American dating ritual, which, in addition, was straining my limited budget. So, there too, I increasingly restricted myself to European girls who often insisted on "going Dutch," who favored cheap little Chinese restaurants, who enjoyed French or Swedish art films and symphony concerts rather than the drunken fraternity orgies following the Big Game. We formed a little group of perhaps a dozen or fifteen francophone students of both sexes and a half-dozen nationalities, to which we admitted a couple of francophile Americans. We met most Saturdays in one or another of the small flats where some of the graduate students lived; we drank cheap California wines at the rate of about one gallon for the evening; and we discussed politics, art, cinema, and books into the early Sunday mornings.

My closest male friend was Alex Kosloff, the son of White Russian émigrés who ran a fashionable Oriental antique shop in San Francisco. We were very different, but we formed a partnership. He was a charming playboy, a spendthrift, a ladies' man, a dashing pilot, an accomplished skier, and a cultured anti-intellectual. French was his mother tongue, though he spoke Russian as well. He was very bright and well read, but also lazy and hedonistic, and he had an aristocratic disdain for effort of any kind, including intellectual. He had both a car and an airplane, and he often took me along on double dates. My first flight was taken, rather foolhardily, in his rickety old World War II trainer. He also gave me my first car-driving lessons. In exchange, I would coach him to pass some of his exams, with minimal effort on his part. He seldom attended classes, never completed his reading assignments, and maintained the requisite C average by balancing his effortless As in French classes with the Ds he earned in practically every other subject. But occasionally he undershot the mark and had to make up an F, as, for example, in biology, a compulsory science requirement. In later life, he became first an air force, and then an airline, pilot. He died of throat cancer in his early forties, after an unhappy marriage. His only son committed suicide in early adolescence with a revolver he had given him.

Between my junior and senior year, in 1951, I spent a summer session in Mexico, the beginning of a lifelong love affair with that country. I thought it was silly to live next to Mexico without knowing its language, so I took a Spanish conversation class at Stanford in preparation for the trip. I also enrolled in a few classes at the Universidad Nacional de

Mexico and at the Mexico City College, then a predominantly gringo institution and the ancestral college to today's Universidad de las Américas. A cut-rate commercial flight (my first long trip by air) took me to Guadalajara, from which I took a bus to Mexico City. There I had an encounter with a clever pickpocket and confidence trickster, who relieved me of $300 in traveller's checks and left me with some 100 pesos in cash. At that time, the rate of exchange was 8 pesos to the U.S. dollar, and prices were very low, but still $12 was a paltry sum to face a city of then some 2.5 million people. Luckily, I had arranged to board in a private home, so I was assured of a roof and meals until American Express refunded my money. Contrary to their advertisements, they took about two weeks. Meanwhile, I was in the embarrassing position of having to explain my temporary penury to the two elderly señoritas who hosted me. My Spanish was then hardly adequate to the task, but they commiserated, expatiated about the *rateros* who sullied the good name of Mexico, and gracefully extended me credit.

Conchita and Incarnación, for such were their names, were exquisite museum pieces of pre-revolutionary Mexico. Both had remained celibate and lived in their parents' large but rather decrepit bourgeois house, in the Colonia Roma, near Insurgentes. Their parents had been large *hacendados* despoiled by the revolution. The sisters still maintained a precarious existence of genteel poverty in the threadbare shell of their childhood home, by taking in three or four boarders (for about $60 a month for room and meals). They were served by two maids, the necessary prerequisite for genteel status, but otherwise, were parsimonious in the extreme. As their highly spiced cuisine was a distinct appetite depressant, I did not bankrupt their food budget. The older of the two, Incarnación, spying the appearance of tears at the corners of my eyes, would always ask me with sly amusement: *"Pica?"* to which I felt obliged to respond: *"No tanto."*

The other guests were Jorge, a cultured and exquisitely polite Mexican accountant, and Joyce, a young woman from Texas on whom I had a fleeting crush. To tease her, I would always join Jorge in taking the Mexican nationalist position on the U.S. annexation of Texas and the War of 1848. Through these political and historical discussions, my Spanish progressed swiftly.

During the week, I attended my classes, but on weekends I took trips to explore Mexico City and environs: Puebla, Cholula, Tula, Teotíhuacan, Taxco, Cuernavaca. The impact of Mexican art, architecture, archeology, and culture was overwhelming. Culturally and linguistically, I felt much more at home in this Latin environment than I did in the United States. Class relations were quite similar to those I had known in pre-war Europe, though poverty made the class distinctions even more pronounced.

Mexico was then a much poorer country than it is now, both absolutely and in relation to the United States. But I had seen enough poverty of an even much starker kind in Africa not to be overly shocked by it in Mexico, as many North Americans are. In poor countries, it is *wealth* rather than poverty I find shocking; the reverse is true in rich countries. Let me explain. The wealth of the few in poor countries is shocking because it was achieved by stealing from the poor; but, alas, redistribution would barely make a dent into the poverty of the many. In the rich countries, on the other hand, the poverty of the few is shocking because it could be so easily eliminated by tax reform and social legislation.

Compared to the tame and bland social canvas of the United States, Mexico was an exciting kaleidoscope of vivid impressions: its stark landscapes of snow-peaked volcanoes, agave fields, and giant cactuses; the stunning archaeological remains of three millennia of urban civilization, especially the gigantic Teotíhuacan; the baroque splendor of its colonial churches and palaces; the magnificent frescoes of its modern muralists. All these vestiges of a turbulent history evoked a cultural diversity and richness that made North America pale by contrast.

That history became a personal encounter when I visited the Chapultepec Historical Museum. There, in this eighteenth-century palace of the last Spanish viceroys, and in the apartments of the ill-fated Maximilian, I could visualize my ancestor, the Général Marquis de Tucé, dancing to a Strauss waltz with Empress Carlota and warning the emperor of impending doom. A few months after my ancestor left Mexico, recalled by Napoleon III who cynically abandoned Maximilian after using him as his puppet, Maximilian faced a firing squad in Querétaro. The Mexicans, with their necrophilia, made a death mask of him, which now stares from its sunken eye sockets at the visitors of Chapultepec. His beautiful widow, Carlota, the daughter of Léopold II of Belgium, became insane but survived her husband by a half-century, haunting her father's castle in Laeken.

By my senior year, I had abandoned my initial plan to follow up a B.A. in political science with law school and a diplomatic career. The conduct of American foreign policy had convinced me that I could not long tolerate such a high level of incompetence. My foreign citizenship also disqualified me, at least for several years. Finally, my mother convinced me that my sarcastic, cynical, iconoclastic turn of mind was a distinct handicap in diplomacy. That is when I started thinking of an academic career in sociology or anthropology.

It was also the time when the shadow of the Korean War draft was visibly lengthening over my Garden of Eden. Even though I was still a Belgian national, my permanent resident status made me eminently eligible to serve in Uncle Sam's army. Deferments had been nearly automatic so long as I was an undergraduate, but now they were becoming more difficult. My hopes of being rejected on medical grounds, on the strength of a positive TB skin test and a dime-size lung shadow, were, alas, dashed after a perfunctory physical examination at the San Francisco Presidio. That event remains one of the low points of my life. To lift my spirits, I had decided that I would go to my physical with some panache. I borrowed a young visiting professor's Buick convertible to drive to the city, accompanied by a rather gorgeous girlfriend. Not only did I pass my physical, but the car broke down on us, much to my embarrassment. That double trauma left a permanent but beneficial mark on my psyche: a prejudice against the American automobile industry. Except for my first car, a 1937 Plymouth, which I bought for $125, I never purchased an American car. The one I did buy soon started smoldering on me when its battery, cleverly lodged under the back seat, next to the gas tank, ignited the upholstery.

Entry into an M.A. program in sociology seemed the safest refuge against the draft, and Stanford was the best bet because I was sure of admission. Such was the inglorious beginning of my professional career. Stanford at that time did not have a sociology graduate program worthy of the name. After an undemanding year, I got a worthless M.A. degree. To be sure, I learned some more statistics from McNemar and a little quantitative methodology from Paul Wallin (my first exposure to the then novel and exciting technique of the Guttman Scale). I also did my first bit of "field work," by participating in Wendell Bell's first major "social areas" project. My contribution consisted principally of ringing doorbells, questionnaire in hand, and hoping that I could convince the prospective respondent to oblige. Not being schooled in door-to-door selling, I stacked up a horrendous refusal rate, which jeopardized the carefully drawn stratified random sample.

Not yet inured to the shameless invasions of privacy to which urban Americans are constantly subjected, I felt very guilty about disturbing people and had none of the brashness required for the job. I simply hated that kind of work. To make matters worse, my diffidence and apologetic demeanor combined with my foreign accent, were likely to arouse people's suspicions. One episode was especially amusing. We were instructed to interview only "male heads of household." Indeed, in those days, "male head" was a redundancy. Innocently, I thought it best to reformulate the pompous question: "Is the head of the household at home?" with a more straightforward: "Is there a man in the house?"

should a woman answer the door. This approach unfortunately resulted in more slammed doors than invitations to come in. One day, the Department of Sociology received insistent inquiries from the police. Did anyone know a suspicious foreign chap lurking around Palo Alto at night who claimed to be doing research for Stanford?

After that fiasco, I was relieved to be reassigned to the home office, the couple of rooms where we did the data analysis. These were the days of the ponderous Friden calculating machines that took about five seconds for a long division and several minutes for a correlation coefficient. In those days, it really paid to think of a good reason before running off a correlation. The biggest monsters in our arsenal of data analysis were the buffet-sized IBM card sorters, and the third main leg of the data-crunching apparatus consisted of the card punchers. This revolutionary technology, the new-fangled methodologists thought, would permanently propel sociology out of the realm of speculation and herald the Comtean millennium of positive, quantified truth. In retrospect, it was merely sociology's first big step in putting the methodological cart before the substantive horse. It propelled sociology into an orbit of theoretical vacuity. Quantitative trompe l'oeil increasingly hid the field's conceptual bankruptcy. As early as 1909, Henri Poincaré had diagnosed the sociological malady. Sociology, he said, is "the science that possesses the most in the way of methods and the least in the way of results." Three-quarters of a century later, the aphorism had lost none of its validity.

The new technology of research had, however, a tremendous advantage that sociologists were quick to seize: it was horrendously expensive, at least by the standards of the day and, thus, provided ample room for the discipline's self-aggrandizement. I was truly an eyewitness to the birth pangs of an academic infant. The methodological baby would soon turn into a gratifyingly voracious consumer of outside (mostly government) resources, which in turn would feed the growth of the entire academic establishment. American academia was trembling on the threshold of affluence. By sheer luck, it was precisely the right time to get in on the act. All I had to do was wait for the balloon to lift me.

CHAPTER 5

Reluctant Soldiering

My two-year spell in the U.S. Army (September 1954 to September 1956) was preceded by a year of graduate work at Harvard. After my Stanford experience, I decided that it was time to attend a really first-class university—and that only Harvard would do. With the overconfidence of youth, I only applied for admission at Harvard, and I was accepted.

By that time much of NATO was breathing hot on my heels. The Belgian Consulate in San Francisco forwarded to me my Belgian draft notice, in Dutch, mailed from Antwerp. As my official Belgian residence was still Brussels, the Belgian army grandly mailed me a one-way, third-class rail ticket from Brussels to Antwerp, worth approximately 75 cents, but left it to me to finance my trip from San Francisco to Belgium. I pleaded poverty for not responding to my country's call to arms, for I was still a Belgian national. A second draft notice ignored my plea and threatened me with prosecution for draft dodging if I did not appear at my appointed time and place in Antwerp. Technically, I have been a Belgian draft dodger ever since.

As I was a permanent U.S. resident, Uncle Sam also regarded me as a prime candidate for the defense of its far-flung empire. I had passed my physical examination and mental test with flying colors, and the board warned me that I might even be drafted in the middle of an academic year. I went to Harvard all the same. With a shooting war still going on in Korea, it seemed much the lesser risk.

RELUCTANT SOLDIERING

For the sake of topical continuity, I shall depart somewhat from chronology and reserve my account of Harvard for Chapter 7. As it turned out, I was allowed to finish the academic year, but I was drafted during the summer vacation of 1954. Technically, I "volunteered for the draft," which only meant that I had some control of the date I would don the uniform, or the "monkey suit," as I preferred to call it.

Needless to say, I was a confirmed anti-militarist, out of both conviction and temperament. My rebelliousness and non-conformity were ill-suited to what I regarded as involuntary servitude. Intellectually, I was not a pacifist, though I was sympathetic to conscientious objectors; but I had been raised to believe that military life was a distillation of human stupidity. I wholeheartedly agreed with Clemenceau's bon mot that war was much too dangerous a game to be played by generals. All my prejudices were soon amply confirmed.

I debated about claiming conscientious objector status, but I decided against it, largely on grounds of expediency. At that time, the army made it difficult to claim C.O. status on grounds other than membership in some religious group, such as Jehovah's Witnesses, and I was not about to become a Jesus freak to avoid carrying a rifle. I did the next best thing, which was to volunteer for the Medical Corps after my Infantry Basic Training. Thus, I spent most of my army service in the company of many upliftingly principled young men with whom I could share my contempt for all things military.

The shock of abrupt transfer from a graduate dormitory at Harvard to basic training barracks in Fort Ord, California, was one of the most traumatic in my life. Rituals of dehumanization inflicted by total institutions have been exquisitely described by Erving Goffman, Michel Foucault, and others. In all essentials, induction into basic training is identical to admission into a prison. One is stripped of all civilian possessions except for what would fit on a small shelf of a narrow locker. One is given a new identity in the form of an eight-digit number to be instantly memorized and stamped on one's equipment. One is left with no doubt at all that, as far as the army is concerned, the cipher *is* the man. One is issued one's quota of uniforms and shorn of all but the last centimeter of one's hair. All this stripping of individuality is concentrated in the space of a few hours and designed to achieve maximum impact and humiliation.

My first revolt against the army came when I was forced to pay (90 cents) for my horrid 45-second regulation haircut. This was adding insult to injury. The ordeal, repeated every week, reminded me of my childhood haircuts in Ghent, but, then at least, it was my grandfather who paid. The clothing line, on the other hand, elicited my reluctant admiration. I was better fitted with uniforms and shoes in the space of some 20 to 30 minutes (including the trying on of boots) than I have been by most civilian tailors in laborious sittings. The practiced eye of a sergeant (who probably had done little else for fifteen or twenty years) sized me up at a glance, and a neat pile of textiles materialized on the counter within minutes. We were only allowed to try on boots and caps, and I was skeptical of the results, but every item was a perfect fit. Not only that, but practically the entire issue, including most of the socks and underwear, outlasted a hundred washings or so and two years of strenuous service. If civilian clothing were made of the same quality, the textile industry would quickly be bankrupted. The same was true of my boots. For the rest of my life, I have been "hooked" on army boots. My current pair of $20 army-issue boots outlasted by far a $150 pair of my son's fancy hiking boots. It has lasted me thirteen years and survived countless hikes through the roughest mountain chains of the Western Hemisphere from Bolivia to Canada. It has yet to need resoling!

I wanted to be fair to the army, and this is the last good thing I shall say about it, except perhaps for its sensible use of the metric system. The first day in the army was spent being separated from one's possessions and individuality. The next ten weeks of basic training were devoted to the maximum possible withdrawal of freedom, privacy, and self-esteem, accompanied by the torture of physical exhaustion and sleep deprivation. We were allowed about five hours of rest a night, but that was only in the best of cases. A sadistic sergeant could decide to spring a midnight "short-arm" inspection (we were asked to "milk" our penises, supposedly as a check against gonorrhea, but what better way to humiliate us?); or we were awakened an hour early for a special rifle-cleaning session; or the company commander decided we should go on a three-day maneuver without sleep; or there was a fire drill at 3 A.M.

The architecture of the barracks was cunningly devised for maximum deprivation of privacy. We were housed in spanking new four-story cement blocks. Each floor consisted of a long room with a row of two-tiered bunk beds on each side of a central isle. At one end of the hall were two small rooms for non-commissioned officers. ("Rank has its privileges," RHIP for short, we were constantly told, as a reminder that we had none.) Each soldier had a footlocker and a locker-room-style metal closet, and one might think that at least these spaces were private. Far from it. They were subject to inspection at any time of the day or night, and the storage of only our military equipment and the barest toilet articles was tolerated. Even the arrangement of the objects inside the closet and footlocker was prescribed in smallest detail.

One compartment of the footlocker, for example, was reserved for a display of toiletries. But these were not the articles we used. Since they had to be in impeccable shape for inspection, we had to buy a second razor, toothbrush, toothpaste, and soap for display, and hide our real toilet kit below a pile of underwear. Our privacy, in effect, was reduced to the contents of our wallets, and even that had to be so thin as not to reveal a bulge through our tight-fitting uniforms. The numerous pockets of our uniforms served not as storage places, but as a constant cause of verbal abuse from sergeants for being unbuttoned.

The architectural showplace of army barracks is the toilet, the "shithouse" in military dialect. Imagine a gleaming white room with rows of white toilet bowls, wash basins, urinals, and shower heads, all totally devoid of any kind of partition walls. The slightest hint of privacy is removed even from defecation. There have been eloquent descriptions of the architecture of prisons, but surely military architecture is inspired by the same systematic search for total control through total dehumanization.

Indeed, our entire existence was practically identical to that of convicts. We were stripped not only of possessions and privacy, but of time itself. Either confined to barracks or marching, we were always accompanied by drill sergeants who unleased a steady stream of abuse. In addition, non-commissioned officers were constantly in our midst to eliminate the slightest hint of leisure. Time, we were constantly reminded, was no longer our own. It belonged to the army. Appropriately, army lingo was the same as prison argot: we were "doing time," "killing time," "filling time." As the military has no use for the old, the army had no "lifers," but the "thirty-year man" was a good approximation. We were, in short, totally alienated from the very essence of our being. Even that most imponderable of commodities—time—was no longer our own.

What little cracks were left inadvertently unfilled by our training regimen were instantaneously filled by an impromptu inspection, "police call" (picking up cigarette butts from the parade grounds, to the accompaniment of a sergeant's invarying witticisms: "Ah don't want to see nothin' but assholes and elbows," or "If it moves, screw it, if it don't, pick it up"), punitive or routine drill or push-ups ("Give me twenty" was perhaps, next to obscenities, the most frequent phrase in the lexicon of sergeants), bed-making practice (another rich source of subtle harassment), or a weapon-stripping and cleaning exercise. If the sergeant's imagination gave out, there were always boots to polish to a gleaming shine. We had two pairs of combat boots, which we were supposed to rotate but never did. One was constantly spit-shined for inspection, the other worn in training. Occasionally, however, a sadistic sergeant made us wear our spit-shined boots, especially when the order of the day called for a particularly dusty 30-kilometer march. This insured one or two hours of sleep robbed from our allotted five the following night.

In one essential way, however, our life differed from that of convicts. Unlike many of our prison counterparts who had picked up the expertise on their own, we had to be trained to become ruthless killers. Any army's principal raison d'être is the production of cadavers. This philosophy was expressed in two different dialects. The official manuals written in officer lingo spoke of "destroying the enemy" or "inflicting maximum damage on enemy targets." At the level of the drill sergeant, this became: "Kill the mother-fucker before he kills you." Bayonet practice was especially graphic. It was not enough to stab sandbags at a fast clip; we also had to produce a satisfyingly bloodcurdling scream, until the sergeant deemed that we had reached a credible level of ferocity. This instruction was accompanied by sound ethological advice: "Don't look at the cocksucker's face, look at his fucking hands." Eye contact might produce a dangerous flicker of humanity.

Our training had three principal components: technical expertise, physical conditioning, and dehumanization. The last two often blended into one another, as when push-ups and marches were used as punishment, but generally the boundaries between these three components of training were fairly clear. Dehumanization was partly verbal, taking the form of a constant stream of demeaning remarks by non-commissioned officers, all peppered with profanities and obscenities. The main formal exercise in this type of training was the "manual of arms" or "short-order drill." It was invented in the eighteenth century, supposedly by Frederick the Great, to train Prussian infantrymen to fire effective volleys of musket fire, in the days when it took one or two minutes to load muzzle-loading weapons. The manual of arms has outlived its utilitarian value in nearly all the world's armies by over a century and now has become a hazing ritual, a ballet of choreographed humiliation. Its lack of any redeeming value has been amply demonstrated by its nearly total elimination from one of the world's most effective armies, that of Israel.

In official army ideology, the short-order drill is a great rite of passage from the lowly status of a clumsy civilian rabble to that of a precise, disciplined soldiery. The message is clear: only by surrendering all individuality of appearance, movement, and timing does one become a good soldier. In a kind of military notion of Nirvana, the good soldier is the one who is proud of having become a cipher, of having lost all claims to uniqueness. Drill is the perfect exercise, aimed at creating complete uniformity in space and time. Even irreducible individual differences, such as those in stature, are made less jarring by ordering the men in descending order of size. Real differences are fused into the optical illusion of perspective in order to create the perfect parade-ground image.

The production of these undifferentiated automata is regarded as the army's ultimate test of leadership, best epitomized by the strutting drill sergeant. It is interesting to note that in this process of dehumanization even the most basic feature of our human condition, namely language, is reduced to its simplest possible form. Commands are best described as barks rather than as speech utterances. The more incomprehensible to the untrained civilian ear these commands are, the more "commanding" they are held to be. The rank and file remain silent, or, at best, are only allowed rhythmic chanting. The climax of this transformation of a human being into a trained killer is, appropriately enough, the great graduation parade in front of the commanding general at the end of the ten weeks of basic training. The greatest compliment of the graduation speech is: "You are looking sharp, men," which really means, "You are looking flat, men, you are totally interchangeable numbers."

The second element of the training triad was physical conditioning, consisting principally of a regimen of calisthenics and marches that was, in fact, the ancestral form of that mania for aerobics that swept the nation fifteen or twenty years later. The more strenuous of these exercises involved 30- or 40-kilometer marches with 30 kilograms of equipment, and three-day maneuvers without sleep. Interestingly, this aspect of training was much less resented than the much less strenuous short-order drill. Far from producing uniform results, long marches "separated the men from the boys." Lasting the course easily became a matter of personal pride and private triumph. It did not for me, for I could never understand masochism. Panting and sweating has never come close to my idea of fun, but many of my fellow soldiers did get some kind of kick out of these tests of endurance. So do many of my otherwise perfectly reasonable-looking academic colleagues who are addicted to jogging, weight-lifting, racquetball, or some such masochistic activity so lucrative for practitioners of "sports medicine."

Finally, there was the technical aspect of our training: map reading, ballistics, explosives, first aid, and the use and maintenance of a wide range of infantry weapons: our basic "piece," the M-1 rifle, but also the carbine, two or three types of machine gun, mortars, rifle grenades, and a half-dozen varieties of hand grenades. Even in those days of a universal draft and fairly simple weapons, the technical part of our training greatly exceeded the competence not only of 90 percent of the soldiers but of most of the instructors. For example, our M-1 rifle was a fairly simple piece of machinery, yet prone to frequent jamming when it came into contact with dirt. It did a nice job of hitting stationary targets at 500 meters on the firing range, especially if you had a couple of minutes to figure out the direction and velocity of the wind and twist the knobs on the rear sight the requisite number of clicks. But after 100 meters through a dusty infiltration course, its combat value was reduced to the bayonet at the end of its barrel. Thus, great stress was put on our ability to dissemble the fifteen or so moving parts of the bolt assembly, preferably blindfolded. We must have gone through the routine two or three times a day, yet that accomplishment still eluded at least 30 to 40 percent of our company at the end of basic training. As for machine guns, I doubt that there were ten of us who could have kept one going for more than a few hundred rounds.

The most "intellectual" subject in our training was map reading. It presupposed, of course, general literacy, which eliminated perhaps 20 to 30 percent of the draftees and 50 to 60 percent of the noncommissioned officers who were training us. But, in addition, you had to master the abstraction of scale, the magic of two-dimensional representation of three-dimensional space, and, most formidably, the sorcery of orientation. The ability to guide a squad successfully through a couple of kilometers of map exercise was regarded by most non-coms as a mark of certifiable genius, or of magic akin to, say, successful waterdowsing. Later, when I was assigned to my permanent unit, I became "professor of cartography," repeating my course every six months as our training schedule called for. This earned me the reputation of being the resident Einstein. The non-coms who were taking the course for the twentieth or thirtieth time still did not fathom the deep mysteries of the compass, contour curves, and symbols. I doubt that more than three or four of the fifty-odd corporals and sergeants in our company could have used military maps in the field. No doubt, in recent years, with an all-volunteer force and more complex weaponry, the working effectiveness of the American army in the field must have been reduced even further.

The level of stupidity of some of the personnel constituted a public menace. I remember two episodes in particular. One involved a borderline moron who was in my basic training company. He had passed the army intelligence test, but he could tie his boot laces only with considerable difficulty, never mastered the ability to make his bed to our sergeant's satisfaction, could not hit a barn with a machine gun at 50 meters, and was, of course, totally incapable of dissembling his M-1. We did all that for him. Meanwhile, I was trying to persuade my company commander that the poor chap was overripe for a medical discharge and constituted a threat to all of us. Sure enough, we soon had a close brush with tragedy on the grenade range. Some twenty of us, behind a protective concrete wall, were to throw live fragmentation grenades at targets. The man pulled the pin, released the handle, and stood there—petrified with fear—with a grenade on a 5-second fuse cooking in his hand. Luckily, his neighbor yanked it out of his hand and threw it over the wall with about a half-second to spare. I was some 5 meters and two men away from him. This time the captain believed me, and the man was discharged.

The second incident involved an officer, a first lieutenant who, incredibly, was a qualified pharmacist and the executive officer of our medical company. The man must have had an IQ of around 90. While literate in a minimal sense, he was incapable of drafting a letter or report and relied entirely on the company clerk for all written communications. His pharmaceutical degree was from a dubious fly-by-night school in New York City. One day, on maneuvers, he started an "enemy alert" by throwing a couple of grenade canisters among our pup tents. Grenades at that time came in two packages: fragmentation grenades were fist-sized "pineapples" of black steel; all other kinds looked like khaki-colored cans of Campbell soup. The inventory included such "flavors" as tear gas, smoke, illumination, and white phosphorus. The latter, designed to burn a hole through tank armor, was undistinguishable, except for the printed matter, from its more innocuous shelf companions. Our executive officer had not bothered to read the labels and severely burned six men, one of whom lost two fingers. His defense was that it was too dark to read the labels. I threatened to file charges of incompetence against him, and I must say that he kept a low profile for the last three or four months of his tenure with us. But I shudder to think of his performance as a pharmacist, assuming that he returned to civilian life.

When I entered the army I was already a trained social scientist with an active interest in social stratification, especially in rigid, despotic social orders such as those of colonialism and caste. The army provided me with an interesting case study of a quasi-caste system operating within an advanced industrial society. I had already been perplexed by, and interested in, the persistence of a racial caste system in the United States. If one were to believe the reigning functionalist theory of social stratification of the time, such rigidly ascriptive status systems were incompatible with, or at least incongruous in, advanced industrial societies. Yet the United States and South Africa (to which I was soon to turn my scholarly attention) were glaring negative cases. I was faced with a rigidly stratified system that seemed to have many of the characteristics of a caste system. Yet it had grown from within a supposedly egalitarian, achievement-oriented, universalistic, urbanized, industrialized society. To be sure, the military was not a genuine caste society in the classical sense. For one thing, it was not a total society but merely a specialized segment of one. For another, the status of officer or enlisted man was not hereditary or ascribed in any strict, legal, prescriptive way. The analytical category of "estate" (*Stand*) gave a better fit to military reality. Yet the army clearly went a long way in creating, maintaining and enforcing quasi-caste barriers between officers and enlisted men.

Apart from a small, anomalous category of warrant officers who were neither fish nor fowl, a chasm clearly separated the commissioned officers from the enlisted ranks. The two categories were, apart from short-term draftees, recruited from different social classes, spoke sharply distinct dialects, had different tastes—in short, belonged to different worlds. Not only that—the army was doing its best to keep them as far from each other as possible. Recreation facilities on the base were separate and unequal. Pay, housing, and all perquisites of rank were kept as conspicuously unequal as possible. Uniforms, for example, differed not only in insignia of rank but in color, cut, and style of headgear, so as to be recognizably distinct at a distance of 100 meters or more. Only combat uniforms were more "democratic" because the army did not want to give the enemy a way of selectively bumping off officers.

One of the first lectures we were given was called "military courtesy," a crash course in the etiquette of rank. Officers were always to be saluted and called "Sir" (or, very uncommonly in those days, "Ma'am," *not,* be it noted, "Madam"). When an officer entered a room, one was to stand "at attention," etc. Non-coms, on the other hand, were to be obeyed, but not saluted as they were not gentlemen. In theory, one could get promoted from non-com to officer, but in practice this was so rare that the exceptions were always noted and invoked to explain unusual behavior.

The army also imposed strict non-fraternization rules between officers and other ranks, in order to keep their private lives as segregated as their professional ones. Officers were never supposed to drink, gamble, or engage in any social activities with soldiers and non-coms. Friendships were strongly discouraged, sexual relations were positively taboo. Indeed, the sexual taboos were extended from army personnel to their relatives and dependents. Officers' wives and daughters, for example, were strictly off-limits. Nurses were a bit of a special case. In a rare reversal of sexual discrimination, male nurses were enlisted men and female nurses were commissioned. But women nurses were not considered "real" officers. Although they were considered to be primarily the sexual preserve of male officers, occasional liaisons with enlisted men were tolerated if kept discreet.

The most interesting aspect of the military quasi-caste system was language. The two groups spoke as different dialects as any two other groups in American society. "Officialese" (in the double sense of being the written "high" language of the army and the spoken dialect of the officers) was close to standard middle-class American English and largely free of obscenities (though not always of profanities). It had a special lexicon of euphemisms and circumlocutions for its less savory activities (e.g., neutralize = kill, interrogate = torture) and a distinct penchant for pretentious, flatulent phraseology; but it was readily translatable into the English that I was familiar with. "Enlistese," on the other hand, was quite a bewildering foreign language. Its basic substratum was rural, Deep South, poor white and poor black, for such were the social origins of a disproportionate number of non-coms. But there was also a large lexical component of army slang (e.g., "piece" to mean both rifle and penis, as distinct from "gun" to mean both cannon and penis) and a profuse use of obscenities as a kind of "phatic noise." I quickly learned that the explicit allegations of incest and homosexual fellatio (all freely used as nouns, adjectives, or adverbs) were quite devoid of meaning and were used only for emphasis or as fillers. For example, "Gimme them motherfuckers" might be translated into standard English as "Please, pass me the binoculars." ("Please" and "thank you," I soon found out, were not part of the Enlistese lexicon.) In this case, "motherfucker" is simply a filler for the unfamiliar "binoculars." If the speaker knew the word "binocular," then the sentence would become: "Gimme them motherfucking binoculars," or, for greater emphasis, "Gimme them motherfucking, cock-sucking binoculars."

Most non-coms were fairly fluently diglossic, that is, they could readily enough shift to Officialese in the presence of, or when talking to, officers. But the reverse was not true: officers did not, and I suspect, in most cases, could not, speak Enlistese. When non-coms used Officialese it was generally with some discomfort and clearly as a stilted second language. Yet many were quite eager to prove their competence in it. This provided me with the opportunity for some harmless fun. For instance, the first sergeant (the top non-com in our outfit) issued an order on the company bulletin board that we must all come in to "signature" our passes. I told him that the verb was "signaturate." He thanked me profusely for saving him embarrassment from those smart-alec, college-graduate, conscientious objectors and retyped the memo!

After completion of my first phase of basic training at Fort Ord, I was given a week's leave, along with orders to report to Fort Sam Houston, in San Antonio, Texas, for the second, "specialized" phase of my training. Amazingly, the army had honored my request for a transfer from the infantry to the Medical Corps. Compared to Fort Ord (nicknamed Fort Pneumonia by the Sea, for its pathogenic coastal fogs), Fort Sam Houston was near-paradise. The south Texas winter was quite pleasant. The base was near a lively town, and we were allowed off base on most weekends. Our training had to do principally with patching up people rather than shooting them up. Our instructors were mostly physicians and nurses rather than Mississippi sharecroppers. My fellow medics were, for the most part, college graduates, and at least a third of them were conscientious objectors. They were quite a pleasant change from the Fort Ord recruits.

To be sure, we still had to go on an occasional march, but we now carried neat little carbines rather than heavy M-1 rifles. When we crawled through the infiltration course dodging the live machine-gun rounds over our heads and the explosive pits around us, we took our first-aid kits along instead of rifles. That meant no rifle-cleaning afterward. Crawling among rattlesnakes was, however, less than pleasant. Still, the relief of spending much of our time in hospital classrooms instead of shooting ranges and parade grounds was welcome. Even the barracks were more tolerable; they were old, wooden, two-story buildings, which, dilapidated though they were, were more comfortable than the damp concrete tombs of Fort Ord. They even had something approaching the charm of antiques.

In my spare time, I took in a couple of operas in San Antonio and even went to Monterey on a three-day pass. It felt like a return to civilization. I keep a specially pleasant memory of a Sunday afternoon spent in the company of a cultured and hospitable upper-class Mexican family. The somewhat rotund matriarch had produced three charming daughters, and she appeared quite eager to off-load one of them on a seemingly well-behaved gringo. *Quien sabe?* Had I been posted in San Antonio a bit longer, I might have married a Mexican.

The next step of my military career was an option: Which "theater" did I want to be shipped to—"stateside," Europe, or the Far East? By then the shooting had stopped in Korea, but, still, I was not eager to go. I had no interest in staying in the states either, so I naturally opted for Europe. Most of my fellow medics thought the army would either pay no attention to our stated preference or even perversely send us elsewhere. Some thought, for example, that the best chance of being sent to Europe was to opt for the Far East. I argued that most would opt for "stateside" and that any preference for an overseas assignment would have a good chance of success. In any case, I got my wish.

After we spent a couple of weeks in a dismal transfer base in New Jersey, a slow troop transport took some 800 of us to Bremerhaven, in a ten-day-long, stormy, late-winter crossing. We slept in four-tiered narrow bunks that reminded me of engravings of slave ships, and the rations were even worse than normal army "chow," but I remember my joy when we sailed past the coast of Belgium. I had not been in Europe for six years, and my excitement at the prospect of family reunions was high.

An old third-class railway carriage with wooden benches took us from Bremerhaven south, none of us knew whereto. I have always felt very uncomfortable at not being able to visualize on a mental map where I am. Luckily, the carriage had a little sketch map of the German railways, and I recognized some names of stations along the way. When we crossed the Rhine and passed through a still war-devastated Cologne, I knew I was quite close to home. We kept going south, however. We stopped at night in Zweibrücken. I had never heard of the place, and it took several frustrating days to find a map detailed enough to list such a small town. A few more days were spent in idleness, waiting for our orders, as we had not yet been assigned to a permanent unit. Finally, the orders came: Bad Kreuznach, they said, to the 517th Medical Company, Clearing, Separate.

I had never heard of Bad Kreuznach either, but I soon located it on the map; it was near Mainz, on what my grandfather would have called the French side of the Rhine. The name of the outfit sounded like jibberish to me, but it turned out to be a mobile field evacuation hospital, exactly the kind of unit later to be immortalized in M.A.S.H. There, with one brief interruption, I was to spend the remaining seventeen months of my military service. There, too, I was to meet my future wife, Irmgard. There, five years later, our first child, Karen, would die shortly after birth. There, eight years later, our second son, Oliver, would be born. My whole destiny was shaped by some army clerk in Zweibrücken whom I shall never meet.

Bad Kreuznach, a quaint town of some 35,000 inhabitants, on the Nahe River, a tributary of the Rhine, was at once a spa and a light industrial town where camera lenses were manufactured. The small base where I was stationed, a mere 3 kilometers from the downtown railway station, was attached to the old *Wehrmacht* hospital. I quickly decided that I was going to spend all my free time away from the U.S. Army; I started learning German through a self-teaching book and practicing on German employees at the base. It came to me rather easily through my school Dutch. Soon, I became the most fluent German speaker in my outfit and the unofficial interpreter with the natives. We were now routinely free from Saturday noon to Monday morning, except once a month or so when we pulled guard duty or "kitchen police." Every six weeks or so, we qualified for a three-day pass, and we could start drawing on our accrued thirty-day-a-year leave time. Things were looking up. The worst of my army time was clearly over, at least for the "chickenshit" part of it.

Tedium was now the main problem. I decided that the best way to combat it was to fight the army through every conceivable technique of passive resistance and to make a game of it. The object of the game was to make the cost-benefit ratio of keeping me in uniform as high as possible for the army, while avoiding punishment. That took some finesse, but, luckily, I was not alone in my subtle war of attrition against authority.

Ours was a very unusual outfit. We were a medical company. In theory our commanding officer should have been a physician and our executive officer a pharmacist, though, in practice, they seldom were. We were a *combat* hospital, but since there was no combat, our medical functions were reduced to naught. We merely had to be prepared to set up a M.A.S.H.-style field hospital, complete with latrines, kitchen, operating room, patient wards, and so on, supposedly in about six hours' time. All our periodic maneuvers followed the same routine. First, we emptied our vast warehouse and loaded some forty tons of tents, surgical kits, bandages, generators, rations, kitchen equipment, camp beds, and so on onto twenty "deuce-and-a-half" trucks and trailers. Then we unloaded the equipment onto some German farmer's rented pasture and started the tedious and strenuous business of setting up long rows of heavy sectional tents, of unfolding hundreds of camp beds for our "patients," of digging capacious latrines, of erecting a "sterile" operating room, and of starting to receive "casualties."

For a week or so, we went through the motion of treating "casualties" brought in by ambulance and helicopter from neighboring units who shared our maneuvers. All the casualties were conveniently tagged with a description of their ailments and sometimes plastered, for the sake of realism, with a gory-looking, Halloween-style plastic patch depicting a gaping wound. When other units could not furnish the casualties, half of us played that role; it was a good opportunity to catch up on one's reading or to play darts against the canvas walls of the tents, using syringes as projectiles. Most of us had an M.O.S., Military Occupation Specialty. Mine was to be a blood transfusion specialist, a job for which I received an additional ten weeks of very good training in Landstuhl some 80 kilometers from Bad Kreuznach. We actually performed transfusions, typed blood, stored blood bottles in large refrigerators—in short, ran a blood bank. Our principal occupation was to roam the wards and take blood samples, an activity that earned us the name of "vampire squad."

One of our best "customers" was a nurse who came to pick up expired blood bottles. She was using them to fertilize her begonias, with splendid results she assured us. Little did blood donors realize that their selfless act was almost as likely to benefit a begonia as a fellow human being.

During my ten weeks in the blood bank, we only "goofed" once, mistyping a blood sample in an emergency. At 2 A.M., a sergeant who had been engaging in horseplay in the guardroom was brought in with a 45-caliber pistol hole in the gut. He probably would have died of massive internal hemorrhage in any case, but transfusion of A-type blood to an O-type recipient did not help. Luckily, I was not on duty that night. As collective punishment, the surgeon in charge made us watch the autopsy the next morning. I skipped lunch that day.

Many specialists were of rather dubious competence. For example, Corporal Lewis (or Louis—he was not sure himself how to spell his name, for he was almost totally illiterate) was a surgical technician, supposedly capable of doing emergency surgery such as tracheotomies. He was the son of black Mississippi sharecroppers, a compulsive crap shooter in debt to half the company, a third-grade graduate, and a perennial tobacco chewer. His principal accomplishment was hitting a wastepaper basket from a distance of about 2 meters with a jet of brown sputum. For a couple of seconds, he looked like a chameleon catching a fly: a brief moment of intense visual concentration on the target was followed by what looked like the flash of an extended tongue. (I shared his room, so I was a reluctant witness to his startling and unerring performance, repeated every fifteen to twenty minutes.)

In between maneuvers (which were repeated every three months or so), our job was to clean and maintain our trucks and equipment. The actual job would have required perhaps one day of work a week, so there was ample room for both "gold bricking" and "make-work." We also repeated cycles of training, so every morning we had one or two classes. I taught map reading and blood transfusions. I was also in charge of adult literacy, my special charge being the aforementioned Corporal Lewis. The problem was that he had been a corporal for seven years and could not pass his sergeant exam because he was illiterate. He was facing the threat of discharge for incompetence. (Yes, the army did have a bottom floor, though it was somewhere in the fourth basement.)

Lewis and I faced two options. The first was to try literacy. We did, but soon gave up by mutual consent. The other was to fake his sergeant exam through a combination of cheating and memory feats. Like many illiterates, Lewis had a highly trained memory. For example, he did not have much difficulty in memorizing the twenty-five or so names in the "chain of command." The photographs of the president of the United States down to the company commander were the principal ornament of the Orderly Room, and we spent a couple of hours rehearsing in front of them. Someone else took the written part of the test for him, and he passed the oral with flying colors. He became Sergeant Lewis for a few weeks, until he was "busted" back to corporal for his part in a drunken brawl over a gambling debt. Corporal was clearly his best level of incompetence. Since he had been a sergeant, however briefly, he had safely warded off a premature discharge before his twenty years of service qualified him for a pension.

My linguistic skills in German, though still quite modest, were amply adequate by army standards. I was called upon to interpret on occasions. A particularly colorful episode sticks in my mind. A German farmer had come to the regimental legal office with a garbled complaint that no one understood. I had a difficult time as well, for he was speaking in a local dialect, but his story slowly emerged. He had noticed that his geese had started bleeding from the rectum. Suspicious of foul play, he had stood in ambush one night and had caught an American sergeant fleeing out of his goat shed. It turned out that the she-goat, too, had received the sergeant's attentions, though with less visible sequels. The farmer gave us a good physical description, as he had been carrying a flashlight, and we readily identified the suspect, a married man with three children. He was court-martialled and given a term in the stockade, and the farmer was given compensation for his ravished geese. My German vocabulary emerged greatly enriched by this interpreting experience.

This case also marked the beginning of my career as a "barracks lawyer." Early in basic training, I had discovered that the Uniform Code of Military Justice could be a powerful weapon against abusive officers and non-coms. I quickly mastered its contents, as the document is only some fifty or sixty pages long, if my memory serves me right. Much like the Soviet Constitution, it contains a long list of rights observed in the breach. Soldiers not only had many legal rights that officers and non-coms constantly violated, but they could also prefer charges against their superiors and obtain redress. For the rest of my military service I made use of that threat to get my "superiors" (and I use the term loosely) to treat me with diffident circumspection.

I quickly gained a reputation as someone the non-coms were wary of "fucking around with," and soldiers facing prosecution approached me for legal advice. My favorite client was the company clown who treated us every morning to an irresistibly funny performance. When "falling out" of the barracks for the morning roll call, he would come out last, about thirty seconds after the roll call had started but just before it reached his name in the alphabet. He would join the ranks in a hilariously funny exaggeration of the military strut and answered the call with a loud and clear "Present, Sir," when most of us answered with a sloppy "Yoh." His genius for timing pointed to a tragic waste of talent. Like me, he was a dedicated anarchist and anti-militarist and a total misfit in the army. He was a New York street kid with a seventh-grade education, and his total disrespect of authority earned my instant sympathy. I could feel that he was on the verge of doing something drastic, much as I urged him to "cool it." One day, he performed a beautiful masterpiece of nonviolent resistance to oppression. He was on a night punishment detail, cleaning the company headquarters including the captain's office. He unscrewed the company bulletin board from the wall, defecated on the duty roster, and neatly placed the entire package on the captain's desk.

I both shared his sentiment and admired his courage, so I was glad to serve as his defense counsel. I argued, apparently with some eloquence, that he was a slum kid with a psychopathic personality, a victim of his social environment, who clearly did not belong in the army, and who should get a medical discharge. He got an undesirable discharge rather than a medical one, but he still got off lightly. Six months in the stockade followed by a dishonorable discharge would have been the more likely outcome. My legal reputation soared.

My campaign of passive resistance against the U.S. Army was far from lonely. Our company was always under strength. Our numbers fluctuated between 120 and 140 men, of whom some 50 were career noncoms ("thirty-year men") with an average educational level somewhere around the seventh or eighth grade. Most were Southerners, about one-third of them black. The rest of the enlisted men were mostly conscripted privates and PFCs (privates first class) serving their two years. As we were a medical outfit, we were a highly selected group. At least 60 percent of the privates were college graduates, and a handful of us even had master's degrees.

Our outfit was also exceptional in its degree of administrative autonomy. We were directly attached to a regiment, whose evacuation hospital we constituted. Thus, we had the autonomy of a battalion-sized unit, although we were a mere company and an undermanned one at that. This meant that one of our platoons was defined as a headquarters platoon, the other three as operational platoons. Nearly all the "goldbricking" jobs were in the headquarters platoon, and, as these jobs required literacy, they were nearly monopolized by the educated draftees. As soon as we got a cushy job as clerk in the company office, the supply room, the warehouse, or the motor pool, we pleaded that the work load required an assistant, and another one of us would find an office sinecure that allowed us to play chess, learn German, read novels, and otherwise pursue our education.

After a few months of this cunning little game, we ended up with a bloated headquarters platoon of 60 or 70 men, leaving three operational platoons of some 20 men (at least half of whom were career non-coms) to do all the "shit work." The day of reckoning usually came after the next maneuvers, when the crippling inefficiency of our unit would become glaringly evident and when the captain would purge the headquarters platoon of its accumulated ballast. Within weeks, however, the cycle was repeated. It was easy for those of us who controlled all the paperwork to create artificial snafus and to plead understaffing.

Meanwhile, the operational platoons, or what was left of them, were supposedly maintaining the motor pool and warehouse in working order and preparing for a dreaded inspection. These inspections were supposedly unannounced, but our man in the inspector general's office could usually give us a few hours' notice. There was always enough time to load all our defective equipment onto our least road-worthy truck and dispatch that vehicle on a fictitious mission intended to keep it on the back roads of the Rhineland until the inspection was over.

Often, there was simply nothing to be done, yet the men had to be kept busy. This gave some creative outlet to the captain's initiative. His best invention was the tent peg episode. With a score of large tents to erect on maneuvers, our tent pegs alone filled most of a truck. Regulation tent pegs were unpainted and made of a light-color wood, faintly visible even at night. Our captain thought that he would impress the inspectors with our good care of the equipment by having us dip the tent pegs in olive drab paint pots. This we did for a couple of weeks—all 10,000 or 12,000 of them. Then we went on maneuvers and disaster struck. At night, the tent pegs blended so well into the landscape that we were stumbling all over them. Something had to be done. The executive officer had a brainstorm. Why not paint the tips of the tent pegs white? The following two weeks were spent on the implementation of this brilliant idea. But then disaster struck again. The inspector came and, far from congratulating our captain on his tender loving care of tent pegs, berated him. The white tips of the pegs were a blatant breach of camouflage. Besides, army tent pegs came unpainted, and that was how they were to be kept.

This time, we were kept busy a full month. A tent peg is far more quickly painted than scraped clean. First, we experimented with scalpels cannibalized from our ten or twelve lavish surgical kits. (Each of those was worth some $10,000 and consisted of hundreds of gleaming instruments lovingly kept in the canvas "pages" of large book-like bags.) We discovered that scalpels quickly dulled when scraped against paint and wood. A better solution had to be found. Yankee ingenuity sprang into action again: broken glass was the solution. To be sure, we had none in our supply room, but we could easily create an adequate supply by breaking a few windows in the warehouse. A convenient windstorm was blamed for the mishap, and our equipment was brought back to its pristine condition, minus, of course, some fifty or sixty dull scapels, which could be hidden away for the next inspection. The ultimate object was accomplished: keeping the company busy for a couple of months.

Perhaps my major triumph against the army was my successful avoidance of being assigned responsibility for one of our twenty "deuce-and-a-half" trucks. As I had purchased a second-hand Volkswagen, I had to pass an army driver's test. Luckily, one needed a higher grade of license to drive a truck. The trick thus consisted in repeatedly failing that higher-level test. Anyone who has tried to fail an army test will testify that this requires ingenuity. Every few weeks, my persistent platoon sergeant would send me to qualify for truck driving, and I had to fail anew, while continuing to drive my own car.

I was only punished once during my two years of service and very mildly at that: two weeks' restriction to barracks. During the weekly Saturday inspection, my platoon sergeant took a look at the display of my equipment by my bed. As usual, my boots had just the bare minimum of shine to pass inspection, and my footlocker was brimming with my library of pocketbooks. The sergeant shook his head at me with an air of resigned desperation and said to me: "You don't take no pride in your job, do you, van den Berghe?" The question was clearly rhetorical, but I could not resist replying, in affable honesty: "Frankly, no, sergeant." That cost me two weeks' restriction to barracks, spent mostly in the music room of the hospital, a favorite hideout known only to a few classical-music afficionados. I also sneaked out at night, using the music room as my alibi, safe in the knowledge that no one would seek me out there.

An insistent problem of the military condition is the search for a stable and satisfactory sexual outlet. The most obvious solution was resort to the scores of prostitutes who happily plied our little garrison town. Quickly adapting to their clients' racial prejudices, German prostitutes belonged to two sub-castes, catering respectively to black ("coon whores" in Enlistese) and to white soldiers. Their presence was most visible at the gates of the barracks just after pay day, but some were very enterprising indeed, with a flair for filling every vacant opportunity. Two or three, for example, specialized in servicing, through the wire-mesh perimeter fence, soldiers pulling guard duty. In those days a 20-mark banknote ($4.75, a little over a day's pay for a private) bought a competent and unhurried blow job. Indeed, during the slack time of the month, just preceding pay day (the day "when the eagle shits" in army lingo), the girls' fee went down to 10 marks. I enjoyed teasing them and practicing my German while on guard duty. A good opener was to offer them 5 marks. This was sure to elicit a lexicon quite unlike anything my other German acquaintances produced. Barmaids were one step up in the hierarchy of "pieces of ass." Some of the better looking ones in the downtown *Gasthäuser* acquired an enviable reputation, but competition for their attention was always keen.

I quickly stopped frequenting the ghettoized bars catering to GIs, first because they were overpriced and rowdy and, second, because the last people I wanted to see during my free time were American soldiers. I always dressed in civvies when I went out, and, although my army haircut still made me sadly identifiable, my improving efforts at speaking German were beginning to be rewarded by a slowly widening circle of civilian acquaintances. This was no easy task, for all middle-class Germans, and certainly all "decent girls," shunned the loud barbarians in their midst. The tables were turned on me now. I was painfully aware of being a foreign occupier, a fact that the pious NATO fiction that we were protecting allies did little to allay. At least, it cut no ice with "decent girls," for whom being seen in the company of GIs was tantamount to a public confession that they had joined the ranks of the world's oldest profession. A number of merry widows left mateless by World War II lived in this demimonde by taking on American lovers, but they were mostly five to ten years older than I, and I had set my sights higher.

As I waited for my turn in the dental clinic, I quickly noticed two attractive German dental assistants who were calling in the patients one by one. Going on dental call was always good for half a day of reading, away from one's regular duties, so I was already predisposed to have my teeth well taken care of. Now an additional incentive presented itself. One of the two girls, a vivacious blonde with a cute little up-turned nose and a curvaceous figure, which even the folds of an oversize hospital gown could not conceal, read out my name and took me in to her dentist, a good-looking chap of about 30. My heart sank, as I thought I had no chance against him. I noted that neither of them wore wedding rings and as he was engaging in a steady sexual bantering with her (thinking I did not understand German), it was easy for me to assume that they were lovers.

Thomas Mann saved the day for me. I was reading a pocketbook edition of *Buddenbrooks,* which I had left on the table next to the dental chair. The dentist, it turned out, was a great fan of Mann and engaged me in a conversation about him. I detected more than a flicker of interest in the assistant, enough in any case to muster my courage and ask the receptionist at the front desk for the dental assistant's name and address.

The receptionist was understandably reluctant to give them to me, but did, three days later, having received the green light from the woman who was to share my life. Her name was Irmgard (Irmi, for short) Niehuis, and she lived in Bad Kreuznach.

The coast seemed clear, yet I took two or three weeks to follow suit, long enough, Irmgard later told me, to make her think that I was merely collecting addresses of likely prospects for future contingencies. When I finally appeared at her door, unannounced but smartly dressed in civvies, I was very courteously received by her younger brother, Habbo, a law student in Mainz. She was out. Habbo and I struck a conversation and found each other simpático. We quickly discovered a common interest in chess, and, by the time his sister came back, we were deeply absorbed in a game, deeply enough in any case to make her believe that perhaps I was mostly looking for a chess partner. I always hated interrupting an ongoing game, so I went on playing after greeting her.

Soon I accepted an invitation for the *Abendbrot* ("cold evening meal") and met the rest of the family: her parents, her older sister, Anna, and her little brother, Manfred. Feeling welcomed by the whole family, I became a frequent houseguest, showing up in the late afternoon and staying for dinner or joining them on Sunday-afternoon automobile outings. I played several more chess games with Habbo (who was an ideally matched partner) and took a couple of solo walks in the woods with Irmgard.

Then, fate struck again. I was suddenly transferred to Landstuhl, some 80 kilometers away, and she and Habbo took off on a month's ship cruise to Egypt. We obviously cared for each other, but nothing "serious" had yet transpired between us. We simply had not known each other well or long enough to make a serious commitment. On the evening of her scheduled return from Egypt, I was waiting for her at her parents' apartment. She came in rather late. We ate, and the family beat a discreet and strategic retreat to bed, leaving us alone in the kitchen. I asked her to be my wife, and we became lovers there and then.

My father-in-law, Gerhard Niehuis, was born in 1898 and died in 1980. His wife, Hanna Aits, was six years his junior and is still alive. Both came from East Frisia and were, thus, technically, not ethnic Germans. They still spoke Frisian to each other, a language close enough to Dutch that I understood much of it. Their children all spoke High German as their first language, but not the local Rhineland dialect. Habbo and Irmgard both spoke English and French in addition to German, but my parents-in-law and the other siblings were only fluent in German. My German had already progressed enough to sustain a rudimentary conversation and improved rapidly thereafter. Thus, we got into the habit of speaking German, and, later, German became the mother tongue of our three children.

My father-in-law, a land-surveyor by profession and a graduate of the University of Bonn, was a senior civil servant (*Oberregierungsrat*). He headed the local branch of the Land Surveying Office, and his life's work consisted of consolidating and rationalizing the magnificent vineyards of the Nahe, the Rhine, and the Mosel, by a process known as *Flurbereinigung* ("ground clearing"). After convincing farmers to exchange small parcels so as to create larger ones, and to surrender enough land to build access roads for tractors, he transformed entire hillsides of messy little patches into neat rows of vines easily accessible to mechanized implements, yielding more wine per hectare than ever before. His youngest son, Manfred, then a lad of 12, grew up to be a zoologist with a keen interest in ornithology and entomology, and a passionate environmentalist. Ironically, Manfred now spends much of his energies trying to arrest the massive slaughter of the fauna that his father unwittingly helped unleash by "sanitizing" large patches of the Rhineland.

Through his professional activities, my father-in-law had become quite a connoisseur of German wines and took me to many *Weinproben* ("wine tastings"). Having been raised in a tradition that claimed for France and perhaps, reluctantly, for Italy, a monopoly of the world's good wines, I quickly had to admit that Germany too produced superlative ones. Most German wines, however, are far too sweet and fruity, especially the quality ones, to make good table wines. They must be appreciated, by themselves, after a meal, in a carefully graded progression of sweet, aromatic fruitiness, from regular wines, to *Spätlese,* to *Auslese,* and *Trockenbeerauslese,* interspersed with taste-neutralizing pretzels. Anyway, I owe to my father-in-law a keen appreciation of German wines, about which I have become far more knowledgeable than French ones.

It took me little time to feel perfectly at home with my yet-to-become in-laws. My future mother-in-law immediately adopted me and started to plant wet kisses on my lips. (Lip kissing, to my lasting distaste, is standard practice between parents and children in Germany and is thus extended to hapless in-laws.) Manfred was so taken with me that it was difficult for Irmgard and me to get rid of him when we wanted to be alone. Habbo and I played chess to our hearts' content. My father-in-law, a benign, easy-going bon vivant, surveyed this domestic bliss with visible satisfaction. My mother-in-law benevolently conspired to keep knowledge of our cohabitation from her husband who was not the most astute of observers and who might have stumbled into compromising situations.

Cohabitation was perhaps somewhat of an overstatement, for our amorous dalliance was always rudely interrupted at 11:30 P.M. I had to be back in the barracks before midnight. Only married enlisted men were allowed to live off the base. As yet, we had no idea of what obstacles we would have to overcome during the four months of our engagement in order to get married. I knew that I would have to do some ground preparation with my family. There was the question of religion. Irmgard's parents were Protestants, and Calvinist rather than Lutheran, as they came from Ostfriesland. On Irmi's side, the only one who cared about my Catholic origins was her 90-year-old grandmother who first greeted me with a conciliatory: "Some Catholics are very decent people too." My mother-in-law is vaguely religious for a mixture of sentimental, superstitious, and conventional reasons, but she is quite tolerant, as indeed is my mother and most of her family. But the Belgian side of my family was a bit more concerned.

Then there was a little problem of nationality. The war had only been over for a bare ten years, and war memories are long. There, if anything, the French side of my family was more sensitive than the Belgian one, a sensitivity quickly allayed on first acquaintance, however. Finally, there was the question of social class. *Mésalliance* might have been somewhat too strong a term to qualify my family's feelings, but there was some sense of disappointment that I was not marrying into a more distinguished and wealthier family. My family tended to regard my in-laws as a little too petit bourgeois for their taste. Irmi's charm later conquered all within an hour's acquaintance, but, of course, she had not yet met any of my relatives. The first to come were my Uncle Paul and Aunt Marie from Brussels, who later attended the wedding along with my Aunt Solange from Paris. My father was in Africa and my mother in California and neither would meet her until long after the wedding.

The main obstacle to our marital bliss, however, was the U.S. Army who, acting in concert with U.S. Immigration and Naturalization Service, saw it as its sacred mission to protect the shores of the United States from an invading flood of German prostitutes. I should perhaps mention here that, in the meantime, I had become an American citizen, duly sworn in at the U.S. Consulate General in Frankfurt. To me, this was a step of convenience devoid of any kind of emotional significance. I have always regarded choice of citizenship as a consideration dictated by expediency rather than sentiment, since a state to me is an abstract entity that does not command any loyalty. In my view, one can be loyal to a person, but not to a state, a firm, or an organization. All of these, I regard as devoid of intrinsic content, beyond the individuals who make them up.

With my father's sister, Marie-Louise Mouson, during my brief and reluctant military career, Bad Kreuznach, Germany, 1955.

In any case, I opened a new front against the U.S. Army bureaucracy. The army had to approve my marriage before I would be allowed to live off the base, and the army, in turn, would not approve until the U.S. consular authorities declared that my fiancée was of sufficient medical, political, and moral standard to be admissible to the United States as an immigrant. We literally spent weeks being subjected to one humiliation after another. My company commander came to inspect my future in-laws' apartment to make sure that it met the army's sanitary standards. Irmi had to submit x-rays and medical certificates to attest that she was free of tuberculosis, syphilis, epilepsy, and some fifty or sixty other conditions. She was asked whether she had ever been a prostitute or a communist, and she had to swear that she did not intend to emigrate to the

Wedding day, January 21, 1956, Bad Kreuznach, Germany. From left to right, back row: father's sister's husband, Paul Mouson; father-in-law, Gerhard Niehuis; brother-in-law Peter; mother's sister Solange; brother-in-law Habbo. Front row: Father's sister Marie-Louise, wife Irmgard, myself, mother-in-law Hanna, brother-in-law Manfred.

United States in order to become one or the other. All this had to be backed up by a good conduct certificate from the German police and the testimony of American character witnesses. Then came an official army investigation. There was no "give me your huddled masses" about it. The United States only wanted the best, physically, morally, and politically, a definition of quality that did not seem to disqualify Nazi war criminals, incidentally. When I showed some irritation, I was sternly reminded that it was all in my own best interest, to protect me against scheming little whores using innocent GIs as their ticket to the great U.S.A. What a great way to make me feel proud of my newly acquired citizenship!

Finally, we cleared all hurdles for our target date of January 21, 1956. We still had to decide what kind of wedding we wanted. My family would have liked a Catholic one; most of my in-laws did not care much, though my mother-in-law's sense of propriety would have been somewhat offended by a purely civil marriage. We considered the possibility of Irmi's official Lutheran pastor, but the man was such an insufferably pompous hypocrite that we both decided he was "out." A Southern Baptist army chaplain seemed a convenient (and cheap) compromise. This was followed by the obligatory German civil marriage in the *Standesamt* ("Civil Registry Office"). Everybody in Germany has to have a title, so I appear on my wedding certificate as *Sanitätsgefreiter* ("Medic–Private First Class"), the only rite of my passage through life that bears an indelible military taint.

My Aunt Solange, who had kindly come from Paris for the wedding and who always showed a keen interest for the biological side of things, asked me in a whisper whether Irmi was already pregnant. Relieved to hear that she was not, she gave me advice on contraceptives and urged me to wait a while. The first years of marriage, she said, were much more fun without babies. Entirely my view, I agreed with her. My Uncle Paul's main concern was whether I had signed a marriage contract. Somewhat startled, I told him that the thought had not entered my head. He was relieved, as he knew that, in the absence of a marriage contract to the contrary, German law limited community property to assets acquired after marriage.

The final act of the wedding took place in a charming old hotel along the Nahe, the Quellenhof (now alas "renovated" into a hideously colorless shell of its former grace), and the next day we were off to our honeymoon in Paris. I spent the following eight months in what anthropologists refer to as "uxorilocal residence," that is, I lived with my in-laws, until the army turned me into a free man once more, in September 1956.

Our next station would be Paris, the site of our honeymoon and the homeland of my maternal family. I opted to be mustered out in Europe. With a couple of thousand dollars in savings and the GI Bill benefits ($135 a month), we drove to Paris in our old Volkswagen. There I was to resume my graduate work, starting with a year at the Sorbonne.

CHAPTER 6

The Left Bank

My university education had been American so far. My first taste of Harvard, just before my military service, was certainly a vast improvement over what Stanford had to offer, and I was determined to resume and finish my doctoral program there. But I also wanted exposure to the European intellectual scene. London would have been a good alternative to Paris, but my Harvard teachers had already exposed me to Malinowski, Radcliffe-Brown, Firth, Fortes, Nadel, Mannheim, Laski, Schapera, Gluckman—all the foreign refugees and colonials who collectively were thought of as the giants of British social science.

Even though my Harvard mentors seemed to think that nothing of any consequence had been said in France since the death of Emile Durkheim, I wanted to have a look for myself. Besides the fact that I had many relatives there, the Paris of the mid-1950s was a highly exciting place. The Latin Quarter was simply bubbling over with ideological, political, and intellectual ferment. The literary scene was dominated by Sartre, Maurois, Camus, Malraux, De Beauvoir, Montherlant, Cocteau, and others. Colette and Gide had only just died. I had not come to Paris to study literature or philosophy, but, still, it was an intellectual scene in which I felt very much at home. I felt reunited with my cultural roots. To this date, French is the only language in which I can truly express my emotions. I can only vibrate to French poetry, for example, and though I can enjoy English theater or cinema, my pleasure is greatly enhanced if the language is French.

Materially, our stay in Paris satisfied all the conditions of romantic indigence. Irmi and I sub-let a single small bedroom in a five-room flat and shared a bath and kitchen with another student. The flat was comfortably bourgeois and was conveniently located on Rue de l'Armorique, across the Boulevard Pasteur from my grandparents' apartment. Its main drawback (and the reason why it had been abandoned by its main tenants) was that the hot water pipes had burst with frost during an unheated war winter and, some fourteen years later, had not yet been repaired. Thus, the apartment had no hot water. We went to my grandparents' flat to take baths.

We had our Volkswagen for long trips (of which we took two, one to Spain, another to Italy; there were also several jaunts to Brussels and to Bad Kreuznach), but gas was so expensive in relation to our limited budget ($135 a month of the GI Bill benefits) that we made little use of it in Paris. By exchanging our dollars on the black market, we could stretch our monthly check by 10 or 15 percent, and, incredible though it may now seem, we managed to live quite adequately on Uncle Sam's bounty.

Frequent dinner invitations from relatives helped, of course, as did the many forms of subsidy that the French government extended to its impecunious intelligentsia. Thirty cents, for example, bought a very decent meal at the Restaurants Universitaires, though at a cost of a half-hour queue. The Metro was quite cheap, especially on a weekly card. So were a number of cultural activities, such as theaters, art cinemas, and concerts, where a student card entitled one to a greatly reduced admission price. In the state theaters, such as the Théatre National Populaire and the Opéra, the cheapest seats cost a dollar or less. Naturally, we made frequent use of these privileges. Come to think of it, our cultural life (in terms of going out to concerts and theaters) has never been as active as it was during this year in Paris. Most important of all, the Sorbonne was virtually tuition-free. Payment of trivial *frais d'inscription* (something like $5, if I remember rightly) gave one the invaluable *carte d'étudiant,* passport to the French state's subsidized cultural bounty.

The contrast between the Sorbonne and an American university was striking. Both the facilities and the structure of the French university were (and still are) minimal, at least from the student's standpoint. In terms of structure, the student formally enrolled and passed examinations leading to various degrees. What happened in-between was of no concern to anyone. Students simply availed themselves of opportunities to educate themselves. Whether they attended lectures, labs, seminars, and the like was left entirely up to them. Qualifications for admission were a French *bachot* or its foreign equivalent (about two years of college in the American case). There was no time limit on one's student career, and a substantial academic proletariat of professional students had been enjoying the privileges of the *carte d'étudiant* for fifteen or twenty years.

As I did not intend to get a French degree but merely to take in the intellectual scene for a year, this situation was ideal. I was free to roam the classrooms and libraries of Paris, not only at the Sorbonne but also at the Musée de l'Homme (the most active center for anthropological research, and the principal lair of Claude Lévi-Strauss), at the Collège de France, and elsewhere. The Collège de France, especially, was a revelation to me and continues to represent my ideal of what a university should be. A chair at the Collège de France is considered the pinnacle of academic distinction, practically on par with election to one of the académies. As a professor, one teaches a single course meeting once a week for something like thirty weeks a year. These courses are open to all comers without even the formality of inscription. One simply steps in from the street, and, during the cold winter months, a few knowledgeable *clochards* take advantage of this citadel of learning to dry their clothes on the radiators. Best of all, the Collège de France gives no examinations and grants no degrees.

The libraries took some adjustment, especially for one accustomed to the open-shelf system of most American university libraries. All the principal public libraries of France guard their books against prospective users through a formidable set of barriers that only the most determined and patient can penetrate. It typically takes a week or longer to obtain a reader's card. Books—a maximum of two or three at a time—are fetched for you; this procedure generally consumes the better part of an hour. Even then, you may only read the books in the library. Reading facilities at the Bibliothèque Nationale and the Bibliothèque Sainte Geneviève, near the Sorbonne, were reasonably adequate. That is, you could normally expect to find a chair after finally getting your book. But the Sorbonne library was absolutely hopeless. There, a permanent crowd of circling students walked around the main reading room, waiting to swoop down on a chair the second any student showed any sign of getting up or merely putting on one's coat.

Luckily, the social sciences were a bit better organized, largely, I think, because many of the professors in those fields had had exposure to Britain and the United States. At the post-graduate level, an institution had recently been created that was principally modeled on an American graduate school or perhaps the London School of Economics. It was called the Ecole Pratique des Hautes Etudes, of which the 6th section was devoted to the social sciences. Tucked away under the roof of the cavernous central Sorbonne building, the Ecole Pratique was an autonomous part of the University of Paris but technically not of the Sorbonne. Its faculty consisted mostly of younger and more dynamic professors, still waiting for a more prestigious chair to open up in the Sorbonne itself or in the Collège de France. The Ecole Pratique granted a diploma, obtainable after a minimum of two years of post-graduate work and called *doctorat du troisième cycle*. (It was a lower-level doctorate, somewhat below a Ph.D. from a major American university and much below the French *doctorat d'état*.)

For all its novelty and relative lack of prestige, the Ecole Pratique was the site of much of the most creative and up-to-date thinking in the social sciences. Roughly half of the seminars I attended were in its precincts. In addition, I spent much time at the Musée de l'Homme, both to attend Lévi-Strauss' seminar on kinship and to draw from the excellent resources of its extensive ethnographic library. That library and a specialized sociology library, Rue de Varennes, were the only ones that allowed books to be checked out, usually for two weeks, and I eagerly went through a half-dozen volumes a week. These were also the only two social science libraries in Paris to have an up-to-date collection of British and American works. (I first read much of Parsons, of Weber, and of my British social anthropology in Paris, for example.)

I also attended several undergraduate courses at the Sorbonne and some series of lectures at the Collège de France, in effect, designing my own program and picking eclectically from whomever I felt could teach me something, without any concern for formal requirements. This lack of structure represents, in my view, the ideal of what a graduate school should be, and I have always been impatient, both as a student and now as a teacher, of the infantilism and dependency fostered by the numerous petty structural constraints of an American higher degree. Despite the limited facilities and services offered by the French system, it has been remarkably productive of first-rate social science. One of my contemporaries in Paris, for instance, was the eminent Mexican sociologist, Rodolfo Stavenhagen, with whom I was later to cross, quite amicably, academic swords concerning my field work in Chiapas, Mexico. Another was the French anthropologist, Claude Meillassoux.

The place was simply crawling with ideas. What would it not have produced with an American level of affluence and services? French social science research was being done on an absolute shoestring. French anthropology students, for example, were expected to survive a year's African field work on a budget of some $500, plus a round-trip ticket on a French cargo ship. Roger Bastide, to name but one, was conducting a dozen or so theses of students who financed their research in Paris solely from their own pockets.

The 1957 *American Sociological Review* article, which I published with Bastide and which was, in fact, my Opus 1, is but one example of zero-budget research. It inspired Louis Guttman to write an extensive methodological piece about it. (Guttman thought we had naively stumbled onto a very useful conceptual framework for the study of attitudes, and he proceeded to make explicit what he thought we had only vaguely discerned!) Anyway, the 500-odd questionnaires in the study were all coded and sorted by hand, by Irmi and me, in the 10 square meters of our cramped Parisian bedroom. Our bed was the sorting counter for the piles of questionnaires. In those days, it really paid off to think before you ran a correlation!

In spite of the lack of funding, obstacles to the use of libraries, total absence of reasonably priced duplication techniques, nearly complete lack of secretarial assistance (even for the professors), unavailability of data-processing machinery, in short, a dearth of the basic research facilities we now take completely for granted, a great deal of interesting research was going on. On top of all the above limitations, student life in Paris was a constant fight against the inertia of physical distance. Paris had the advantages neither of an American campus, that marvellously efficient concentration of academic facilities, nor of the small British or continental university town like Cambridge, Oxford, Louvain, Tübingen, or Heidelberg. There is, to be sure, a geographical concentration of institutions of higher learning in the Latin Quarter, but, by the 1950s, Parisian intellectual and academic life had already exploded well beyond the narrow confines of the Left Bank.

Much like rats in the sewers, tens of thousands of students daily scurried between lectures and libraries in that other famous system of underground Parisian tubes, the Metro. After a few months in Paris, I carried a mental map of Metro topography that included not only the train lines I used most frequently but also the length of corridors and the number of steps to be climbed in making connections. A seemingly short connection was sometimes defeated by a long walk between trains, notably at Montparnasse and the Chatelet.

Basically, I had three intellectual objectives in Paris. First, I wanted to resume my reading in general sociology and anthropology to prepare for the generals on my return to Harvard. Having gained a good idea of what was expected of me during the 1953–1954 year at Harvard, I was, from a distance, picking up my studies where I had left them. This, I did, largely by working my way through the libraries of the Musée de l'Homme and the Rue de Varennes. Next, I wanted to soak in the French intellectual scene, especially in the social sciences. Thus, I regularly attended

Raymond Aron's vastly popular Sorbonne course on industrial societies, Georges Gurvitch's dogmatic and pompous lectures on the history of sociology, Claude Lévi-Strauss' scintillating pyrotechnics in kinship analysis, and a number of others more episodically. Finally, having already developed a strong special interest in race, colonialism and, most particularly, Africa, I knew that Paris was, with London, the most seminal setting in the world for these subjects, and I wanted to make the most of that opportunity.

One of the features that made French intellectual life so much more exciting to me than its American counterpart was its direct, unabashed linkage to politics and ideology. French intellectuals do not apologize for being political; they thrive on it. Instead of disclaiming ideology for the sake of objectivity, they state their political position quite clearly and proceed to make it the explicit point of departure for their analysis. The events of 1956 and 1957 were ideally suited to bring ideological issues to the forefront. France was experiencing the death throes of its colonialism in those years. The memory of Dien Bien Phu was still fresh. Yet, soon after losing one colonial war, France was dragged into another one in Algeria and plunged with alacrity into a brief third one in Suez. The Suez adventure was quickly aborted when it failed to get the approval of the imperial center in Washington. The Algerian War, conducted with the benevolent support of the United States, was to last seven years. Like the British in Kenya and Malaysia, the French proved in Algeria that, with ruthless brutality, a guerrilla movement *can* be defeated; there is no question that the French won militarily in Algeria. But it was a Pyrrhic victory (in which, incidentally, my future brother-in-law, Alain Brucker, took part as a paratrooper officer). Politically, however, defeat was inevitable.

An extraordinary "wind of change" was sweeping the African continent, three or four years before Harold Macmillan turned the phrase into a cliché. A bare six years earlier, I had experienced a seemingly unshakable colonialism in the Congo. Now the whole edifice was on the verge of collapse. Egypt had gained control of the Suez Canal. Algeria was on the move. Britain was peacefully preparing to quit Ghana and Nigeria. Three or four years later, only the southern tip of the continent would escape the tidal wave of independence.

Clearly, Paris was, along with London, at center stage in this process. Momentous political events were taking place in Africa, but the Left Bank was the very vortex of intellectual ferment, as virtually every African intellectual in the francophone world went through it at one stage or another of his life. In this climate, *engagement* was de rigueur. Detachment was tantamount to cowardice or immorality.

Most intellectuals were, of course, on the left, which at the time was still predominantly Marxist. Hardly a week went by without Sartre issuing a pious pronouncement on some crying injustice. But there was also a right and, to my amazement, an *intelligent* right. My American experience had led me to associate the right with ignorance, provincialism, and stupidity, as epitomized by Republican Party politics. Now I discovered that there existed in France a highly articulate and intelligent right, represented by such people as Jacques Soustelle, Raymond Aron, and André Malraux. (Some of them, of course, had youthful antecedents in the left, but let that pass.) And interestingly, this right was nearly as anti-American as the left. The main difference between left and right was that the left was internally divided as to how anti-Soviet it dared to be (an issue brought to a head by the 1956 rumblings of Soviet tanks in Budapest), while the right had no difficulty in making up its mind on that issue.

Equally interesting was how conservative the French left was on colonial issues. Leading colonial intellectuals like Aimé Césaire and Léopold Senghor (both of whom I was to meet many years later—the first in Martinique in 1980, the second in Tübingen in 1983) were singing Négritude in their poems, but were, in fact, pursuing a political course of continued close association with a pro-colonialist French left. Throughout the 1950s, the French Communist Party's vision of the association between France and her colonies was within an assimilationist framework of a *union française*. Sékou Touré was definitely the odd man out. Even Frantz Fanon, who had recently published his *Peau noire, masques blancs* (1952), had discovered how angry he was, but his anger was very much that of a black Frenchman humiliated by racism, not of the Third World revolutionist who was yet to emerge out of his Algerian experience. *Les damnés de la terre* (1961) was still several years in the future.

The Négritude movement and its literary journal *Présence africaine* were clearly more at home in the Latin Quarter than anywhere in Africa. Even much of the incipient ideological protest against colonialism was born and bred on French soil and within a Gallic cultural framework. Paradoxically, Paris was (along with London) the birthplace of Pan-Africanism and the best place to be if one wanted to read into the cloudy African crystal ball. Nor was this very surprising. Paris and London were the principal meeting places of African intellectuals who, at that stage, shared little beside their colonial language and education and their common experience of colonialism.

Luckily for me, Paris was also the meeting ground for a whole group of top-notch social scientists—sociologists, anthropologists, geographers, historians—with a vast African expertise. They taught me that the view of Africa from Paris and through its intellectuals was a grossly distorted one, that African societies had a dynamic of their own, and that colonialism was much more than a political and ideological superstructure.

The leading influence on my thinking was that of Georges Balandier. His work, *Sociologie actuelle de l'Afrique noire,* which had just been published in 1955, remains, I think, a towering landmark in the analysis of colonialism as a process of economic, social, and political change affecting African societies down to their grassroots. His lectures made the "colonial situation" come to life dynamically and from the African perspective, unlike so much of the then-prevalent Africanist scholarship that looked at Africa either Eurocentrically, or, in the British anthropological tradition, as a catalog of tribes in pristine isolation. Balandier clearly showed us that it was precisely the complex interaction between Europe and Africa that was the master key to understanding the dynamics of contemporary Africa. A few years later, I was to discover that closely parallel approaches were almost simultaneously being developed in southern Africa by Max Gluckman, Monica Wilson, Hilda Kuper, Clyde Mitchell, and Philip Mayer and in Mexico by Gonzalo Aguirre Beltrán, Julio de la Fuente, and other members of the Mexican school of anthropology. But I owe to Balandier my first exposure to this dynamic social science grounded in direct field work experience.

There were other Africanists from whom I learned much. Paul Mercier, a young sociologist, was very much in the emerging Balandier school. Germaine Dieterlen, a student of Marcel Griaule, was more in the traditional ethnographic tradition, but her enthusiasm in communicating the richness of Dogon cosmology left a deep imprint. Her course was certainly a vivid illustration of the lack of correlation between the degree of complexity of thought systems and technology across societies. Pierre Gourou's course in tropical geography at the Collège de France was a model of informative clarity.

I should also acknowledge here a special debt to Roger Bastide, who introduced me to Brazil and more generally to the African diaspora in the Caribbean and Latin America. I collaborated with him in analyzing Brazilian data, as I mentioned, and his main contribution to the graduate program at the Ecole Pratique consisted in encouraging students to do research and in guiding their efforts. Unlike most of his colleagues, he was modest, unassuming, and generous of his time. He advanced his own ideas only with diffidence, but his long stay in São Paulo had made him a walking encyclopedia on Brazil and especially on Afro-Brazilian religion. He was also interested in social psychiatry and directed an unfunded study program on African students in Paris. A decade later, Bastide was to become my sister's thesis director. Gwendoline wrote her doctoral dissertation on the upper class of Lima, and a couple of years after her stay in Lima, I was to do field work in Cuzco, Peru. In fact, our anthropological careers had already intertwined once before: she followed me in the field in Chiapas, Mexico.

In sharp contrast to Bastide, Georges Gurvitch was dogmatic, arrogant, sarcastic, inaccessible to students, and altogether unpleasant. I attended both his undergraduate course on the history of sociology and his graduate seminar at the Ecole Pratique, because he was the living heir to Durkheim's chair and because Balandier respected him and said I should get exposed to him. But I got very little out of it. Gurvitch formed a mutual admiration society with his friend, contemporary, and fellow Russian émigré from the Bolshevik Revolution, Pitirim Sorokin, but no other living sociologist found grace in his eyes. I was soon to encounter his alter ego in Harvard, and the two men were extraordinarily alike in character and demeanor. Both spoke all the main European languages badly. Gurvitch's French was grammatically correct but acoustically painful, as was Sorokin's English. Both men made a virtue of being cantankerous, abrasive, insulting to their colleagues, contemptuous of all ideas except their own, and haughtily frosty and dogmatic with students. Of the two, however, I benefited much more from Sorokin because Sorokin was the more erudite, the less intellectually formalistic, and the more original.

Gurvitch saw himself as the heir to a tradition that began with Saint Simon, progressed to Comte, climbed on to Durkheim, and culminated in Gurvitch. His course on the history of sociology, the necessary prerequisite to a *certificat* in the field, devoted all but the last two hours of lecture to French Durkheimian positivism. The last two lectures in the year, which were devoted to a summary dismissal of Weber's "psychologism" and "Anglo-Saxon functionalism," were laced with the heavy-handed sarcasm that was Gurvitch's trademark. In my second month or so in his weekly post-graduate seminar attended by seven or eight students, I could no longer constrain myself from expressing disagreement with his blatant distortions of "Anglo-Saxon functionalism." I knew better than to interrupt him in his undergraduate lectures, which at the Sorbonne, have all the hallmarks of a sacramental rite. The professor does not lecture; he officiates. But I thought that the seminars at the Ecole Pratique were intended for discussion rather than professorial monologues. Indeed, that is how Balandier, Bastide, Mercier, and others understood them. In any case, I raised objections in my most restrained and deferential manner. The other students looked at me with dumb astonishment at my temerity. Gurvitch stared at me for the two minutes or so I spoke, then he resumed his monologue, completely ignoring my remarks. That is the closest I came to an intellectual exchange with Gurvitch.

The main liability of Gurvitch is that, having sat on the most powerful sociology chair in France for many years, he used his position to stultify and petrify the Durkheimian tradition into a highly formalistic scholasticism bereft of meaningful connections to empirical reality. Like Parsons, whom he so sarcastically attacked, his main concern was for the erection of a grand scaffold of shaky analytical abstractions. This reified system of abstract categories became, in fact, Gurvitch's social reality. Unlike Durkheim and Mauss, whose thinking was greatly enriched by a mastery of ethnography, Gurvitch was ignorant of non-Western societies. Gurvitch managed to fossilize Durkheim's reifications through his concept of *phénomène social total* (whatever that meant) and to empty these reifications of empirical content. Unlike Parsons and Sorokin, who had flashes of intuitive brilliance and dazzling erudition during their excursions into the real world, Gurvitch always remained in the conceptual stratosphere, where, to make matters worse, he chose to remain incommunicado.

My contacts with Raymond Aron were more distant but far more fruitful. His writings were my first serious introduction to German sociology, and it was in Paris that I began to read Weber and to make sense of him. My closest approach to Aron was in the vast Sorbonne auditorium where he was teaching his comparative course on industrial societies to an overflow crowd. Unless you came ten minutes early, you could not find a seat, and the doors were shut on the pressing multitudes at the stroke of the hour. This charismatic appeal was all the more surprising, as Aron's ideological stance was clearly right of the Left Bank mean and his course was being simultaneously broadcast on the radio. Yet hundreds of students braved the Metro to hear him in person.

In French intellectual circles, Aron was branded a man of the right, largely because, unlike Sartre and the other darlings of the left, he had the courage to be unpopular and honest. He scrupulously held the communist countries to the same rigorous standards of decency as the capitalist ones, and, in the last analysis, he always remained a libertarian. On the American political spectrum he would clearly have been a liberal. In any case, his lucid comparative analysis of capitalist and communist societies, his uncompromising criticisms of both, and his unblinking intellectual honesty in the face of ideological attacks impressed me enormously. He was that rare bird, an engagé scholar combining brilliant intellect with ruthless honesty and total contempt for ideological fashion.

Another major intellectual figure of my Paris days was Claude Lévi-

Strauss. He too was a rare bird in the French scholarly aviary: the ostensibly apolitical intellectual, the anti-Sartre. It is ironic that Lévi-Strauss later inherited in many ways Sartre's mantle as the pre-eminent darling of French intellectual salons. In 1956, he had not yet achieved that exalted status. He was merely a highly respected anthropologist, at the apex of his profession to be sure, but still barely read outside of it. Even within anthropology, Lévi-Strauss' impact was still largely limited to France and Britain. His major early work, *Les structures élémentaires de la parenté* (1949), was not translated into English for twenty years, and most American anthropologists do not read French. It was the publication of *Tristes Tropiques* in 1955 that heralded the entry of Lévi-Strauss on the wider literary scene, ushering his way to the Collège de France and the Académie Française. But all that was still to come, though the impact of *Tristes Tropiques* was already quite wide in 1956. (The first English edition was not published until 1961.)

In 1956–1957, Lévi-Strauss' teaching was mostly confined to advanced seminars on kinship and on myth analysis given to smallish audiences of fifteen to twenty devotees (prominent among whom were a half-dozen attractive young women). It was impossible to listen to him without coming under the spell of his sparkling intellect. For sheer brilliance of content and elegance of expression, he had few peers. To him, I owe a lifelong interest in kinship analysis, one that remained dormant for a long time, however, and did not surface until my 1979 book, *Human Family Systems,* and several recent articles on incest avoidance.

Even then, I was more seduced than convinced by Lévi-Strauss. I felt that his elegant dualistic models were too neat to correspond either to actual behavior or even to the mental construct of that behavior in the mind of the putative native philosopher. Nambikwara and Tupi-Kawahib thought processes, cosmologies, and accounts of their social world always came out incredibly Cartesian, Gallic, in short, Lévi-Straussian. But what mental pyrotechnics! Arcane systems of matrilateral cross-cousin marriage or esoteric myths were so much putty artfully reshaped into an elegantly closed system. Out came a harmonious synthesis of pairs of opposites: nature and culture, raw and cooked, dead and alive— anything really, and all interconnected by neat tables of equivalences.

True dialogue with Lévi-Strauss was also difficult, not because he was arrogant like Gurvitch but because hardly anyone could meet him on his level. The actual nature of empirical evidence, for instance, was seldom at stake. When a student would report on recent field work in a seminar, the facts were rarely at issue. Before they could be discussed on their own terms, Lévi-Strauss set off another intellectual rocket in which the Bororo, the Caduveo, the Tupi-Guarani, and the Nambikwara all exploded into a fresh shower of dualistic sparks.

There was more to my Paris life than libraries and lectures. The political context was especially fascinating for a budding Africanist. As the Algerian War was warming up, it increasingly came to dominate French politics, much as the Vietnam War was to do in the United States fifteen years later and ironically out of the same colonial antecedents. A recurrent event was the Saturday noon demonstration inside the main Sorbonne courtyard. It was a well-rehearsed bit of political choreography. Around 10 or 11 A.M., a long row of black Renault trucks filled with *gardes mobiles* ("riot police"), dressed in dark blue uniforms, would park outside the Sorbonne building, just in case. By tradition, the police never entered the Sorbonne building proper but were always on the spot, to prevent any disorder from spilling into the "Boul Mich" (Boulevard St. Michel) and the Luxembourg Gardens nearby.

Inside the courtyard, as the late Saturday morning classes came out, two camps of students would form on opposite sides of the courtyard. The right, appropriately, tended to form on the church side of the yard, while the left held the other side. As the entire courtyard is only 50 or 60 meters across, it was quickly filled with a few hundred students. The larger the crowd, the smaller the distance that separated the two sides. For about twenty or thirty minutes, there would be a crescendo of rhythmically chanted slogans: *"Le fascisme ne passera pas"* was countered by *"Algérie française."* A few isolated protagonists on each side would step out from their respective groups and occasionally engage in a bit of desultory scuffling and fist fighting. Meanwhile, the *gardes mobiles* would make a show of deployment just outside the doors of the courtyard. Then it was time for lunch, and the two sides slowly dispersed toward a *restaurant universitaire,* a Boul Mich café, or the Odéon Metro station . . . until the following Saturday noon.

In the summer of 1957, it was time to move on. My mother and sister, who had come to Paris on an extended visit from California, embarked with Irmi and me on the *Liberté* at Le Havre. Despite the fact that we were travelling tourist class, we were treated to five days of non-stop gastronomy and service worthy of the Crillon. Though I had already sailed the Atlantic three times, it was the first time I was doing it in style. A little over a decade later, jet travel would sweep this last vestige of prewar bourgeois decadence onto the junkpile of history, but it was very nice while it lasted.

CHAPTER 7

The Yard

As I mentioned before, my stay at Harvard was rudely interrupted by Uncle Sam's ineffective attempt to turn me into a trained killer, but for the sake of continuity of place, I shall fuse my two Harvard episodes (1953–1954 and 1957–1960) into one. Immediately upon arrival, it was clear to me that Harvard was a major intellectual center and a firstrate university, altogether in a different league from Stanford. I had begun to doubt that such a place existed in North America, but now I had clearly found one.

In retrospect, it was a singular piece of luck that I stumbled into the vortex of the great mid-century attempt to integrate the behavioral sciences into a grand unitary model. The Department of Social Relations ("soc rel") had just been founded and the latter years of my graduate work, in the late 1950s, probably marked its apogee. A decade later, the attempt had clearly failed, but it was a glorious failure and, in the 1950s, the going was great. Harvard soc rel was not alone in this quest for the grand synthesis of psychology, sociology, and anthropology, but it was central to it. And the handful of other centers engaged in this enterprise, such as the homonymous Johns Hopkins department, the Committee on Social Thought at Chicago, and the Columbia and Berkeley sociology departments, all had at least a few Harvard connections, through Parsons students (such as Robert Merton and Robert Bellah), Harvard Junior Fellows (such as Edward Shils), or in some other capacity.

Not coincidentally, this was also the time when the Center for Advanced Study in the Behavioral Sciences was conceived (1952) and founded (1954), under a Ford Foundation grant. The center was to be the Western thinking spa where all the great minds in social science would mesh to spawn the grand new paradigm. It was to take me fifteen years or so to begin to understand why the brave attempt ended in failure, and it is somewhat ironic that the center now provides me the setting for a post-mortem. Indeed, the shelves of the center's library are a distillation of that glorious failure, containing as they do the intellectual ashes of departed Fellows. It is customary for Fellows to donate copies of their books to the library. At the rate of forty-five to fifty prolific Fellows a year, responsible for perhaps a half-dozen books each, the book collection is a fair sample of the more notable failures in American social science.

Let us leave for later an analysis of that failure and try to recapture the attempt, from the perspective of Emerson Hall, then the home of soc rel on the Harvard Yard, next to Widener Library. The "holy trinity" (my term) of soc rel consisted of Talcott Parsons, Gordon Allport, and Clyde Kluckhohn, high priests respectively of sociology, psychology, and anthropology. Parsons was clearly the father in that trinity, the leading architect of the lofty edifice of "structure-functionalism." But within Parsons' theoretical system, he had carved out three great domains: the personality system, Allport's territory; the social system, Parsons' own preserve; and the cultural system, Kluckhohn's turf.

The three domains were seen as both levels of analysis and functionally differentiated sub-systems that intertwined to form an overarching "theory of action." The social structure emerged out of the individual interaction but was not reducible to it. The cultural superstructure in turn emerged out of the social structure and fed back to the personality system through the mushy psychoanalytic morass of a field known as "culture and personality." No one except Parsons found his way through a maze of transformations linking four-fold tables at various levels and sub-levels, but all the faculty in the core group of soc rel nodded gravely in assent and apparent comprehension when Parsons expounded all these hidden correspondences. As to students, they jolly well had to plow through *The Structure of Social Action* and *The Social System* and try to make sense of it all. The general feeling prevailed that we were all witnessing the opening of a sweeping new vista of understanding about human behavior.

The aura of revelation was all the more awesome to me as, during my first year at Harvard, Parsons was away in the other Cambridge, setting back the cause of sociology in Britain by a generation, said some irreverent wags. Not everyone was taken in, but I certainly was, and my years at Harvard were profoundly marked by my close association with both Parsons and Allport. My relationship to Parsons was always somewhat ambivalent and inhibited. In my third year at Harvard, I became his research assistant and he my thesis co-director. Thus, we saw a great deal of each other, averaging perhaps two conversations a week. Parsons was always very kind to me. He invited me to his home for dinner; he never gave me the impression that I was wasting his time; he read the chapters of my thesis promptly and commented on them sparingly but constructively; his manner was mild, unassuming, and totally lacking in sarcasm and arrogance. Yet we never really hit it off, and we never could get a real discussion or argument going, either in seminars or privately.

Parsons immediately felt that I would never become his disciple. Many aspects of his thinking left me dissatisfied, especially his assumption that no society could long persist without a broad consensus about basic values. I was intimidated by his ceaseless productivity, and my pace of reading him always seemed to lag behind his output. Furthermore, I was inhibited in my criticisms of him as I felt I did not fully understand him. In the climate of veneration that surrounded him, I attributed my lack of comprehension to my shortcomings rather than his.

In Parsons' case, partly because of the opaqueness of his prose and the turgidity of his thinking, but also because of his considerable erudition and his flashes of intuitive brilliance in his more informal seminars, it took me the better part of a decade to deflate his theoretical balloon. In the end, I resented having spent so much time to discover how little original substance Parsons had to offer. That is why, even though we never quarrelled and we parted on cordial terms, our association essentially stopped after I left Harvard in January 1960.

My thesis, I had decided, would be an analysis of the evolution of South African racism, in terms of a dichotomy of "competitive" and "paternalistic" types of race relations. The methodology was to be in the Weberian, ideal-typical tradition, and that was congenial enough to Parsons; but the central theoretical theme was a refutation of Parsons' value consensus assumption. Parsonian functionalism simply did not fit my colonial experience, and South Africa seemed a good test case. Besides, I had decided that I wanted to go back to Africa.

Allport became my thesis co-director for two reasons. First, I had presented my typology of race relations in his course on the social psychology of prejudice, the course around which his great classic, *The Nature of Prejudice* (1954), had grown. Second, he and Tom Pettigrew (my classmate in 1953–1954, who, in the meantime, had raced ahead of me in the Ph.D. program and become a junior faculty member) were just back from a stay in South Africa. In the normal course of events, I should have left for South Africa in 1959 and then come back to Harvard to defend my dissertation. Somehow, I persuaded Allport and Parsons to invert that sequence: I would write and defend my dissertation first and then go to South Africa to check on whether it made sense. After a few months ensconced in a carrel of Widener Library, I thought I had sufficient materials for a library dissertation, and, in December 1959, Allport, Parsons, and Pettigrew decided that I had indeed a passable dissertation. I have never looked at it since; both my 1965 book, *South Africa, A Study in Conflict,* and my 1967 work, *Race and Racism,* were written from scratch, neither of them being a published dissertation as some have assumed. The dissertation, I am afraid, is written in the turgid style that most graduate students assume is de rigueur for this kind of exercise.

Allport's input into it was unstinting and sometimes excruciatingly painstaking. We enjoyed a cordial relationship, and his generosity and devotion to me were well beyond the call of duty. His firsthand knowledge of South Africa was, of course, invaluable, but his contributions extended to the smallest details of style. On a par with Bill Gum, Allport was an excellent editor and it is a measure of his modesty and of his devotion to his students that his comments ranged from lofty points of theory to disquisitions on the use of semicolons and the avoidance of "which." It was also Allport who put me in touch with Leo Kuper, enticed him to offer me a lectureship in his Durban department, and helped me obtain a scholarship to go to South Africa with a freshly baked Ph.D.

Allport was interested in my thesis, as was Tom Pettigrew, because it demonstrated that racism was at least as much the product of social factors, especially of relations of power and of production, as of personality traits and psychological experiences. Today, this hardly seems a very startling conclusion, but then the study of prejudice was largely dominated by *The Authoritarian Personality* and the murky Frankfurt-school psychoanalysis of frustration-aggression. Allport, always the prudent and sensible eclectic, was carefully critical of that position and quite open to consider other theories. Pettigrew, his main protégé and future successor at Harvard, went even farther in exploring the social-structural dimensions of prejudice, and, thus, my work dovetailed with their interests.

Parsons, however, was far from convinced that South Africa refuted his consensus assumption. Yes, he conceded, South Africa was a rather unusual kind of society. Perhaps consensus existed below the surface, and I had simply not dug deeply enough to find it. Alternatively, South Africa was perhaps so unusual as not to be a real society at all, but a composite of several societies. He too passed my dissertation without raising any serious objections and even cited it a couple of times in subsequent years. Whenever we seemed to come to a theoretical issue or impasse, Parsons always avoided an incisive discussion or argument. He often gave one the impression that one's arguments were sinking in, because he seemed to listen patiently and politely and nodded with avuncular benevolence. When one was finished, he invariably commented: "Very interesting." And that was the last of that argument. Although Marcuse's concept of "repressive tolerance" always seemed an overstatement, Parsons' style of intellectual non-exchange came close.

But Parsons had his great moments, almost always improvised disquisitions in his seminars. An interesting empirical issue would be raised, and Parsons would take off, dazzling us with his erudition and intuition. At other times, he could be dismally dull, or the entire session would bog down on some truism or tautology. I remember trying to nip a tautology in the bud. Parsons started the seminar with one of his famous "Isn't it interesting . . ." openers. "Isn't it interesting that no other religion ever successfully challenged the world's great religions: Islam, Judaism, Christianity, Hinduism, Buddhism." A wave of assenting nods rippled around the seminar table, and a minute of ruminative silence followed. My impudent impishness got the better of me, and I could not help but break that reverential mood. The statement, I suggested, was a complete definitional tautology. No, not really, said Parsons; he still thought all the world religions shared a special greatness that rendered them immune to competition from the not-so-great ones. Universalism, probably. Judaism, I suggested, was not very universalistic. Oh, yes, it really was, and the proof was that it spawned two highly universalistic religions, Christianity and Islam. And so it went.

My association with the third member of the "holy trinity," Clyde Kluckhohn, was more distant and indirect. Even though soc rel advocates were intent on erasing disciplinary boundaries in the social sciences, they were realistic enough to encourage most students to opt for one of the four tracks within the field: clinical psychology, social psychology, sociology, or anthropology. I was very much torn between the latter two, but I opted for the first. Throughout my career, I have always felt that the distinction between sociology and anthropology had no intellectual justification and was a residue of nineteenth-century racism and colonialism. If one studied dark colonials, one was an anthropologist; if one studied Europeans and their white colonial offshoots, one was a sociologist.

One of the reasons for opting for the sociology tag was that I knew I wanted to spend a lot of time in Africa, where the academic label of anthropology is shunned because of its colonial connotations. Outside of

South Africa, there are few, if any, departments of anthropology at African universities. Anthropology is conducted under the sociology label. Thus, the sociology option for me was, in part, a political choice. But there was another reason. Anthropology at Harvard was split between soc rel and a residual Anthropology Department housed in Peabody Museum and incorporating archaeology, physical anthropology, and some linguistics and cultural anthropology. In short, anthropology was only half in soc rel, if that much, and was, thus, the weakest of the four tracks. Kluckhohn was the central figure in soc rel anthropology, but I was more attracted by British and French *social* anthropology than by the American *cultural* anthropology epitomized by Kluckhohn. Perhaps my resistance was based on the fact that much of my exposure to him came secondhand through his wife, Florence, a sociologist. In any case, I quickly tired of her endless rehashing of their "value orientation" scheme in the five cultures project. Besides, I was not interested in the U.S. Southwest.

Yet I knew that I wanted to do field work and that I needed to perfect my methodological skills in the anthropological direction. The Department of Social Relations was remarkably broad-minded and eclectic in its conception of methodology. We all had to become competent in statistical analysis of quantitative data. Frederick Mosteller, Sam Stouffer, and, briefly, Louis Guttman (on a sabbatical from Israel) exposed me to the best quantitative methodology of the time. Mosteller was probably the best teacher of statistics I encountered, and I greatly enjoyed my year as his TA. (In fact, Lore Colby was a student in my section, and it was through her that I initiated a close, lifelong relationship with Benjamin [Nick] Colby.)

Sam Stouffer was much more effective in his graduate seminars than in his undergraduate classes. His thinking always raced ahead of his speech, which was further slurred by the perennial presence of a cigarette between his lips. He did not even take it out to flip away the ashes; the latter simply fell randomly over his shirt or sweater. He had a memorable opening shot to his methodology seminar: "Ideas are a dime a dozen. Give me data." I spent much of my subsequent career rejecting this naive kind of nose-counting empiricism, both as an epistemology and as a quasi-exclusive type of methodological training for graduate students. But it was necessary to become competent in this methodology in order to understand its limitations. My doubts about it were of long standing, but Stouffer equipped me to reject it intelligently.

All graduate students in soc rel were required to complete six months of field work. For sociology students this usually meant low-level participation as interviewers and data analysts in the Cambridge-Somerville study of the impact of high school motivation and achievement on social class mobility aspirations. My participation in the project was fairly desultory. I could not become excited about the problem, and urban America was not my kind of research setting. I did learn the basics of how to record, transcribe, and analyze interviews, however. This was definitely a step up from ringing doorbells and administering ready-made questionnaires as I had in Stanford.

Still, it was not "real" field work, as I wanted to do. I wanted to do a long stretch of field work in South Africa after completing my dissertation, and I felt the need for a prior experience in learning that methodology. As luck would have it, Evon Vogt ("Vogtie" to us all), then a young Kluckhohn protégé and Kluckhohn's future academic heir, was just getting the Harvard Chiapas project under way. Nick and Lore Colby and myself were among the first group of students in the project, soon to be followed by many others like Frank and Francesca Cancian (also my contemporaries at Harvard), Duane Metzger, Robert Laughlin, George and Jane Collier, and others who collectively were to gain much prominence in Meso-American anthropology.

What began as a dry-run for South Africa developed into an enduring interest in doing field work in Latin America and merely the first of several stints in that region. Both Nick Colby and I were interested in ethnic relations, and we knew that the highlands of Chiapas were a particularly fascinating area. We were both greatly impressed with Gonzalo Aguirre Beltrán's recently published *El Proceso de aculturación* (1957), in which I recognized many points of convergence with Balandier (attributable in part, no doubt, to a common Marxian ancestry). In any case, we immediately established a fruitful division of labor between us. Lore Colby would study Tzotzil linguistics; Nick would do an ethnography of Zinacantán and look at ethnic relations from the Indian perspective; I would concentrate on the Ladinos in San Cristóbal de las Casas and look at ethnicity from the viewpoint of the politically and economically dominant group.

In June 1959, Irmi and I purchased our second Volkswagen "beetle" and took some ten days to cover the seemingly interminable distance between Boston and the Mexican Southeast. It was her first exposure to Mexico and my third. Once more, I felt very much at ease in this Latin environment and was eager to initiate my field work. I certainly experienced no culture shock. If anything, my culture shocks have always come on returning to the United States from the field. This long automobile journey gave me a much better sense of the ecological and cultural variety of Mexico than my previous trips, which had been largely confined to the Central Valley or the northern border area. This time we drove through the semi-desertic north and the lush tropical isthmus, as well as the central highlands, with stops in Oaxaca, Mitlá, and Monte Albán. We stayed in cheap but often charming little hotels on the way. One delightful vignette sticks in my mind: an intensely green tree frog perched on the shower head of our hotel bathroom in Juchitán.

The last leg of our journey took us to the highlands again, on the spectacular stretch of Pan-American Highway rising from Tuxla Gutierrez to San Cristóbal de las Casas. The Instituto Nacional Indígenista, which had a regional station in San Cristóbal, extended us the most gracious hospitality in the form of a rent-free room, and its local director, Alfonso Villa Rojas, was a delightful host. The town, with a population of about 30,000, was an ideal research setting for my purposes. It was small enough for one to gain an overview of its social structure, yet large enough to be sharply stratified. It was also the dominant political center and market town of a region whose rural population was almost entirely Indian, in the Mexican sense of native speakers of indigenous languages. The population of San Cristóbal, on the other hand, consisted almost exclusively of Spanish-speaking mestizos, or *ladinos,* as they were locally known.

As I already mentioned, I feel much at home in the Mexican (or, more generally, Latin American) bourgeoisie. It is a world sufficiently close to the one in which I grew up to enable me to understand it without much "cultural translation." This has greatly facilitated my Latin American field work, but it has also given it a slant and a flavor that some of my colleagues have criticized. I am simply not very good at participant observation among peasants, nor have I cultivated the kind of field work mystique fashionable in some anthropological circles. I do not feel that field work is a mystical rite of passage rendered more formative for having been traumatic. To be sure, distance from one's own society helps to give one perspective and insights not so easily acquired otherwise. I would go so far as to say that one cannot be a competent social scientist without having had the experience of prolonged participant-observation in at least one foreign culture. On the whole, the more numerous the cultures to which one has been exposed, and the more alien to one's own, the richer one's perspective becomes.

Stress is, I think, an inevitable part of field work. Field work is always a period of intensification and acceleration of one's life. One must do things at a frantic clip: learn a new language and culture; adapt oneself to new situations; record one's observations in field notes; continuously reinterpret the flood of fresh information into some kind of cognitive coherence; mediate the inevitable conflicts and misunderstandings that arise from one's intrusive presence; and solve the mundane problems of health, diet, shelter, and the like. To do all this, day after day, generally under conditions of lesser physical comfort than one is accustomed to is not without its trauma. But I do not subscribe to the masochistic school of anthropology that holds that the quality of field work is a direct function of the amount of trauma. You have to cope with difficulties and discomforts when they arise, but there is nothing wrong in avoiding them if you can.

I must have been fairly successful in my hedonistic brand of field methodology because the dominant feeling that I have experienced in the field has generally been a "high" of mental exhilaration created by a constant overload of new experiences. This was stressful and often irritating, to be sure, but, on the whole, not painful. The main exception was in South Africa, but then only because of the kind of society that South Africa is. Indeed, my best time in South Africa was when I was most deeply engrossed in my community study of "Caneville."

The three months of work in San Cristóbal passed very quickly and very pleasantly. Our reception in the San Cristóbal social and intellectual elite was exceptionally cordial; the municipal authorities were most cooperative; and we enjoyed a warm relationship with local Mexican and foreign scholars. Among them, I should like to mention the Danish archaeologist, Franz Blom, his dynamic and unforgettable Austrian wife, Trudy, who outlived him for many years to become San Cristóbal's slightly eccentric *grande dame,* and Prudencio Moscoso Pastrana, a distinguished local historian. Both Blom and Moscoso put their extensive libraries at our disposal with extraordinary graciousness.

Although I spent most of my time in town and observed Indian-Ladino interaction in the urban setting where much of that interaction took place, I frequently accompanied Nick and Lore to Zinacantán, Chamula, and other Indian *municipios* to get a glimpse of the Indian world. But, of course, in the limited time at my disposal, I could not hope to penetrate it at any depth. Nick's work and mine complemented each other's neatly, and we published a couple of articles out of that collaboration, one in the *American Anthropologist* and another in *Social Forces.* The AA paper attracted some interesting criticisms from my old Paris classmate, Rodolfo Stavenhagen, who was later to reach the pinnacle of Mexican academia as director of the Colegio de México.

So far, I have stressed my contacts with the "holy trinity" at Harvard. At the time, they seemed the most formative and important contacts and I suppose that, like most graduate students, I let my judgment of intellectual quality be somewhat contaminated by the Realpolitik of departmental power. To my lasting benefit, however, I also cultivated a relationship with the "terrible three" (again, my term) of soc rel: George

Homans, Barrington Moore, and Pitirim Sorokin. The word to the wise in soc rel graduate student culture was that one associated with any of them only at considerable risk to one's career. Sorokin and Moore were marginal outsiders to department politics, and all three terrorized students with their displays of intellectual haughtiness. Each of them was, in his own inimitable way, a vastly colorful character and a legend in the oral tradition of the department. Most of the anecdotes, however, were not of a nature to encourage contact.

The most unapproachable of the three was Sorokin, who by that time had withdrawn into contemptuous isolation from all except his client, Carl Zimmerman. His bitter feud with Parsons was proverbial. Sorokin accused Parsons of having destroyed the Sociology Department, which Sorokin had founded, in order to create soc rel. He also accused Parsons of thinly veiled plagiarism not only from his own writings, but also from William I. Thomas, Florian Znaniecki, and many others. Sorokin was a man of prodigious intelligence and erudition that was matched only by his megalomania. His colorful past was quite enough to create the legend. He had been a secretary to Aleksandr Kerensky during the brief first phase of the Russian Revolution and had the distinction of having been condemned to death by both the Czar and the Bolsheviks. He was enough of a political figure to have been the target of one of Lenin's more vituperative pamphlets.

Naturally, the rest of his life as an American academic was a pallid aftermath to this youthful Sturm und Drang. Hardly anyone found grace in his eyes except a handful of like-minded Russian émigrés like Kerensky and Georges Gurvitch. His opinion of his own contributions was epitomized in a frequently cited anecdote. In lecture, he would inveigh against his critics for referring to him as "Professor Sorokin." "Why," said Sorokin, "do they always call me '*Professor* Sorokin'? They won't say 'Professor Aristotle,' would they?" Few of his colleagues escaped his ponderous, embittered sarcasm. Nearly all were, in his eyes, fools, knaves, or often both. Unfortunately, his sarcasm also extended to students. He was known to possess a rubber stamp marked "Utter nonsense," which he would use profusely on the typescripts of his helpless students. Few survived that ordeal by ridicule. I certainly did not. After one or two attempts at intellectual exchange, I gave up.

Barrington Moore was a model of approachability by comparison with Sorokin. A mere untenured lecturer, he was politically marginal to soc rel and made little effort to hide his contempt for many of his colleagues, especially for Parsons; but his independent wealth allowed him the luxury of total impudence unsullied by the merest hint of sycophancy. Although he had a justifiably high opinion of himself and did not suffer fools gladly, he was not, like Sorokin, a paranoid egomaniac. He set high standards for students, but was easily mollified by a show of scholarship and originality. In any case, he rather liked me, and my knowledge of French and German raised me considerably in his esteem. The A− he gave me in his political sociology class was a signal mark of favor. (Mine was the only grade above B in a class of about seventy.) Emboldened by such recognition, I invited him to join my General Exam committee—a foolhardy move, my classmates warned me.

With Homans, I had a relationship approaching warmth. This stupefied many of my fellow graduate students who thought that with both Moore and Homans on my exam committee I was courting disaster. They were very nearly right, but it was Homans who came to my rescue on the fateful day of my exam. The third member of the exam committee was Tom Pettigrew who was benevolently disposed, but a political lightweight in the presence of these two formidable figures. Moore asked me a treacherously general question in the oral on comparative sociology: "What would you say are the main differences between an industrial and a pre-industrial society?" On the spur of the moment, I thought that Parsons' "pattern variables" were a reasonable conceptual coatrack on which to hang my answer. Given what I knew of both Moore's and Homans' opinion of Parsons, this was a tactical blunder of the first order. Moore let me squirm for an interminable five or six minutes and then interrupted with a devastating: "Now, Mr. van den Berghe, did you tell me anything I would not have known from reading the *New York Times*?" Luckily, Homans saved the day by interjecting in his stentorian voice: "But Barrington, you didn't ask anything which could not be answered in those terms." After that, the rest of the exam was a piece of cake.

It is difficult to think of two intellects as different as Homans' and Moore's, yet both had an important impact on me and, in both cases, a delayed one. Moore's great works of historical synthesis were still to come, but his incisive, sophisticated political analysis was already evident in his recently published *Soviet Politics, The Dilemmas of Power* (1950). I much admired his scholarship, and, more than anyone, he instilled in me respect for historicism at one end of the intellectual spectrum. Clearly, if you try to give a complete contextual analysis of a complex, unique and non-repeatable historical situation, you *must* be a historicist.

Homans, or at least the famous Homans, is commonly put at the reductionist end of the spectrum. Homans-the-behaviorist was interested in reducing social structure and culture to individual interaction. At the time, however, I was at least as interested in the "other" Homans, the historian of *English Villagers in the Thirteenth Century* and of Frisians in East Anglia. Homans' little book with David Schneider, *Marriage, Authority and Final Causes* (1955), an attack against Lévi-Strauss' *Les structures élémentaires de la parenté* on matrilateral cross-cousin marriage, further reinforced my interest in kinship and my sense that kinship was a promising domain in which to look for cross-cultural uniformities of behavior. (I was also very impressed with Murdock's *Social Structure* (1949), which I read in those years.)

The famous Homans of *The Human Group* (1950) had the appeal of parsimony and common sense and stood in stark contrast to Parsons' *The Social System* (1951) for both lucidity of thinking and elegance of style, but it left me dissatisfied by its stress on sentiment as the cement of sociality. It might be true that interaction often led to liking and that leadership sometimes rested on popularity, but liking and popularity seemed to provide weak explanations of sociality—weaker ones, in any case, than the more conventional utilitarian, hedonistic, and maximizing models current in classical economics and behaviorism. In short, Homans' social behaviorism did not seem to add anything to classical behaviorism and seemed to be missing an important element. Not until I turned to evolutionary biology did I discover, some fifteen years later, what that missing element was.

Certainly Homans' own life was a refutation of his theory of sociality. Long-standing interaction with his Harvard colleagues had increased neither his liking of them nor theirs of him. Homans' behavior did little to enhance reciprocal liking and tolerance. A famous anecdote has Homans interrupt a Parsonian homily at a formal soc rel gathering. As Parsons was expatiating on how nice, congenial, collegial, cooperative, and consensual a department soc rel was, Homans rudely interjected in his booming voice: "Come, come, Talcott, you *know* we all hate each other!"

Still, I owe a great deal to Homans. He stimulated me to think about important issues; he kept the voice of common sense audible through the thick obfuscatory blanket of Parsonianism, and ultimately he led me to an even more radical (and, I would argue, much more productive) brand of reductionism than his own. Beyond my penchant for alliteration, it was in tribute to him that I entitled my 1974 *American Sociological Review* article "Bringing Beasts Back In," in obvious pastiche of Homans' famous "Bringing Men Back In." At the same time, both Moore and Homans helped me see that reductionism and holism, nomothetic theory construction and historicism, were best regarded as the poles of a *methodological* continuum, not as dogmatic a priori positions between which one had to choose. Different levels of social reality called for different methodologies. What superficially looked like incompatible positions boiled down to complementary research strategies. The Homans of the *English Villagers* was the same as the one of *The Human Group*. It was only small minds that created the split personality.

Little did I yet know that later my colleagues would also insist that there were two van den Berghes, the second one supposedly emerging from his "conversion" to sociobiology! No amount of reasoned argument succeeds in disabusing a human mind bent on finding oppositions. The dualistic frame of thinking seems deeply wired in our brain structure.

There was more to our life in Cambridge than Emerson Hall, Widener Library, and the other amenities of Harvard, but our social life was more restricted than in Paris. For one thing, the American university is much more of a self-contained ivory tower than its European counterpart. Harvard, while clearly *in* Cambridge, is not *of* Cambridge. In that respect the American Cambridge is very unlike its great British homonym. The English Cambridge *is* the university with all of its colleges. The American Cambridge is a decrepit, grimy, working-class, industrial suburb, which just happens to house Harvard and MIT on opposite sides of its unremittingly ugly center. Happily, the subway (itself a grim, ungracious relic of an earlier industrial age), linking Harvard Square to Boston permits one to traverse that ugliness quickly and be spared the very sight of it. The American campus is an island of privilege, typically located in either a sea of urban decay (as Columbia, Chicago, Harvard, and MIT) or in a cultural desert of cornfields (as many large state universities). To live in a place like Cambridge, Massachusetts, is not conducive to partaking of its non-academic life. The banks of the Charles River are but a pale replica of the meadows and commons of the English Cambridge.

We lived at 41 Dana Street, in a vintage eighteenth-century house rendered ugly by new siding and shabby by its transformation into a student slum. What had once been a functionally gracious bourgeois house had been converted into seventeen cubicle-sized flats sharing approximately half as many bathrooms, each renting for some $60 or $70 a month. The entire operation was under the management of an Irish couple, the male half of which was named Pat and was the stereotypic drunkard. Between binges of alcoholic stupor followed by spells of detoxification in the hospital, Pat desultorily fixed the leaking pipes, the hot wires, the squeaky doors, the overflowing gutters, the plugged drains, and the various other hazards that constantly threatened the denizens of this decrepit tenement. A mere six or seven blocks from the splendor of the Harvard Yard, we were living under conditions of precarious overcrowding on the fringes of a declining, industrial semi-slum. I say "semi-slum" because student inhabitation saved the immediate neighborhood from total squalor, but another ten blocks further away from the Yard there was nothing "semi" about the slum anymore.

All our daily movements took us away from central Cambridge and toward Harvard Square. This was true not only of my studious activities, but also of recreational ones and of Irmi's job. When we went out for an evening concert, for example, it took place either in Harvard's Memorial Hall or in Boston. Harvard Square was also the hub of a little ghettoized shopping district for Harvard students and faculty. It had its full complement of student pubs and hash joints, the Harvard Coop (a combination bookstore, drugstore, and haberdasher, as most American college "bookstores" are), an art cinema, a few mediocre ethnic restaurants, a couple of delicatessens, and a few boutiques and specialty stores.

In one of these stores—Miss Cannon's Shop—Irmi earned $250 a month selling expensive toys and children's clothes to rich grandmothers. The students unlucky enough to be saddled with young children were far too impecunious to shop at Miss Cannon's (whose owner, incidentally, was the spinster sister of the *Wisdom of the Body* Cannon). But Miss Cannon, a lady, was not in it for the money. She preferred to run her shop on the brink of bankruptcy and to pay her sales staff subsistence wages rather than lower the class of her store by attracting a student clientele through lower-priced articles. Irmi was constantly reminded that the "nice people" she met on a daily basis were ample compensation for her meager wages. She dared not tell Miss Cannon that she would not have minded a little student riff-raff in exchange for a 25 percent raise.

Between her wages, my GI Bill benefits, and a paltry teaching or research assistantship (which went mostly toward paying Harvard tuition), we led a life of genteel indigence, unsubsidized, alas, by relatives as it had been in Paris. We were nominally earning four times as much, but living worse. Luckily we did have a few well-heeled friends who invited us to good dinners. Among them were Serge Elisséeff, the distinguished Harvard Sinologist and father-in-law of my Aunt Francine, and the famous Belgian ophthalmologist at Massachusetts General, Charles Schepens. This charming and cultured man often invited us to his seashore home in Nahant where we spent many a delightful evening with his no less charming family.

During the few months when we had our Volkswagen, after our return from Mexico, we took some outings into the New England countryside and historic villages. But most of the time we were simply too busy to travel. Even our forays into Boston were relatively infrequent. We went there mostly for meat and for concerts. The latter require no explanation, but the former is easily explained. Before Faneuil Hall was converted into a tourist trap, it was surrounded on all sides by cheap little butcher shops where we restocked our larder about once a month. Twenty dollars would buy two bulging bags of flank steaks, tongues, kidneys, brains, sweetbreads, and other delicacies unobtainable at the "A & P" and unbelievably cheap because most Americans then considered these to be barely suitable as dog food. Living among barbarians had its advantages!

Our social life also included some dinner parties at fellow graduate students' homes. Besides the Colbys, we associated with Harvard Japanologist Ezra Vogel, economist Kenneth Kauffman, sociologist and Andeanist Oscar Alers, and a number of others. These parties were held at our shabby flats and were lubricated by gallon jugs of cheap California wines. But the intellectual action was great!

Harvard, a great place for meeting the high and the mighty, is one of those rare sites in American society where power and intellect intersect and, what is more, where intellect occasionally leads to power. The old Harvard anecdote of a *Crimson* headline stating: "The President Meets Mr. Coolidge" has not lost its *pointe*. In other countries, the linkages between government and higher education are taken for granted. All the ruling elites of French society, for instance, come from a handful of *grandes écoles,* whose graduates form an overlapping directorate of technocrats. In the United States, these links are far looser, and only Harvard seems to have a direct pipeline to the White House and, then, mostly during Democratic administrations.

Power has never fascinated me. Unlike the pursuit of wealth, which buys a measure of security, freedom, privacy, and independence, the pursuit of power brings a loss of all of these. Power is only any good if it is absolute, and, even then, it is very dangerous. Why anyone should seek power through the electoral process, however, is even more incomprehensible to me. That kind of political game, it seems to me, is a fool's delusion. Courting the favor of others is perhaps the most demeaning and futile of all pursuits. It is demeaning because one cannot be true to oneself; it is futile because favor is the most evanescent of all commodities. Anyway, I always held power mongers and popularity seekers in great dislike and contempt, and I have never sought them out.

My closest encounter with world power, however, took place at Harvard and even then it was fleeting. I was looking for a research assistantship to tide me over the summer. Someone—I think it may have been Barrington Moore—suggested to me that Henry Kissinger was hiring indentured servants and that my knowledge of French and German might be useful. Henry and I had a fifteen-minute interview in his lair, the Littauer School. He had already developed a dose of professorial arrogance that exceeded even the Harvard norm. His elephantine social grace made the moment even more awkward. Kissinger was still an obscure political science professor, but his power-mongering was already oozing through the pores of his skin. In any case, I was relieved not to get the job and not to have to work for the man.

In January 1960, thanks to Allport's efforts, I was ready to leave for South Africa. My thesis had just been successfully defended. I had a little scholarship ($3,600) to defray the travel expenses and an offer of a lecturership in Leo Kuper's Sociology Department at the University of Natal in Durban. Irmi was pregnant with our first child. We had planned its arrival to coincide with my Ph.D., and everything seemed to be right on schedule. We left Harvard for an intermediate stop in Germany. There, as was our plan, Irmi would give birth in the midst of her family while I went on to Durban to prepare for her arrival with the baby. I was 27 years old and felt on top of the world.

CHAPTER 8

Apartheid

No other period of my adult life has marked me as deeply as the twenty-two months I spent in South Africa, from February 1960 to December 1961. I arrived just in time to experience the abortive revolution of Sharpeville and its aftermath, and I left on Blood River Day, the anniversary of the 1838 bloodbath inflicted by the Boers on the Zulu, now celebrated as a great military triumph of Afrikanerdom. In between those dates, two-thirds of Africa, including my native Congo, gained political independence. I could hardly have picked a more interesting time to be in Africa.

It certainly looked then as if the days of white South Africa were counted and as if a promising new era of African history had dawned. Yet, a quarter of a century later, white domination in South Africa seems as securely entrenched as ever. The nominally Marxist regimes to South Africa's north—Angola, Mozambique, and Zimbabwe—far from constituting a threat to South Africa are so politically shaky that one had to be propped up by 50,000 Cuban troops and the other two can be destabilized almost at will by South Africa. Further north, much of the continent is staggering under a combination of political, economic, ecological, and demographic catastrophes of unprecedented scope and severity. As the human and bovine population explodes, desertification ravages vast stretches of land at an ever-accelerating pace. Deforestation, wind and water erosion, soil exhaustion, drought, man-made disasters (such as the Aswan Dam), and sinking water tables combine to make famine a chronic condition for tens of millions in Ethiopia, Chad, Niger, Mauritania, Uganda, Rwanda, Burundi, and elsewhere. Civil wars and international conflicts have ravaged the Sudan, Zaïre, Nigeria, Ethiopia, Somalia, Rwanda, Burundi, Angola, Mozambique, Algeria, Morocco, Egypt, Chad, Uganda, and a few more. What little wealth is created (or imported in the form of foreign aid) is siphoned off by a corrupt "kleptocracy," which plunders the public weal for private gain.

Could it be that the racists I had known in the Congo and whom I met daily for my two years in South Africa were right all along? Was colonialism the best thing that ever happened to Africa? Were Africans incapable of self-rule after all? I always refused to believe any of these statements and I continue to do so. But I can no longer be the optimist I was then. A quarter of a century ago, Asia, especially South Asia looked like the world's prime basket case. Africa, while desperately poor, seemed to have more space and more scope for development. To be sure, even then, there were non-racist pessimists, like Stanislav Andreski and René Dumont, who warned that Africa was headed for disaster. I was not one of them because I accepted the liberal and radical analysis of the African predicament.

Basically, analysis of Third World poverty came in two ideological bottles—a liberal one and a radical one. The liberal theory of "modernization" was that the Third World was poor because it was backward, isolated, technically unskilled, and weakened by disease and illiteracy. But the vicious circle of poverty could be reversed. Development could be achieved through the infusion of human skills, capital, and technology, combined with family planning, "modern" values of diligence, initiative and motivation, and international philanthropy. A few thousand Peace Corps volunteers spreading the Protestant ethic and Yankee ingenuity and millions of hardworking natives pulling themselves up by their sandalstraps could turn things around. The radical analysis was known as "dependency theory." The Third World had been pauperized, not through backwardness and isolation, but through its integration into the capitalist world system. Underdevelopment of the Third World was simply the other side of the development of the First World. The two stood in direct causal relation to one another. Poverty was the result of exploitation at two levels: internationally by the rich countries of the capitalist core and locally by the dependent bourgeoisie of the poor countries. The radical analysis, like the liberal one, presented a solution and a seemingly easier and much more ideologically appealing one than modernization: revolution. Since poverty grew out of social structures of unequal relations of production and terms of trade, the problem was not to increase the resource base but to destroy the social structures. And since those who profited from these social structures were understandably attached to them, violence was the only way out.

When I first came to South Africa, my thinking was more in line with modernization theory, then dominant in American academic circles, and my politics were roughly those of universalistic liberalism with perhaps a dash of European social democracy. This was still the ideological context within which I analyzed South Africa in my 1965 book, *South Africa, A Study in Conflict*. But my South African experience gradually radicalized me into an increasing acceptance of dependency theory.

By now, however, it is clear that both modernization and dependency theories were half right in their diagnosis and, alas, more than half wrong in their optimistic solutions. Underdevelopment is the result of *both* exploitation and technological backwardness, plus a multitude of ecological and demographic factors, and the proportions of these causal factors vary widely from place to place. The lack of a simple, direct relationship between exploitation and underdevelopment is made evident by countries like South Africa, the most super-exploitative country on the African continent, and yet also the most developed by far, *even for its black population*.

"Modernization" does not work. It is premised on the abundance of the scarcest of all resources in the Third World, namely capital, and it cannot effectively harness its most abundant resource, namely labor, even when that labor has been "educated." A country like Israel can modernize because half of its population was "modern" to start with and because its patron infused massive amounts of capital into it. Currently, Israel annually receives about two or three times as much U.S. *aid* per capita as the per capita *income* of most African countries. That is enough to make the Negev bloom, but not the Sahara. In addition, modernization does not work because what it assumes to be a major precondition of development, namely population control, is demonstrably a consequence of development. People never became richer by having fewer children; they always started getting richer and *then* begat fewer children. Nothing short of the massive coercion now practiced in the People's Republic of China seems likely to reverse that causality, and even the Chinese experiment is still far from a demonstrable success. So far, it only seems to have held catastrophe at bay a while longer.

But revolution does not bring about development either. Sometimes, revolution redistributes wealth and reduces inequality, at least for a while, until a new ruling class repeats the cycle of using power to accumulate wealth. However, redistribution in poor countries means largely downward leveling, not development. There are a few exceptions, as in some Latin American countries when large unproductive estates are redistributed among land-hungry subsistence peasants. In most cases, however, redistribution means that a few people are much poorer, but that hardly anyone is any richer for it.

There are two things that Marxist-inspired regimes do well and that *do* improve the quality of life of the majority, namely mass literacy campaigns and mass preventive medicine. These are by no means negligible accomplishments, as recent Cuban and Nicaraguan history has shown. But, in Africa, Marxist revolutionary regimes have dismally failed even in those aims (e.g., in Ethiopia, Angola, and Mozambique). So far, there has not been a *single* case of a successful *economic* development of a Third World country under a revolutionary Marxist regime, while there have been a dozen or so cases of moderate success stories of dependent capitalist development in Asia and Latin America (e.g., Mexico, Brazil, Korea, Taiwan) and *one* in Africa. Lest all this sound like a paean to capitalism, let me stress that I reject the development ethic common to both capitalism and socialism. It is, alas, more likely that the People's Republic of China is the wave of the future than either the United States or the Soviet Union. Given the fact that we are consuming our habitat at an irreplaceable rate, poverty and tyranny are more likely to spread than wealth and freedom. As an anarchist, I find the increasing centralization of state power in both capitalist and communist countries equally repugnant. And the scarcer resources become, the greater the scope for tyranny.

Assuming that we avert a nuclear holocaust, we shall still have to face the fact that we are eating ourselves out of our only known survivable planet. Unless the developed world starts "undeveloping" fast and inventing a neo-agrarian technology of renewable resources, we do not have much of a future as a species. Both capitalism and socialism are barking up a dying tree. And it is the statist developmentalism common to both systems that will kill us all, either quickly in a mushroom cloud or slowly under an acrid smog blanket. The Sahel drought, the dying forests of Europe, the acid rain of the northeastern United States, the destruction of the Amazonian rain forest, the desertification of India, and the suffocation of Los Angeles are the intertwined aspects of a process of global necrosis. The global problem is the development of underdevelopment through overdevelopment.

What does all this have to do with South Africa? Perhaps the fact that exceptionally rotten societies help one see problems in stark contrast and attain a degree of lucidity about the basis of the social order otherwise not easily achieved. A tyrannical, exploitative society like South Africa exposes its sinews of power and privilege to social analysis better than one that hides under a thick blanket of ideological mystification.

Let me try to recapture the ideological and theoretical context within which I approached South Africa. My previous colonial experience in the Congo was crucial in giving me a preliminary insight into South Africa, for, despite the argument that South Africa is not a colonial society, it seemed obvious to me that the similarities greatly overshadowed the differences. Other labels given to South Africa, such as "fascism" (a favorite of the left), seemed a much poorer approximation to reality than that of colonialism. South Africa was clearly a case of "settler colonialism," and the quasi-indigenous status acquired by the white fifth of its population did not fundamentally alter that fact. It merely made the colonialism *internal* rather than external.

Many neo-Marxists think they invented the notion of internal colonialism in the late 1960s or 1970s, but the concept was used in South Africa as early as the 1950s by Leo Marquard among others. There was one central feature of the South Africa polity that required focused analysis, it seemed to me, and that was the contrast between the ostensibly representative institutions of the white population and the openly despotic colonial institutions applied to the black population. South Africa was *at once* a parliamentary democracy of sorts for whites and a colonial empire for non-whites. I coined the term "Herrenvolk democracy" to refer to this type of polity. Over the years, I was gratified to see that others, such as William Wilson, Eugene Genovese, and George Fredrickson, have adopted large chunks of my analysis.

Some have made a career out of attacking me, even when their stated disagreements were mere restatements of my own work. (Bernard Magubane is a good example.) Of late, I have become a favorite *bête blanche* of many neo-Marxists who attack the "plural society" school while merely restating in turgid Marxist jargon many of the arguments made by Leo Kuper, Michael G. Smith, and myself. Most amusing in this respect is the recent rediscovery of the "autonomy of the state" by neo-Marxists. This latest fad in contemporary Marxism is merely a restatement of the obvious, namely that differential relations of power more often lead to differential relations of production than the other way around. Anyone familiar with the anthropological literature of the 1960s on the origin of the state has known that for at least twenty years. The works of Karl Wittvogel, Elman Service, and others are cases in point. In any case, my published works on South Africa have exerted considerable influence (if often as a target) not only on the literature on that country, but also on the field of race and ethnic relations at large. A good deal of my perspective on race and ethnic relations in plural societies was developed in South Africa and through intellectual associations in the years immediately following.

The most central figures in that development have been sociologist Leo Kuper, in whose department I taught during the last two years of his stay in South Africa, and anthropologist Hilda Kuper. Our association was much more than simply intellectual. It was also political. Both were prominently involved in the South African Liberal Party. Their open house on Sunday afternoon was the meeting place of the Durban liberal intelligentsia. Fatima Meer, Alan Paton, Peter Brown, Jordan Ngubane, Violaine Junod, Edna Bonacich (then Miller), Ben Magubane, and Tony Ngubo were among the habitués. Week after week, we discussed political developments in a context where personal involvement was so intense that, even for an outsider like myself, analysis and ideology were inevitably intertwined. Hardly a week went by without some issue being raised that required some action.

For example, Leo Kuper, as head of the Sociology Department at the University of Natal was running the only academically integrated department of the university. The principal, E. G. Malherbe, an Afrikaner "liberal" constantly compromised his stated opposition to apartheid by imposing a brand of "voluntary" segregation of his own. In effect, Malherbe's policy was to try to forestall government intervention into the affairs of his university by running a racially segregated institution. There was a lily-white campus in Pietermaritzburg and a "mixed" campus in Durban. But even the "mixed" campus (where I taught) was hardly integrated. The Medical School was for non-whites only (and was, in fact, the only medical school in the whole of South Africa to admit Africans, "Coloureds," and Asians). The other faculties at Durban admitted some Africans, Asians, and Coloureds, but non-white students only made up some 10 percent of the Durban students. They were housed in a segregated hostel located out of town in old army barracks, under the wardenship (yes, that was his title) of sociologist Hamish Dickie-Clark, a senior lecturer in the Sociology Department. Sport facilities were totally out-of-bounds to non-white undergraduates, as were indeed the main library, the classrooms, and the labs on the breezy hilltop where the main campus was located. Non-white students had to attend classes in a dingy, crowded, downtown building—a converted warehouse, in fact. Teachers duplicated their courses for their white and non-white students, commuting by car between the white campus and the non-white warehouse. In the latter place, a room the size of a classroom served as a "library."

Naturally, Leo Kuper found this blatant discrimination intolerable and did his utmost to alleviate it within the narrow tolerance limits of the system. His position was made doubly difficult by the fact that his own department covered the entire political spectrum from Chris Jooste, an ardent Afrikaner nationalist, to Fatima Meer, a prominent Congress Alliance activist. Leo's scrupulous personal fairness to Jooste was little short of saintly, as the man openly supported the government. In any case, Leo decided that his department was to be academically integrated. Neither he nor his lecturers would duplicate their classes. Since non-white undergraduates were not allowed on the "upper" campus, white students who wanted to take sociology (some eight or ten of them) would have to come to the downtown warehouse. (Leo and I offered them lifts in our private cars, and one of them, incidentally, was Edna Bonacich, the daughter of Reformed Rabbi Meyer Miller of Durban.) Since non-whites could not enter the "white" library, then the entire sociology collection of some 3,000 books would be moved downtown (where it constituted about 80 percent of the "non-white" book collection). Furthermore, Leo insisted that his two black graduate students and research assistants, Tony Ngubo and Ben Magubane, be given access to the upper campus facilities.

In addition to these little internal battles fought within the confines of the university, the Kupers and nearly all their friends and associates were continuously living in the shadow of search without warrant, police surveillance and intimidation, and arrest and detention without trial for their political activities in the strictly non-violent Liberal Party. In this climate, the line between sociological analysis and political action was indeed a thin one and was made all the thinner by a whole string of laws that cared little for such fine distinctions. The 1950 Suppression of Communism Act, for example, defined communism (a criminal offense punishable by five years of imprisonment) as follows: "any doctrine or scheme which aims at bringing about any political, industrial, social, or economic change within the Union by the promotion of disturbance or disorder, by unlawful acts or omissions or the threat of such acts or omissions." A mere analysis of South African race relations, for instance, could easily be construed as the promotion of disorder if it suggested that, perhaps, blacks had good reasons to be angry at the government.

This was also the period when the government, through the Extension of University Education Act of 1959, sought to exclude all non-white students from the "white" universities, thereby closing the last loopholes in South African educational apartheid. The act also created government-controlled "bush colleges" segregated not only by race, but also by ethnicity, one each for the Coloureds, the Indians, the Zulu, the Xhosa, and the Sotho. Leo Kuper privately published a little satirical novel, *The College Brew* (1960), set in one of these yet-to-be-created bush colleges.

The would-be satire turned out to be one of the most uncannily accurate pieces of prediction in the social science literature. It anticipated in detail every feature of these institutions. South Africa is one of the countries that defeats any attempt to be satirical. Reality always outstrips imagination in the production of absurdity.

My study of South Africa began, as I mentioned, in a challenge to Parsons' idealist and consensual view of society and ended in my 1965 book, *South Africa, A Study in Conflict,* with a rather clumsy eclectic mixture of idealist American functionalism and conflict-oriented dialectical materialism. This ungainly hybrid of a theoretical formulation was originally meant to be the last chapter of my book, but a wise editor convinced me that it would best be published as a separate article. It therefore appeared in the *American Sociological Review* (1963) and became my most often cited and reprinted publication, inspiring (along with a half-dozen other statements by Lewis Coser, Ralf Dahrendorft, David Lockwood, and others) scores of equally clumsy attempts to reconcile theories of conflict and consensus. It still lingers on as a debased fifth-hand formula for writing those ghastly pieces of intellectual rubbish known as introductory sociology textbooks.

The book, too, was quite influential, if only because it was the first attempt to present a *sociological* analysis of South African society as a whole. Its liberal attack against apartheid was very much in the ideological mainstream of academia. In fact, the book was probably a bit to the left of that mainstream, at least in North America. Gwendolen Carter, a political scientist who had written a somewhat comparable book to mine, *The Politics of Inequality* (1958), and was respectfully listened to in Washington by those at the African desk of the State Department, strongly advised me to tone down my language. "Oppression," "exploitation," "tyranny," and so on, did not, in her view, belong in the scholarly vocabulary. I am glad I did not take her advice.

Now the book has become the standard butt of criticism by the neo-Marxists who collectively dominate South African scholarship. If I were to rewrite the book today, my interpretation would undoubtedly give less weight to ideological factors and more to material ones. In particular, I would modify the part of my analysis that saw, as a major source of strain in the system, the contradiction between the ideological dictates of apartheid and the economic imperatives of capitalism (requiring a skilled, mobile labor force responsive to market forces, and so on). As my good friend and critic Heribert Adam has demonstrated, I greatly underrated the resilience of the economy and the political pragmatism and adaptability of Afrikaner nationalism, though I still do not believe that the present system can indefinitely bend with the wind and gradually evolve toward some form of consociation. My timing of revolution was clearly off, but I still do not see compromise or peaceful evolution as a probable outcome. I do not think the system will crash down in an apocalyptic collapse, but I believe it will be ground down by ever-mounting waves of urban and rural insurgency, an ever-escalating cost of repression, patterns of birth rates and immigration favoring blacks, and a mounting white emigration starting with the younger, better educated, more dynamic and more enterprising. Whites have already declined from 20 to 15 percent of the population in the last thirty years. More and more whites are getting tired of living in a garrison state, especially when more attractive alternatives beckon in North America or Australia.

Marxist analysis is typically compelling to the degree that the society it seeks to explain resembles nineteenth-century Europe. It is powerful in Latin America, which still has, to a large degree, the class structure of Europe in Marx's time. In the "post-industrial" societies of Western Europe and North America, Marxist class analysis has become obsolete, and, of course, Marxists have, with few exceptions, suspended their critical analysis of socialist countries. Asian societies, while highly stratified, lend themselves much less well to Marxism than Latin America because they are so different from Europe and because Marx's views on the "Asiatic mode of production" have always been extremely nebulous. As for Africa, it presents the greatest challenge to Marxist thinking, a challenge only intelligently met by some French Marxist anthropologists like my Paris contemporary at the Ecole Pratique, Claude Meillassoux, who tried to develop the concept of a "lineage mode of production."

Within Africa, however, South Africa provides the best fit to a Marxist mode of class analysis. Class formations are well and prominently developed, and the level of industrialization makes the South African economy in some respects a fairly good analog to nineteenth-century Europe. Furthermore, the tight integration of South Africa in the "capitalist world system" has made South Africa an excellent "semi-peripheral" exhibit for dependency theorists. Some Marxist scholarship on South Africa is solid and creative, especially in the historical field (e.g., the work of Stanley Trapido). But the sociological literature is, on the whole, dismally plodding, unimaginative, and doctrinaire. Ben Magubane's work is a good case in point. After completing his Ph.D. under Leo Kuper at UCLA, he made a career by producing a series of articles against the "pluralist school" (mostly Leo Kuper, Max Gluckman, Clyde Mitchell, M. G. Smith, and myself) and by writing a turgid, Stalinist book on South Africa. Like Leo Kuper and other "pluralists" who have written about South Africa, I quite agree with Marxists in stressing the importance of relations of production, and I would go much further now than I did twenty years ago in accepting the Marxist argument that many features of apartheid (and its ancestral forms, such as the migratory labor system in the mines), far from being obstacles to the development of capitalism, were, in fact, early adaptations of "extractive" capitalism to minimize the labor costs of production. But on two fundamental points, I would continue to disagree with mainstream Marxist analysis.

One concerns the issue of the causal priority of economic over political relations. To me, this is an empirically open question, but the burden of evidence tends to show that relations of production are derivative of relations of power rather than vice versa. (The rise of Afrikaner capitalism in relation to English capitalism since 1948 is a case in point.) The Marxists are belatedly and reluctantly coming to realize this in their recently fashionable concept of "the autonomy of the state." But that more creative and flexible Marxism has not yet reached South Africa.

The second point of disagreement with South African Marxists is on the issue of class reductionism. Any attempt to reduce race and ethnicity to class and to explain solidarity based on these as archaic residues of "feudal" (in Africa!) societies and expressions of "false consciousness" so distorts South African reality as to make the analysis lose all touch with reality. Even the *best* Marxist work in that tradition, such as that of H. J. and R. E. Simons and Harold Wolpe, has so much conceptual rigidity as to make for a very loose fit to reality. The most creative conceptual innovation in the Marxist tradition is split labor market theory, as represented in the work of Edna Bonacich, a former student of mine, and Leo Kuper. But I find even it too class-reductionist in its disregard of Afrikaner ethnic solidarity as an autonomous basis of group formation. Besides, split labor market theory is ideological anathema to the party-line Marxist, since it makes the white working class the villain of the racist farce instead of the misguided co-oppressed brothers of the black proletariat.

The one conclusion that seemed inescapable in South Africa was that the society was deeply fragmented along race and ethnic lines. Furthermore, these social categories, whether forcibly imposed from the top (as "race") or pre-existing white domination but manipulated for political purposes (such as ethnicity), had an irreducible reality of their own and overlapped only partially with class. A new analytical framework had to be developed to explain, first, how such deeply fragmented societies could persist despite conflicts and lack of consensus, and, second, how these multiple dimensions of cleavage and stratification related to one another. The result emerged in the 1960s as the "plural society" approach, which produced an abundant and valuable literature dealing principally but not exclusively with colonial or ex-colonial societies, but also applied as a general theoretical framework for the analysis of all societies.

J. S. Furnivall's *Colonial Policy and Practice* (1948) is usually cited as the original source of that approach, and its confines remained largely bounded by the British colonial world. My name is generally associated with that of Leo Kuper and of Jamaican anthropologist Michael G. Smith as one of the principal theorists of the school, and my short 1967 textbook *Race and Racism* was probably the most widely read statement of that position outside British colonial academia. (Some 60,000 copies of it were inflicted, largely on American undergraduates, as a text in race relations classes.) The most representative collective work of the school is the book *Pluralism in Africa* (1969), co-edited by Leo Kuper and Michael G. Smith, that arose from a truly seminal colloquium held at UCLA in 1966. In the 1960s UCLA was the academic home of M. G. Smith, Hilda and Leo Kuper, Jacques Maquet, and a number of other scholars who turned it into the greatest American concentration of academic talent devoted to Africa.

Eventually the analytical model was used, modified, and amplified in scores of articles, empirical monographs, and theoretical treatments and came to include a number of Americans like Leo Després and Richard Schermerhorn, Israelis like Sammy Smooha, and others. It soon generated a cottage industry of criticism coming principally, but not exclusively, from Marxists, and, in a curious and roundabout way, it wormed its intellectual way into the totally different American tradition of political pluralism derived from Tocqueville. Lastly, it came to roost back in South Africa to become adopted as a more palatable euphemism for apartheid! This, in turn, gave ammunition to our Marxists critics who, of course, knew all along that we were crypto-fascists.

The intellectual context of my encounter with South Africa is, of course, inextricably intertwined with its ideological matrix. As I mentioned, most of my associations, as well as sympathies, were with Liberal Party and Congress Alliance intellectuals who gravitated around the university, the legal profession, the leading Indian and African secondary schools, the trade unions, and the other institutions with which I came into contact in the course of my teaching and interviews. I also attended numerous Liberal Party and Congress political meetings, met informally with student groups, interviewed numerous political leaders, and otherwise participated in countless political discussions during the course of my field work.

Political neutrality was simply not an option in the context of South African society. Not only did I find apartheid ethically abhorrent; it affected—nay, poisoned—every aspect of my daily life. Jan Smuts once said that one had to be "quite mad" to ignore race in South Africa. Perhaps he should have said that one became quite mad (though not quite in the sense he meant) if one started questioning the validity of "race" as a social category. Apartheid is such a cradle-to-the-grave system that, as a "white," one faces two basic options. One can accept the system and sit back to enjoy its privileges, carefully repressing dangerous little twitches of conscience that might disturb one's serenity. Conversely, one can question the system, in which case life becomes increasingly untenable.

The first course, that adopted by all but a tiny liberal minority, is by far the easier. The whole might of the state and of white opinion sustains it. Apartheid's material advantages to whites are glaring, so why buck a system so slanted in one's favor? One can, I suppose, quietly enjoy the advantages of a system of which one disapproves, but this requires a level of intellectual lucidity and cynicism of which few people are capable. I have met a handful of "apolitical liberals" in South Africa, who came close to that position, but most of them were, in the end, pushed over the edge and emigrated. The stable, comfortable position for enjoying white privilege in South Africa is racism.

One best rationalizes racial privilege by making a *categorical* distinction between whites and blacks. Blacks are so different from whites that the same standards need not apply. Sure, blacks are poor, but they are used to a much lower standard of living, so it does not hurt them. We whites should not put ourselves in their places or project how we would feel because there is *no common measure* between whites and blacks. South African blacks should compare themselves not to whites, but to blacks elsewhere in Africa. That comparison should make them feel very good. And so on, ad nauseam. This is the comfortable ethic of "racial relativism." Each race must be measured by its own standards; each race is incommensurable with any other one.

The end result of this *Veldanschauung* (as Subithra Moodley cutely put it in her thesis; *Veld* is the Afrikaans word for "field" or "countryside") is, of course, total dehumanization of blacks, which suffuses the whole of South African life. There have been a few cosmetic changes in racial etiquette in recent years, but in the 1960s, one was constantly exposed to such news bulletins as: "Mr. Piet Du Toit, aged 37, a farmer in the Bloemfontein district, was killed in an automobile accident as his lorry was hit by a train at a crossing. He leaves behind his wife Henrietta, and three children, Piet, Claas, and Anna. Four Bantu in the back of the lorry were also killed." "People" in the South African press, radio, and television almost always referred to "whites," unless qualified. South African whites managed to ignore the very presence of blacks. Whites living in a densely populated rural district, for instance, would tell you that their nearest neighbor lived 10 kilometers away when thirty servants and farm workers were housed within 500 meters of them.

Again and again, I have watched whites speak of the most intimate details of their own lives, or, worse yet, make disparaging comments about blacks in general or their servants in particular, *in the very presence of servants*. Cognitively, they knew the servants understood them because they would speak English or Afrikaans to them on a daily basis, yet they treated servants completely as non-persons, much as a dog or cat. This behavior often did not preclude a high level of paternalistic "kindness." When servants were being "well treated," they were in a very real sense being *petted*.

At the political level, this *Veldanschauung* gets translated into what I termed a "Herrenvolk democracy," that is, a dual political system in which the ruling ethnic group maintains a representative government with a façade of formal democracy (albeit a badly eroded democracy in the case of South Africa) for itself and rules the rest of the population as colonial subjects. The ideology corresponding to the Herrenvolk democracy is "Herrenvolk egalitarianism," the notion that all whites are created equal and that government of whites, by whites, and for whites shall not perish from the face of the earth. The Constitution of the Transvaal (Boer) Republic put it clearly: "There shall be no equality between white and black in either Church or State."

Later, incidentally, I extended the notion of Herrenvolk democracy to the United States, Israel, and other countries. In the United States, the ideological climate was ripe for acceptance of the concept and the related one of internal colonialism, and the term has been picked up by many sociologists and historians. But whenever I extend it to Israel, I evoke howls of protest from many of my colleagues, including many "liberal" ones. Even more amusing and interesting is that the Israel–South Africa comparison arouses much more anger in the United States than in Israel itself, where, in 1976, I had many dispassionate discussions on this very topic with a number of Israeli social scientists.

Apartheid is more than a political and economic system. It is a way of life, as many white South Africans repeatedly stress. Precisely because it is so all-inclusive, it must be either accepted or rejected in toto. And rejecting it means confronting the entire might of the system. Blacks have, of course, no sensible or self-respecting option except total rejection. But whites have very little realistic or livable option *other* than acceptance of apartheid. Not only do they benefit from it, which, by itself, is reason enough to expect that most would accept apartheid, but the burdens of rejection are even greater than for blacks. Not only do they face the state machinery of repression; they also face the ostracism of the only group with whom they are *allowed* to associate, without a corresponding benefit of acceptance by blacks. Finally, they face the burden of guilt for continuing to enjoy racial privileges that are forced on them whether they want them or not. Even if you prove your bona fides by going to jail, you go to a privileged white jail with a standard of accommodation vastly superior to a black jail. And if you commit suicide, your body is driven to a white cemetery in a whites-only hearse. Emigration is the only escape.

There have been essentially three ideological rejections of apartheid: the black racist, the liberal, and the socialist. The simplest form of rejection of white supremacy is, of course, the antithesis of black power. The argument in its favor is disarmingly simple: you have to fight fire with fire. Since apartheid is racially based and is directed against blacks, blacks must organize as blacks against it. Coalitions with white liberals and radicals can only weaken and divide blacks. Besides, there are not enough non-black allies to make any difference.

The amazing thing about South Africa is how little ideological resonance black racism has had. There have been elements of it in the Pan Africanist splinter from the African National Congress and, more recently, in very mitigated form, in the black consciousness movement. Some would argue that there is a lot of black racism at the grass root level and that the militant leadership only avoided taking a racist stance because, given the demography of a population that is over 70 percent black, the ostensibly universalistic position of equal rights irrespective of race would de facto result in black government anyway. Even if this were the case, it is still surprising that leaders managed to become such without resorting to a facile racial appeal.

The two universalistic platforms on which to oppose apartheid have been the reformist liberal and the radical socialist one. Both share a total ideological rejection of the principle of race or ethnicity as a basis of social organization. The liberal alternative stresses individual rights and defines them primarily in legal and political terms (e.g., habeas corpus, universal adult suffrage, and so on). The socialist program stresses class conflict and aims primarily at the transformation of relations of production, treating the political realm as merely a means to the end of destroying capitalism.

In the early 1960s, the Liberal Party had recently moved to the left; many of its members espoused the Congress Alliance's Freedom Char-

Visiting Albert Luthuli, South African Nobel Peace Prize Winner and President of the African National Congress, under banning order in Stanger, South Africa. From left to right standing: Ben Magubane, Mrs. William Benghu, Edna Bonacich (nee Miller), Chief Albert Luthuli, and myself. Sitting in front: our host, Mr. Mohammed, of the South African Indian Congress. Taken in early 1961.

ter. At that time, both groups were ideologically very close. The Liberal Party had a social democratic left wing, and the Congress Alliance was an internally diverse, united-front type of organization with both liberal and socialist currents within it. Both were firmly committed to a Gandhian ideology of *satyagraha* and non-violence, although the Congress Alliance was on the verge of accepting violence as a last resort. Indeed, Gandhi had himself honed the techniques and philosophy of passive resistance during his twenty-year stay in South Africa, and his moral aura remained enormous until the 1960s. Even then, Congress was, on the average, slightly to the left of the Liberal Party, in that it had a small but disproportionately influential cadre of communists, many of them whites, incidentally. But the difference was not large. For example, the great Albert Luthuli (whom I was privileged to visit in his place of internal exile in Stanger, Natal) was clearly in the mainstream of liberalism, deeply influenced by Christian and Gandhian morality and passionately committed to non-violence.

The main ostensible line of cleavage between the Liberals and Congress was a tactical one. Congress judged it opportune, within the constraints of apartheid, to organize the masses along racial lines and was thus an umbrella of five sub-organizations, four of which were monoracial, joined by an executive committee with two members from each of the five constituent units. The Liberal Party, on the other hand, adamantly refused to accept race in any form and was thus the only multiracial political organization in South Africa, apart from the miniscule Communist Party. Contrary to some assertions, it was not a predominantly white party. At its peak it had some 12,000 active members, of whom some 7,000 were blacks, most of them Natal peasants; several hundred were Coloureds and Indian, mostly professionals and merchants; and 4,000 to 5,000 were whites, mostly but not exclusively, English-speaking academics, lawyers, students, and other professionals.

A few years later, the Liberal Party disbanded because the government had made it illegal for a multi-racial (and non-racial) party to function. Congress was driven underground or into exile after the massive repression that followed Sharpeville in 1960. Over the years, it gradually became at the leadership level what it had been incorrectly accused of being, namely a communist-dominated, Moscow-leaning organization.

During my South African years, my politics were most clearly in sympathy with the left wing of the Liberal Party, in that I favored a social democratic platform of land reform in addition to the formal democracy of universal adult suffrage, but I was committed to non-violence and to a totally uncompromising stance on the issue of recognizing the legitimacy of race as a political category. In later years, my politics have moved from socialism to anarchy, but my ideological rejection of race in any shape or form has remained intact. If there is *one* thing of which South Africa has unalterably convinced me it is that the official recognition of race is *always* noxious and invidious. This unbending conviction was, in later years, to bring me into sharp conflict with the American mainstream of academic "liberalism" on the issue of affirmative action, as we shall see.

South Africa, in short, was the setting of my first massive involvement with an entire society at a level that totally engulfed me both as a scholar and as a person. I found the experience so traumatic and so emotionally draining that I never repeated it. Irmi was conscious that it was taking its toll on me while we were there, and it is a tribute to her patience that she put up with my irritable self during these years. This was doubly meritorious as she had just undergone the wrenching experience of losing a newborn baby. Soon after arriving in Durban, I received my father-in-law's joyous telegram announcing the birth of our daughter, Karen. The next day another telegram brought me the news of her death. The German hospital claimed that the baby had a defective heart; it suddenly turned blue a few hours after a seemingly normal birth. But no autopsy was conducted, and I still suspect hospital negligence. Some fourteen months later, on April 18, 1961, our son Eric was born in a whites-only Durban hospital, the second generation of our family to be born into the dying world of colonial Africa. By *jus soli,* Eric is a South African, though we never pressed the point.

Teaching and conducting field work in South Africa proved so draining an experience that, thereafter, I never allowed myself to become so personally involved in my subject and, conversely, I never did field work again in societies where I would be likely to become personally involved, such as Belgium or the United States. At the same time, my South African experience was immensely formative and enriching. For one thing, it taught me a great deal about doing field work.

Studying South African race relations involved playing a non-stop cat-and-mouse game with the police and the government. The object of the game was to collect the best data possible while avoiding extradition. First, I had to obtain a visa, which was finally granted but subject to renewal every three months. The threat of discontinuation was thus constant. In order to get the visa, I said I was interested in South Africa's spectacular economic development. My experience with the South African government, incidentally, left me with a very dubious view of professional "codes of ethics" that require a blanket condemnation of deception in social research. My own code of ethics agrees with the principle of informed consent for *individuals,* but not for organizations, firms, or governments. These entities do not command any respect or loyalty in my view. In any case, my South African research was one long series of acts of deception of the government, especially the police, who were frequently on my tail. On several occasions, I was stopped by the police for being in African "locations" or "reserves" where I was not supposed to be without a permit. (But the permit would have been refused if my intent had been known.) I usually got out of that by claiming to be the innocently lost American, rather naive about South African folkways.

Attendance at Liberal Party or Congress meetings, while still legal, invited police suspicion, tailing, and questioning. This, in turn, opened my eyes to the collusive relationship between the South African police and U.S. diplomatic authorities. Within days of such an encounter with the

Special Branch, the American vice-consul in Durban expressed a desire to see me, ostensibly for a formality of passport renewal. In a seemingly social conversation, he asked me what I was doing in Durban, and soon the direction of his questions made it clear that he was checking up on me at the behest of the South African police.

Many of my colleagues were under much greater strain than I was. Fatima Meer and Leo Kuper, for example, were under constant surveillance. Daily, they faced the possibility of arrest and indefinite detention without trial, "banning," internal exile, or house searches rather than merely expulsion as I did. The state of siege that lasted for months after Sharpeville was not conducive to intellectual serenity. The university campus overlooked the ghastly African slum of Cato Manor, and the hillcrest was constantly patrolled by Saracen armored cars and police and army vans, so that the campus itself was under virtual military occupation.

My closest brush with actual physical danger was when I joined, notebook in hand, a demonstration of some 10,000 to 15,000 African workers marching from Cato Manor to the Central Prison to demand the release of political prisoners. The march was amazingly peaceful and disciplined. I was one of perhaps five or six white faces in a black ocean, and yet no hostility was shown to me. Quite the contrary; I was accepted as a sympathetic journalist. The crowd marched through affluent white neighborhoods without a single act of aggression or vandalism. As we reached the downtown area (next, in fact, to the non-white campus of the university), the crowd faced a cordon of police. After giving a perfunctory order to disperse, the police started shooting into the crowd, killing two and wounding a dozen. I only heard the shots because I was in the rear of the crowd, around a street corner. But I had just witnessed a routine act of police repression, virtually a weekly occurrence in South Africa.

Our university classes were infiltrated with government spies. Because of Leo Kuper and Fatima Meer, the entire Sociology Department was a target for police suspicion. Naturally, this situation had a dampening effect on intellectual exchange in the classroom. I lectured mostly about American race relations, but the implications for South Africa were nonetheless quite clear.

Despite these strained circumstances, I retain fond memories of my teaching days in Durban. The intense interest and motivation of students, especially of the Indian and African students many of whom came from desperately impoverished circumstances, was a nice change from bloated and blasé American students. And among my undergraduates were two who became close friends and distinguished colleagues. One was Edna Miller (later Bonacich), who at that time wanted to go on to a

With Heribert Adam, Vancouver, B.C., Canada, 1984. Photo by Kogila Moodley Adam.

B. Litt. at Oxford, but whom I convinced to become my research assistant. After that, I talked her into doing a Ph.D. in sociology at Harvard. She was thus my first professionally successful student and I can claim a major role in turning her away from English literature and toward sociology. The other was Kogila Moodley who later married Heribert Adam and got a Ph.D. in anthropology at the University of British Columbia where she now teaches. They later visited us in Nairobi (in 1968), and we have been close friends ever since. Heri and Kogi settled in Vancouver and their proximity to Seattle has enabled us to sustain a never-ending dialogue on South Africa that is punctuated by friendly, creative disagreements. The relationship became even closer when Kogi's younger sister, Subithra, became in turn my doctoral student at the University of Washington.

One little episode involving my colleague Fatima Meer is also worth relating because it reveals another facet of South Africa. Both she and I were young lecturers in Leo Kuper's department. Irmi and I lived in a modest little brick cottage at the foot of the hill from the university, and I had invited Fatima in for a cup of afternoon tea (already a breach of social etiquette, but luckily our immediate neighbors, also young university staff members, were liberals). Then I offered Fatima a lift home, since she had no car. She accepted but suggested that Irmi join us. I assumed that, being a Muslim, she did so on grounds of propriety, though I was a bit surprised to find her so "traditional," knowing her politics.

I soon discovered that her reason was altogether different. Until 1985, South Africa had an infamous law (one of many) called the Immorality Act. It punished with up to seven years of imprisonment heterosexual relations between whites and non-whites. (Homosexual relations were not covered, presumably because they could not sully the Herrenvolk's bloodstream.) In fact, a mere *intent* to have sexual relations constituted sufficient grounds for conviction. The South African etiquette of race relations did provide a loophole for whites and non-whites of opposite sex to sit safely in the same vehicle. (White "masters" frequently took their African servant "girls" along to go shopping, for example, or to escort white children as "nannies.") The rule was that the non-white woman had to sit on the back seat of the car. Otherwise, South African courts interpreted sitting side by side as evidence of intent to have sexual intercourse and, therefore, an offense under the Immorality Act. In the case at hand, it would have been inconceivable for Fatima to sit in the back seat of my two-door Volkswagen while I sat alone in front. Irmi's presence resolved the dilemma. I still asked Fatima to sit next to me in front, as our guest, while Irmi sat in the back. Thus, we were again violating etiquette. Indeed, when a traffic policeman saw that shocking sight, I noticed in my rearview mirror that he was making a dash for his motorcycle along the curb. He thought he had a good Immorality Act pinch, until he saw Irmi's blonde hair through the car's rear window and desisted.

Our car was also an unforeseen source of embarrassment. I had bought what I thought was a common and inconspicuous car, a beige Volkswagen beetle. It turned out that this was the official model and color of Special Branch (secret police) vehicles. Needless to say, its appearance in African and Indian areas did not exactly awaken people's trust.

I also had to live down my surname, as I had many Afrikaner namesakes (usually spelled "van den Berg"), not the least embarrassing of whom was a brigadier and chief of the South African police! Most people naturally assumed that I was an Afrikaner and, therefore, a racist. (By an extraordinary long shot, our next door neighbor, Johann van den Berg, who was indeed an Afrikaner, was also one of the perhaps one hundred Afrikaner members of the Liberal Party in the whole of South Africa!) I have had to live with that stereotype long after leaving South Africa. Many people assumed that I was an Afrikaner and therefore, by definition, a bigot. Anything that I might have said to the contrary was dismissed as deceit and insincerity, and the most tortuous imputations of motives were repeatedly read into the plainest, most universalistic anti-racist statements. Over the years, I learned to stop caring about what most people thought of my politics. The problem is especially acute in America where the level of ideological sophistication is often quite low, even among academics. Most Americans get irritated if you fail to fit into their stereotypic, uni-dimensional conception of either a "liberal" or a "conservative," and they will force you into the category opposite to the one they claim membership in. The more annoyed they get at their own failure to understand your position, the more extreme their ascription of political labels. I have gotten used to being described simultaneously as a dangerous ultra-radical and a crypto-fascist. One of the more imaginative labels created to describe my politics has been that of "right-wing Leninist"!

All of this used to disturb me, but I now find it amusing. I have stopped expecting either rationality or honesty in political discussions. When I occasionally encounter both I am pleasantly surprised. Most Americans who react to politics do so at the level of emotional knee jerks. And that only describes the intellectual minority who can be said to have any kind of ideology at all. This critical view of American politics has been exacerbated by prolonged contact with other societies with a much higher level of political consciousness and sophistication, of which South Africa is a prime example.

My activities in South Africa were split between half-time teaching (for a salary of £50—at the time $140—a month!) and travel and field work. Every break in the academic calendar was taken up by long car trips, the two principal ones to the Cape and to the Transvaal, with extended stays in Cape Town and Johannesburg, and shorter ones at most important points in between: the Transkei, Grahamstown, East London, Port Elizabeth, Paarl, Stellenbosch, Kimberley, Bloemfontein, Pretoria, Zululand, Swaziland, Mozambique, and Lesoto. We even took a fortnight for an excursion into Zimbabwe (then Southern Rhodesia) to visit Bulawayo, the Wankie Game Reserve, the Zambezi Falls, and the impressive ruins of Zimbabwe and Kilwa. We found Rhodesia to be a miniature South Africa, with an essentially identical social and political structure but a much less developed economy.

The impoverished High Commission Territories, as Swaziland, Lesoto (Basutoland), and Botswana (Bechuanaland) were then known, were indistinguishable from the Transkei, Zululand, and other South African "native reserves," except for size. They presented the same picture of "colorful desolation": a beautiful landscape ravaged by overpopulation, overgrazing, and erosion. Their population of old people, women, and pot-bellied, undernourished children, whose fathers were working in the South African mines, showed the same picture of rural destitution. There, if anywhere, was dependency theory in action: a sub-subsistence agriculture subsidizing the sub-subsistence wages paid by the capitalist mining economy. The native reserves, now restyled as Bantustans, are in a direct sense the cheap nurseries for the urban sub-proletariat. They spare the employers the costs of the biological reproduction of the labor force.

The urban areas were even grimmer—first, because the social reality of the city was starkly undisguised by the gorgeous natural backdrop of the South African landscape as it is in the countryside; and second, because the juxtaposition of white affluence and black poverty is physically much closer. At that time, the government was in the initial phases of implementing the Group Areas Act, a blueprint for erasing the last residual "black spots" from the map of "white" South Africa.

The program consisted essentially, under the guise of slum clearance, of expropriating and bulldozing the few desirable and centrally located areas where some urban Africans, Coloureds, and Asians had acquired some free-hold tenure. Another important "fringe benefit" of group areas was the expropriation of the small Indian merchant class. Non-white areas would then be redeveloped for white occupancy, and new "model townships" like Soweto and countless others would be built to accommodate the displaced non-whites. It is true that some (but by no means all) of the "black spots" were squalid shanty towns, totally neglected by their respective municipalities and lacking paved roads, electricity, and even, in some cases, piped water. Municipal neglect was a long-standing tradition for the areas occupied by non-whites. Some of these shanty towns, such as Cato Manor in Durban, were densely packed conglomerations of corrugated iron shacks, each housing ten or twelve people in an approximately equal number of square meters. Those areas were often permanently bathed in a haze of atmospheric pollution created by the charcoal burners used for cooking, and some of these slums were veritable antechambers of hell. The shanties were connected by a maze of narrow alleys, where criminal bands of *tso-tsis* ("thugs") roamed almost at will. The police, who were also frequent visitors, intimidated people, raided the illegal bars, and checked people's passes, but did not protect them against crime.

It is also true that the hundreds of square kilometers of "model townships" built by the government since the 1960s, although grim and starkly ugly by any civilized standards, represent a vast *material* improvement over what they replaced. But the motivation for the operation was not altruistic. The stated aims of this gigantic scheme were, first, to deprive non-whites of their few residual free-hold rights in the so-called white areas; second, to increase the degree of physical segregation between whites and blacks in urban areas; and, third, to facilitate police control over urban blacks. The government built what were in effect controlled camps for urban blacks. These were (and still are) surrounded by wire-mesh fences; subject to curfew regulations and pass control; sprinkled with strategically located and fortified police stations; and carefully designed to have wide, rectilinear (though unpaved) thoroughfares with clear fields of fire and ample maneuvering room for armored personnel carriers.

These camps, of which Soweto (for "south-western townships"), 60 kilometers from Johannesburg, is but one of the largest, were meant to house only a limited number of African families and, then, only on a supposedly temporary basis, as long as the adults in the family were working for whites. The overwhelming purpose of providing urban housing for blacks was to furnish the black *labor* needed by white-controlled mining and industry. Anyone else was deemed "redundant" and forcibly sent back to the "Bantu homelands," *including* the wives and children of employed workers, unless they could document a decade of continuous urban residence and employment. Mothers even had to send their children back "home," to some rural dustbowl, after age 5 or 6. This systematic, brutal disruption of black family life under the guise of the "migratory labor system" and the insistence that 87 percent of the land area of South Africa belongs to the 15 percent of the population who are white is perhaps the most bestial feature of apartheid and is still fully enforced, despite all the talk of "liberalization." By any civilized standards, apartheid is a crime against humanity, only one step below genocide. It attacks and destroys the very fabric of intimate relations between spouses and kinsmen. It simply cannot leave a decent human being unmoved or uninvolved.

Some seven months of my stay in South Africa were spent doing a detailed community study of the sugar town of Tongaat, some 35 kilometers north of Durban. Edna Bonacich was my assistant, and the study was published in 1964 under the title of *Caneville, the Social Structure of a South African Town*. With a population of some 10,000, only a few hundred of whom were white and some 70 percent of East Indian background, Tongaat is certainly not typical of South Africa. It is, I believe, the only town anywhere in Africa to have an Indian majority (except for the artificial ghettos created by the Group Areas Act). It is also unusual in that it is a company town dominated by a single firm and it is connected to an industry that is rather marginal to the South African economy.

The study was primarily concerned with the effect of industrial paternalism on the social stratification of this extremely diversified community. Among the 10,000 people were represented four "racial" groups, segregated by South African legislation; a dozen or so languages (English, Afrikaans, Zulu, Xhosa, Swazi, Shangaan, Sotho, Hindi, Urdu, Gujarati, Tamil, Telugu) belonging to four major linguistic families; three major world religions (Christianity, Islam, and Hinduism), and among Hindus, some 80 castes and sub-castes (of mostly residual significance, however). In short, this was a sociologist's dream and an anthropologist's nightmare. Obviously, I could not get at any depth into the cultural world of all these communities, nor did I attempt to do so. Mine was a study essentially of the relations of power and of production that linked these groups in a plural society controlled paternalistically by a small English capitalist class.

My access was relatively free and unimpeded, as the patriarch controlling the Tongaat Sugar Company had given me the green light, largely, I think, on the basis of what I would describe as a working misunderstanding. I openly stated my liberal politics and my opposition to racial discrimination. But then Mr. Saunders, a scion of one of the arch-conservative, English, Natalian, United Party families saw himself as a benevolent despot and an upright opponent of apartheid. He saw no conflict in our perspectives, and I felt under no obligation to disabuse him. The company's blessing was obviously a mixed one. It opened all doors, but it also shut many mouths. I had to spend several weeks gradually gaining people's confidence and friendship. With Africans, I largely failed, with a half-dozen exceptions. Most Africans were non-literate Pondo (a Xhosa sub-group) migrant laborers who spoke no English, only stayed for a few months at a time, and had ample reason to distrust anyone with a white face. I also largely failed with the dominant whites, again with a half-dozen exceptions. The principal reason was that I found their smugness and bigotry so abrasive that it was difficult to hide my prejudice against them. I delegated the unpleasant job of interviewing them mostly to Edna Bonacich, who shared my politics, but whose Natalian upbringing equipped her with savoir faire in handling whites.

For my part, I concentrated on the Indian community, or, more accurately, communities. This was by far the largest and the most complex and interesting sector of the town. The study of Tongaat thus led to a wider, long-standing academic interest of mine and of Edna Bonacich. Ever since then, we have both been vitally interested in the comparative study of "middleman minorities" and, in my case, especially of the Indian diaspora. A few years later, in Kenya, I had an opportunity to reactivate that research interest.

APARTHEID

The complex and subtle factionalism of Tongaat Indians was also a good introduction to the politics of field work. The main cleavage was between Muslims and Hindus, and I was almost inevitably drawn into the Hindu community, which I found both congenial and hospitable. Again, it was difficult to hide my sympathies, which, in turn, made my relations with Muslims somewhat stiffer and more formal. This bias, too, is one that has accompanied me for the rest of my life. For example, in Nigeria, I felt much more comfortable in the largely non-Muslim south than in the solidly Muslim north.

As a non-religious person, I find all forms of deeply committed religiosity uncomfortable to live with and difficult to understand. But I can easily respect and ignore an internalized religiosity that makes no attempt to proselytize and passes no public derogatory judgment on the behavior of those outside the fold. Religion, I feel, should remain in the private domain and not be worn on one's sleeve. Thus, I found a highly tolerant, private, non-proselytizing religion like Hinduism easy to live with. With Hindus I was an outsider, but not an infidel. With Muslims, I would often be treated to a short condescending lecture on how, as a Christian (which they assumed me to be), I was a notch higher than a heathen, but that, of course, the path to raising my status through the True Faith was wide open. Hindus took it for granted that I was not one of them, but no one seemed to mind. All I needed to do was fulfill my *kharma* as a decent human being. Fair enough, I thought.

My reception in the Hindu community was indeed warm and hospitable. Not a day of field work passed without my ingesting eight or ten cups of sweet tea enriched with condensed milk. It was totally unthinkable to turn this bounty down. Both within the context of South African race relations and Hindu caste relations, commensality was one of the main tests of social equality and acceptance. Besides tea (which, ever since, I have drunk the Indian way, with plenty of milk and sugar), my Tongaat field work exposed me to the incredibly wide and subtle range of Indian cuisine. I became a regular guest at humble family meals and at elaborate wedding feasts, sampling super-hot Tamil non-vegetarian dishes one day, Gujarati vegetarian delicacies cooked in ghee the next. When I returned home in the evening, Irmi could tell by the tell-tale spots on my shirt with whom I had eaten that day, for I never completely mastered the art of eating daintily with three fingers of my right hand. (As a genetic southpaw, I am handicapped here, and I knew better than to use a left hand supposedly reserved for more lowly functions!)

Every three months, the sword of Damocles hung over my head, in the form of my South African visa renewal. Once I shared the queue in the passport office with Alan Paton who had to renew his passport in order to accept a prize in the United States. He whispered in my ear that he doubted his passport would be renewed; but, to his surprise, the employee extended the validity. Within hours of his returning home, the police were at his door ordering him to surrender his passport. The lowly clerk in the passport office had not recognized that dangerous enemy of the state, but someone higher up quickly remedied his oversight. I was luckier; my visa was routinely extended to the time of my final departure in December 1961.

A few months before we left the freshly baked Republic of South Africa (the Republican referendum and ceremonial exit of South Africa from the Commonwealth also took place, to much fanfare, during our stay), we sadly escorted Hilda Kuper and her daughters to the Durban railway station, along with some fifty or so other friends. Leo had already left a few weeks before. The Kupers and we had, in the meantime, become close friends, and we knew that Durban would be sadly impoverished by their departure. Like much of the moral and intellectual cream of South Africa, the Kupers had been hounded into exile. Even their departure was a pointed reminder of the world they were leaving. They were taking the train to Johannesburg and then a plane to England and the United States. The South African Railways are one of the fiercest bastions of apartheid, as railroad personnel are drawn mostly from lowly skilled, semi-literate Afrikaners who are otherwise unemployable. (The South African police is their other major employment outlet.) Everything in the railways is segregated: coaches, waiting rooms, platforms, ticket windows—you name it. The farewell party for the Kupers had to split at the entrance of the railway station. Only their white friends could escort them to the train platform.

Our own last moments on South African soil were anxious ones. We had booked a cheap charter flight on South African Airways, but we were to pay dearly for our parsimony. First, the departure was delayed by nearly a full day. As we were trying to catch a wink in the spartan departure hall of Jan Smuts Airport and to keep a restless 7-month-old infant fed and pacified, I kept wondering whether, at the last minute, our baggage would be searched and two years of field notes and documents confiscated. I had taken the precaution of mailing duplicates of some of the most important papers ahead of us, but that too was risky and expensive in the days before cheap copying. (Our total income for two years, incidentally, was about $11,000, which included my teaching salary; two scholarships; and a little research grant for my Tongaat study. Out of that we had to cover all our travel expenses.)

Finally, our plane, a four-propeller DC-6, took off, to our intense relief. It was December 16, Blood River Day! We felt we had vanquished not the

Hilda and Leo Kuper, Los Angeles, 1985.

Zulu but the Afrikaners! But our troubles were not over yet. The old airplane began to develop one trouble after another, mostly in its air-conditioning and heating systems. We were delayed several hours at Entebbe (on the very site of the 1976 Israeli rescue mission), and I can testify to the acute discomfort of that particular airport. The attempt to fix the air conditioning having failed, we proceeded north and spent some eight or ten hours shivering over the Sahara, with a hungry and squirming Eric. At Benghazi, Libya, another fruitless delay ensued, during which we were treated to a display of exceptionally surly behavior by the Libyan authorities, who did not take kindly to this unscheduled landing by a "racist" airplane.

With a still unfixed heating system, we shivered across the Mediterranean to Rome, where another fruitless attempt at repair was made. Several hours later, not daring to fly over the Alps, where we might have become frostbitten, we made a detour over the Côte d'Azur and finally arrived at our destination, Düsseldorf, fifty-six hours after leaving Johannesburg. Our South African ordeal was over.

CHAPTER 9

Scrambling Up the Academic Ladder

Irmi and I felt we deserved a few months of rest and recuperation in Europe. It would have been almost impossible to find academic employment in the United States in January. Besides, through a slight breakdown in contraceptive technology, Irmi was pregnant again. We wanted another child, but not so soon. We felt it best to stay in Europe until her expected August delivery; meanwhile I would explore American job openings and work on my South African material. My Tongaat monograph was already written, but the "big book" was, as yet, just a chapter outline. We bought another Volkswagen, made the rounds of relatives and in-laws in Germany, Belgium, and France, and settled down in Paris for six months.

This was an occasion to renew my old ties, especially with Balandier, Bastide, and Lévi-Strauss, all of whom had been promoted into more prestigious chairs during the intervening years. Balandier had succeeded Gurvitch in the main Sorbonne chair of sociology; Bastide now had a Sorbonne chair on American civilizations; and Lévi-Strauss, whose resonance had by then reached the literary salons, was now holding forth on the analysis of myths at the Collège de France to a mixed audience of elegant young women and *clochards.* Balandier secured a temporary post for me as *maître de conférences,* and I was to give a series of lectures on South Africa.

UNESCO was also quite interested in my South African work. Its headquarters were in Paris and, over the preceding decade, it had sponsored a lot of research on race, mostly in Brazil. Alfred Métraux held an important post at UNESCO: director of social science research. I had known him only slightly in 1956–1957, as my interest in South America was than distinctly secondary to my African concerns. He invited me to a conference near Munich in 1962, was impressed with my presentations, and tried to interest me in applying for his job. He was then already a sadly discouraged man (indeed he committed suicide not long after). In any case, he was tired of his UNESCO job and was concerned that his successor be academically respectable and not a political appointment. He warned me that, because I was a U.S. citizen, the cards were stacked against me. I applied for a job, which had a tax-free salary of some $12,000—at the time a truly fabulous sum for a young academic—but, as Métraux had predicted, nothing came of it, although I was, in his eyes, the most qualified candidate.

Meanwhile, Allport was at work trying to find me employment in the United States. At that time, most academic jobs were not advertised, at least not the good ones, and the "old-boy network" was alive and thriving. Still, it was a hindrance not to be on the spot for interviews. Assistant professors were, however, sometimes hired sight unseen, and, in the seller's market of the early 1960s, I soon had two offers to choose from. The alternatives were Columbia with a nine-hour teaching load and a salary of $6,500, or Wesleyan with a six-hour load for $7,200. The prospect of genteel poverty with two infants in New York and of academic exploitation with little prospect of tenure at Columbia was not appealing. Neither was Wesleyan, of which I had barely heard, but at least Middletown, Connecticut, was survivable on $7,200, and we thought that it might not be a bad base from which to look for better alternatives.

Our months in Paris were pleasant and interesting. The Algerian War was winding down as de Gaulle had started the negotiation process in Evian, but the military revolt in Algiers and the Organisation de l'Armée Secrète (OAS), the swan's song of the reactionary *pieds noirs,* ensured that the French exit from Algeria would be accompanied by a big bang. Indeed, the bang reached Paris, as usual a hotbed of political ferment that involved some prominent academics. Jacques Soustelle, in particular, was ostracized by his colleagues for siding with the OAS, which, during these months, was liberally sprinkling Paris with plastic explosives. One charge exploded some 200 meters from my grandmother's apartment, giving her a terrible fright. She was not alone in consigning the OAS to hell. The entire French metropolitan population was, by that time, heartily sick of the war and wanted a political settlement at any cost. The OAS's totally inept campaign of terror backfired and alienated even conservatives. The Sorbonne's political temperature was, as usual, very close to the boiling point, but now the demonstrations came mostly from the left. The right had ceased to be respectable. *Algérie française* was now the cry of the ultras, a mere handful of last-ditch fanatics. The game was over, even though the French had won the war militarily. Only stupid army officers and settlers had failed to see it. Soon a million *pieds noirs* (including, incidentally, much of the cream of Sephardic Jewry) were to flood Corsica, Marseille, Lyon, and the rest of France. French colonialism in Africa was over. The era of neo-colonialism had begun.

By July 1962, we were vacationing at my Aunt Solange's summer villa in Vierville, Normandy (the Omaha Beach of D day, next to the vast Arromanches American military cemetery). Eric was now a highly mobile 15-month-old toddler, but was still in diapers. Irmi, very pregnant, began to hemorrhage, nearly two months before term. We decided to drive back to Bad Kreuznach where her obstetrician was, and the next few weeks were full of anxious moments. The German obstetrician decided on an eighth-month cesarian. Thus, Oliver was born on July 21, a mere 15 months after his brother, Eric. Though the two of them now get along famously and share, among other things, a passion for fishing, they were to spend the next three or four years in nearly non-stop quarrels. Their noisy disputes over toys and the like were to punctuate most of my attempts to get some writing done. The end result was, however, amply rewarding, a powerful argument against infanticide.

I left Irmi in Bad Kreuznach with the two boys and departed for the U.S. to prepare for their arrival. I shipped our car and household goods from Antwerp and flew to New York, arriving at Wesleyan in early September in time to furnish the apartment that the university was renting to us. Soon after, Irmi arrived with the two boys, dead tired, after another harrowing charter flight by propeller plane that was delayed many hours in Reykjavik.

Both Irmi and I took an instantaneous dislike to Wesleyan. The very afternoon of her arrival, the president was holding his ritual garden party to open the academic year. My department head had let me know that this was definitely a command performance, especially for incoming assistant professors and their spouses. A mere matter of physical exhaustion was no excuse. The college would provide a baby-sitter and thus deprive us of the only acceptable excuse. I practically had to carry Irmi over and take her through a line of some 150 or 200 faculty hands to shake in "welcome." After an hour or so of this bad imitation of an English garden party, the level of inebriation of the senior faculty was rising noticeably. What was even more astonishing was that this intoxication was produced by a California sherry, the only alcoholic beverage being served. I judged that a situation that would drive so many to alcoholic stupor with so little provocation was not a happy one. Before the afternoon was over, one of my senior colleagues was so incapacitated by drink that his wife asked me to drive him home. As I had walked the 500 or 600 meters between our flat and the president's house, I had to fetch my car before I could oblige.

These inauspicious beginnings were, alas, sad portents of things to come. Wesleyan was the epitome of pretentiousness. First, its title of "university" was rank presumption. To be sure, Wesleyan gave a few master's degrees to bored faculty wives, but it was clearly an undergraduate college and a small one at that. Total enrollment barely amounted to 1,000 students. Second, though it prided itself on its elite status, Wesleyan was, in fact, principally getting students turned down by Yale, Princeton, Columbia, Harvard, Dartmouth, Amherst, Brown, and a few other snob-appeal colleges. It was, in short, a haven for snubbed snobs. Many students had a superficial veneer of education acquired in New England prep schools, but, for the most part, they were anti-intellectual, blasé playboys whose college life centered on fraternities, football games, and weekend dates with women from the neighboring female colleges such as Smith, Mt. Holyoke, and Wellesley.

Rowdy, inebriated brawls rocked every fraternity every Friday and Saturday evening. Not only were the fraternity houses interspersed with college faculty housing (we had one within 50 meters of our flat), but the faculty were expected to take turns chaperoning the fraternity parties. As an inducement to join in the revelry, the fraternity in question gave the faculty chaperone a bottle of the liquor of his choice. In exchange for this bribe, the professor was to douse himself into an indulgent, unseeing stupor.

Third, faculty-student relationships were predicated on a paternalistic model that perpetuated infantilism rather than promoted intellectual growth. The faculty were supposed to be available to the students, because access was what the students' parents were paying for. In effect, the faculty were much like Greek slaves hired by rich parents to impart a semblance of education to a horde of young barbarians, who, for the most part, could not care less. The 10 or 15 percent of the students who *did* want to learn, on the other hand, considered you to be on call fourteen or fifteen hours a day, roughly from 8 A.M. to 10 P.M.

In self-defense, we did not get a telephone, but again my department head soon let me know that this was unheard of. If it was the expense that stopped me, he suggested, he would be glad to pay my telephone subscription, but a telephone I must have. I was adamant on that score, but little good did it do me. Students simply came to ring my doorbell, though probably in smaller numbers than would have telephoned.

Fourth, the absence of female students not only made for a much duller campus for faculty and students alike; it also created a totally artificial milieu in which student preoccupation with finding dates in the women's colleges of the region and driving to and from their chosen playmates took precedence over all other activities, except perhaps sports. Students started preparing for their weekend expeditions on Thursday afternoon and needed Monday to recuperate from their hangovers and sleeplessness. They were intellectually alive on Tuesday and Wednesday.

Fifth, town-gown relations approached class warfare. The college, located on a hill along High Street, overlooked a run-down New England textile mill town devastated by a succession of economic crises. The principal factory still in operation was a tire plant, which liberally belched its malodorous fumes over the neighboring slums and the dilapidated commercial main street. Contacts between the town and the college took mainly the form of resentful stares between high school and college students during occasional encounters in cafés or stores and noisy demonstrations of class resentment by high school kids driving their jalopies along High Street. The university was clearly a gilded ghetto made more painfully obvious by the ambient decay, poverty, and unemployment.

Lastly, and most difficult to take, was the combination of pretentiousness and mediocrity that was Wesleyan's hallmark. On a five-point scale, Wesleyan was clearly third-rate. The sources of this mediocrity were multiple. Wesleyan lived in the shadow of a great university (Yale, a half-hour away by car) and necessarily suffered by comparison. But there were a number of internal causes that made it much worse than it need have been, and many of them had to do with its grossly inflated self-image.

The library, with its 400,000 or so books, was, like that of most elite liberal arts colleges, about one-fifth the minimum necessary size to constitute a decent research collection. Had it not been for nearby Yale, I would have suffered intellectual paralysis. The Wesleyan library could best be described as a vast Swiss cheese: blobs of substance pitted with spheres of void. The collections in some specialized subjects, say, early Byzantium or eighteenth-century Portuguese literature, were surprisingly good, while others (e.g., the whole of Africa, when I arrived) were terra incognita. The islands of strength were mute mementos to bright young assistant professors, long since departed, who had to build up the collection in their specialty to survive, but who quickly found the place so stifling that they departed after one or two years. The library did not have a specialized staff and the faculty were expected to act as acquisition librarians. I spent many hours trying to build up the African collection, almost from scratch, and, by the time the books were catalogued, I was gone. My story was far from unique, the head librarian told me. He described his collection as a graveyard of assistant professors.

The inadequacy of the library was matched by the departments. Averaging five or six professors, they were, with two or three exceptions, far too spotty to offer a balanced and diversified undergraduate program, and certainly not one that would leave its graduates equipped to enter a first-rate graduate program. Wesleyan was in effect a finishing school for young gentlemen. It gave a reasonably decent education in music, English literature, economics, and government among the social sciences, and perhaps in one or two additional fields; but its natural sciences were a joke, as were foreign languages, psychology, sociology (I was the first sociologist in Wesleyan history), anthropology (there was one anthropologist, only tolerated because he was an ethnomusicologist), and most other disciplines. Wesleyan *did* manage to attract many good assistant professors. For example, my cohorts included historian Harvey Dyck, and political scientist, Nelson Polsby, both of whom soon left Wesleyan for Toronto and Berkeley respectively. But any research-oriented scholar quickly realized that salvation was only to be achieved by a precipitous exit. Few assistant professors with any drive lasted longer than two years. I lasted the nine months of my first academic year.

The pretentiousness of Wesleyan came through in its response to outside offers. When the State University of New York at Buffalo offered me an associate professorship with a light teaching load and a salary nearly double that of Wesleyan ($12,000 to Wesleyan's $7,200), my dean responded that Wesleyan never even *considered* its assistant professors for tenure until after four or five years; furthermore, the State University of New York was not in the same league as Wesleyan and called for no serious counter-offer at all. But everyone was pleased with the good job I was doing at Wesleyan; I could count on a $1,000 raise the next year, and my prospects for tenure in another five years looked favorable if I kept up the good work. In one respect, Wesleyan was right, though not quite in the direction it meant. Buffalo and Wesleyan were *not* in the same league. Buffalo was second rate; Wesleyan, third.

The outcome of such an attitude was that the faculty was sharply split between a bright, upwardly mobile junior faculty (kept out, incidentally, of all significant decision-making even at the departmental level) who revolved through Wesleyan with something like a 40 percent turnover per year, and a largely unproductive senior faculty. The end result of this attrition was that only the dregs of each assistant professor class survived to get tenure at Wesleyan. Wesleyan prided itself on only promoting one assistant professor out of eight or ten, just as in the Ivy League. What it had not yet come to realize was that it was promoting its *bottom* 10 percent. Nor was the trend a new one. Woodrow Wilson was Wesleyan's great man. He had taught political science at Wesleyan . . . for one year as an assistant professor, before going to Princeton.

The only island of quality (and one of the main sources of income) at Wesleyan was the University Press. By far the largest branch of it published the immensely profitable "Weekly Reader" for grammar schools and high schools across the country. The much smaller scholarly side of the operation published my first two books, *Caneville* (1964) and *South Africa, A Study in Conflict* (1965). The latter only took off two years later, however, when the University of California Press published a paperback edition. Anyway, it was a nice feeling at the end of my Wesleyan year to have the bulk of my South African data all written up and accepted for publication.

The move from Wesleyan to Buffalo was an easy one and an obvious step up. For the first time, I earned a salary that ensured a comfortable life-style, even with two toddlers growing out of clothes and shoes almost as fast as we could buy them. Made cautious by our Wesleyan experience, we rented a flat (rather than bought a house), the upstairs of a duplex owned by an upper-lower class Italian-American family, in an Archie Bunker–style neighborhood. Indeed, the site was historic: less than 100 meters from our flat, William McKinley, twenty-fifth president of the United States, stopped an assassin's bullet in 1901.

Ethnic stereotypes came to life with embarrassing regularity. Our new landlords were as caricaturally Italian as our manager in Cambridge had been situation-comedy Irish. Once a week or so, our landlady would treat us to an explosive tantrum dominated by her shrill voice and the crash of kitchen utensils against the walls. The presumed target of her projectiles was her husband, whom she called a lazy womanizing bum, but her aim must have been bad, as our landlord always emerged unscathed and unruffled. These outbursts would often break out on Sunday morning. About an hour later, the entire family, including the stereotypic half-dozen children, would file out in their best clothes, pile into their ostentatious, gas-guzzling chariot, and leave for a fashionably late High Mass at the neighborhood Catholic Church. Come to think of it, this was the last true "ethnic" neighborhood we inhabited in America, and all our subsequent locations have been pallid and non-descript by comparison.

One thing we did not escape in Buffalo was foul winter weather. The winter months were perhaps marginally warmer than in Connecticut or

Massachusetts, but they more than made up for it in precipitation. We had white Thanksgivings, Christmases, and Easters for two years in a row. From late November through mid-April, Buffalo streets were narrow canyons of black slush flanked by meter-high banks of bespattered snow. Galoshes ("rubbers" to some) were an indispensable article of clothing; snow chains were the mainstay of motoring; air travel was always a risky gamble with the weather. Indeed, any form of transport was misery for nearly half of the year.

The university had its problems, but it was a vast improvement over Wesleyan. The old University of Buffalo, a third-rate private institution, had just been gobbled up by the many-headed hydra that the State University of New York was fast becoming. The idea was to create a major university in New York State within a decade. This was done by buying the best possible faculty, by offering them low teaching loads and good working conditions, and by building or expanding campuses at breakneck speed. In addition to some fifty local four-year colleges, SUNY was to have three "flagships": Albany, Buffalo, and Stony Brook, and these were to rival Berkeley, Michigan, and Wisconsin, given time. Money was no object, or so it seemed for a while. In the end, the attempt failed. Only Stony Brook came within sight of academic distinction, and even *it* missed the mark by a sizeable margin.

Still, compared to Wesleyan, there was a recognition of what it took to make a real university: a bright research-oriented faculty with access to good libraries and laboratories. Students were not the pampered, bloated brats of the elite, but the industrious, upwardly mobile offspring of the working and middle classes. The faculty was there, not to bottle-feed them a cultural veneer between fraternity dances and football games, but to show them how to read and think between part-time jobs. Many, to be sure, had been badly miseducated, but most tried hard to make up for their deficiencies. The others sank and made room for the serious students. I have been repeatedly called an intellectual elitist because I always insisted on dedication, rigor, and disciplined effort from my students; but I have always detested teaching at *socially* elitist institutions. Much of American education has the worst of both worlds: social elitism and intellectual egalitarianism. My priorities and values are precisely the reverse. Hence, the great superiority of a Buffalo over a Wesleyan in my eyes.

The principal problem at Buffalo was that, due to the frantic pace of construction and expansion, everything was in shambles. The old campus was bursting at the seams for lack of buildings. The tiny library was being flooded under the tons of new books ordered by the expanding faculty; there simply was no shelf space to accommodate the new acquisitions. Office space was at such a premium that even full professors sometimes had to double up. My space consisted of about six square meters screened off from two secretaries by a flimsy opaque glass partition and well within earshot of a brisk student traffic. Sustained work was only possible at home, when Eric and Oliver would let me.

In the classroom, the situation was no better. Every lecture was delivered to the accompaniment of hammer blows, electric saws, compressor engines, and other instruments in the great symphony orchestra of campus construction. All this was irritating, but we put up with it in fairly good cheer because we felt it to be a temporary predicament and a necessary inconvenience on the way to a better future.

I was compensated for all this by the salary, which was great by the standards of the times, and the low teaching loads: two classes per semester, usually a graduate seminar one afternoon a week, and an undergraduate course meeting for three 50-minute sessions a week. That left much time for reading, writing, and research. During my two years at Buffalo I put together a reader, *Africa: Social Problems of Change and Conflict* (1965), in which I translated Balandier and Mercier into English for the first time and republished the work of many leading Africanists of the 1960s.

It was also in Buffalo that I wrote *Race and Racism* (1967), a short undergraduate text that I dashed off in six months. It was a comparison of race relations in Mexico, Brazil, the United States, and South Africa, from the "plural society" perspective. The approach, then considered radical, soon became mainstream, especially the thesis that the United States was, like South Africa, a "Herrenvolk democracy." Most subsequent attempts, in both Britain and the United States, to approach race and ethnic relations comparatively bear a trace of that book, as evidenced by the work of William Newman, E. K. Francis, Phillip Mason, Richard Schermerhorn, George Fredrickson, William Wilson, John Rex, and others.

Race and Racism not only threw my career into high gear, but was also the start of a long-standing relationship with the best commercial editor I ever knew. The recent death of Bill Gum was a sad blow to me. We were not only friends; we made a great team, so much so that I faithfully followed him from publisher to publisher. The imprints of my books read like a vita of Bill Gum: Wiley, Basic Books, and, lastly, Elsevier. Bill belonged to a vanishing species of editors. He had a flair for intellectual quality as his sociology lists at the above publishers clearly demonstrate, and he always took up the cause of his authors vis-à-vis his employer, the publisher. He meant it when he said he was interested in originality, even at the expense of sales. Quality always came first. His editorial hand was remarkably light; *not once* did he push me in a more commercial direction, even when the heat was on him from the publisher. Twice or three times, he was fired for being "too creative" and for pushing too hard for his stable of mavericks. I salute the memory of one of those rare figures: an honest intellect.

The amazing thing about Bill was that this discriminating connoisseur of knowledge hid behind the mischievous mask of a Southern bigot. He delighted in outraging others by violating intellectual taboos, and, in this respect, we were blood brothers. But his favorite ploy (which he would also use with me, just to watch me squirm, with a mischievous glint in his eyes) was to make outrageously racist remarks. We generally met at conventions; he was famous for organizing parties in his hotel suite, and he always took me out to a good dinner. Such was the favorite setting for his calculated ethnic "faux pas." Thus, when I complained about the slowness of the mail, he would retort, with a subtle exaggeration of his University-of-Virginia, *Gone-with-the-Wind* accent: "What do you expect with all these Negrahs in the post office? Half of them can't read." Then he would pause for a response, which was, of course, impossible without making a sanctimonious ass of oneself.

Anyway, I was glad that, after Bill Gum's death, his place in American sociology received recognition in the form of several prominent obituaries. I was also amused that all of them included a posthumous apology for his "tasteless" ethnic jokes. That sardonic iconoclast had unerringly discovered the supreme obscenity of American academia, and he enjoyed it to the hilt. The more shocked one was, the more delicious his pleasure. I am sure he would have relished these obituaries. So, here is to my favorite white cracker! May he enjoy his dry gin martinis to the heavenly choir of happy singing slaves!

The Sociology Department at Buffalo was very much of a mixed bag. Its chairman, Llewelyn Gross, was a genial, avuncular figure who had a genius for keeping everyone relatively happy and, what is more, talking to each other. This was no mean achievement in a department of some twenty members covering a rather broad intellectual and political spectrum. Among the other senior professors was Costas Yerakaris, a jovial Greek and excellent host who was a better cook than sociologist, and John Sirjamaki, a quiet, gentlemanly figure who had just come from Minnesota. My closest associates were Lionel Lewis, a fellow iconoclast and young Turk, Mark van de Vall, a Dutch industrial sociologist, and Marian Lockwood, a British sociologist of religion.

There was also a group of three youngish radicals, with whom I agreed on a number of political issues but not on their pedagogy of laxity. One day, to tease them, I planted in my colleagues' mailboxes the vita of a fictitious Polish sociologist as a candidate for one of our senior vacancies. I made him a Gomulka refugee of exactly the kind of anarcho-syndicalist politics to appeal to the New Left radicals, and I made up an impressive trilingual bibliography for him. Sure enough, they took the bait, and at the next departmental meeting they started pushing his candidacy.

Anthropology, too, had some very good people, especially Marvin Opler and George Trager. But much of the department was devastated by the ravages of alcoholism, an occupational disease of anthropologists it seems, particularly of Americanists who do their field work in societies where the intake of spirits accompanies every festive occasion. (Indeed, though I always managed to remain fairly sober, I could only remain so by turning down thousands of unwanted drinks in Mexico, Guatemala, Peru, and Bolivia.) At Buffalo, prospective candidates for a teaching position were taken to the faculty club for their rite of passage: they had to prove that they could still hold an intelligent talk after three martinis on an empty stomach. The Anthropology Department, by itself, accounted for some three-fourths of the bar clientele, day after day.

Among my students, a few stick in my mind. One of my best undergraduates, M. Kay Martin, went on to a Ph.D. in anthropology, a teaching career at UCSB, and a number of first-rate publications. Another, in a different and much sadder vein, was my first classroom casualty. He collapsed of an asthma attack during a seminar and died shortly thereafter. A third was an accomplished kleptomaniac and compulsive gambler. He supported his gambling by emptying his fellow students' pockets, but he also built himself a nice library by "borrowing" books from the faculty. Several young ladies offered to do *anything* for a change of grade, an opportunity that Wesleyan had denied me. I tried to make them understand that I preferred to be loved for myself. Finally, I had the novel experience of having a father phone me to make an appointment to discuss his daughter's grade. He must have thought that he was in a police precinct fixing a traffic ticket, because he bluntly took out his wallet and pulled out a $50 bill "for the kiddies." (The interview, at his insistence, had taken place in my home, and the "kiddies" provided audible background noise.)

Politically, two main issues preoccupied the campus. One was a stupid loyalty oath imposed on its teachers by the State of New York. With my anarchical contempt for loyalty oaths, I hardly thought the issue was worth fussing over, so I signed it as one of those ludicrous documents for which American government authorities show a great predilection, in the style of: "Are you or have you ever been a spy for the Soviet Union?" A group of colleagues wanted to test the oath in court, but, again, I hardly thought that it was worth my money in legal fees to prove the government stupid.

The other issue was far more important, and I did lend my support to collecting signatures and sponsoring advertisements in the *New York Times*. It concerned the embryonic protest movement against American involvement in Vietnam. To me, it was obvious that the United States was merely taking over from the French an absurd colonial war, which could not be won except by the virtual annihilation of the Indochinese population. In those days, I still had illusions that a reasoned presentation of evidence might sway government policy. In the 1980s, when I saw the same path of idiocy being followed in Central America, I had already lost any hope that reason might affect U.S. foreign policy.

In the heady days of the mid-1960s, and with my publications breaking out in quick succession, it was clear that I could do better than Buffalo. Two possibilities presented themselves in the early months of 1965. Dartmouth was one. I went there for interviews, and I enjoyed the Orozco murals in the library, but it was clear that Dartmouth was the same sort of place as Wesleyan, though perhaps one notch better. I had had my fill of "gentleman Cs" and sherry at the dean's. Some of my friends like my old Harvard classmate Bernie Segal and anthropologist Jim Fernandez were there and they liked it, but that did not convince me. Besides, Dartmouth was no way to get out of the snow.

Seattle was something else. I left a Buffalo blizzard to be interviewed at the University of Washington, and the Seattle drizzle that greeted me on arrival appeared almost sub-tropical. Seattle and Buffalo were of approximately equal size, but there the resemblance ended. And the comparison was not in Buffalo's favor. In addition to a mild climate, a magnificent hinterland, a spectacular city, and a manicured park for a campus, the University of Washington offered the intellectual setting of a first-rate institution, or, at least, something very close to it. UW was one of a score of leading large state universities that entered a period of rapid expansion after World War II and by the 1960s, had entered the big league—not quite at the level of Berkeley or Michigan perhaps, but not far behind.

For elusive reasons, the state of Washington has long had a better university than it deserved. Despite lagging academic salaries and periodic budget cuts by an obscurantist State Legislature, UW manages to retain a first-rate faculty. The physical attractions of the region help, of course, and we all have to suffer what I call the "Mount Rainier discount" from our pay checks. In 1965, when UW offered me $15,000 for a tenured associate professorship, the money looked quite good. Little did I know that, at age 32, I had reached the peak of my earning power. More than

With Irmgard, Bad Kreuznach, Germany, 1965.

twenty years later, I make marginally less in constant dollars. The only aspect of my finances that has improved in relative terms is the thirty-year, 5.25 percent mortgage on my house.

In any case, resigning from Buffalo was one of the easiest decisions of my life, as had been resigning from Wesleyan two years earlier. In the intervening summer (1965), we took a trip to Europe, where, besides the usual round of in-laws and relatives, we bought our fifth Volkswagen and drove it to Istanbul and back, via Prague, Belgrade, Sofia, and the Adriatic coast. This was our first trip in communist countries. We found the experience so depressing and restrictive that we have no wish to repeat it. The splendor of Baroque Prague was worth the trip, but the rest of Czechoslovakia looked like a movie set for a World War II film: economically stagnant, politically stifling, and culturally dead. The Sudetenland, emptied of its German population, was still largely vacant, and most farmsteads were in ruins. Yugoslavia was much more tolerable and did everything to attract tourists, but still the fate of Milovan Djilas and countless other intellectual dissidents made the tyrannical nature of the regime obvious to those who cared to look below the tourist scene.

SCRAMBLING UP THE ACADEMIC LADDER

Bulgaria is probably, along with Haiti, the most depressing country I have ever seen, because of its combination of tyranny and poverty. Perhaps the phrase "Third World Stalinism" captures the situation best. Sofia juxtaposes the grim ugliness of Soviet-inspired architecture with the squalor of a city with one foot in the Middle East. But the Middle East squalor had been sanitized and rendered flat, lifeless, and colorless. Thank goodness, there was Istanbul at the end of our trip. Taken as a whole, Istanbul is not a beautiful city, though it is intensely vibrant (especially after Sofia). But the individual monuments are like so many jewels scattered over a vast field of urban congestion and ugliness. The overwhelming beauty of Hagia Sophia, the marvels (and the Kitsch) of the Topkapi Museum, the great seventeenth-century mosques, the bazaar, the gorgeous Byzantine mosaics in the old churches are moving relics of 2,000 years of civilization.

Refreshed by our European holiday, we shipped our car to New York, flew over the Atlantic, and then crossed Canada by car on our way to Seattle. On arrival, we rented a spacious house near the university (for $135 a month!), and I happily settled into my new academic routine. My appointment was in sociology, but anthropology was in the same building (Savery Hall), and I quickly established very good ties with my fellow Africanists Simon Ottenberg and Edgar (Bud) Winans, and with Jim Watson. For the first time, I was in an American university with enough of a critical mass of faculty and students to sustain a small African studies program. The library, with its 2.5 million books, was quite adequate for research in almost any field.

The students were uneven in quality, but on the whole a notch above the ones in Buffalo. Both sociology and anthropology had well-established, thriving, well-funded graduate programs, and each department, with its faculty of some twenty members, was diversified enough to offer balanced graduate training. Only a handful of our graduate students were brilliant, but most were solid. In short, UW had the faculty, the students, and the facilities to conduct a real university-level operation.

Some construction was going on but not at the disruptive (and deafening) pace of Buffalo. Existing space was adequate enough to give all faculty members individual offices with telephones (then by no means a generalized luxury); even our TAs were well-lodged in individual cubicles. Our TAs' main complaint was that their offices were windowless. Full professors at Buffalo would have been delighted to swap with them, I told them to pacify them—unsuccessfully, of course. Social comparisons, I should have known as a sociologist, are always made upward. Downward comparisons serve no political purpose.

As I entered the Sociology Department, it was on the threshold of a drastic transformation. My first year was the last of an incumbency of over ten years by Bob Faris as chairman. George Lundberg had been in retirement since 1963 but his positivist shadow was long indeed. Stuart Dodd, one of those brilliant individuals trembling on the borderline between the genius and the inspired crackpot, was still active in his concern to reduce all human behavior to the universal laws of physics. He and Faris exerted a strong influence on Otto Larsen and Bill Catton (who was promoted the following year). Clarence Schrag and Calvin Schmid, two other senior professors, were both entirely in the mold of naive nineteenth-century positivism. Of the full professors, only Frank Miyamoto and Norman Hayner (who was on the verge of retirement) were of a broader and more flexible intellectual disposition.

Set against this old guard was a growing, but as yet totally powerless, group of associate and assistant professors pushing to widen the intellectual boundaries of the department and increasingly impatient with the rigid authoritarianism of Faris's chairmanship. Among the principal iconoclasts were Ernest (Tom) Barth, Dick Emerson, and Bill Chambliss, joined in 1965 by Ed Gross, Ron Akers, Bob Burgess, and myself. The critical mass now existed to start the sparks flying. Within a few months, Faris was relieved of his chairmanship and was succeeded by Frank Miyamoto. The old regime was over, and the department was now wide open to intellectual fresh air. Over the next five years we hired Travis Hirshi, Stan Lieberson, Phil Blumstein, Rodney Stark, Guenther Roth, Michael Hechter, Bill Kornblum, Dan Chirot, and others who completely changed the climate. Many of them have since left, and the 1971 appointment of Tad Blalock gave a newer version of methodological positivism a fresh lease on life, but the department was never the same again. The Sociology Department at Washington probably peaked in the early to mid 1970s and declined since for a combination of reasons to be examined later.

I was most certainly not the prime mover in unseating Faris. Indeed, by the time of my arrival, he had already managed to antagonize all but one or two members of his department. But Faris and I soon locked horns on an issue that further undermined his position. Faris had a notion that, unless we spent ten hours a week in the classroom, we did not earn our keep. He set himself up as an example by teaching a full load on top of his chairmanship, and he was adamant that we all do likewise. With a quarter system, this teaching load translated into six courses a year—two per quarter—each meeting five days a week. At most, one of them per year could be a graduate seminar meeting once a week. That load represented a large increase over what I taught at Buffalo, and it seemed out of line not only with other universities of the first rank but also with other departments at UW.

The issue came to a head when Faris insisted that, to fill my schedule, I split my large race relations class. I argued that no pedagogical argument could be made for two sections of 150 students as compared to one of 300, which was my proposed alternative. Faris' argument was that students benefitted from a smaller class and from an option of times and that I should be glad to have only one preparation for two classes. He did not tell me "no" point blank. Instead, he said he would think it over. Three days later, I received a three-line note saying that he had thought it over and had not changed his mind. Next, I raised the question at our faculty meeting. Such a public challenge was apparently unprecedented. Faris curtly cut off discussion by saying that, in any case, the question was out of his hands. The dean insisted, he said, that we carry the regular load. That assertion was a fatal mistake. Immediately after the meeting, I contacted the dean by telephone, and he confirmed what I had suspected: that uncompetitively high teaching loads were Faris' idea. At the next faculty meeting, I gave a verbatim report of my phone conversation with the dean, and a red-faced Faris took a couple of minutes to regain his composure. He never fully recovered from this public loss of face, and it took several years before we would exchange another word. Happily, Frank Miyamoto soon took over the chairmanship, and things went smoothly under his tactful, considerate, and gentle guidance.

In the summer of 1966, a marvellous opportunity presented itself to renew my collaboration with Nick Colby. He was just initiating his Ixil project in the Guatemala highlands (Department of El Quiché), and I obtained a small faculty research grant from UW to join him via Santa Fe, New Mexico, where he then resided. Because of the danger of guerrilla activities and the logistical difficulties of bringing young children into the field for a relatively short time, I left Irmi and the boys with Lore and her children, and Nick and I proceeded to Guatemala. Our plan was again to study ethnic relations between Ladinos and Indians, as we had in Chiapas seven years earlier, and with the same division of labor between us. Nick would concentrate on the Ixil and I on the Ladinos. Our findings were reported in a monograph published by the University of California Press, *Ixil Country, A Plural Society in Highland Guatemala* (1969), and in a couple of articles.

Chiapas and the adjacent Guatemala highlands present many similarities, so, in a general sense, the area had an air of familiarity. But from the literature, Guatemala had the reputation of representing a much more rigid (though non-racial) type of ethnic relations than Mexico and other Latin American countries. Some, such as John Gillin and Melvin Tumin, even used the term "caste" to refer to the supposedly unbreachable line dividing Indians and Ladinos. Our work demonstrated that the whole question of "passing" from one group to the other received very different answers depending on whether one focused on the local or the regional and national level. What looked like a rigid system from the point of view of the local community did not preclude a high rate of both assimilation and acculturation of Indians into the Ladino group at the national level. But an Indian had to leave his home to "pass." That tens of thousands did so was clear from the decennial census data. Many of these people, mostly men of working age, actually "commuted" between the Ladino and the Indian world, depending on whether they were at home or away at work.

This finding was but another illustration of a methodological point: the necessity to move away from the traditional anthropological focus on the local community treated as an isolate and to incorporate into one's analysis the larger regional framework. Nowadays, this perspective is taken completely for granted and has been extended even further to the international scene by "world system" theorists, but then it was still definitely a non-conventional approach in anthropology.

Our field headquarters were in the *municipio* of Nebaj, a small market town of some 5,000 people and one of three "urban" centers in the area occupied by some 45,000 speakers of Ixil (one of the twenty-eight living Maya languages). In Chiapas, virtually no Indians lived in town; however, in Ixil country, all three *municipios* had Indian majorities, though the Ladinos held disproportionate political and economic power. The main problem for Indians was the insufficiency of arable land under the double pressure of land appropriation by large (and often unproductive) *haciendas* and population explosion. Indian agriculture had become increasingly sub-subsistence over the preceding thirty or forty years, while cash crops like coffee, sugar, cotton, and bananas covered more and more land under a latifundiary system hiring "migrant" Indian workers at famine wages (about 75 cents a day). This was another clear illustration of dependency theory: the development of one sector exacerbated the underdevelopment of another.

We were witnessing the economic roots of the revolution that is now engulfing the whole of Central America. In 1954, the CIA supported a counter-revolution to overthrow the mildly reformist government of Jacobo Arbenz and thereby ensured the continuation of oligarchical control by large *hacendados*.

In 1966, the guerrillas were still largely confined to the eastern lowlands, and the Indian highlands presented the tranquil picture of a rural idyll. The physical beauty of the region and the striking color of Indian textiles make the Guatemala highlands one of the most spectacular parts of the world. Each woman carried on her back a work of art of her own or of a neighbor's creation: her *huipil* ("blouse") and other articles of homespun clothing.

This enchanting world, of which I have so many fond memories, was brutally shattered by political repression, including massive forced displacements of population and massacres of thousands of men, women and children by government troops. In the late 1970s, the insurgency spread to the highlands, and during the last few years, the Ixil and many other Indian groups have become engulfed in the simmering Guatemalan civil war. In the summer of 1987, I was to see the devastation firsthand when I revisited Nebaj with Oliver. The fighting has largely stopped, but the area was still under army occupation. The Ixil are but a footnote in the vast revolutionary process that Central America is undergoing. The U.S. responsibility in increasing human misery by supporting reactionary regimes and forcing insurgents into the communist camp is glaring. U.S. policy is not only totally indefensible on moral grounds, it is monumentally stupid. In the cynical words of Talleyrand apropos of his master Napoleon: It is more than a crime; it is a mistake.

Now, our kind of field work would be impossible. In 1966, it was still relatively easy, despite frequent guerrilla activity in both the Atlantic lowlands and in Guatemala City. The Ixil ostensibly wanted to stay out of national politics and sought to be left alone by pretending to be loyal to whatever government was in power in the capital. The main lines of conflict were religious and largely imported from the outside: both Protestant fundamentalists and the Catholic Church competed with each other to turn the Indians away from their "pagan" practices. As anthropologists, we were caught in the middle of these cross-currents of intolerance, and we had much difficulty extricating ourselves from our ascribed religious roles. Like the itinerant Catholic priests in the region, we drove a Landrover. Many people thus assumed that we were Catholic priests. Children would greet me: *"Bendígame, Padre"* ("Bless me, Father"), as soon as I stepped out of the car. Our other unwitting "mistake" was to rent a house that had been previously occupied by Protestant missionaries. This gave us another ascribed religious role that we would gladly have shed. Somehow, a rumor spread that I was blessed with the gift of prophecy. I became aware of it when an old lady approached me and asked me in a shaky voice, "Is it true, *papacito,* that you can foretell the future?" Luckily, I couldn't, or I would have wept.

Shortly after my return to Seattle in the fall of 1966, I had to face another academic battle, this time not with the chairman over teaching, but with the full professors over my promotion from associate to full. Thanks to the chairman, Frank Miyamoto, who supported me against the overwhelming majority of the full professors, I won the fight and made UW promotion history to boot. By that time, I had published three books and approximately twenty-five articles; a fourth book was in press and a fifth was in the making. I thought I was ripe for a full professorship, and, in fact, I had anticipated the issue of promotion when I accepted an associate professorship in 1965. Faris reassured me in writing that, with my rate of productivity, I could well expect promotion within two years.

Needless to say, I was mildly shocked when the full professors let me know that they were not going to present my case to College Council, the higher (and largely determining) body in tenure and promotion decisions. Tenure was not at issue since I already had it. I asked the full professors to reconsider. They did and their previous vote of 5 to 0 shifted to 4 to 1, with the chairman not voting. I then took the unprecedented step of presenting my own candidacy to College Council. I consulted with Frank Miyamoto before doing so, and he first advised patience, but he rallied to my viewpoint and wrote in my support. The case was a puzzling and embarrassing one for College Council to deal with. Of some forty such cases in front of College Council that year, mine was, at least on paper, the strongest. Yet most of the full professors had declared themselves against me. Some dark secret must hide behind the apparent incongruity. College Council invited the full professors to state their opinion of me. Only two obliged: Faris and Catton. From the echoes I received, I gathered they told College Council that my status as a sociologist was dubious. I rejected positivism and the scientific status of sociology, and I was really an anthropologist in sociological disguise.

At this stage, I took great pleasure in mailing College Council a copy of Faris' glowing letter expressing delight at my acceptance of the UW job in 1965 and prognosticating a prompt promotion. Faris had painted himself into a silly corner. He had to explain how, a mere eighteen months before, he could have been so wrong as to offer me, a non-sociologist, a tenured position in the Sociology Department he then headed. Surely, if I was not a sociologist, that fact would have been apparent then. And yet, his whole faculty, himself included, had enthusiastically approved my appointment. I never knew the exact contents of Miyamoto's letter to College Council, except that it was supportive. I imagine he tried to tell College Council that I represented a different brand of sociology than the tradition represented in the department. In any case, thanks to his support, I won.

At age 34, seven years after getting my Ph.D., I was a full professor at a major university. It was rather nice going, assisted, of course, not only by my aggressive chutzpah but also by the seller's market in the academic world of the 1960s. I described this market in my scurrilous little book, *Academic Gamesmanship* (1970). Alas, as the book came out, the end of the go-go years was already in sight, but the book nevertheless attracted an extensive readership. It went out of print rather quickly, but secondhand copies still trade briskly. The book is very much an insider's joke on academia, in the style of a jocular ethnography. Except for the chapter on publication, which had appeared earlier, the book was written in ten consecutive evenings. There seems to be a steeply inverse relationship between the amount of effort I put into a book and its readership. My two or three best-selling books have all been produced in a few months at most. On the other hand, my dozen or so serious monographs and theoretical statements that are the product of one or two years of field work followed by another two years of analysis and writing have typically sold only two or three thousand copies.

The year 1967 marked the end of the old regime in UW sociology. Faris withdrew from all public participation in departmental affairs for the last few years of his career. There were other issues that scandalized him, such as the presence of elected graduate student representatives at departmental meetings. Faris thought that even assistant professors should be seen but not heard. Since Faris' retirement, we are again on speaking terms, and, in fact, the longer Faris was out of power the more of a Mensch he became. I am sure that, had it not been for his position of authority and his outdated conception of a departmental chairmanship, we could have had a decent relationship.

The irony of the promotion fight is that I was more of a sociologist then than I am now. In a sense, the Faris excommunication decree was prophetic. Over the years, I became increasingly impatient with, and marginal to, a discipline whose practitioners have defined themselves narrowly and provincially. An irreversible process of growing alienation was set in motion by that promotion fight. I gravitated increasingly toward anthropology, the only discipline that could accommodate my range of intellectual concerns. Unfortunately, the structural rigidities of a university in which the established disciplines are forced to fight over academic turf in their competition for funds make it virtually impossible to relocate internally in keeping with one's evolving interests. I now hold an adjunct appointment in anthropology, but even that took a decade of delicate negotiation and slow infiltration.

In the end, Faris won. His definition of the field triumphed over mine. Insofar as I was, willy nilly, forced to remain in a sociology department, I had to keep fighting over the same intellectual issues again and again. The fights became increasingly quixotic over the years. As my marginality to the discipline increased, my respect for it continued to sink. By now, my role of gadfly has been firmly institutionalized. Like the court jester, I go through the motions of amusing my colleagues by being intellectually outrageous. But the ground for common discourse has become so tenuous that scarcely any sociologist can afford to take my strictures against the profession seriously. By now, I have even stopped caring.

Of course, I am not a "mainstream" anthropologist either, certainly not a mainstream American *cultural* anthropologist. But at least I can claim this much: I share more of my diverse interests with different sub-sets of scholars who call themselves anthropologists than with any other sub-sets in other disciplines. In addition, this overlap of diverse interests has become greater over the years, so that, by now, only anthropology covers the entire range of them. Let me make one more grandiose claim. I think that my vision of anthropology is much broader than the currently fragmented field projects and returns to the grand view of the late nineteenth century. Anthropology must recapture its claim to be *the* science of Man *as an evolving biological and cultural creature.*

By 1967, the "call of the wild" was again too strong to resist. Five years of nearly continuous academic residence in the United States had tested my tolerance limits. I longed for another taste of Africa. The Rockefeller Foundation gave me the opportunity to participate in its "university development program" in Africa, and I was game for it. Off we were, to Nigeria we thought, via Europe.

CHAPTER 10

Africa Again: Kenya and Nigeria

After our usual round of family visits in Europe in June 1967, I went on to Africa alone, setting up shop for Irmi and the boys to join me in a few weeks. I also wanted to make some stops on my way to Nigeria, where I was to take up the professorship of Sociology at the University of Ibadan. I particularly enjoyed a fortnight in Morocco, which I spent visiting the four imperial capitals (Rabat, Fes, Meknes, and Marrakech) and the Roman ruins of Volubilis. There is no better place than Morocco to see medieval Islam in all its unspoiled splendor.

To be sure, the Maghreb has become somewhat peripheral to the Muslim world, and other large centers like Cairo, Istanbul, Damascus, Bagdad, and Teheran have eclipsed Maghrebine cities in the intellectual and political sphere. But although these other great Muslim cities have monumental architecture and a vibrant social and intellectual life, Islamic civilization is somehow diluted and partially hidden behind a shabby facade of non-descript, ubiquitous, Western-influenced "modernity," which defaces most Third World cities. That ugly world of corrugated iron shanties, garish publicity panels, stinking diesel buses, "prestige-project" airports, pot-holed grand boulevards, and concrete boxes of government and office buildings has given much the same look to many large Third World cities. A few are redeemed by a beautiful natural setting, but creeping ugliness, alas, characterizes most of them.

The old cities of Morocco have been spared that fate (as has old Jerusalem in the Middle East). What saved them was that they were already tightly packed inside their walls long before the brief colonial period and that the French version of modernism introduced by General Louis Lyautey was artistically sensitive and sympathetic to Islam. Lyautey was quite an aesthete and connoisseur of all things Islamic, including incidentally little Arab boys for whom he had a very special penchant. Whatever else he did, he helped save the beauty and grandeur of medieval Islam in Morocco. Fes and Marrakech are especially impressive, though very different from each other. Fes is clearly linked to Moorish Andalusian culture (the Kairouan University courtyard is a virtual duplicate of the Court of Lions in Granada's Alhambra), while Marrakech is the antechamber of the Sahelian Muslim world to the south, the one I was soon to discover in northern Nigeria. No other country so clearly bridges two continents and more vividly illustrates the deep artistic and intellectual links between Europe and Africa.

In the vibrant urban life of the old Moroccan cities, the Middle Ages come to life better than almost anywhere else on earth. One would only need to remove the inevitable aerial maze of electric wires, telephone poles, and television antennae to create a perfect movie set. The medieval world of the merchant and artisan guilds, each in its separate quarter, of labyrinthine alleyways, of teeming tenements, of overwhelming religiosity totally engulfs the visitor in a time capsule five or six centuries old. Neither the technology nor the relations of production have substantially changed since, except for a little electric motor here and there. Even the visiting hordes of scantily clad blond barbarians cannot spoil the picture, though they undoubtedly arouse both the lucre and the lubricity of the Faithful. (On a second, more leisurely, visit in 1985, with Eric, the charm of Morocco was still intact. It seemed that a combination of economic stagnation and Islamic revival was keeping Morocco pristine for European tourism.)

From Morocco, I went on to Dakar for a four-day stay in Senegal (including the old slaving port of Gorée) and Ghana. While I was working my way down the coast of West Africa, fate intervened in the form of the outbreak of the Nigerian Civil War. Initial Biafran successes brought Ibo troops close to Lagos and Ibadan, and the Rockefeller Foundation was understandably reluctant to send new people into that unstable situation. I spent a fascinating fortnight in Ghana waiting for instructions.

Kwame Nkrumah had recently been overthrown (in 1966), but his imprint remained quite visible. He had essentially bankrupted the country through a series of grandiose, ill-conceived, megalomaniacal prestige projects (such as the Accra airport and his palaces), and Ghana never recovered from this wasteful mismanagement. But I was quite taken by the vibrancy of Akan culture, by the sexual allure and elegance of the women (a pleasant contrast with my recent Moroccan trip, that!), by my renewed encounter with the lush African tropics, and by the historical richness of the place. Particularly memorable were visits to the Asantehene's palace in Kumasi, the Ashanti capital, and to the old Portuguese (and, later, Dutch) slaving fort of El Mina. One might be surprised to find that the main fortification and the artillery of El Mina faces outward to the sea, not inland. But then one is reminded that the West African slave trade was, by and large, a peaceful trade partnership between Africans and Europeans and that nearly all the conflicts pitted Africans against Africans and Europeans against Europeans. Slaving was no black-and-white morality play. Africans were just as good as Europeans in making a fast buck out of it.

The campus of the University of Ghana at Legon, where I stayed much of the time, was also a revealing place. A quaint relic of British colonialism, it presented the picture of an Oxford-under-the-palms. Undergraduates still went about in short academic gowns, despite the sweltering African heat. They lived in British-style colleges, served by a vast staff of servants. Meals, especially the evening meal in hall, had retained all the formality of High Table: grace in Latin, the whole Oxbridge scene. Faculty and students were segregated in Senior and Junior Common Rooms, sipping endless cups of tea with milk. In fact, the scene was more that of a Victorian than a contemporary Oxford or Cambridge. And all that in an institution founded in 1948!

Finally, the telegram came from New York: "Proceed to Nairobi," said the Rockefeller Foundation. Both the geographical and the mental leaps from Nigeria to Kenya were large ones. People unfamiliar with Africa have little conception of the continent's cultural and ecological diversity. West Africa and East Africa are about as different from each other as, say, Japan is from Afghanistan or Uruguay from Canada. In addition, the internal differences *within* each of these countries are *much* greater than anything found within these other four countries. Mentally, I was all set to teach and do research in Nigeria; Kenya required an abrupt reorientation, though my stay there in 1949 helped create a set of anticipations.

Physically, Nairobi is not difficult to adjust to. Despite its proximity to the equator, its altitude of some 1,500 meters gives it a mild sub-tropical climate, but because of that proximity, the seasonal variation is in precipitation rather than temperature. Thus, the climate is close to ideal nearly all the time. Even the rains come in short tropical thunderstorms, usually in the mid-to-late afternoon. As one of Africa's leading centers of neo-colonialism and unbridled capitalism, Nairobi brings all the luxuries and amenities of the First World to its native and expatriate elite and its hordes of tourists. It constitutes an artificial island of parasitic affluence in a sea of grinding poverty.

Unlike Mombasa, an old Arab city on the coast, which grew organically out of several centuries of Indian Ocean trade, Nairobi was the arbitrarily chosen site of a colonial capital, along a railway line linking Mombasa to Kampala. Nairobi has no roots in African or Arabic culture at all; it is a pure exotic flower, a flamboyant orchid drawing its substance from the tree of African society and giving it little in return. Even most of the tourist wealth and foreign aid is either appropriated by the ruling elite and transformed into conspicuous consumption or re-exported to the capitalist world. A graphic Swahili neologism describes the ruling elite as the *wabenzi* (*Wa* is the plural prefix; the term means "drivers of Mercedes-Benzes").

It is difficult not to be taken with the spectacular landscape of East Africa. Its mountain peaks (Mounts Kenya and Kilimanjaro); the Great Rift Valley; the luxuriant lakes (like Nakuru and Naivasha) swarming with flamingos and other bird life; the vast savannahs teeming with zebras, impalas, and gnus all combine to produce unmatched natural beauty. East Africa is the last great reservoir of large wild mammals on this planet. Indeed, it constitutes the last vestige of the Garden of Eden, which cradled our hominid ancestors, as the paleontological discoveries of the last decades proved.

A mere twenty minutes' drive from downtown Nairobi, one can literally step into the footprints of Australopithecus afarensis, surrounded by giraffes, lions, cheetahs, hippos, rhinos, buffaloes, zebras, antelopes, and baboons. Lions happily copulate to circles of shutterbugs shooting through the open roofs of zebra-striped Volkswagen microbuses. Baboons jump on the hoods of cars in the hope of handouts. We were even chased by a rhino, while a terrified Oliver hid under the back seat of our Peugeot. A family photograph shows my contribution to the most recent hominid generation, Eric and Oliver, walking through Olduvai Gorge, at the end of millions of years of evolution on that very site. Nowhere else in the world can one literally touch the roots of one's humanity, as if in a Pleistocene time capsule. The splendor of Tsavo, Ngonrongoro, Serengeti, Manyara, and the other great national parks of Kenya and Tanzania is unmatched anywhere else.

Materially, we were wallowing in affluence. The Rockefeller Foundation not only put at our disposal a Peugeot and a luxurious four-bedroom house at a greatly subsidized rent. It matched my American salary and gave us all kinds of additional travel, expatriation, and other allowances. We reluctantly hired two servants, the absolute minimum in the world of neo-colonial luxury. In short, our standard of living was much higher than we had ever experienced. Whopping tax exemptions enabled us to save most of that income during two years and to return to the United States with sufficient funds to buy both a house in Seattle and a weekend cottage in the Cascade Mountains.

This sybaritic luxury was justified by the need to attract competent expatriate experts to help Africa develop. In fact, it made Kenya a much more pleasant place for Europeans to inhabit than before independence. Europeans kept all their economic and social privileges, while shedding all their political responsibilities. The neo-colonial African elite could now be blamed for everything that went wrong. Never mind that these *wabenzi* were themselves the creatures of colonialism. The cosmetic change in skin pigmentation at the top passed for "independence." *Plus ça change, plus ça reste la même chose.*

My father was a prime beneficiary of that dolce vita, neo-colonial style. He had bought a small farm in Karen, on the outskirts of Nairobi, where he raised saddle and race horses for the other members of his social set; he was surrounded by some forty African servants and grooms and their dependents. (That year—1967–1968—was, in fact, the last period of sustained contact we had.) Like all the members of his expatriate set (gentlemen farmers, disgraced scions of the British aristocracy, retired Indian army colonels, and the like), he praised to high heaven the inspired political leadership of Jomo Kenyatta who, but a few short years before was an imprisoned "Mau Mau terrorist." Now Kenyatta was reverentially referred to as *Mzee* ("old gentleman").

Racial segregation had officially disappeared with independence in 1963. All the elite bars, hotels, schools, and other public facilities were now patronized by Europeans, Asians, and Africans alike. Money bought anything—from Jaguars to European call girls. And the principal source of money for the *wabenzi*, apart from the exorbitant salaries and "fringe benefits," was, of course, the systematic plunder of the public purse made possible by a monopoly of the state apparatus of control and repression. To mention but one glaring example among many, the wife of Jomo Kenyatta was widely known to have been the principal beneficiary of ivory exports generated by poaching in Kenya's national parks. And this was merely a hobby. The entire Kenyan government was an ethnic mafia drawn from the same district of Kikuyu country, an organized "kleptocracy."

Aside from this small, racially desegregated public sphere at the elite level, Kenyan society in 1967 was virtually unchanged from what I had known in 1949. The private sphere of leisure, parties, and so on was still almost entirely segregated between Europeans, Asians, and Africans. Schools were now desegregated at the top, but economically stratified.

The former European schools now admitted the children of rich Asian merchants and African senior civil servants. The former Asian schools catered to the rest of the Asian population and middle-class African urbanites. The other 95 percent of Kenyan schools remained vastly inferior in academic standards and facilities and stayed all-black. Indeed, most of my university colleagues, black and white, were surprised when we sent Eric and Oliver to the nearest primary school, hitherto an all-African one, though probably the best African primary school in Nairobi. Eric and Oliver had a marvellous time, though they resented having to wear British-style school uniforms with neckties.

The contrast between a social setting that I abhorred and a physical world that I found enthralling made for a great deal of moral unease. In fact, next to South Africa, my year in Nairobi was probably the most trying of my professional career. It confronted me with ethical dilemmas directly related to my activities at the university. I suppose I could have ducked these problems, but to do so would have been an abdication of my responsibilities as I saw them. My task was to establish in the briefest time possible a Department of Sociology at the Nairobi branch of the then three-campus University of East Africa (now the University of Nairobi). I was, in fact, the first Professor of Sociology at Kenya's only university. Upon my actions depended in part the intellectual development of an entire discipline (or rather two, because anthropology was implicitly included in my department) in a whole country. This was a heavy as well as heady responsibility.

Four principles guided my conception of what an African university should be. First, I felt that Africa deserved the best and that at least one university in each country should maintain the most rigorous, internationally competitive standards of academic quality. I was, therefore, extremely critical of any condescending notion that, in the name of democratization of higher education, standards should be lowered. There was, I felt, a place for lower-level technical and vocational education, but that place was not the country's premier university. Next, I considered it crucial that the university maintain as much political independence and academic freedom from the government as possible. Any government interference in university affairs had to be resisted to the utmost, I firmly believed, because otherwise the university would become a mere training school for the bureaucracy, a nursery of sycophants.

Third, I was fully sympathetic with the idea that an African university could not be simply an imitation of a European one. It had to develop a curriculum with African content and relevance to the society it served. I definitely agreed that the university served *societal* needs (but not governmental ones). I also resisted the misuse of "Africanization" of curriculum as a euphemism for dilution of standards. Last, an African university, I believed, should be entirely open to talent, irrespective of economic or social condition, even if that meant that most students would have to be supported by government bursaries or loans. That last condition was actually closest to being realized, at least for more "modernized" ethnic groups, especially the Luo, the Luhya, the Kikuyu, and the Kamba.

In theory, my goals were accepted by most of the faculty and were indeed not very revolutionary. In practice, my attempt to implement these objectives, even in the very narrow sphere of my own small department (of four members, including myself), immediately clashed with the aims of the university authorities, some of my colleagues, and, of course, the government. The problems were many, but the principal ones were the constant interference of the government in university affairs and the government's view of the university as a hotbed of subversion. As might be expected, the social sciences were a special target of government suspicion and constant surveillance by police informers among both staff and students.

The principal, a Sierra Leonean, and the registrar, a Kikuyu, were both government appointees and stooges and were thus in the position of headmen in a police surveillance operation. They saw their role as one of keeping the faculty and students in line. The main source of government suspicion was that a disproportionate number of Kenyan professors and lecturers belonged to the rival Luo ethnic group and sympathized with the Luo opposition leader, Oginga Odinga. The university was thus seen as the intellectual mecca of the political opposition, a view that became increasingly accurate as resistance to government control over the campus grew. Police surveillance dampened intellectual exchange in classes, of course. Many students—indeed most African students—were on government bursaries and knew that any critical comment about the established order would result in immediate suspension of their scholarship. About one-fourth of the students were Asians, and they were typically not on scholarships, as they came mostly from the merchant class; but they felt even more vulnerable than the Africans because of the government's mounting campaign of squeezing the Asians out of the Kenyan economy. Thus, their parents were at the mercy of corrupt officials who could revoke their trading licenses or even expel them from the country if they were not Kenyan citizens.

The quality of both faculty and students was excellent. Most of the teaching staff (about equally divided between Kenyans and expatriates) were trained in Britain, often at Oxford, Cambridge, London, Edinburgh, Manchester, Sussex—in short, the very best universities. The examinations standards were those of the University of London, and the British system of external examiners was effective in keeping up a demanding level of performance. My battles on matters of curriculum, examinations, and the like were mostly with the some 20 percent of the teaching staff who were Americans or American-trained Kenyans and who, in the name of democracy, wanted to Americanize the university, by which they meant essentially to lower its standards. A few of the Kenyans, in particular, had gone to the United States because they could not qualify for a British or African university, and they often went to third- or fourth-rate institutions (often Protestant colleges associated with missionary societies).

As for the students, their average level of intellect and motivation was extraordinarily high. The best undergraduates I encountered in my teaching career were in my Nairobi (and, the following year, my Ibadan) classes. The reason was not far to seek. They were all the survivors of a fiercely competitive system of primary and secondary schools in which less than 1 percent of those entering first-grade classes completed secondary school. Naturally, only the most intelligent and highly motivated survived this drastic attrition. Most, however, still came from illiterate peasant homes and were, thus, not socially privileged at all.

Many students had big lacunae in their educational background, and their main shortcoming was an overemphasis on rote memorization and a reluctance to express critical ideas. But their intelligence and motivation made up for these deficiencies. Indeed, they could scarcely be blamed for their limitations, because their entire prior education (largely in Christian mission schools) had stressed dogmatism and regurgitation. Most members of non-literate societies excel at feats of memory (or, better perhaps, reliance on the written word atrophies memory skills). This situation led to the European stereotype of Africans as uncreative parrots and imitators and perpetuated an old-fashioned mission pedagogy of learning by rote.

In addition, as I mentioned, students were scared to speak out on any topic that could be construed as political. Given that oppressive climate, it was remarkable that any intellectual discourse could survive at all. But after a few weeks of acquaintance, when I had gained their confidence, students would come and see me in private and open up to reveal subtle, creative, mature, and, indeed, cynical minds. Incidentally, my African teaching experience led me to reject the notion that poverty or a modest social origin as such is a hindrance to intellectual development. What is crippling is outcasting and social stigmatization, a point brilliantly developed by Nigerian anthropologist John Ogbu whose *Minority Educa-*

tion and Caste (1978) constitutes, in my view, the best analysis and diagnosis of what is wrong with American schooling for blacks, Hispanics, and other "minority" groups.

My first clash with university and government authorities took place over the issue of academic recruitment. Under a British-style system, academic posts are advertised; applications for vacancies are sent to the registrar; an ad-hoc committee of a half-dozen professors is appointed by the university Senate (itself a strictly academic body) to review the applications; and the Senate appoints, guided by the recommendations of the committee. The committee always includes the professor who heads the department where the vacancy exists, but he is not the chair of it nor is his department ever more than a significant but a minority voice on the committee. The principal (or vice-chancellor) and registrar often sit on the committee, but the majority of the membership consists of academic members of the Senate. The system is somewhat gerontocratic, but puts the recruitment process clearly under academic control of the Senate as a whole, not of individual departments, nor of the university administration.

The recruitment issue was especially crucial in sociology. Four or five lecturers were to be appointed as quickly as possible to create an effective undergraduate program. Preference was to be given to Kenyans, holding qualifications constant, to insure continuity; thus, recruitment to several junior positions would determine the direction of the department for several decades. It was my mandate to ensure the best possible outcome. Abruptly, the principal called me to a meeting, with something like two hours' notice. I discovered that he and the other government stooge, the registrar, had already decided who was persona grata and were determined to railroad their choices through the Appointments Committee *without any prior consultation* with any of the four or five academic members of the committee. None of us had even seen the files on the candidates, and two of us could not make the meeting on such short notice. I protested and walked out of the meeting. At the next meeting of the Senate, I made my inaugural political speech. This was an egregious violation of all academic procedures, I stated, and Kenya would never have the university it deserved if it was to be run in an authoritarian manner like a mission school. My little speech was a bombshell. No one had dared to speak that bluntly before. The principal took it as a declaration of war, but much of the faculty, especially several of the senior Kenyan professors (who happened to be mostly Luo), supported me, albeit mostly privately. The lines were clearly drawn.

James Coleman (the political scientist, not the sociologist) who was the Rockefeller Foundation representative in East Africa was in a delicate position, and I felt badly about putting him there, but the issue was simply too important to ignore. In the end, my intervention only delayed the appointments by a couple of months. The principal and registrar were riding roughshod over the university with the support of the police, and the Senate was emasculated and cowed.

From that point on, my relations with the principal were reduced to a minimum, but we had a second major clash. This time the issue was one of political intimidation of the teaching staff. There was a fund-raising drive for the Jomo Kenyatta Hospital, a pet charity of the president. Contributions were supposedly voluntary, and I knew that most of the faculty did not support the political sponsorship of the charity. I received a form memo from the principal enjoining me, as head of the department, to collect "donations" from my staff at the following "suggested" rates: professors, £5; senior lecturers, £3; lecturers, £2. I replied that I would do no such thing, as this would be an unwarranted act of political pressure that I could not condone. This time, I felt the issue was relatively minor, and I did not publicize it.

My third political involvement in Kenya, and the most serious one, almost got me expelled from the country and made me persona non grata since. (Many years later, I learned, for example, that a student of mine from Seattle had been refused a visa to Kenya on the strength of a letter of recommendation from me. I don't think I ever had so much negative clout with any other government since. Academics are really taken seriously in Africa, which is why so many land in jail or in exile.) University students had organized a political demonstration of protest against the Rhodesian government's hanging of freedom fighters during the Zimbabwe War of Independence. The students intended to march peacefully from the campus to the Parliament building some 2 kilometers away. The cause was one of which the Kenyan government officially approved, so it looked like everything would pass smoothly. However, the government was not prepared to have a crowd of students (many of whom were known to be Luo opposition supporters) demonstrate close to Parliament, where the events would surely be covered by the foreign press and where protest could find more local targets.

About half way along the students' intended route, the marchers encountered a police block made up of some 200 men (still under white officers, by the way). The white police commander told the students to turn around and return to campus. As the students began to obey, the police moved forward, nudging students with their baton tips and herding them like cattle. Both the students and the police increased their pace to a run, and soon the police were visibly chasing students and swinging their batons, just for the fun of it. I was standing in front of Taifa

Hall, a large glass building on one edge of campus when I saw the melee of students and police approach campus. At this point, the students' patience was exhausted. They were determined to be chased no further and to stop the police at the edge of the campus. Again, by tradition, the campus was off-limits to the police (at least to the uniformed police). Some students turned around and started to pelt the police with a few small stones. Scuffles escalated and police brutality mounted, but the students kept retreating, though more slowly, and posed no threat to anyone.

At this point, the police were in a quandary. Had they simply withdrawn, calm would, in all likelihood, have returned. Only a small minority of perhaps 100 students were visibly angry and even they would probably have been content to withdraw to campus. But the police felt that they had to make a few arrests to prove they had "won." The police also knew that it would have been inflammatory to arrest the visible leaders, who were all Africans. The old scapegoating trick was invoked. It would be safe to arrest *Asian* students. The problem was that few Asian students had taken part in the demonstration. There were, however, a number of Asian spectators who, like me, were watching the events from the fringe. Suddenly, I observed a white police officer enter Taifa Hall and reemerge from it holding an Asian student by the scruff of his neck. The charge was that he had stoned the police (from inside a glass building that did not suffer a single broken window). It turned out that the student was Tanzanian, not Kenyan, and thus faced the threat of deportation as well as jail and the total disruption of his university career. I was not the sole witness to the events. I had noticed a couple of my Asian secretaries among the spectators inside Taifa Hall. But for them to testify as defense witnesses was risking immediate loss of their jobs. In short, I felt duty-bound to be a defense witness for the student, naively expecting that he would receive a fair trial. Needless to say, except for a couple of Asians who appeared as character witnesses, I was the only defense witness. The student was the only one the police preferred charges against, so the authorities were determined to make a show case of the trial. The magistrate, by the way, was Asian, and the prosecutor, British.

When I started describing the behavior of the police, the prosecutor objected and the magistrate ruled my testimony prejudicial to the police and inadmissible evidence. Then the prosecutor cross-examined me, seeking to establish, first, that I had been a leader of the student demonstration, not a dispassionate observer as I claimed, and, second, that I was a dangerous anarchist. Two high-ranking police officers, one white, one black, blatantly perjured themselves, stating that they had seen me leading the march in the front row of the crowd. A third police officer, from the CID (secret police), then read statements critical of the government I had made in the Senior Common Room over the last few months. These were not perjured. They indeed sounded like verbatim transcripts of things I *had* said. This meant that the Senior Common Room of the university was wired. Some of my Kenyan colleagues had warned me that it was, but I had dismissed their warning as slightly paranoid. The magistrate warned me to shut up or face perjury charges, and the student got a six-month suspended sentence, a fine, and an immediate expulsion from Kenya. His studies were obviously at an end.

Not all of my stay in Kenya was this grim. Aside from several trips to the game reserves with the family, I was external examiner twice, once at Makarere in Kampala and once at the Dar es Salaam campus of the University of East Africa. Thus, I got to know the Ugandan capital (before it was ravaged by Idi Amin) and the Tanzanian one. Tanzania, under Julius Nyerere's experiment in "African socialism" was a very different country from Kenya. If anything, it was even poorer and more underdeveloped, but at least Dar es Salaam had none of the obscene ostentation of wealth so evident in Nairobi. Tanzanian cabinet ministers were driving their own Peugeots 404, instead of being chauffeur-driven in black Mercedes limousines as were their Kenyan counterparts.

Also, there was a pride in using Swahili as the new national language, even on the university campus and even among the expatriate staff. In Kenya, English was almost the exclusive public language of the black political elite. Jomo Kenyatta sometimes spoke in Swahili at political rallies, but only because that was the only way to be understood by more than a few thousand people. African socialism dismally failed to pull Tanzania out of its poverty, and the Ujama villages (cooperatives) were marred by much political coercion and economic inefficiency. Still, the Tanzanian ruling class seemed remarkably austere, honest, and altruistic by comparison with the Kenya mafia.

Kampala was also a fascinating city and much more of an African intellectual center than Nairobi. First, it was the traditional capital of the Ganda state, one of the great "interlacustrine" monarchies of central Africa. Second, Makarere College (established in 1948) was the oldest and best university in the whole of East Africa and had a number of leading intellectuals, like Kenyan political scientist Ali Mazrui. Lively literary and scholarly journals like *Transition* and *Mawazo* ("Thoughts") were published in Kampala. Such distinguished masters of fiction as Paul Théroux had their literary debuts in *Transition,* for example, under the inspired editorship of Rajat Neogy.

The large and thriving Asian community of Kampala made the city a booming commercial center, and the rich agricultural land around Lake

Victoria made southern Uganda one of the more prosperous regions of Africa. But the political problems were mounting. The Baganda were restive under Milton Obote's increasingly despotic rule. When Idi Amin deposed him in 1971, Ugandans cheered . . . but not for long. Obote was a rational, modern, educated despot; Idi Amin was a murderous, erratic, illiterate buffoon combining the intellectual maturity of a 10-year-old with the emotional stability of a psychopath and the physique of a punch-drunk prize fighter. He ran Uganda as a hippopotamus on a rampage. Soon the expulsion of the Asian merchant community transformed downtown Kampala into a ghost town. Little did the Ugandan Asians know then how privileged they were to be allowed to leave Uganda alive. Uganda was in for a generation of brutal massacres, civil war, famine, and impoverishment. There was a brief hope that Amin's ouster and Obote's return would lead to an improvement, but Obote's second period in office proved much more tyrannical than his first one.

There was relatively little I could do in Kenya by way of research. All research required government permission. Aside from the fact that I always found it repugnant to get government clearance to do what I regard as my central scholarly activity, I also knew that it was pointless to request a permission that would surely be denied. That meant that my research had to be inconspicuous and surreptitious. It was largely limited to some observational and archival work on the East African Asian community and a questionnaire study of students' class origins and attitudes on the three campuses of the University of East Africa. I was greatly interested in the role of higher education in determining the character of the emergent bureaucratic ruling class of newly independent African countries.

Meanwhile, in Nigeria, the Civil War had bogged down to a slow war of attrition in the heartland of Ibo country in the southeast. It was clear that the Biafran army was hopelessly outnumbered, outgunned, and encircled and that Ibo secession was doomed. The Rockefeller Foundation and I decided that it was safe for us to revert to our original plan. I would go to Ibadan in September 1968 to help develop a post-graduate program in sociology there. I would occupy the chair (in the British sense), but a Nigerian senior lecturer, Olu Okediji, would relieve me of administrative responsibilities by assuming the departmental headship. This was ideal for my purposes, as it would shield me from the political unpleasantness I had faced in Nairobi and leave me freer to teach and do research.

With three months of free time between these academic posts, Irmi and I decided to make the most of one of the Rockefeller Foundation's many "perks"—the "home leave." The "home leave" was actually not a Rockefeller Foundation invention; it was a hallowed British colonial institution, extended to the new African elite of the Senior Civil Service after independence. Every senior civil servant was entitled to a free annual passage home for himself, his wife, and his children, supposedly to recuperate from the hardships of colonial service. "Home" meant "Britain," of course. When Africans began to be promoted into the Senior Service, they insisted on equal conditions of employment with their British colleagues. For a number of years after independence, thousands of Nigerians, Ghanaians, Sierra Leoneans, Kenyans, Ugandans, and others thus annually went "home" to Britain at African taxpayers' expense. The Rockefeller Foundation followed suit, simply redefining "home" as the United States for its American staff. We found ourselves with four tickets from Nairobi to Seattle to Lagos or their equivalent to any other intermediate destinations. We put Eric and Oliver on a plane to Frankfurt to spend the summer with their grandparents, and Irmi and I took a marvellous six-week trip to Ethiopia, India, and Lebanon.

Two of these three countries have been changed out of recognition since then, neither of them for the better unfortunately. Ethiopia is rid of its feudal empire, but its several civil wars rage on and its new status as a Soviet client state, far from ameliorating the desperate plight of the population, has plunged the country even more deeply into chronic famine. Only Western philanthropy shields millions of Ethiopians from dying of hunger through a mixture of ecological disaster, demographic explosion, human corruption, brutality, and incompetence. Actually the Marxist regime in Addis Ababa is not at all displeased to see the dissident northern populations in Tigre country and Erytrea decimated by famine. By 1968, when we were there, Ethiopia already exhibited the worst destitution we had experienced in Africa. The country was not simply poor; it was desperate. Both humans and livestock were emaciated as nowhere else on the continent. The spectacular mountainous landscape was even more denuded and overgrazed than the South African Bantustans.

Total absence of garbage is always a telling symptom of absolute destitution. Extremely poor countries are amazingly clean. Every scrap of metal is eagerly scavenged for reuse; every bit of paper is picked up for fuel; tin cans are flattened into roofs, cigarette butts are recycled in pipes; excrement is treasured as fertilizer or fuel. Whatever humans might have overlooked is quickly lapped up by roving dogs reduced to walking rib cages. Addis Ababa, Gondar, and other cities of the Ethiopian heartland are simply spotless. They are so poor as to produce no garbage. The whole surface of the land is licked clean and bare.

The appearance of vast garbage dumps, as, for instance, in Latin America, is the first sign of development. However, the garbage dumps of semi-developed countries are still quite different from those of developed countries. They support armies of specialized scavengers. (Mexico and Cairo are good examples.) By their garbage, you shall know them, as archeologists have long known. But there is also a systematic comparative *ethnography* of garbage creation and disposal begging to be done.

The Ethiopia we saw was clearly very different from the rest of sub-Saharan Africa. It was the only truly feudal country in black Africa, with 3,000 years of class exploitation, dense population, and agrarian technology behind it. Its problems were, in a sense, much more Asian than African, resulting not from horticultural *under*development nor from recent colonial exploitation, but from a long, homegrown history of ecological depletion of resources under a relatively advanced agrarian technology and super-exploitation by a large parasitic class of feudal landlords and priests. Up to 20 percent of the adult male population of the Christian parts of Ethiopia consisted of Coptic priests, who were not only largely parasitic on the peasantry but did not even have the saving grace of being celibate.

The Conquering Lion of Judah (as Haile Selassie styled himself) was obviously on his last leg, but so was his sprawling, ragtag empire. The communist regime that was to follow inherited a basket case. But what a beautiful basket! For sheer physical attractiveness, the population of the Horn of Africa has, in my view, no match anywhere else on earth. Women are almost monotonously beautiful and graceful. I remember an evening in a traditional restaurant in Addis. We shared the large circular room (a converted palace) with some 50 female students from the university holding some kind of class reunion. At least 75 percent of them would easily have made the finals of the Miss Universe contest.

One of our delightful discoveries in Ethiopia was the subtlety and delicacy of Amhara cuisine, truly one of the world's most refined culinary traditions. The grandiose ruggedness of the landscape also has few rivals. A striking feature of the Ethiopian highlands is the prevalence of high plateaux. Unlike most other mountainous regions of the world, many of the flattest areas of Ethiopia are high plateaux separated from one another by steep, craggy gorges. Flying over these in a rickety old DC-3, as we did, is an unforgettable, if unsettling, experience. As the safe operating ceiling of a DC-3 is well below much of the Ethiopian landscape, pilots fly by the seat of their pants, with dangerously souped-up engines. They negotiate a passage through mountain crevasses with perhaps 50 meters to spare between the plane and rock outcrops. Rains prevented us from landing in Lalibela, but the splendors of Gondar and Axum were well worth a few skipped heartbeats and the nausea of bumpy flights in a cabin reeking of vomit and goat cheese.

Lebanon was another story. We saw it before the years of civil was and foreign invasions, which have since ravaged it. Lebanon in the 1960s was the much vaunted success story of the Middle East, the political and economic Switzerland of the Levant. Its political system was seen as a great experiment in "consociational democracy," demonstrating the possibility of peaceful coexistence between diverse religious communities. It was advanced as a successful alternative to the sectarian Muslim and Jewish states around it. As for its thriving economy, it represented triumphant mercantile capitalism, a contemporary extension of the Phoenician genius for trade and commercial enterprise. Beirut was the glittering playground of the eastern Mediterranean with its bikini-bespattered bathing beaches, its nearby gambling casino, its sumptuous hotels and restaurants, its luxury boutiques, and its lavish embassies. The most common make of taxi was the Mercedes!

The teeming Palestinian refugee camps were neatly tucked out of tourist sight, though our taxi driver, a Maronite, amply bemoaned their presence, pointing to the hills beyond the airport. We simply sat back in his Mercedes and enjoyed Tyre, Sidon, Baalbek, and all the other sights. We also met my Seattle colleague, Stuart Dodd, whose son Peter had succeeded him to the chair of sociology at the American University of Beirut. We conversed with some of the most articulate members of the highly urbane, polyglot, westernized Lebanese elite. That such a highly intelligent, suave, and educated class should have transformed this island of peace and affluence into a charnel house pockmarked by artillery shells is a sad comment on the fragility of civilization. Of course, the Lebanese are not entirely to blame. The Israelis, Syrians, and Palestinians vied with each other to make Lebanon their favorite shooting gallery. Still, the unravelling of civil society in Lebanon is a terrible negative lesson on ethnic coexistence. A multiethnic society more easily survives, it seems, under centralized tyranny than under consociational democracy.

The highlight of our trip was India. With my long-standing interest in the Indian diaspora in Africa, it was high time I saw Mother India herself. India requires a strong stomach, both gastrically and morally, to be enjoyed. It is the ideal locale for the seeker of what the French call *les émotions fortes*. Few other countries so starkly juxtapose the glories of their past and the squalor of their present. Indianist friends and colleagues, like Paul Brass and Morris Morris, tell me that I overreact and that conditions are not only not as bad as all that, but that they are markedly improving. Statistics, of food production for example, back up their statement, and it is also true that India has a remarkably advanced and sophisticated industrial, commercial, and educational infrastructure for a poor country. The Indian railways, for instance, are a marvel of lumbering efficiency for a tropical country of such enormous size.

Its political coherence in the face of religious, linguistic, and caste fragmentation is nothing short of phenomenal. Even after the assassination of Indira Gandhi and the continuing Punjab troubles, the cohesiveness and professionalism of the Indian army prevented Humpty Dumpty, once more, from having a great fall. (There is a great book on the Indian army, by the way, written by an urbane former pro-consul of the British empire, Philip Mason. Published in 1974, its title is *A Matter of Honour.*)

Our three-week stay in India was too short to gain anything but a superficial view, and only of northern India at that. We plane-hopped from marvel to marvel, starting in Bombay with a side trip to Ellora and Ajanta, crossing over to Calcutta, and then backtracking westward to Benares, Delhi, Agra, and Srinagar. The architectural splendors of the past are simply overwhelming in India. We were duly impressed with the caves of Ellora and Ajanta, those monumental sculptural excavations from mountainsides. Whole temples are monolithic carvings hollowed out of the rockface. One of these consists of a herd of life-size elephants holding up a temple. The great Mughal architecture of Delhi and Agra is no less impressive, especially the Taj, of course, but also the Red Fort of Delhi. All of these in juxtaposition with the ambiant squalor are stark reminders that all civilization grew out of poverty, misery, and oppression. The freedom of the few was always built on the slavery of the many. In Europe, the rise of living standards in the past century enables us to forget the human misery that built the cathedral of Chartres or the Palace of Versailles. In India, the social conditions that produced the Red Fort or the Taj still surround these marvels. The perfume of the flower still intermingles with the stench of the manure that produced it.

Coming from Africa, one is tempted to look at India through Afrocentric eyes. Superficial similarities of climate, ecology, and poverty encompassed in that huge grab bag we call the Third World do not carry understanding very far, however. The internal contrasts within the Third World are far more illuminating, and, in that sense, Africa is a useful *foil* for looking at India. In a nutshell, the contrast is best expressed in levels of technology: most of the differences in terms of population density, social stratification, societal size and complexity, and internal differentiation between elites and masses (not only in wealth but also in culture) are simply reducible to the differences between what Gerhard Lenski has called horticultural and agrarian societies. The continued relevance of that distinction (based on the *pre-colonial* level of technology) for present conditions of development is demonstrated in an article by G. Lenski and P. D. Nolan in *Social Forces* (1984, vol. 63, no. 1).

One of the most vivid first impressions that hits one in India, especially if one comes from Africa, is the sheer density of population. Not only are the cities much larger and more numerous than in Africa; they are also much more densely packed. African shantytowns are made up of one-story shacks. Indian proletarian quarters are stacked up four or five stories high. Indian streets are permanently crowded, for they serve not only as avenues of travel and transportation but also as places of commerce, foraging grounds for roaming cows, and outdoor dormitories for the destitute.

If the pit of Indian poverty can be said to have a bottom, Calcutta is probably it. Admittedly, we hit it at the worst time of the year, in early July, when the monsoon transforms the city into a swamp. (Calcutta was a British creation, and the British seem to have had a knack for siting their colonial capitals on swamps. Lagos is another good example.) Our bus trip from Dum Dum Airport to the center of the city was an excellent introduction to the aquatic hell of Calcutta. It took nearly two hours for the Air India bus to slalom its way through a dense flow of lorries, taxis, pedicabs, oxcarts, wandering cows, and pedestrian hordes. For at least half of the trip, we were wading through 30 to 50 centimeters of water. A gondola would have made the trip faster. Downtown, skeletal shadows of human forms roamed the streets in ragged loincloths, their only worldly possession. Since they could no longer stretch on the pavement of flooded streets, they took refuge on window sills and steps of buildings. This is the city where refuse trucks make rounds each morning to pick up the daily crop of human cadavers. Yet on its outskirts, a large complex funded by the government caters to orphaned calves.

Another overwhelming impression that India creates, especially for the visitor from a secularized society, is the ubiquity of religion. Muslim societies also give the impression of moving in an oppressive cloud of religiosity, and so do some great centers of pilgrimage like Jerusalem. But Hinduism is sui generis. It is true that Hinduism is a private and familial religion, made up of countless little rituals of daily life rather than great public ceremonies. But as private life promiscuously spills into the streets of crowded India, the frontier between private and public life is difficult to draw.

Benares may not be a fair example, because it is the mecca of Hinduism, but it merely intensifies experiences encountered all over the sub-continent. The atmosphere of Benares is simply unforgettable. The endless rows of beggars squatting behind their empty food bowls; the crowds jostling down the steps of the temples for a chance to bathe in the Ganges; the upper caste widows in white saris who have come to Benares to await death; the mixed aroma of burning flesh and fragrant herbs emanating from the scores of funeral pyres; the bands of rhesus monkeys roaming the temples in search of food offerings—all of these transport the Western visitor into a world that is powerfully *sensed* but not understood.

The miracle of India is that this huge, implausible, ungainly, disparate, overcrowded, magnificent monstrosity of a society that, by all rational expectations, should have collapsed into chaos long ago, *works*. Indeed, by African standards, it works remarkably well. The British are given much credit for the efficiency of the railways, the army, and other governmental institutions. In no other former British colony have I met so many Anglophiles as in India, at least in elite circles. Yet this is clearly a partial explanation at best. Nigeria, too, was a British colony, and yet it is a shambles compared to India. (If you don't believe it, just *try* to fly Nigerian Airways, and then take Air India.) In Nigeria, everything that does *not* work is blamed on the British; in India everything that works is credited to them. The explanation must lie elsewhere, principally in precolonial history and indigenous institutions.

Still, the imprint of the British Raj remains extraordinarily strong. This was driven home to us when, thanks to the good offices of a Permanent Secretary in the Maharashtra State Government to whom we had been introduced by Kenyan Asian kinsmen, we stayed in a government Rest House in Aurangabad. The Rest House in question was one of the many erected by the British, in that inimitable neo-Mughal Victorian style, to cater to travelling British officials. It continues to serve that function for senior Indian civil servants, but remains a museum to British India, complete with the slowly revolving ceiling fans, the plush red parlor furniture, the tent-shaped mosquito nets around the beds, and the vast retinue of obsequious servants scurrying about to anticipate one's slightest whim.

One last contrast between India and Africa is worth noting, namely the much narrower gap between the top and the bottom of the income distribution in India. Except for a tiny group of entrepreneurs and industrialists, the Indian elite lives at a much more modest level than its African counterparts. This is especially true of senior civil servants, teachers, and the rest of the university-educated professional elite. A university professor in Nigeria earns roughly *one hundred times* his country's per capita income. His Indian counterpart makes perhaps ten or twelve times as much as his average countryman. Let me illustrate by comparing a Nigerian and an Indian high school principal. The Nigerian lives in a spacious, three-bedroom, Western-style house with electricity, a modern bathroom and kitchen—in short, all modern conveniences. That house is amply furnished at government expense, and he pays a nominal, subsidized rent amounting to perhaps 5 or 6 percent of his salary of $600 or $700 per month. He drives a late model European or Japanese car, for which he receives a generous monthly allowance. He sends his children to elite schools (probably not the one where he teaches), and his house is full of Western consumer goods: several radios, a color television set, a typewriter, an electric sewing machine, a large refrigerator, toys, books, pictures, magazines, and so on.

By contrast, let me describe the life-style of an Indian secondary school principal I visited in a small town near Aurangabad. His housing, too, was provided by the state, but it consisted, like the rest of the school, of holes in the outer wall of a Mughal ruin. Indeed, the high school was lodged in what used to be the stables of a Mughal palace, a series of open arcades, each some 20 square meters in area, on the inner side of a town wall. Two such arcades, enclosed by a flimsy wood partition on the courtyard side, housed the principal, his wife, also a teacher at the school, and their four children. His salary was about $50 a month; his wife's $25. A bare 40-watt electric bulb hung from the ceiling of each room, but the only source of water was a communal tap in the courtyard. Latrines were communal as well.

Their most conspicuous consumer goods were a bicycle, a small transistor radio, a little kerosene stove for cooking, and a meager complement of cooking and eating utensils. Each had three or four changes of clothing hung on a string behind a curtain in the corner of the sleeping room they shared with their four children. The parents slept on an old Western-style bed, the children on mats on the floor. The other room was a combination kitchen, dining room, and parlor. Its furniture consisted of a small cooking table, a larger dining table, and four simple chairs, all clearly made by a local carpenter. A mirror, a few family photographs, a gaudy Hindu calendar, a small shelf with a few toilet articles, and another one with a dozen or so school books completed the inventory of the house.

Both the principal and his wife, incidentally, were university graduates and spoke flawless English in addition to Hindi and their native Marathi. He headed a school of some 3,000 pupils and 50-odd teachers, and he was privileged because, as principal, he was the only teacher to be provided with official housing. By Indian standards, they were probably in the top 5 percent of the population. By American standards, they were living well below the level of the most destitute denizens of Indian reservations. There is simply no common *objective* measure between the poverty of rich countries and that of poor countries, and the subjective aspects of poverty in the First and Third Worlds are also very different.

Nearly twenty years later, in 1986, Eric and I took another, more extensive and leisurely, five-week trip through India. We travelled about 7,000 kilometers, mostly by rail, through Uttar Pradesh, Himachal Pradesh, Rajastan, Tamil Nadu, and Kerala. India had not changed much. It was not noticeably more "modern" or Western. Indeed, use of English seemed less widespread than a generation earlier. But the Indian miracle continued unabated. The trains ran, slowly but reliably. Famine had been safely averted. Living standards were creeping upward. Cities, despite their ever-increasing populations, continued to be supplied with water, electricity, and food, and remained remarkably free of garbage. The army, the police, the postal service, and the other agencies of government, though slumberingly and archaically bureaucratic, and moderately corrupt, creaked along through riots, monsoons, and epidemics. By African standards, all this is little short of miraculous.

When Irmi and I were on our way back to Africa after our 1968 trip to India, we picked up Eric and Oliver at Rome Airport, and we soon landed at Ikeja Airport, near Lagos. There we were met by a Rockefeller Foundation chauffeur and driven to Ibadan, some 150 kilometers to the north. The driver, Johnson, a burly, jovial, loquacious Bini who spoke a colorful Pidgin English, had an irresistibly contagious good nature, and I owe him many hours of delightful companionship on Nigerian roads. I would bombard him with ethnographic questions, which he always accepted in his cheerful spirit, but then he would turn the tables on me and ask me about life in America. Why was it that Americans had only one wife, he would ask, when they could obviously afford several? Was it because they were so stingy? He, for example, a mere chauffeur, had two wives, a young one in Ibadan with whom he lived most of the time and an older one in Benin City whom he periodically visited, laden with gifts for her and their children. I told him that if I married a second wife, I would be thrown in jail. Johnson looked at me with a stupefied expression of surprise. Then, after a five-second pause, he burst out in uncontrollable laughter. He had never heard of anything so ridiculous.

He was not alone in his assessment of Western marital mores. During my year in Nigeria, I was repeatedly propositioned by young women offering to be my wife. When I mentioned that I was already provided for, they cheerfully volunteered to be my junior wife. This was not as true of university students who mostly came from Westernized, monogamous, mission-educated families and were often alumnae of prim Victorian boarding schools; but market women, sales girls, postal clerks, and other lower-middle class urban women were among the most aggressively seductive I encountered anywhere.

For this, and a number of other reasons, I immediately found myself very comfortable in Yoruba society. Compared to my year in Kenya, my stay in Nigeria was remarkably free of tensions and conflicts, and my relations with Nigerians, both on and off campus, were much more free, open, and easy than was the case with Kenyans. Given the Civil War raging in the country, I expected the political situation to be much more tense and fraught with suspicion of foreigners than in Kenya, but the very opposite was the case. I was allowed to do research in a totally unrestricted manner; my teaching was unhampered by political pressures; and I felt that my students and colleagues enjoyed a climate of unbridled intellectual freedom. All this was a most pleasant change from my Nairobi experience.

It may sound callous to state that I thoroughly enjoyed my year in Nigeria, during which hundreds of thousands of people were dying (mostly of disease and starvation) as a result of the war, but it is true. By late 1968, the Biafran cause had become totally hopeless. Only Ojukwu's obstinacy imposed the untold sufferings of the blockade, not only on the Ibos, incidentally, but even more on the non-Ibo minorities of the Eastern Region, especially the Ijaw, Efik, and Ibibio. The only significant success of the Ibo during the conflict was in waging the propaganda war. The ruling secessionist clique and the Ibo intelligentsia abroad, such as Harvard history professor and former Ibadan vice-chancellor, K. O. Dike, cleverly manipulated the human misery and starvation that their conduct perpetuated to attract overseas sympathies. They were remarkably successful in swaying European and American opinion in their favor. The myth most successfully propagated by Biafrans was that the Ibos were being persecuted throughout Nigeria and that surrender would mean genocide. Even the Vatican departed from its usual position of neutrality, believing Biafran propaganda that Muslim troops on the federal side were conducting an anti-Catholic Jihad.

It is quite correct that extensive anti-Ibo pogroms *did* take place in the Hausa cities of northern Nigeria *before* the Civil War, making perhaps 6,000 victims and causing a panicky exodus of nearly a million Ibo back to their Eastern Region homeland. No doubt, this was the main catalyst for Ibo secession. But there is no evidence of genocidal policies or intent by the federal government during or after the war, nor even of widespread massacres of civilians by federal troops. At least 90 percent of the casualties were indeed civilian, but they were caused by disease and starvation rather than by military action. The last eighteen months of the war were bogged down in a military stalemate, and the rain forest of the Ibo heartland made large-scale military operations virtually impossible. The federals simply blockaded the Ibo heartland into surrender, though they allowed Red Cross humanitarian flights into Biafra.

When peace finally came, the federal government proved what it had claimed all along. The whole world was "surprised" to note that no genocide or even reprisals took place. Few peace settlements in history have been as magnanimous as that offered by the federal government to the Biafran rebels. The hand of friendship and reconciliation was extended by General Yakubu Gowon to his "brother officers" at the very surrender ceremony.

Needless to say, I made myself unpopular with some of my Africanist colleagues by denying the accuracy of the Biafran propaganda and by expressing my admiration for Yakubu Gowon, the Nigerian head of state. I still assert that Gowon, at the time a young officer in his early thirties, proved the most humane, uncorrupt, and capable head of state that Nigeria ever had and deserves recognition as one of the great African statesmen of his generation. A man of common sense, humility, and wisdom well beyond his years, his voice was always one of moderation, generosity, and reconciliation. He was that rare figure in world history: the warrior who hates war, and the statesman who hates politics. To my knowledge, he was the only head of state who ever had the humility to become a graduate student after being deposed from office. He enrolled for a Ph.D.—in political science, no less—at the University of Warwick.

When he was in office, he lived, not in a palace, but in the officers' quarters of Dodan Barracks, his headquarters. One little anecdote will give the measure of Gowon's character. For many months, the University of Ibadan had been paralyzed by petty personal quarrels between the vice-chancellor and the registrar. Finally, exasperated by this academic chicanery, Gowon summoned the University Council to Dodan Barracks to try to settle the dispute. He gently addressed them, saying, in effect, that they were all grown men, far wiser and better educated than he, and that, surely, they could come to a settlement. A member of council asked what arrangements had been made for lunch. With a suave smile, Gowon told them: "None, gentlemen," and left the room. By evening, the crisis was settled.

Throughout the year, we travelled extensively by car in Nigeria, in every major region, except in the war zone. The closest we came to the war was Benin City, and there the signs of conflict were evident: heavy military traffic on the roads; the flow of wounded to the hospitals, and so on. In the rest of the country, the principal signs of war were the newspaper headlines and military roadblocks on major highways. On the campus, life was completely normal, except for the frequency with which young officers came to pick up women students for an evening in Lagos. The male students resented this competition from the dashing young warriors in their khaki Mercedes.

Incidentally, hundreds of Ibo (including our own house servant) lived on the university campus throughout the war, and I did not hear a single story of harrassment or threat against them. In fact, if anything, the opposite was the case. We later learned that the Ibo domestic servants, who had an ethnic monopoly on the American families on campus, served as informers for a well-organized gang of Ibo burglars, who came to steal when they knew that the houses would be unoccupied. We escaped being burglarized, however, and our servant was a delightful person of whom we grew very fond. That, too, was a pleasant change from Kenya, where there had been serious trouble between our two servants. They were brothers-in-law, so we thought they would get along, but soon one accused the other of wanting to poison or bewitch him, and he grew so paranoid that we had to sack him. From then on, we tried to get along with just one house servant, well below par for an expatriate family. But our servant problems abruptly stopped.

Our travels in Nigeria revealed the extraordinary heterogeneity of the country. The contrast between the Muslim north and the largely non-Muslim south was particularly striking. The two sides of the Niger are about as different as, say, Israel is from Jordan. The great Hausa cities of the north, like Kano, Katsina, and Zaria, are still a closed world, hostile to infidels, and frozen in uncompromising, fundamentalistic, medieval Islam. It is an impressive world of culture and scholarship, but scarcely one that welcomes the outsider. As one moves south, the picture begins to change even in the southern fringe of the Muslim world, as in the Nupe capital of Bida or the Muslim Yoruba emirate of Ilorin. Children begin to chase your car in joyous curiosity. Women move about freely in the marketplace, which they dominate. The stranger is met with a gleaming eye, talked to, bantered with, followed with a mixture of speculation and interest. In Yoruba country, itself a richly diverse area, one clearly encounters an open society. There is no hostility, no servility, no haughtiness. People simply accept and approach you with no inhibitions of race, sex, religion, or culture. They try to take advantage of you in the marketplace, because, after all, that is what marketplaces are for. But they freely banter with you without any reserve or hypocrisy. They do not hesitate to make fun of you or to criticize you if the occasion calls for it, but they also accept you on your own terms, with no barriers of status.

Though the utter frankness, cynicism, nepotism, and manipulativeness of Yoruba culture shocks many outsiders, I must confess that I found this ungarnished expression of human nature refreshingly honest and that I was impressed with Yoruba political sophistication and absence of ideological delusions. In retrospect, Yoruba society helped me develop my utilitarian conception of human behavior based on selfish individualism and imbedded in a matrix of kinship and ethnicity. It also helped me understand the *nested,* multi-layered nature of both kinship and ethnicity and see how the latter was merely an extension of the former. This idea later became the central thesis of my 1981 book, *The Ethnic Phenomenon.* Both nepotism and "tribalism," far from being aberrations, are at the very root of human sociality. The Yoruba have the decency and intelligence openly to admit and recognize these as the basis of their society and the explanatory principle of their own and other people's behavior. They, in short, taught me a better brand of sociology than the one I was being paid to teach *them.* And they certainly put Talcott Parsons to shame as social and political analysts.

Through my many extracurricular contacts in Yorubaland, I got to know and like the area better than any other in Africa. It was not like the north, where the mantle of Islam and the Fulani Jihad of the early nineteenth century imposed a hegemonic cast on the region; each Yoruba city was, until a century ago, the capital of a statelet. Every Yoruba town is still a vibrant center of culture, art, politics, and commerce and has a unique individuality. Through my interest in Yoruba art, especially wood sculpture, I was privileged to know a number of obas ("kings"), artists, praise-singers, traditional priests and diviners, and others. Always, I was struck by the ease with which one could establish a relationship uninhibited by barriers of language, wealth, religion, education, status, sex, age, and, least of all, race.

The Yoruba are refreshingly free of what we French call complexes. They have a disarmingly candid good opinion of themselves and need no external confirmation to assert their tranquil self-confidence. One of my students expressed it well in a short autobiographical account I asked him to write: "As I was the brightest pupil in my class, there was no question that I would be successful." I have never seen a Yoruba, or indeed a southern Nigerian, express self-doubt or show any trace of an inferiority complex. Yet there is no arrogance or haughtiness either; just smiling, optimistic self-confidence. In Kenya, the sequels of colonialism were still so clearly visible; in contrast, in Nigeria the colonial trauma seemed totally erased in a few years.

Most of my time was spent on campus. The University of Ibadan was a self-contained residential community. Professors, lecturers, students, and even the "intermediate and subordinate staff" nearly all lived in accommodations rented to them (at very nominal rates) by the university. The campus, literally cleared out of a beautiful rain forest, is located some 15 kilometers outside the traditional city of Ibadan. This city of a million is a sprawling maze of narrow unpaved alleys connecting assemblages of compounds with mud walls and corrugated-iron roofs. The city and the university seemed worlds apart, one an apparent anarchical universe of vibrant, cacophonous, fragrant disorder, and the other an orderly, manicured, serene, tropical Cambridge luxuriating in its stately halls, its air-conditioned senior staff bungalows, and its jacaranda-shaded avenues. Yet the two were connected by a constant stream of dilapidated Toyota taxis, and nothing could be more deceptive than the university's appearance of being an ivory tower. The university was, to be sure, an island of glaring privilege in a poor society, and it was clearly the training ground of that society's new elite. But it was continuously embroiled in Nigeria's political maelstrom. More plots were probably hatched on the University of Ibadan campus than in army barracks, at least until the mid-1960s.

Indeed, the university played so central a role in the country's politics, in its ethnic conflicts, and in its emergent class structure that I decided that there was no better (or easier) object of study. For the first time in my field experience, I was turning ethnographic research inwardly on the very academic world that had spawned my discipline. Never have I been more thoroughly a participant-observer. And never, I might add, did I enjoy doing field work as much as in Ibadan. Helped by a British and three Nigerian assistants, I produced what I believe is the only ethnographic community study of a university (*Power and Privilege at an African University,* 1973).

My study of Ibadan had two complementary aims. On the one hand, by analyzing the class and ethnic divisions within the university, I wanted to show that it was a microcosm of the society around it, albeit a highly privileged microcosm. On the other hand, I wanted to indicate how the university, by training the new ruling elite of bureaucrats and technocrats, was powerfully shaping the present and future of Nigeria and had contributed to plunging Nigeria into its wrenching Civil War. The topic could not have been more sensitive, yet I was given virtually untrammelled freedom in probing it. My high status as professor and member of Senate gave me practically full access to all university documents and ensured the willing—nay, eager—cooperation of many colleagues, especially of the savvy academic politicians who delighted in exposing to me the Byzantine intrigues of our colleagues. My student assistants, for their part, were doing the same among their peers with equal ease and fun.

University Senate meetings, in particular, were a constant source of intellectual delight. In an inimitable mixture of British and Yoruba styles of oratory, a score or so of political virtuosi fenced with each other in a dazzling display of devastating irony and Machiavellian cunning. The vice-chancellor, Tom Lambo, a scion of an Abeokuta elite family, was a consummate master of this style of elegant ferocity. One episode is worth recounting. A member of University Council (a smaller body than Senate, composed for the most part of government appointees and entrusted mostly with running the financial and non-academic affairs of the university) had presented to the Senate for consideration a thoroughly inappropriate proposal. He was a senior civil servant in the government's medical service and proposed to introduce within the university the procedures for reprimanding subordinates that prevailed in the Civil Service. Within the academic context, his proposal was totally ludicrous and out of conformity with the collegial structure of the university.

Many members of the Senate were concerned that Council was serious about introducing this bit of authoritarian nonsense; they wondered how Lambo would introduce the matter in the Senate, as his position forced him to do. Lambo slowly read the text of the proposal with a deadpan expression, letting every ridiculous phrase sink in. There was a stunned silence as he finished. Then, with a genial smile, he said: "Now, gentlemen, I trust there will be no objections!" After a three-second pause, the whole of the Senate burst out in a fit of hilarity. Lambo had deftly killed three birds with one stone: he had used his political rival's own words to make him a laughing stock; he had permanently buried a ridiculous proposal in less than five minutes; and he had won much sympathy and admiration from his faculty. Not all of Lambo's actions were that effective, for he had at least a dozen equally skilled rivals to contend with, all of whom gladly confided in me when they saw how much I enjoyed the game myself. Naturally, not all of them liked my book when it came out, but several let me know that it was a fair and accurate picture of the university. That is all the praise I expected.

My teaching duties were also a pleasure. As in Nairobi, my students were both extremely bright and highly motivated. They not only wanted to graduate but to get the "high pass" that would secure them a job in the Senior Civil Service, a lifelong sinecure at high pay, with ample opportunity for corruption and nepotism. They were refreshingly cynical in their aspirations, but they applied their sharp intellect to an analysis of their own society with a degree of lucidity and a total absence of ideology that I never encountered in such a young group elsewhere. They accepted only one defense that someone was telling the truth: the other person had no *interest* in lying. "Why should I tell a lie?" was the most common profession of good faith.

Student government was widely regarded as an apprenticeship in political corruption. Every student expected his elected representatives to be corrupt, but each year a new slate of student officials got elected on a platform of rooting out corruption. The favorite racket of student government officials was to organize a chartered flight to London during the vacation. In order to generate free tickets for themselves and their girlfriends and a bit of spending money to boot, they would sell 20 or 30 percent more tickets than there were seats on the plane. Pandemonium broke loose on the day of departure at Ikeja Airport, but by then the funds had vanished. As the scam yielded mere peanuts by the standards of their elders, the students got off with a light tap on the wrist. In fact, I have *never* taken a Nigerian Airways flight that was not grossly oversold. There are basically two ways to get on a Nigerian plane: a "dash" (bribe) or a show of force (if you are an army officer or a high government official).

Another anecdote will convey the pervasiveness, brazenness, and imaginativeness of Nigerian corruption. A newly arrived Rockefeller Foundation employee was flagged down on the main road by a policeman. He was driving the foundation Peugeot assigned to him, but the policeman told him that he would have to go to the police station for a check on his papers. Terrified of being held incommunicado by the police, the man asked the policeman if he could make a telephone call from his office to warn his wife. The policeman gracefully agreed and rode with the man in his car to the office. As the man stepped out, the policeman politely asked him to leave the keys in the car. The man left to make his call, and when he returned, the car was gone. Accompanied by another foundation employee, he then went to the police station, asked to see the chief of police, and explained what had happened. The chief of police genially offered to set up a lineup of his men. The victim actually recognized the thief in the lineup of uniformed policemen. The chief of police smilingly asked the foundation person whether he was new to Nigeria. Upon being told that, indeed, he was, the police chief suggested that it was obviously a case of mistaken identity. All Africans looked alike to Americans, he had frequently noticed. No constable of his could conceivably be guilty of such a crime. In actual fact, the entire police station was running a car-theft operation, immediately smuggling the stolen vehicles into neighboring Dahomey (now Benin), where the cars would, within hours, be stripped down for parts.

But there was an amiable bonhomie and cleverness about Nigerian corruption, quite unlike the thuggery of the Kenya mafia for example. In Kenya, cabinet ministers assassinated each other over rackets. In Nigeria, the kleptocrats stashed their loot in Zurich bank accounts and merely absconded on the next plane to London when the heat was on. The next government would come in on a platform of honesty, and, within months, the cycle would repeat itself.

Eric and Oliver also enjoyed their year in Ibadan. Together with the two sons of a Nigerian neighbor, they would explore the rain forest for hours at a time. We trembled that they might catch schistosomiasis in a polluted stream or, worse, encounter a Gaboon viper. But they miraculously escaped all harm and developed a taste for fishing and beetle collecting. To this date, the rain forest has remained their image of paradise. By the end of their stay, they had become totally adjusted to Nigerian society. They even picked up Pidgin English, with the total linguistic adaptability of 7- and 8-year-old children.

Another facet of their Nigerianization was their treatment of animals. Nigerian children often take delight in torturing animals, and their parents too are, for the most part, totally callous about animal suffering. A favorite game, for instance, is to capture a bird, tie a long string to its leg, let it fly off, and then yank repeatedly on the string until the bird dies of exhaustion or injury. Another great favorite of children is to tie two lizards together and throw them on a much travelled road. The animals pull in opposite directions, cancelling each other's efforts, and get run over. Then their blue and red heads are cut off and strung into a colorful, if grisly, necklace. One day, as we drove through campus, we encountered tied lizards on the road. Irmi was in an indignant rage at the Nigerian kids and said she could strangle them. I stopped the car and started haranguing seven or eight boys hiding behind trees. Suddenly, two distinctly lighter heads appeared behind a bush. They belonged to Oliver and Eric.

One feature of Nigerian behavior that our boys did not adopt from their peers was filial respect. In fact, their lack of it, by African standards, once put us in an acutely embarrassing situation. We were visiting at the court of the oba of Benin. The occasion was the state visit of the oba of Lagos. We sat among the Benin nobility, all dressed in their white togas and red coral jewelry. Some 3,000 people were tightly packed in a palace courtyard about 50 meters square. There the main festivities were to take place, supposedly around 4 P.M. Unfortunately, the oba of Lagos used Nigerian Airways for the ninety-minute flight and he did not appear until 7 P.M., three hours late. There was simply no graceful or unobtrusive way of sneaking out as we were the only pale faces in a black ocean and were, in addition, sitting not far from the king, among the honored guests. Eric and Oliver were understandably hungry and impatient. Finally, Oliver broke out in a tantrum of impotent rage. He flew at Irmi and started ripping her clothes off. She was very lightly dressed and she barely escaped being stripped naked before I could contain Oliver. All eyes converged on the scene for lack of a better diversion, and a look of horrified scandal appeared on hundreds of faces, as if they had been witnessing a scene of incestuous rape. Several people started shouting at me: "Punish the child! Punish the child! This is intolerable." So, of course, was the interminable wait for the Nigerian Airways flight!

In June 1969, we reluctantly left Nigeria. Our flight from Ibadan to Lagos was predictably overbooked, so Johnson drove us for our last trip to Lagos. Our international flight, prudently booked with Pan American, got us out of Ikeja Airport almost on schedule. We stopped over in Europe for the summer, picked up a Peugeot in Paris, vacationed with my Aunt Solange in Normandy, visited the family and in-laws, flew back to the United States and, once more, drove our new car across the continent to Seattle.

We were coming back from Africa tremendously enriched, both culturally and materially. The bounty of the Rockefeller Foundation had enabled us to save enough money to purchase our first pieces of real estate: our Seattle home and our mountain retreat. And, luckily, we had all escaped injury and disease. It had been a most interesting and exciting two years.

CHAPTER 11

Back in Seattle

The next three years in Seattle marked the beginning of a slightly more sedentary existence than we had experienced to that date. So far, the boys had never been anywhere long enough to call any location home. Home was simply wherever we happened to be at any given time. It was not a place. Now we were in a position to buy a house and to sink roots. Presumably most of my career advances were behind me. We all liked the Pacific Northwest and Seattle enough to face the prospect of an indefinite stay. Our savings gave us the resources to buy a comfortable house near the university without otherwise overtaxing our budget. We picked a conventional, but spacious and functional, colonial-style house within walking distance of the campus, and then we started exploring the hinterland in search of a weekend retreat.

Until then, we had not really taken advantage of the outdoor resources of the region, and we felt that ownership of a mountain cottage would greatly improve the quality of our life and that of our children. Eric and Oliver were already quite interested in fishing, so we picked a place along the Skykomish River, one of the region's great fishing streams. Located near the village of Index, at the foot of a spectacular snow-capped peak by the same name, the mountain home soon became our favorite weekend and vacation spot. For me, it became a place to write, free of the electronic and human interruptions that nibble away at my time in the city. It allowed Irmi to indulge her green thumb. As for the boys, it took them away from much of the silliness of their contemporaries, and without the slightest regret on their part. As soon as they got out of the car, they would make a beeline for their fishing poles and the river.

The basic pattern of our existence was comfortably set, in a way that enabled us to combine our diverse interests with a shared family life of a quality and persistence that few urban Americans manage to create for themselves. The drug culture, adolescent peer pressures, and all the other concerns of so many of my colleagues passed us by altogether. Many of our friend both envied us and wondered how we managed to create such a nice family cocoon for ourselves. Other than a conscious effort on our part to isolate our children from what we saw as the silliness and misplaced values of the ambient culture, we have no secret formula to share. I suppose we were fortunate in having sensible children who accepted our values without rebelling and who, at the same time, became strong, self-confident individuals. The fact that Oliver and Eric were so close in age and kept each other company helped, but, very early, their closest associates were mostly adults, principally fellow fishermen.

Professionally, two series of events and developments profoundly marked this period of my life. One was mainly political and ideological, but it impinged directly on the main thrust of my scholarly specialty. The other, primarily intellectual, led to a considerable widening of my interests; but political events served as a catalyst nudging me in that direction more rapidly than might otherwise have been the case. As both developments represent good illustrations of the unity of theory and practice, I shall dwell on them at some length and, I hope, with a maximum of candor and a minimum of smugness.

Both developments, incidentally, put me in a more ideologically embattled position than ever before. They certainly put me squarely outside the "liberal" mainstream of academia and into a rather idiosyncratic niche. Many have facilely defined my position as "conservative," but I hope to convince my readers that it defies any conventional classification on any simple continuum of right or left. I suppose my pessimism and cynicism help create a superficial impression that my position is conservative. It is also true that I distanced myself from, and had little intellectual sympathy for, several ideological currents of the 1970s that were supported by the left, but then I detested the ideologies of the right even more.

The New Left, in particular, always struck me as an inchoate, romantic, anti-rationalist, hedonistic, personalistic ideology espoused by spoiled middle-class brats who turned to "radicalism" to solve personal problems, to escape serious intellectual engagement, and, not least, to escape the Vietnam draft. When, after the 1970 Kent State massacre, students came to ask me whether a boycott of classes would affect their final grade, I knew that, far from representing the vanguard of a social revolution, they were playing a deliciously titillating game of self-indulgent, self-righteous, late-adolescent rebellion.

My own politics in those years were those of the European Social Democratic old left, which rejected the psychologistic anti-rationalism of the gurus of the New Left. But I was also beginning to lean toward a more radical stance of anarchism. All states, I increasingly felt, represented degrees of corruption and tyranny; their professions of democracy and legitimacy were but thin disguises for the perpetuation of privilege by ruling elites. Some were more vicious than others in their means of repression, but all were repressive. Basically, all modern states were more alike than different, and all were increasingly despotic. None could claim my allegiance. Freedom could only exist in the vanishing interstices of state power. It could only survive in a constant and conscious rejection and subversion of state authority. In a sense, I was merely generalizing the lessons I had learned in the army, in Jesuit schools, and in other clashes with authority: that organized state power and authority are the supreme social evils. The ethical and free life was one that sought disengagement from relations of power and, therefore, from politics, since politics is competition for power. Any revolutionary movement that merely seeks to change the social base of state power merely achieves the circulation of tyranny.

The first set of events that engaged me on my return from Africa was primarily ideological and political. Much as my distaste for politics (and contempt for the American brand thereof) might have led me to avoid the issue, I simply could not because it touched the very core of my integrity as a teacher and scholar and attacked a central tenet of my value system. The set of events was the sudden shift, around 1968, of the civil rights movement from an ideology of individual rights and radical rejection of "race" as a legitimate category for social action and social policy to an ideology extolling group rights, collective guilt, and the legitimacy of race and ethnicity as principles of both political organization and social policy.

When I had left the United States in 1967, black power advocates were regarded as a lunatic fringe. When I returned in 1969, they seemed to have taken over the center stage of the civil rights movement. Worse yet, the conservative white establishment, partly in panic, partly in cunning Machiavellianism, seemed to respond with alacrity to demands for the re-racialization of American society. Most astonishing of all was the fact that this abrupt reversal of all fundamental ideological tenets of the civil rights movement, these demands for self-imposed apartheid, were being accepted as a mere extension of past developments, a logical radicalization of the movement for non-racial equality.

Let me say, first, that I did not object to the black power movement as such. I found it misguided and self-defeating and I rejected its racism, but any group is entitled to organize any way it sees fit, even if the strategy it pursues is suicidal. What I objected to, however, was the establishment's response to it. In my view, all demands for racialization of American society should have been ignored. Yet they were largely met, sometimes in panic, sometimes reluctantly, sometimes with alacrity. From the late 1960s, the United States embarked on a vast scheme officially to reinstate race and ethnicity in assigning pupils to schools, in admitting students to colleges and universities, in hiring and firing employees, and in many other domains. Suddenly, race and ethnicity questions started popping up on all kinds of public and private documents, and the era of quotas and "affirmative action" was launched. It now became *mandatory* to discriminate on racial ground. An interesting case was the issue of busing for school desegregation. This policy is usually said to have its legal base in the 1954 Supreme Court decision of *Brown v. Board of Education*. In fact, Brown was an *anti*-busing decision. It said, in effect, that no children could be categorized by race and bused out of their neighborhood to racially segregated schools. The new policy, on the other hand, forced racial assignment of pupils and racially based busing out of their neighborhoods in order to achieve desegregation. Brown abolished racial discrimination; busing re-institutionalized it.

My position has been so widely misunderstood that it bears restating. I fully support the total elimination of racial and ethnic discrimination, but I firmly believe that this aim cannot be achieved by official recognition and entrenchment of racial and ethnic criteria of group membership, and allocation of resources on the basis of group affiliation or categorical membership. Quite the opposite: any step in the direction of officially recognizing race or ethnicity is retrograde because it entrenches the very categories it purports to eliminate. Before expanding on my reasons for opposing race or ethnically based "affirmative action," I would like to spell out what I am *for*. I fully support:

1. Vigorous prosecution of all acts of discrimination and *individual* redress for such.

2. Policies seeking to reduce inequalities by the adoption of *economic* or *class* criteria of selection or qualification. Even if these policies are indirectly intended to benefit disproportionately certain disadvantaged racial or ethnic categories, the test of their equity is that they do not *exclude* anyone on racial or ethnic grounds.

3. A policy of complete tolerance of linguistic and cultural diversity,

including state support for bilingual education and the like, provided again that participation in any such programs be entirely open and voluntary and that there be no state-mandated assignment to any racial or ethnic category.

4. Complete freedom for any collectivity to organize *privately* along ethnic, religious, linguistic, or "racial" lines, provided they do not interfere with the rights of outsiders or infringe on the public domain. Ethnic or racial collectivities should have complete freedom to organize for political action, but should receive no more official recognition than any other pressure groups.

5. Absence of any official recognition of race and ethnicity as *criteria of group membership* or qualification for access to any resources in the public domain. Race and ethnicity questions should not be asked in the U.S. Census. My position does not preclude state protection and support of language and cultural rights. For example, the recognition of Spanish as a language of instruction in schools in no sense requires a definition of who is Hispanic. Spanish classes should be freely open to Anglos, and English classes to Hispanics. Yet the two systems of schooling could exist side-by-side, with complete freedom of parental choice.

My arguments against official recognition of race and ethnicity categories and entrenchment of group rights are multiple. Some are ethical, some ideological, some pragmatic. As early as 1971, I predicted the failure of affirmative action and foresaw many of the problems it would inevitably create or exacerbate. To avoid any confusion, let me stress here that I am defining affirmative action as it increasingly came to be practiced, namely as a policy of granting or denying access to social resources on the basis of membership in an ascriptively defined race or ethnic group. (Sex-based affirmative action, despite numerous attempts to lump it with racial or ethnic policies, has, in fact, taken a substantially different direction and has had quite different consequences. I am not concerned with it in this discussion.)

In brief, these are some of my principal objections to racially or ethnically-based affirmative action:

1. My South African experience convinced me that categorical distinctions based on race are always invidious and noxious to the subordinate groups. Therefore, any invocation of the principle of race, even ostensibly for purposes of redress of past wrongs, inevitably has stigmatizing consequences and perpetuates the inferior status of the stigmatized categories. In effect, to invoke race in order to bring about equality is an intrinsic contradiction. It does the opposite: it perpetuates and entrenches invidious distinctions.

This argument applies less to ethnic categories, which, unlike race, are not *intrinsically* invidious, but even for ethnicity, the conditions under which "egalitarian institutionalization" of ethnic categories can be successful are extremely limiting and not met in the United States. For one thing, the ethnic groups must be highly territorialized, and for another, they must have relatively equal status to start with. "Consociational democracy," as this system has been called, can only work, in short, if there is not much inequality to start with. And, even then, the system is extremely fragile and vulnerable to even slight shifts in the status quo.

2. Because affirmative action is based on categorical membership and group rights, it conflicts frontally with the principle of individual rights that underlies the entire legal system of Western societies. It, therefore, affronts the sense of equity of millions of citizens who are not racists, but who are in danger of becoming so when they are constantly reminded that race *is* a relevant social category and that it works against them. Affirmative action inevitably heightens racial and ethnic consciousness and creates a vicious boomerang effect. [of course]

3. Affirmative action inevitably unleashes a competitive process *between* underprivileged groups and, therefore, divides them much more than it unites them. A frantic game of preemptive claims and manipulative strategies to capture what are, in any case, doubtful "advantages" leads to ethnic fragmentation. Eventually, the game engulfs virtually all the groups in the society. Once the process is institutionalized, even the privileged groups organize ethnically in self-defense.

4. By emphasizing race and ethnicity, affirmative action detracts attention from fundamental class inequalities and, therefore, deters organization along class lines. A true "rainbow coalition" must necessarily be based on class, not on race, ethnicity, or gender.

5. Affirmative action benefits not the underprivileged, but the middle class among the minority groups and thus accentuates class divisions within racial and ethnic groups. These groups become increasingly polarized between a coopted bourgeoisie and a redundant Lumpenproletariat.

For all these reasons, affirmative action, far from being the progressive policy it purports to be, is, in my view, the most retrograde one that the United States experienced since the post-Reconstruction era at the end of the nineteenth century. Not only was it unsuccessful in any of its stated aims of equalizing the distribution of, and access to, resources; on some indices, the gaps widened during its supposed implementation. One can, of course, question whether those who enforced affirmative action ever *meant* it to succeed. I am personally doubtful, if only because so much of it was implemented under the very dubious sponsorship of the Nixon administration. What affirmative action *did* do was create a small coopted class of "profiteers of apartheid," minority group professionals, bureaucrats, and the like (overwhelmingly in university and federal government employ) who have a vested interest in perpetuating their particularistically gained privileges. Their dubious gains have been purchased at the cost of paving the ground for the massive swell of reactionary politics practiced during the Reagan era.

This analysis now seems like the wisdom of hindsight, but I actually predicted most of these developments as early as 1970. I was convinced even then that the new course could only lead to disaster, and I sounded the alarm in the classroom, in scholarly journals, on television interviews, in open letters to my university colleagues, in personal acts of resignation from professional bodies, in newspaper articles, in private correspondence with university authorities, and so on. Never have subsequent events so completely validated my most pessimistic predictions and seldom have my actions been so totally futile and ineffective. I became the target of a torrent of ideological invective (and even physical threats), a semi-ostracism from the "liberal" academic mainstream, and now I receive the belated, unwanted, and embarrassing kudos of the New Right. I was virtually alone in the United States in attacking affirmative action from the *left,* not from the right, and I was so far out of line with all main currents of American political thinking that hardly anyone understood my position, not even those who belatedly agreed with me.

Because the main thrust of both my teaching and research interests was focused on race and ethnic relations, the issues were not simply academic and ideological ones to me; they affected my whole existence. In a sense, I was reliving my South African experience, which had led me to my uncompromising stance on the refusal to legitimate race as a social category. I was fighting the same battle against racism, but this time it was the left that attacked me and accused me of being a racist for refusing to discriminate on the basis of race. Some even managed to see in my completely consistent position an ideological reversal from my earlier opposition to apartheid and an alleged conversion to "racism." The irony was not lost on me, and I never allowed myself to become as deeply involved in the American politics of race as I had been in South Africa. Nevertheless, the American episode of the early 1970s left a legacy of increased alienation and disaffection from the society and its political process. I am now more convinced than ever that American academics are merely the court jesters of a decadent society. They are allowed their little enclave of freedom, precisely because their actions are so inconsequential.

A brief recounting of some personal involvements of the period will document, once more, the intimate unity of theory and practice. One of the opening shots came at the 1969 Montreal meetings of the African Studies Association (ASA). A group of largely Afro-American students disrupted the meetings and demanded the "Africanisation" of the association and exposure of its "neo-colonialism." Indeed, I shared some of their concerns. I had misgivings about the involvement of many members of the ASA with unsavory intelligence activities of the U.S. government, and I had expressed in print my concern about CIA and State Department infiltration into the ASA. I had myself been approached twice, in the early 1960s, about my willingness to be a consultant on counter-insurgency operations in Zaïre. In one instance, I was approached by the notorious Rand Corporation and, in the other, by another "research" outfit, the Atlantic Research Corporation, directed by a German with impeccable academic credentials: he had a Nazi-vintage doctorate in geopolitics from the University of Freiburg. When I turned him down and said that I regarded his activities as unethical, he wrote an outraged letter to my department head, asking him to punish me for insulting him.

In short, I sympathized with some of the criticisms of the student militants. But I could not accept their racist demands that skin pigmentation was to be a criterion for membership on the council of the association. What scandalized me most, however, was not the list of student demands, but the alacrity with which most of my prominent colleagues in the association acceded to the student demands for racialization and accepted a principle of racial parity on the council. That body, they agreed, would henceforth consist of six "Africans" (meaning dark faces) and six "Europeans" (meaning pale faces). I remember a moving statement by an anguished Hilda Kuper that she was a Swazi and thus an African, but her voice, like mine, was drowned in an orgy of racist hysteria. There was no option, I felt, but to resign from the ASA and, although I did not realize it at the time, that episode was probably decisive in reorienting my scholarship away from Africa and toward Latin America. Indeed, I did not return to Africa until 1985, although I continued to write about it.

A few years later, I likewise felt constrained to resign from the DuBois-Johnson-Frazier Award Committee of the American Sociological Association, when I discovered that the majority of the committee was determined to reserve this award for blacks, but was too hypocritical to admit it. My reasoned letter of resignation mailed to the editor of *Footnotes*, the association's newsletter, was never published. To my knowledge this was an unprecedented act of censorship. Almost any reasonable letter by a Fellow, which deals with an important issue, is almost automatically accepted for publication unless it duplicates another in content. Mine certainly did not! The amusing postscript to the incident is that, in 1978, I was myself the recipient of the Spivak Award, the much better funded but racially unpegged prize for distinguished work in race relations. The principle of internal apartheid had, by then, thoroughly suffused the entire association, not only in such things as racial representation to elective office, but even in its awards structure.

However, the climax of the racial crisis for me came in spring 1971 and occurred on my home campus. The events that led to it were complex and multiple. On my return from Nigeria in 1969, I found that a Black Studies Program had been created in my absence. My name was listed on its faculty and my courses on its curriculum, both without any prior consultation with me. I protested not only at the arbitrary and unauthorized use of my name, but also at the fact that the black studies faculty, as I soon discovered, consisted of two sub-groups, a core group (which happened to be darkly pigmented and made all the decisions) and a peripheral group (lightly pigmented, never even invited to meetings). The director of the program, a totally marginal acting assistant professor without a Ph.D., curtly told me that he would remove my name from the list of faculty, but that the courses I taught did not belong to me and that, therefore, I had no say as to whether they should be listed in the black studies curriculum. This was a key issue because my course on race and ethnic relations drew several hundred students each year and singlehandedly made up some 40 percent of the total enrollment in "black studies." Never mind that I considered my course to be one in *human* rather than black studies. The enrollment in my class could be used to justify the great demand for black studies.

In the meantime, the University of Washington had also created a full-blown machinery of internal colonialism to deal with its newly increased clientele of "minority" students. Sam Kelly, a retired army lieutenant colonel without a Ph.D., was hired to be the "native chief" of black students. The School of Education was cajoled into giving him an associate professorship, and he was made vice-president of the Office of Minority Affairs. This apartheid bureaucracy quickly proliferated and became internally compartmentalized into five divisions: one for blacks; one for Amerindians; one for Chicanos; one for Asians; and a token "poverty" division for whites (making up about 5 percent of the total operation). In short order, the entire office was controlled by self-styled black "radicals."

The vast majority of our "minority" students—something like three-fourths—were of Asian origin, and they had long been admitted according to universalistic criteria. Indeed, students of Japanese and Chinese origin tended to outperform the general student population and to be over-represented in the reputedly tough fields of mathematics, engineering, and the physical sciences. The trick was to count them in as "minority" students when there was a need to demonstrate the success of the Office of Minority Affairs, but to exclude them from the program's benefits. Most Asian students did not, in any case, want to be associated with minority affairs and they resented being manipulated to political ends.

Although Chicanos outnumber blacks in the State of Washington, they definitely got the short end of the minority affairs stick and so did the Amerindians despite sizeable numbers of potential beneficiaries. Together, they were only about one-third as numerous as black students, and they never mustered the critical mass to make any political difference. There was only one mild flurry of Chicano political activity ending in the trashing of a dean's office. The "poverty" division was, of course, a total farce. Even though poor whites in the state outnumber all the other "disadvantaged" groups put together, they were represented at the university by some 40 or 50 students out of 37,000!

This situation left blacks in virtually total control of special admissions, remedial instruction, and all the other supposed "support" facilities for "special" students. The office's self-assigned task was to bring up the black enrollment at the university to the national average—in a state where blacks only made up 2 percent of the population. Since our undergraduate population was (and still is) overwhelmingly drawn from state residents, the aim was a five-fold over-representation of blacks in the student body. Indeed, in the 1960s, our black enrollments under universalistic admission standards were very close to proportional, and there was not a shred of evidence of racial discrimination on campus, though sex discrimination was indeed widespread.

Naturally, such a crash program of special black admissions called for the cajoling and bribing of black youths off the streets of the nation's ghettoes. Functional illiterates were begged to enroll in order to demonstrate the success of the Office of Minority Affairs. Once enrolled, they were steered to special remedial courses and to black studies courses, of which I taught one, whether I wanted to or not. Several minor episodes all contributed to the climatic crisis in spring of 1971. One was a request by the administrator of the black studies program that I conduct a racial census of my class, which I refused to do. Another was the involvement of five black students in a crude attempt to tamper with a grade sheet of my class. (They changed their grades in their favor, but, luckily, I was prepared. I had made a photocopy of the grade sheet, and I turned the students in to the Discipline Committee.)

By mid-term, it was obvious that a major crisis was brewing. My class had about 300 students, of whom around 80 were black. The mid-term exam results, when plotted on a graph, revealed *two* grade distributions with two modes about three standard deviations apart. The papers themselves revealed a group of about 40 or 50 functional illiterates, who could charitably be described as having the equivalent of a seventh grade education. (I said "eighth grade" at the time, but in retrospect, I was overly generous in my estimate.)

In a long letter to the provost, I expressed my concern about the situation, anticipated trouble, and stated my inability to teach a university-level class to a mixed audience of college students and functional illiterates. I got in reply a bureaucratic expression of concern for my pedagogical predicament combined with a pious expectation that I would find a way to handle the situation to everyone's satisfaction. Most of my colleagues, of course, were doing just that, by the blatant adoption of double racial standards of evaluation or, alternatively, the suspension of all standards for everyone. Indeed, small goon squads of black students were patrolling the campus and intimidating professors into changing their grades. I had already been visited by three such squads of 3 to 5 students, who became vituperative when I refused to budge. Either course (no standards or double standards) was unacceptable to me. For good measure, my letter to the provost was passed on to the Office for Minority Affairs, where it entered the file of exhibits later to be produced and misquoted from in an attempt to prove that I was a racist.

Predictably, the excrement hit the proverbial fan when the final grades in my course were released. An open letter was published in the local press, with numerous signatures headed by that of Sam Kelly, vice-president for Minority Affairs. It demanded my dismissal from the university as a racist. I quickly counter-attacked, refuting with ease allegations of racial discrimination in grading. I simply offered for inspection the examination papers themselves. They were sadly eloquent. Significantly, none of the signatories took me up on my offer. Nevertheless, for the next fortnight or so, I "made" the campus *Daily*, the two Seattle newspapers, and/or the local news on one or more of the television chains almost every day. The media fanfare was naturally accompanied by the usual complement of telephone calls ranging from vituperative and threatening (presumably by angry blacks) to supportive by such organizations as the KKK and the John Birch Society.

My colleagues distinguished themselves by their resounding silence, but for two notable exceptions. My chairman, Frank Miyamoto, forthrightly supported me, both in private and in public statements, and the History Department issued a collective statement of support as well.

Most others preferred to ignore the issue. Some even hinted that perhaps I had been a bit inflexible and had needlessly exposed my department to public embarrassment. Surely, with a little more tact and diplomacy, I could have avoided all this brouhaha. Perhaps I was secretly relishing the publicity, they suggested. Also revealing was the reaction of the provost when I asked him for an official university statement concerning the demand for my dismissal by one of the university's vice-presidents. To my knowledge, it was totally unprecedented that a senior administrator of the university demanded the dismissal of a member of the tenured faculty. Was Sam Kelly, I asked the provost, speaking in his official capacity? I pointed out that his name on the open letter was followed by his title. No, answered the provost, both Sam Kelly and I were speaking for ourselves, not for the university. Kelly's attacks and my self-defense were equated as private acts.

The total lack of principled response from the university administration even when the most fundamental issues of academic integrity were at stake was no great surprise to me, but it permanently destroyed the last shred of respect I might still have had for academic administrators. Academia, thy name is spinelessness! I taught the course on race to a large group for one more year because I did not want to give the impression that I had been successfully scared away from it. But I decided that, from then on, I was never going to teach another large undergraduate course. I simply created a higher-level, more selective course on comparative race and ethnic relations, with an enrollment of about one-tenth that in the old course. If my colleagues did not want to support me in an issue of intellectual integrity, let them carry the burden of "educating" the students in the most "diplomatic" way they saw fit. Twelve years later, my new chairman expressed regret that so few students were exposed to me, a world-renowned authority on race, and asked me if I would not, please, start teaching the large undergraduate course on the subject again. Had he forgotten, I asked him, the circumstances under which I ceased teaching it? Yes, he confessed, he had forgotten. I haven't.

The second major development of this period of my life was the increasing intellectual dissatisfaction with the reigning orthodoxy of cultural relativism and determinism in social science, and the beginning of my search for a broader and more satisfactory framework in the direction of evolutionary biology. I began with Lorenzian ethology, focusing primarily on the works of Desmond Morris, Robin Fox, Lionel Tiger, Robert Bigelow, and others, and I canvassed the literature on behavioral primatology for a comparative basis. In primate studies, I was especially impressed and influenced by the work of Hans Kummer on baboons. *Age and Sex in Human Societies* (1973), subtitled *A Biosocial Perspective*, was a product of that period, as were an article in *American Sociological Review* (1974, vol. 39, no. 6), "Bringing Beasts Back In," and the 1975 edition of my textbook, *Man in Society*.

My ideological critics have interpreted that expansion of my intellectual horizon as a "conversion" to "social Darwinism," as a recantation of my previous "liberal" writings, and as a move consistent with a general ideological turn to the right. In their minds, any concern for the biological evolution of human culture is, by definition, a rightist undertaking, and no amount of evidence or reasoned argument to the contrary will disabuse them. My politics were indeed moving away from liberalism, but in the radical, anarchist direction, not in any way recognizably identifiable with any conventional rightist movement. Typically, I find all political candidates presenting themselves in American elections to be so far to the right of my opinions as to present me with no real choice.

Yet intellectual honesty impels me to give political ammunition to my critics and to note that there was a definite ideological catalyst to that extension of my interests in a biological and evolutionary direction. I have readily admitted (in both my aforementioned 1973 and 1975 books) to the effect of my engagement with 1970s feminism in prodding me toward a serious examination of the biological bases of human behavior. My tolerance threshold for intellectual silliness has always been low, and the dominant feminist line of the 1970s amply qualified. The dogma that virtually all significant social and behavioral differences between men and women were the result not of the biology of sex, but of the cultural construction of gender, was such an arrant half-truth that it could not be ignored. Because all significant differences between males and females have ultimately to do with each sex's specialized role in its species' reproductive system, the feminist myth of biological trivialism could only be sustained by ignoring reproduction and by treating fetuses and children as irritating nuisances. Not surprisingly, the ideological nonsense was largely propagated by young, childless women.

There was, thus, a profoundly anti-child and anti-humanist dimension to some strains of strident feminism. If one accepts ideological claims of feminism to humanism, then the very term "feminism" is a misnomer. If the aim of feminism is the liberation of both genders from socially defined roles, inequalities and inequities, then it should no more be called feminism than the search for racial equality should be called blackism. Humanist feminism is simply a contradiction in terms, and one that becomes immediately evident if one tried to define what one might mean by humanist masculinism.

Another bit of ideological nonsense bothered me, namely the facile and fashionable equation of racism and sexism. Racism had a clear meaning to me: it meant the attribution of social importance to biologically trivial differences such as skin pigmentation. But the fundamental difference between racism and sexism that is so facilely glossed over is that sex differences are *not* biologically trivial. They evolved in millions of animal and vegetable species over hundreds of millions of years. This is hardly the evolutionary homolog to selection in a single species for a few genes controlling melanin production. Any ideologue who pretends that the two are the same and who draws conclusions from this false analogy must either remain resolutely ignorant of biology or abandon the stance.

The immediate catalyst that goaded me into professional activity on the sex front was a proposal by a group of female graduate students in the Sociology Department to teach a course on women in society. As were most of our graduate students, that group was largely ignorant of human biology, palaeontology, archaeology, anthropology, and other fields essential to an intelligent teaching of the proposed topic. I agreed with the students that the dimension of sex and gender differentiation (and the related topic of *age* differentiation, another fundamental and biologically non-trivial feature of all societies) had been badly neglected in our sociology curriculum, and that this lacuna must be filled as quickly as possible. But I also felt that the topic was far too important to be taught by half-baked graduate students who, in addition, had a vested ideological interest in talking rubbish, beyond even what their level of ignorance of the subject would lead one to expect.

As for myself, I clearly had an enormous amount to learn on the topic, but at least I had a reasonable command of ethnography to give me a broad basis of cross-cultural comparison. This was my chance to devote a year of intensive reading in human evolution and in primate ethology to broaden that comparative understanding. I, therefore, volunteered to introduce into the sociology curriculum a respectable class on age and sex differentiation (for which I wrote my 1973 book as a text). After my proposal cleared the departmental and college curriculum committees, the "women's caucus" made an unsuccessful last-ditch attempt to prevent me from teaching the course by petitioning my chairman to that effect. This latest attempt to interfere with my academic freedom was, I am glad to say, treated with the contempt it merited and the women in society course was relegated to the Women's Studies Program where it belonged. My reputation as a sexist as well as a racist was now firmly established in campus radical circles. The latter, having signally failed either to make me budge or to have me displaced, has left me in peace ever since.

In the end, it often pays to stand one's ground. There are two things of which I am particularly intolerant: nonsense and dishonesty. I continue to be amazed at the willingness of so many of my colleagues to put up with and to compromise with both, but, then, many of them regard me as a priggish moral absolutist. Naturally, I prefer to see myself as defending a rational position based on a pragmatic view of reality. Perhaps what distinguishes me from many of my colleagues is that I care more strongly about some issues and that, when I do care, I try to make intellectual sense of issues. That is, I cannot rest until I develop a reasoned, internally consistent position about the issue in question. This, in turn, means articulating a set of values with a set of empirical realities and recognizing any dilemmas that the analysis may reveal. Such a course often incapacitates one for action, as action often requires ignoring the irreducibility of dilemmas. Unlike Marx for whom understanding was a necessary step toward action, I am often content to stop at understanding. For one thing, I am too pessimistic about the indeterminacy of action. It is easy to change things, but difficult to change them for the better.

The political events to which I just alluded did not in any way change my outlook or affect the direction in which I went, but they prodded me into exploring new fields faster and earlier than I might have done otherwise. After a couple of years of reading human and primate ethology, the prima facie case for the biological evolution of social behavior seemed quite strong to me. The old cultural determinist orthodoxy was no longer tenable. Neither was that apparently incurable malady of social scientists to force explanations into a false opposition of nature versus nurture, genes versus culture, heredity versus environment. Nothing short of an evolutionary and *interactive* model could account for behavior. Behavior, including human behavior, was obviously the product of an interaction of genes and environment.

Culture for humans was, equally obviously, an important part of that environment, but culture itself could only be understood as the outcome of a long process of biological evolution by natural selection. To be sure, culture had emergent properties not directly reducible to the biology of genes; the linkages between genes and culture were no doubt still exceedingly obscure and, most likely, indirect, multiple, and complex. No simplistic instinct theory or attempt to link individual cultural traits with specific genes would serve as a general model. The crudeness and theoretical fiasco of the "psychometricians" and their IQ studies, for example, were a clear path *not* to follow.

Interestingly, I had been groping for a theoretical model that had been in existence since 1964; it was only through Edward O. Wilson's 1975 book, *Sociobiology, The New Synthesis,* that I became aware of the path-breaking work of William Hamilton, John Maynard Smith, George C. Williams, Robert Trivers, Richard Alexander, and others. In the early 1970s, I was still thinking within the largely descriptive framework of classical Lorenzian ethology and implicitly accepting group selectionist arguments.

Ethology left me with an uncomfortable feeling that, while it was generally on the right track, it could never hope to get very far in an account of human culture. It could help us, through cross-specific comparisons, in establishing the probable pre-cultural basis of some human behavior and in setting species-wide boundaries on human culture, but none of that was terribly exciting. What was needed was not simply more painstaking observational studies to refine the human "ethogram" and more inferential speculations of evolutionary origins of, and genetic limits on, behavior based on cross-species comparisons; the field cried for a genuine theoretical framework that meaningfully *incorporated* culture into the evolutionary process. Culture, I felt, was neither a "tale told by an idiot" nor a deus ex machina propelling our species out of the orbit of biological evolution, but something in between. Human language was neither a complex bark nor a totally arbitrary symbolic system invented by a tabula rasa of a mind. Culture and language were the products of a very special and unique kind of brain with many non-random propensities that evolved by natural selection. To achieve a greater level of understanding, human ethology had to become more theoretical and less descriptive, and it had to go beyond the stage of "studying humans as if they did not talk." It is one thing not to believe what people tell you; quite another not to listen to what they have to say. Looking for the lie and learning from it is a great source of data in the field, I had learned long ago.

All this groping for a way to put the social sciences squarely in the mainstream of evolutionary theory, where I felt they belonged, was still nebulous between 1970 and 1972; but every new area I glimpsed at suggested tantalizing possibilities and convergences: structural linguistics, brain physiology, developmental psychology, human palaeontology—all seemed to point to a single interactive model of the evolution of man as *both* a biological and a cultural animal. To ignore either component was to retard the social sciences.

My three years in Seattle (1969–1972) were not all travail and political turmoil. In many ways, they marked the apogee of the UW Sociology Department. Bright and diverse people joined the faculty, like Guenther Roth, Michael Hechter, Pepper Schwartz, Phil Blumstein, Karen Cook, Stanley Lieberson, and Sam Preston. I was fortunate to have my quota of excellent graduate students like Cullen Hayashida, George Primov (who was soon to accompany me to Peru as my field assistant), and Gary Hamilton (who is making his mark as a Sinologist and comparative sociologist). Funding was still adequate to support a lot of "frills," especially several flourishing inter-disciplinary programs. I was particularly involved in our small but very active and dynamic African Studies Committee, which gave me a chance to associate closely with several members of the Anthropology Department: Simon Ottenberg, Edgar Winans, Carol Eastman, and David Spain.

Even more central to my intellectual interests was the Committee on Comparative Studies in Ethnicity and Nationalism, which a small group of us formed in those years. The main early members of the group were Paul Brass, political scientist and Indianist; anthropologist Charles Keyes, who specialized in Southeast Asia; Africanist anthropologist Simon Ottenberg; sociologist Michael Hechter; and myself. We developed an interdisciplinary graduate program in ethnicity and produced a dozen first-rate doctorates. We held an advanced symposium each spring, and most of the symposia were published as books or special issues of journals. In short, we constituted an active and visible forum for the exchange of ideas in the burgeoning field of comparative ethnic relations. The list of our visitors became a "who is who" in the field: Heribert Adam, Leo Kuper, Michael Banton, John Rex, Nathan Glazer, St. Clair Drake, Crawford Young, and some forty more.

By 1972, I felt the urge to go into the field once more. A grant from the National Institute of Mental Health to go to Cuzco, Peru, for a study of class and ethnicity was approved. George Primov, my assistant, and his wife, Karen, left first in June; I followed in July and Irmi and the boys brought up the rear a couple of weeks later. A new research adventure was to begin.

CHAPTER 12

Los Caminos del Inca

The title of this chapter is the name of Peru's most famous car race, on an even more gruelling circuit than the more fashionable East African Safari. Between July 1972 and December 1973, I was to drive some 40,000 kilometers of Peru's and Bolivia's roads, at an *average* altitude of some 3,500 meters. Some roads reach 4,700 meters, higher than the summit of Mont Blanc. Because of their proximity to the Equator, the Central Andes can sustain human life at higher elevations than other mountain ranges. Thousands of people spend most of their lives at over 4,000 meters, relying on alpaca herding and on some hardy varieties of potatoes and high-altitude cereals for sustenance. The high Andes of Peru and Bolivia are without question one of the most beautiful and fascinating regions of the world, although I never felt comfortable in Andean culture.

Flying down to Peru, I took the opportunity to make a few intermediate stops: Mexico City, Guatemala City, Cartagena, Bogotá, Quito, and finally, Lima. The stop in Guatemala enabled me to fulfill my dream of seeing Tikal, perhaps the greatest Maya city and the most aesthetically appealing archaeological site in the Americas. Previous Mexican trips had taken me to Palenque, Uxmal, Chichén Itzá, and other great Maya sites, but the grandeur of Tikal is unique. Cartagena, the great Spanish port of entry into South America, is a monument to the colonial past and perhaps the most African city in the Spanish Americas. Bogotá is a bustling megalopolis, high in an Andean valley, and its Museo del

Oro alone is well worth the stop. The colonial city, a substantial one since it became a vice-royalty in the eighteenth century, is now smothered in a sea of high-rise modernity, and, unfortunately, the city's reputation for violent crime is well deserved.

In Ecuador, I spent a week in Quito, Ambato, Riobamba, Otavalo, and Puyo and got my first view of both Andean peasantry and the Amazonian jungle. The Otavalo Indians, famous for their entrepreneurial savvy, were especially interesting. They are one of the few Indian groups in the Americas that both resisted assimilation *and* became economically successful in the commercial world. They now cover the globe with their commercialized homespun textiles; in 1981, for example, I saw a group of Otavalos selling their textiles during the fiesta of Pamplona, Spain. One of them, still proudly wearing his long pigtail, told me that there is a community of some 200 Otavalos centered in Madrid, who live by making the rounds of fiestas and peddling their wares throughout the Iberian Peninsula. By 1988, Otavalos were successfully playing music and selling cassettes in the Paris Metro.

Quito is a jewel of colonial architecture; it is the best preserved capital city in Latin America, saved from ugliness and modernity by the presence of bustling Guayaquil on the coast. It also has a beautiful Museo del Oro, albeit a smaller one than Bogotá's. The descent, in a somewhat rickety bus, from Quito into the *yungas* ("rain forest") was also a memorable adventure. I was soon to repeat similar trips in Peru and Bolivia, and every one of them has been breathtaking, literally, because of the perils of automobile traffic on narrow, unpaved, precipitous mountain roads, and, figuratively, because of the ever-changing vegetation as one descends from a 4,000-meter-high, treeless *altiplano* to lush rain forest at 1,500 meters, via tree ferns, bamboos, and cacti. In Ecuador, the adventure is enhanced by the omnipresence of jittery little military garrisons, prepared to defend the jungle frontier against Peruvian aggression. Indeed, poor little Ecuador has already lost half of its territory to its greedy southern neighbor. In 1941, for instance, Peru gobbled up a huge chunk of Ecuador when the rest of the world was busily facing World War II. Peru emerged one of the biggest victors of the war at virtually no cost.

Finally, I arrived in Lima where I spent a few days establishing contact with Peruvian anthropologists at the Instituto de Estudios Peruanos and the universities of San Marcos and La Católica. José Matos Mar, Fernando Fuenzalida, Giorgio Alberti, Julio Cotler, and others received me quite well and I found them a most stimulating group. I also spent a couple of days getting our project's Volkswagen microbus out of customs in Callao, visiting the sights and museums of Lima, and enjoying some of its excellent restaurants (in particular its *chifas,* or Chinese restaurants, and its seafood eateries).

Traces of the pre-Columbian past only survive in outlying archaeological sites and the collections of four main museums, one devoted to the few gold objects that escaped the rapacious Spanish crucible, another to the astonishing pottery of Mochica, Chimú, Nazca, Paracas, Chavín, Inca, and other Peruvian civilizations, and one to textiles recovered largely from mummy bundles. Peruvian pottery and textiles rank among the finest artistic creations in the world and are certainly the most exquisite in the Americas.

The colonial past has survived in the lavish baroque architecture of churches and palaces. These stand as tangible remnants of the immense accumulation of wealth that flowed from the mines of Potosí to the capital of the vice-royalty of Peru. The mummy of Francisco Pizarro, the man who started it all, lies exposed to tourists in the cathedral. The cadavers of the millions of Indians who perished during the three centuries of colonial predation have vanished without trace.

Compared to Arequipa, Cuzco, Ayacucho, and other smaller towns, colonial Lima is poorly preserved, however. The Baroque churches and the elaborate carved-wood balconies of old palaces are but fragments of the past, smothered in a thriving, bustling commercial metropolis. Despite the poverty and chronic unemployment of much of its population, Lima still constitutes the greatest concentration of wealth, education, talent, and expertise in Peru. As in all Latin American countries with their highly centralized political structures, the lion's share of the country's resources converges on the capital. Even the most destitute, unemployed sub-proletarians of the capital are probably marginally better off than most peasants because they have some access to educational and medical services that simply do not exist in the interior.

As a rough approximation of the pyramid of power, wealth, and privilege, Peru (and other Latin American countries) might be pictured as a four-tiered system, differentiated both socially and spatially. At the base, a broad peasantry, scattered in thousands of villages, bears the burden of the entire structure. One step up, small market towns and district capitals spawn petty entrepreneurs, artisans, and bureaucrats who are the first link in the chain of surplus expropriation. Regional cities (generally departmental capitals, in the French sense) are ruled by a mercantile and bureaucratic bourgeoisie. They are major hubs of both economic and political power, with a well-defined rural hinterland, and they are real urban centers with the full range of amenities from airports and universities to hospitals and supermarkets. Yet compared to the national capital, they are small, provincial, powerless, and insignificant. Arequipa, the second largest city in Peru, for example, is only one-tenth the size of Lima.

All the decisions of any consequence are made in Lima. Even department prefects (the equivalent of state governors in the American governmental hierarchy) are but glorified flunkies appointed and fired by the minister of the interior. Successful people in every field gravitate toward the capital. All the top universities, technical schools, hospitals, and other services are found in Lima. All of the political and commercial oligarchy resides there. As a rough measure of scale of population, services, wealth, and power, one might say that each step up in the four tiers of the system multiplies size and resources by a factor of ten.

Lima, like other Latin American capitals, is also fundamentally different from provincial cities in that, together with its port of Callao, it is the center of most manufacturing industry. Thus, it is the only city in the country to have a sizeable urban proletariat, much of it of recent peasant origin. Miserable though the condition of that chronically unemployed or underemployed urban proletariat and sub-proletariat is, the working class in the Third World belongs to a privileged minority compared to the peasantry. This is particularly evident in a country like Peru, with its sharp ecological cleavage between *costa* and *sierra*. Lima is not only the industrial, mercantile, and political heart of a country, but also the center of an ecologically privileged region within the country. Coastal Peru not only has a monopoly of industry, but also the lion's share of large-scale commercial agriculture. The costa generates a per capita income roughly twice as high as the sierra. Coastal Peru has an economy (and a class structure) comparable to that of late nineteenth-century Europe. By contrast, the sierra is still basically in the eighteenth century, but for an extremely thin technological veneer of modernity that affects perhaps one-tenth of its population. Yet costa and sierra, despite the tremendous ecological and technological hiatus between them, are intertwined in a centralized political and economic system that perpetuates and accentuates the internal class and regional disparities.

It was, indeed, the source of these inequalities that I was coming to Peru to study. I agreed with much of what the dependency theorists (who completely dominate Latin American social science) were saying, but I could not accept a position that seeks to reduce ethnicity to class. I wanted to show that inequality in an ethnically stratified and ecologically differentiated country like Peru had both a class and an ethnic component. To be sure, class and ethnicity are often empirically intertwined and both have important ecological correlates, but each is an analytically distinct principle of social organization. Overlap between the two factors is an empirical question, not one to be settled through an a priori theoretical position seeking to reduce one to the other. In the case of Peru, there is, indeed, a large amount of empirical overlap between being an Indian and being a peasant, and thus neo-Marxist analysis gives a relatively good fit to reality. But in other situations, notably in Africa, the autonomy of class and ethnicity is quite evident.

Even in Peru, the linguistic and cultural marginality of the Indian peasantry to the mestizo-dominated society reinforces the class subordination of the peasantry and makes it qualitatively different than a system of domination based on class alone. This work resulted in my 1977 monograph co-authored with George Primov, *Inequality in the Peruvian Andes: Class and Ethnicity in Cuzco*. Our study focused on the Department of Cuzco, a region inhabited by some three-quarter million people, of whom some three-fourths were Indian peasants living in scattered villages and haciendas and one-fourth mestizos residing in urban centers. The city of Cuzco, capital of the department, had a population of 125,000 and was the only real city within a radius of 300 kilometers. There were many reasons I picked Cuzco as the locale of my study. In the southern Andes of Peru (and adjacent areas of Bolivia) is the largest concentration of monolingual speakers of indigenous languages in the Western Hemisphere. Some eight to ten million people are native speakers of Quechua and Aymará and at least half of them speak little or no Spanish. Any study of the effect of language and culture on social stratification would be best conducted in an area where the ethnic differentiation was most pronounced.

The regional scale of the study was also dictated by both methodological and practical considerations. A small-scale community study would only tap the bottom of the social hierarchy, and a very special subsegment of it, such as an hacienda or an Indian village. At a minimum, I wanted a regional city and its hinterland in order to capture all but the topmost echelon of the system. I also wanted to cover a wide range of social situations, including the regional city, small market towns, haciendas, and Indian communities of varying altitude zones. Anything beyond the departmental level would become too unwieldy for the resources at my disposal ($97,000 for a year and a half in the field for myself and three assistants, including a preposterously high "overhead" cost charged by my university). Also, as the study was to be based almost entirely on field methods of participant observation and interviews (rather than questionnaires), there were methodological constraints on scope as well. In any case, the apex of the system, the national oligarchy, had already been extensively studied by several social scientists in the Instituto de Estudios Peruanos and by the French sociologist François Bourricaud.

Finally, the specific choice of Cuzco was dictated largely by historical considerations. Cuzco was the capital of the Inca Empire, the largest centralized polity of pre-Columbian America. After the Spanish conquest, it remained an important colonial city, becoming a bishopric, and since the eighteenth century, an *audiencia* ("high tribunal"). Cuzco thus offered exceptional archival documentation, covering nearly half a millennium of ethnic relations. There are not many places where ethnic relations can be studied in such historical depth. And, as an extra bonus, the Cuzco region is one of the healthiest and most beautiful places in the world. I firmly believe in doing field work in pleasant locations.

My first exposure to the Peruvian hinterland was an 1,100-kilometer trip by road from Lima to Cuzco via Huancayo, Ayacucho, and Abancay. The distance by air is only a little over 500 kilometers, but I do not recall a stretch of straight road along the way. Within 100 kilometers or so of Lima, I had climbed to 4,700 meters of elevation. The rest of the distance was a vast roller coaster with a dozen or so major climbs and precipitous drops between 3,000 and 4,500 meters of altitude. The dirt track was between 2 and 4 meters wide, liberally strewn with landslides and nibbled at by swollen torrents. A pick and a shovel, I soon discovered, were the most important tools of Andean motoring. Miraculously, our Volkswagen microbus withstood 40,000 kilometers of such abuse, fording innumerable rivers and surviving two frontal encounters with bovines. One left behind a bent front axle; the other a long horn streak on the port side. The region around Ayacucho, Abancay, and the canyon of the Apurimac must be among the most stunning on earth, and I mean this literally. I was so dizzy and unsettled driving through it that I could scarcely enjoy it. Ayacucho, incidentally, which is now the hotbed of the Maoist guerrilla movement, *Sendero luminoso,* looked then like a time capsule out of the seventeenth century, an almost untouched colonial town.

On arrival in Cuzco, I found that George Primov had skillfully negotiated the rental from a Cuzco physician of a spacious, though somewhat dilapidated, mansion in the town of San Jerónimo, 12 kilometers from the city center. Built of thick adobe walls and a heavy round tile roof in the traditional Spanish style of an upper-class dwelling, it occupied half a town block and enclosed an inner patio and small orchard. It also contained three of the five flush toilets in the entire town of 5,000 inhabitants. The parlor had a 5-meter-high ceiling and was dominated by a large colonial painting of the Assumption of the Virgin. There we set up our field headquarters amidst stately, though not very comfortable, Spanish colonial furniture.

The Primovs occupied one wing of the house and we another, and our palace soon became a favorite stopping place for a number of British,

Anthropologists in the field, Cuzco, Peru, 1972. From left to right, Liz Long, son Oliver's hair, Ben Orlove, Jorge Flores Ochoa, Abraham Valencia, my son Eric, and my student George Primov.

American, and other anthropologists working in the region. Among regular visitors were American Ben Orlove, who was working in Sicuani and who became a close friend, and Briton Sean Conlin, who was working in the nearby hacienda Angostura. We employed a succession of typists, mostly short-term, counter-culture tourists on the "hippies' circuit" who were in need of a little cash. Our two Peruvian assistants, Narciso Ccahuana and Gladys Becerra, and various Peruvian colleagues from the University of Cuzco, especially Oscar Nuñez del Prado and Jorge Flores Ochoa, were also frequent visitors. As most of them were young and as some stayed overnight, our field headquarters soon acquired the reputation of being the venue of wild drug and sexual orgies.

Our low rate of reproduction also made us a valuable source of contraceptive information.

We soon organized our daily routine. Our boys attended a nearby boys' Catholic school, the Colegio San Antonio de Abad, where they were the only pale faces. It was their first exposure to Spanish, which they picked up in three to four months, and to religion, which left them much amused and bemused. Oliver could do a hilarious imitation of his mellifluous religion teacher. He and Eric were nicknamed *los gringos de San Jerónimo,* or, more affectionately, *los paganos* ("the heathens").

Irmi occupied her time cooking, shopping in Cuzco's odorous market, and satisfying her lifelong ambition of raising chickens. Not content with merely raising them, she also observed them and became a barnyard Konrad Lorenz. She even managed to get 2-week-old chicks purchased on the market to imprint on a hen whose brood had just been ravaged by disease. Productivity was low. If disease did not claim her protégés, a ferret would visit our chicken coop, leaving behind disemboweled fowls. Most of the survivors were spared the cooking pot for sentimental reasons. As the hens were virtually feral, egg production was equally low. They just laid a dozen and started brooding. What we lost in dietary benefits was amply made up by our rapidly mounting knowledge of gallinaceous ethology and pathology. I never knew hens could be so interesting.

Shopping was also both an adventure and a challenge. The Cuzco central market could well qualify as the filthiest on earth. Its public toilets (the only ones, incidentally, in a city of 125,000) were visited daily by thousands of Indians and mestizos from neighboring communities and were so pungent that its attendants had to wear gas masks. Vegetables and fruits were cheap, abundant, and of excellent quality, but the ongoing land reform program resulted in chronic scarcities of meat followed by brief, sudden gluts. Bargaining for meat was both a lesson in anatomy and a culture shock, especially to Karen Primov who had been raised to believe that meat grew in neat cellophane packages springing by spontaneous generation from refrigerated supermarket counters. In Peru, the price of meat was set by the government at some 50 cents U.S. per kilogram, and the art of bargaining consisted of maximizing the meat-to-bone ratio. If you wanted tongue or brains, for instance, you had to purchase the entire head. Mutton had to be bought by the half carcass and butchered at home. A rumpsteak came with a hipbone. These bones would then be boiled in potato soups. In rural eateries, for example, I frequently stumbled on such unexpected tidbits as half of a sheep's lower jaw in my potato soup.

A delightful delicacy of the region and interesting human symbiont is the guinea pig, locally known as *cuy* or, in Spanish, *conejo de India* ("Indian rabbit"). Most Andean kitchens are warrens of *cuyes*. Each housewife breeds her own, and a special warm hiding place is reserved for them underneath the adobe bench that serves as cooking surface in the kitchen. The kitchen floor is alive with agile little balls of fur scampering in and out of their hiding place. On festive occasions, their numbers are depleted by human predation, but the rare feelings of sentimentality that I have seen Peruvians display toward animals are generally directed at their pet *cuyes*. Our maid, for instance, was visibly disturbed when her uncle, our neighbor, killed her favorite animal to feed us.

Treatment of animals exposed Irmi to rude culture shocks. On the very day of her arrival in San Jerónimo, she was greeted by the plaintive yelps of a nearby dog. She was being initiated into the old Andean custom of executing dogs by slow strangulation on the death of their masters. The filth of the town also taxed to the limit Irmi's fastidious sense of cleanliness. In the nearly total absence of latrines, the streets serve as public lavatories. The entrance to our patio was especially convenient as our outer wall was recessed some 2 meters from the street and provided a nice little niche. Almost every morning, excrement piles greeted us when we opened the door. At first, we took it personally, but our maid assured us that there was no hostile intent. As proof, she pointed out that the side walls of the church were the town's favorite urinal. Indeed, the adobe wall showed visible signs of erosion at a height of about one meter.

The streets were paved with rough stones and had a drainage ditch about 50 centimeters wide and 25 centimeters deep in the middle. These drainage ditches were the only method of handling sewage in town and, in turn, fed into the Rio Huatanay, the main stream of effluents irrigating the Valley of Cuzco. The river (if a thick flow of refuse still deserved that name) also received the offals from the town's putrid abattoir. After a heavy rain, it was a common sight to see market women use the flow of filth to "wash" their vegetables, stamping on them with bare feet.

Andean peasants practically never bathe or wash their bodies. Even hair is infrequently washed. Toddlers walk about, their hair matted in filth, until their first haircut ceremony around age 3 or 4. That so many survive this regimen is a tribute to the healthy climate of the high Andes and a triumph of natural selection. All of this was hard to take and quite a contrast to the high standards of bodily cleanliness we had experienced in Africa. The rural Andes are also one of the few places on earth where I think I could reconcile myself with celibacy. Nowhere else have I found women so consistently unattractive. Apart from their lack of bodily hygiene, their stodgy, squat physique and their staccato gait are the very antithesis of gracefulness. To make matters worse, peasant women walk about in up to eight or ten layers of seldom, if ever, washed woolen dresses, exuding the pungent sex appeal of peripatetic onions.

I have already mentioned callousness to animal suffering, which is indeed a widespread human trait. But Andean culture is more than averagely dour, nasty, and aggressive. One rarely sees Andean Indians laugh, but when they do, their hilarity is usually excited by the misfortune of others. Widespread inebriation accompanies all festive occasions, as is true nearly everywhere in Latin America, and staying sober as a participant-observer is always a problem. But whereas in Mexico and Guatemala, the drunkenness is joyous, in Peru it seems to bring out anger and aggression. The only occasions when I remember people having a genuinely good time was when the possibility or actuality of pain or misery to others arose.

One memorable such occasion was a ritual fight, repeated three or four times a year, between two communities in the Langui area of the Cuzco Department. The two communities repair, in a kind of vast village picnic, to a high altitude area that is their traditional meeting ground. Each community takes possession of a knoll where the women start spreading their food and *chicha* ("maize beer") pots, while the men warm up for the fight. More and more men confront each other across a small stream, gradually escalating their conflict from hurling insults to throwing well-aimed stones with their slingshots. Broad-brimmed felt hats and ponchos dampen the impact of the stones, leaving only the shins vulnerable. The object is to try to break an opponent's leg with a stone.

The combatants fight on two lines: a front line of infantry hurling stones and a rear line of cavalry ready either to capture the enemy wounded or to rescue their own. The unlucky few who get captured are taken back to the rear where they are sometimes stoned to death, with the women egging on the men. One or two policemen of the Guardia Civil are usually in attendance to ensure that things do not get too far out of hand, and they sometimes try to intervene to prevent killing, but they are seen as spoilsports. The fight is supposed to be an ancient fertility ritual: if human blood is not spilled, it will be a bad year for the crops. But ritual or not, the event is clearly great entertainment, a kind of institutionalized "snuff" game.

My other anecdote put me in the role of intended victim. I was driving along Lake Titicaca, between Puno and La Paz, when I noted that a small town was having a fiesta. I stopped, got out of the car with my camera, and walked to the central plaza where a crowd of some 3,000 or 4,000 people were having an inebriated good time, watching masked dancers and play-bullfighting with young oxen. As I was photographing, a masked dancer started merrily gesticulating in front of me. How nice of him to pose for me, I thought. I should have known better. He was, in fact, trying to attract an ox toward me while simultaneously distracting me, so that I could be gored for the crowd's amusement. The horn missed me by about 10 or 15 centimeters, much to the crowd's disappointment, though they still had a good laugh seeing me take a frightened leap back. A gored gringo would have made their afternoon, all the more so as I was five hours away from the nearest hospital. Again, there was nothing personal in the incident. My goring would have been more entertaining than that of a mere peasant because my high status would have lent some chic to the occasion, but there was no animosity against me at all. In fact, people immediately started offering me *chicha* and joking about the episode. It was all in an afternoon's good clean fun.

It may be surmised from the preceding remarks that I could never warm up to Andean culture. For anthropologists to admit a dislike of the people they studied is, to say the least, unfashionable. Anthropologists are supposed to love "their" people. At the risk of incurring my colleagues' censure or excommunication, let me say that I have never felt proprietary toward any of the groups I studied and that I have always rejected the demeaning paternalism implied in much "advocacy" anthropology. In some foreign cultures, I have felt very comfortable and at ease, for example, in Yoruba culture or in Mexico. Others irritate me a great deal, e.g., the United States, Islamic societies, and the Andes. But wherever I have been and however I might have felt, I never espoused the guilt-ridden attitude fashionable in much "liberal" anthropology that, as a representative of a powerful and rich society, I should apologize for my presence, make amends for the sins of my compatriots (whoever *they* might be), suspend my standards of criticism, pull my intellectual punches, and gush out with sympathy.

It seems to me that the only truly humanistic attitude is to eschew all double standards of evaluation, to take people on their own terms, and to base relationships on a premise of equal worth and competence. Indeed, far from having felt powerful and exploitative in the field, I generally felt at a severe disadvantage in relation to locals. During one's first weeks or months in the field, the anthropologist must blunder almost blindly through a social mine field. A wrong step can mean sudden and unpredictable disaster. To be sure, there is an intrusive and manipulative quality to ethnography, and the enterprise is frequently of little or no value to those studied. I do feel that ethnographers have a responsibility to ensure that their presence will do no harm, and I believe that their interactions should be based as much as possible within the local context of reciprocity and status relations. But within this context of reciprocation, I have consistently felt as manipulated by the natives as vice versa. Such advantages as relative wealth gave me were often cancelled by the crippling handicap of ignorance of local conditions, especially in the early phases of field work.

Let me illustrate the tenuous contingencies of field work through our experience in Cuzco. We entered Peru on an "official visa," given to scholars on government research grants. This was a double-edged sword: on the one hand, it gave us quasi-diplomatic status; on the other hand, it opened us to suspicions of espionage. Repeatedly, when I came to a village or small town and met local schoolteachers (who, in Peru, overwhelmingly behave like petty bourgeois but talk like Maoists and Trotskyites), I had to defend myself against accusations of being a CIA agent. How can one prove that one is not a spy? My best ploy was to argue that if I were, I would be in Lima, not out in the sticks. As most teachers are urban mestizos who consider rural postings punishment duty, this argument was often convincing. After a couple of bottles of beer, those Maoist radicals would start telling me how stupid and backward the Indians were. *El indio es el animal que mas se parece al hombre,* they would say, quoting a mestizo aphorism. ("The Indian is the animal that most closely resembles man.")

Another constant dilemma was how to deal with the political authorities. Peru has a highly centralized government, and the standard procedure when arriving in a community is to pay a courtesy call and introduce oneself to the *autoridades,* a loose category of "notables," which in a small town would include the mayor, the governor (a low-level, unpaid government appointee), the parish priest, a couple of schoolteachers, the commander of the Guardia Civil post, and two or three of the leading merchants or land owners who would also be town councillors. All these people are mestizos, except in Indian villages. Without their consent, field work is impossible because everyone clams up for fear of incurring their wrath. With their consent, one is automatically associated with them. Indians, for example, simply regard the anthropologist as another mestizo on some kind of official (and probably disagreeable) mission. There is, thus, little possibility of avoiding being forced into a position of perceived authority.

Indeed, the anthropologist has an institutionalized, if somewhat nebulous, role. Many students of the University of Cuzco engage in little field projects in the region, notebook in hand. The *antropólogo* is thus generally regarded as a kind of minor and generally harmless bureaucrat who asks many silly questions. Mestizos often greet one with their favorite pun: *"Usted es antropófago?"* ("You are a cannibal?")

Even observing all the rules of propriety of those in power is not foolproof. My first contact with the mayor of San Jerónimo was nearly disastrous. He was immediately suspicious of me and reported me to the Guardia Civil, who, in turn, sent two police inspectors to check on my credentials. Things looked grim, for even residence in town would become difficult without the good grace of the mayor. Luck was on my side, however. The man, a portly and pompous retired Guardia Civil noncom, was cordially detested by the entire population. He had been appointed by the prefect in total ignorance of local politics, and he was openly ridiculed by everyone. His nickname was *el elefante blanco* ("white elephant," in devastatingly apt reference to his uselessness, his large size, and his light skin color). Within a fortnight of my arrival, he had become so unpopular that the prefect had to depose him and appoint one of his rivals. My clash with the "white elephant" immediately worked wonders with the new administration. We got along famously for the rest of my stay, but that was just a fluke of good fortune.

My next step up the political ladder was a courtesy call on the departmental prefect in Cuzco. By local standards, he is an exalted figure, the central government's first representative and executive head of one of the 23 departments into which Peru is divided. But he too is virtually bereft of autonomy and can be sacked by telephone from the Ministry of the Interior in Lima. I put on my best suit and was kept waiting the protocolar half-hour in his antechamber before his secretary led me into his office. On our first meeting, he was extremely stiff, formal, and cagey. I showed him my passport and official visa and asked him for a letter of introduction to his subordinates in the department. He asked me to come back in a couple of weeks.

Obviously, the prefect did not want to commit himself without Lima's approval. This required another police check, and a couple of telephone calls to the Ministry of the Interior. When I came back for my second visit, he not only received me immediately; he came out of his office to greet me effusively, positively gushing with the elaborate courtesy formulas characteristic of upper-class Spanish discourse. Obviously, I was in Lima's good books. He gave me the letter of introduction that ordered all his subordinates to extend their full cooperation. I tried to use it as sparingly as possible, but whenever I produced the document with its impressive official seal, it worked wonders. Surliness, suspicion, and arrogance melted into abject servility. Luckily, the prefect's tenure in office outlasted my stretch of field work.

The next crisis we had to resolve was with our landlord. We almost got evicted from our stately quarters (just as we were comfortably settling in) through an unwitting political blunder. Our landlord, a gracious and well-to-do physician, had rented us what he considered his *casa de descanso* ("vacation place"), largely because he was afraid that a large, unoccupied house might be expropriated by the Velasco government. At the same time, he wanted to rent it to transient foreigners who would not stake a permanent claim on the house. In addition, we were a handy source of scarce and valuable dollars to help finance his son's medical studies in the United States. Thus, we formed a perfect symbiotic relationship.

Our blunder was inviting a local woman with a radical reputation inside our house. San Jerónimo had a radical reputation, as it was the home town of Hugo Blanco, the leader of the peasant movement in nearby La Convención Valley, a few years before. The local high school was also a hotbed of radical rhetoric. Our landlord feared that exposing the wealth of his house to the greedy and envious eyes of radical leaders would precipitate expropriation. Indeed, we soon discovered, several of the teachers were arguing that our house would come in handy to relieve overcrowding in the nearby high school. This was obviously a ticklish situation. I wanted our house to be open to all visitors as far as possible, but I could sympathize with my landlord's concerns. I reluctantly agreed to keep "radicals" out and then went to see them individually to apologize and explain the source of my new inhospitability. They laughed the matter off, and our relations improved.

"Radicalism" in Peru was a most interesting phenomenon, especially in the context of mestizo-Indian relations in the highlands. In 1968, a Revolutionary Government of the Armed Forces had overthrown by military coup the elected civilian government of a moderate Christian Democrat, Fernando Belaunde Terry (whom I was to meet in Seattle in 1987). The leader of the coup, General Juan Velasco Alvarado, installed a reformist military government bent on expropriating both foreign interests and large land holdings. By 1972, the expropriation of haciendas was in full swing. I witnessed, in fact, the last few months of operation of traditional haciendas in the Peruvian highlands. Government policies were a complex blend of old-fashioned nationalism, military authoritarianism, home-grown populism in the Aprista tradition, Marxist dependency theory, and corporate state fascism.

The land reform program was indeed sweeping and remains the military regime's major achievement. For the purposes of my study, it was a crucial test case of my thesis that the subordination of Indians was not simply one of class, but was also rooted in ethnicity. The implementation of land reform was orchestrated by an organism known as SINAMOS, a Spanish acronym for the National Syndicate of Support for

Social Mobilization, which, in a clever pun, also meant "without masters." It was, in fact, a bureaucracy largely staffed with young, inexperienced, radical university graduates whom the government was trying to coopt to its ends.

Supposedly, the haciendas were to be transformed into cooperatives, not into small-scale peasant holdings as the peasants wished. In fact, the outcome was not even cooperatives, but rather incompetently, and sometimes corruptly, run state farms under the chaotic direction of mestizo technicians, mechanics, agronomists, veterinarians, and political organizers. These bureaucrats were mostly recent university graduates from the coastal area, who lacked Andean experience, spoke no Quechua or Aymará, and had no knowledge of Indian culture. They presumed to tell peasants with generations of accumulated experience what to do or not to do.

The consequences were predictably catastrophic. In many cases, the *hacendados* had left their estates stripped of livestock, tools, and machinery when threatened with expropriation. Many of these haciendas had already ceased to operate as unitary production units and had, in effect, reverted to small-scale subsistence farming when they were transformed into pseudo-cooperatives. Technical blunders, corruption, and old-fashioned peasant resistance resulted in a collapse in surplus food production (especially of meat).

The political outcome was the alienation of the peasants who were the supposed beneficiaries of the land reform. The land was not given to the peasants as they had hoped. As several of them put it to me: before the reform, peasants had one master, now they had ten or twenty. Their relation to the means of production had been altered by the land reform, according to Marxist theory. They were no longer called *indios* or *indígenas,* but *campesinos,* in the regime's Marxist class terminology. Yet their subordination to mestizos had not changed at all. A Marxist-inspired land reform had demonstrated my point: the subordination of Indians was based on *both* class and ethnicity, and a mere circulation of mestizo elites at the top would not appreciably affect the Indians' social, economic, or political position.

Naturally, the traditional land-owning class and the urban bourgeoisie had opposed the military regime from the start. The peasantry became alienated for the reasons I just mentioned. Now the government proceeded to antagonize the last influential civilian sector from which it had originally drawn its support: the intelligentsia. Composed largely of university students, teachers at all levels, and university graduates in public employ, that intelligentsia, in Peru as in the rest of Latin America, is almost entirely Marxist. At least, the politically active and vocal members of the intelligentsia claim allegiance to one brand or another of Marxist ideology. Marxist phraseology is the lingua franca of Latin American intellectual discourse.

The intelligentsia soon outflanked the government on the left and started mounting teacher strikes, student demonstrations, and the like. The government retaliated by closing down universities and high schools, thereby paralyzing much of higher education. With all the interruptions in their studies, it regularly took students seven or eight years to complete four-year degrees. Any semblance of a regular school calendar vanished. A colleague of mine who was supposedly a Fulbright professor at the University of Cuzco ended up teaching six weeks during his year of tenure, just long enough to be accused by the students of being a CIA agent.

The most salient features of this Peruvian "radicalism" were its urban, petty bourgeois, mestizo character, and its total divorce from Indian peasant masses. Radical rhetoric was totally divorced from behavior. Trotskyist teachers, for instance, behaved like authoritarian martinets in the classroom and found nothing incongruous in forcing their students to march in a poor imitation of military drill. A newspaper article captured this contradiction neatly. It reported on the graduating class of a high-status, religious, girls' school. The class (*promoción* in Spanish) gave itself the name of a public or historical figure, as is customary in Peru. The caption under the class photograph read: *La promoción Vladimir Illich Lenin del Colegio de Señoritas Virgen del Rosario* ("The Vladimir Illich Lenin class of the Young Ladies' College Virgin of the Rosary"). The irony was seemingly lost on most Peruvian radicals.

Another vignette sticks in my mind. The university had organized a protest march from the campus to downtown. The orderly procession was led by two stylishly dressed female students holding up a large red-lettered banner. (Having pretty young women in front of a demonstration is an effective deterrent of police brutality in *macho* Peru.) Then came the corps of professors all impeccably attired in suits and ties. Behind them came a bevy of secretaries, followed by a large mass of mostly male students, more informally dressed, but still very clearly middle-class urbanites. Closing the march was a small group of some thirty or forty Indian peasants in ponchos, day laborers at the university's experimental farm. What slogan were the demonstrators chanting in unison? "*Campesinos, obreros, estudiantes; unidos venceremos.*" ("Peasants, workers, students; united we will win.") Obviously, victory was still a long way off.

Perhaps a brief account of the dynamics of ethnic relations in the region is in order here. The fundamental paradox of the situation is that ethnic boundaries between Indians and mestizos are both permeable and stable. An Indian is defined as a native speaker of Quechua, Aymará, or some other indigenous language, who speaks little or no Spanish, is illiterate, lives on the land, and is a peasant. A person of Indian origin who learns Spanish, becomes literate, leaves his village for a neighboring town, and becomes a craftsman, a trader, a truckdriver, a soldier, or whatever, will, in a matter of a few years, cease to be regarded as an Indian. To be sure, his status and his own self-definition may remain marginal for a while, but most assuredly his children will be fully accepted as mestizos. So will he, if his Spanish becomes fluent enough. Most mestizos are fluently bilingual in Spanish and Quechua (or Aymará) and are probably only one to three generations removed from being Indians.

The mestizo-Indian distinction is clearly *not* racial or phenotypic. A few recent immigrants from Europe look different from the mass of the population, and mestizos are on the whole a bit taller than Indians, in part because they enjoy a better diet, but most mestizos are not physically distinguishable from Indians. "Passing" into the mestizo group is usually achieved in the second decade of life, either through the school system (where instruction is in Spanish), through the army (which drafts principally Indian peasants and turns them into mestizo proletarians), through labor migration to the coast (where Spanish is the overwhelmingly dominant language), or, for girls, through domestic service in mestizo households. At any given time, hundreds of thousands of individuals are in this transition process, which necessarily involves spatial as well as social mobility.

These opportunities for *individual* upward class and ethnic mobility paradoxically ensure the stability of the *system* of class and ethnic inequality. Since, by social definition, there can be no such thing as a literate, Spanish-speaking, well-to-do, urban Indian, the Indian population constantly loses its most intelligent, enterprising, adventuresome youth. Generation after generation of potential Indian leaders are "lost" to the mestizo world, which explains the lack of an Indian nationalist movement, for example. Each peasant community remains politically atomized and confronts a national system that is entirely mestizo-controlled. The mestizos form a vast, complex system of class relations that tightly integrates the local, regional, and national levels. Indians are the fragmented, marginalized, geographically isolated, bottom stratum of a double structure of class *and* ethnic domination. Indians necessarily always remain at the very bottom, in part because the individuals who rise above that bottom cease to be Indians. Individual mobility perpetuates social inequality.

There is another essential ingredient of Indian subordination that explains systemic stability despite considerable individual fluidity. As Marxists rightly point out, Peruvian Indians have not simply been isolated, atomized, and marginalized. They have been intensely exploited, first by native ruling classes during several millennia of indigenous state formation, then during three centuries of mercantilistic capitalism under Spanish colonialism, and finally for 165 years of laissez-faire capitalism since independence. Marxists have been good at analyzing the system of production that gave rise to *class* relations, but they have not understood the specific mechanisms of domination across *ethnic* boundaries. As in most agrarian societies, class domination has been greatly reinforced by a particularistic, paternalistic system of clientage linking individual members of the peasantry with individual patrons.

Clientage and paternalism are ubiquitous features of agrarian societies, and they have been insufficiently studied. Indeed, clientage is at the very root of the stability of agrarian regimes. Paternalism is much more than a legitimating ideology seeking to reconcile despotism with benevolence by making use of false familistic analogies. Paternalistic patron-client relationships one-sidedly atomize the lower class without affecting the class solidarity of the upper class. In Latin America, the official state religion of Catholicism was the principal vehicle for the formation of these inter-ethnic patron-client ties. Known as *compadrazgo,* the system links mestizo patrons to Indian clients through godparental ties established at baptism, confirmation, and marriage. These ties, often between *hacendado* and *peón,* consolidate and legitimate existing relations of domination and exploitation by injecting into them an ideology of parental concern and benevolence.

The interesting feature of *compadrazgo* is that these ties of ritual kinship are used not only to reinforce relations of inequality across ethnic lines, but also to cement friendships between class equals or near equals. This is especially true in the upper class, which is a vast national network of *compadrazgo* ties. Indians, too, have *intra-*ethnic *compadrazgo* ties between peasants, but these tend to be confined to the local community. One can see how the same system of *compadrazgo* serves to legitimate and buttress ethnic inequality between mestizos and Indians (and thereby to atomize the peasantry) *and* to cement class solidarity in the upper class. *Compadrazgo* suffuses the entire social pyramid, but with antithetical effect at the bottom and at the top.

Our field work called for a lot of travel. As neither George nor I spoke Quechua, we each took one of our bilingual Peruvian assistants, Narciso or Gladys, with us in the field, and we usually separated into two teams to insure wider coverage. One of us would generally stay behind in San Jerónimo to work on the urban side of the study, to transcribe and trans-

Participant observation in San Jerónimo, Cuzco, Peru, 1972. The statue of the patron saint carried in procession appears in the center background. Photo taken by George Primov.

late the field notes, to supervise the typing, and so on. The other team would, in the meantime, visit small towns, haciendas, and Indian communities, and attend fiestas, for periods ranging from a few days to a few weeks. A half-dozen of these outlying places were studied more intensely and visited several times.

Although the *selva* ("rain forest") on the eastern slope of the Andes was outside the purview of our study, we took several short trips into it, to the delight of Oliver and Eric who avidly collected butterflies and beetles and who could never see enough of the tropical jungle. Their delight surprised their school friends, who, with the prejudice of highlanders, called the *selva, el infierno verde* ("green hell"). From Cuzco, we also took several trips to Puno, to Arequipa, and to Bolivia. Puno is a rather drab, almost treeless, town on the shore of Lake Titicaca, but the setting—the altiplano and the lake around it, at some 4,000 meters of altitude—is one of the most starkly beautiful places on earth, with colors rendered more intense by the thin, crystalline air. Arequipa, at a balmy 2,500 meters, offers a semi-tropical vacation from the highlands and is one of the most beautifully preserved colonial cities in the Americas. Built in resplendent white stone, it has a unique architectural elegance, and its convent of Santa Catalina, now a museum, provides an idyllic island of monastic serenity in a bustling city.

Bolivia deserves its old colonial name of Alto Peru. Much poorer than its northern neighbor, it lacks a coastal zone and its highlands are even more barren than Peru's, being both further from the Equator and of higher average elevation. The old colonial cities of Sucre and Potosí are the most spectacular. The honey-combed mountain of silver ore that overlooks Potosí was the grave of hundreds of thousands of Indians, and the royal mint in town was the source of the bullion that flooded world trade for two centuries, from Europe to China. Silver, it was said, was so abundant, that it was used to shoe horses and mules. The massive silver chamber pot was a standard item in the inventory of urban households. The mountain swallowed human flesh and belched silver ingots. Populations were decimated by the *mita* ("forced labor") in a 1,000-kilometer radius, in one of the most sustained genocides in world history.

Santa Cruz is Bolivia's booming jungle frontier and the golden mecca of its cocaine smugglers. Like all "development" areas in the Amazon Basin, the region around Santa Cruz is being devastated by logging, followed by a few years of wasteful farming, and then successive grazing, first by cattle and lastly by goats. This development scheme is guaranteed to convert jungle into semi-desert in 20 or 25 years. Meanwhile, the generals, principal wholesale dealers in the cocaine traffic, are getting rich quickly.

Oruro is a non-descript tin-mining town, but at carnival time it comes to life for a few days with a dazzling and deafening display of color and sound. Lavishly costumed groups in their twisted-horned, "devil" masks prance around the streets and compete with each other. Bourgeois families hire taxis on which they mount their silverware for public display. More modest families tie their silver to weavings carried on the backs of cows and donkeys. Beer and *chicha* flow in torrents down people's throats. I shall always kick myself for missing by a few seconds the picture of the year: a man simultaneously urinating in the middle of the street while emptying a beer bottle down the other end of his anatomy.

In contrast to Sucre—Bolivia's other capital and a sedate, dormant, patrician city—La Paz is bustling, garish, and "modern." A favorite haunt of old Nazis like Klaus Barbie, it has spawned coups d'état at the rate of about one a year. Soldiers armed with automatic rifles are permanently posted at all of the main intersections and lend the city a suspenseful aura of imminent political change. From Cuzco, La Paz was a two-day drive, via Puno, but we took the trip several times as we yearned for a decent restaurant and a little whiff of cosmopolitanism. We also learned to like La Paz in its own right and in spite of its unsavory political climate. The physical setting of La Paz is unique. The city hugs the slopes of a steep cleft in the altiplano. One approaches La Paz from a flat, high plateau at 4,000 meters. Nothing suggests its presence until the whole of it suddenly comes into view over the edge of the plateau. The city consists basically of a continuous main street, some 20 kilometers long, winding down from 4,000 to about 2,500 meters of elevation, along an enormous crevasse. In a reversal of the usual social topography of cities, the slums and the industry concentrate in the chilly higher elevations while the foreign embassies and cocaine barons bask in the palm trees and swimming pools of the semi-tropics at the bottom of the canyon. "Downtown" is in the middle, along the scant kilometer or so of the main street that is almost level.

A number of momentous international events occurred during our stay in Peru. It is amusing how one's sheer physical location changes the perception of events. The 1973 Arab-Israeli war broke out during one of my short visits to Lima, but it seemed a curiously distant and irrelevant event. Even the oil embargo had little local impact as, by then, Peru was producing some oil of its own. By contrast, the bloody overthrow of Allende in nearby Chile seemed a cataclysmic event. Political refugees brought back horrifying tales of massacres. I had to try to reassure my radical teacher friends that I had no hand in Pinochet's coup, but I am not sure I succeeded. Certainly, I was in a bad position to dismiss their fear of the CIA as paranoia.

At a more mundane and personal level, it was also in Cuzco that I learned of the death of my Aunt Marie, my father's sister. By an irony of fate, the same mail delivered her last letter to us and the telegram announcing her death in a streetcar accident. She was my last close Belgian relative, and her death ended the last significant Belgian chapter in my life. I have been to Belgium several times since, but somehow it never felt like home any more. In fact, the alienating feeling of being in a place that once was mine, but no longer is, was so unsettling that I have avoided going to Belgium in the past few years.

On rereading the pages of this chapter, I fear I have painted too negative a picture of my stay in Cuzco. I failed to acknowledge the friendships and stimulating intellectual contacts I had with a number of Cuzqueños, especially anthropologists Oscar Nuñez del Prado and Jorge Flores Ochoa of the University of Cuzco, my assistant Gladys Becerra, her husband, Abraham Valencia, and Narciso Ccahuana. I learned an enormous amount from all of them; together they spared me much ethnographic spadework, and my debt to them is great. Their good cheer often made up for the rigors and irritations of the field. I also failed to convey how engrossingly interesting and hauntingly beautiful the region is. The archaeological sites—Sacsahuamán, Pisác, Machu Picchu, Tiahuanaco, Ollantaytambo, Pictillacta, and, of course, the very foundations of Cuzco itself—are perhaps not as awe-inspiring and artistically moving as those of Meso-America, but they certainly are engineering marvels, all the more impressive for the primitive stone-tool technology with which they were achieved. The colonial architecture of Cuzco and environs is also among the finest in the Americas, and the great religious pageants of Holy Week and Corpus Christi transform the Plaza de Armas of Cuzco into one of the greatest *tableaux vivants* of Christendom.

The modern artisanal traditions of Cuzco are a vibrant testimony to the creative vitality of Andean culture. We grew especially fond of the sculpture of Hilario Mendivil and Edilberto Mérida. Some of their works now adorn our house and permanently enrich our lives. A masterly *Last Supper* by Mérida is the centerpiece of our living room and excites the admiration of practically all our visitors. Let these lines be a feeble homage to his genius. Peruvian textiles have also "grown on us" over the years. Several weavings adorn the very study in which I am now writing. Andean music, hauntingly melancholic, also stays with one, once one has learned to appreciate its totally idiosyncratic tonal system. It deserves a prominent place in the world's repertoire of great musical traditions.

In September 1973, Irmi and the boys left Peru, in time to start the new school year in Seattle. I stayed behind for another two months to wind up my research, and I took three weeks on the return trip to fulfill my long-delayed desire to visit Brazil. I took off from La Paz for São Paulo and then travelled by bus to Rio, Belo Horizonte, and Salvador da Bahia. From there, I plane-hopped to Recife, Belém, and Manaus and flew on to Mexico City and Seattle.

A heterogeneous sub-continent of 130 million people can scarcely be fathomed in three weeks, but my extensive prior reading and research on Brazil helped in organizing the stream of direct experience. My main interest was in race relations and in the African impact on Brazilian society. Brazil is very different from both Spanish and Anglo America. Unlike most Spanish Americans, Brazilians are, on the whole, very race-conscious, in the sense of continuous concern for, and attention to, even minute and subtle distinctions of skin color, facial features, and hair texture. They are also racist in that they often derogate African phenotypes. But this very concern for small differences in physical appearance has led to a complex racial nomenclature of at least fifty or so racial terms, which are individually applied as terms of reference. Frequently, members of the same family will be described by different racial terms. The result is that racial categories, like white and black in the United States, are almost totally absent and, therefore, race cannot become the base of social action or even of corporate group formation. Brazilian race relations are thus totally different from those that exist in, say, the United States or South Africa, where corporate racial categories suffuse the entire social structure.

I was most taken by Rio, perhaps the world's most beautiful city in terms of its natural site, and by Bahia, that vibrant cultural blend of Portugal and West Africa. The Afro-Brazilian population of the Northeast is also a very handsome one, despite grinding poverty and malnutrition. The economic contrast between the industrial megalopolises of the south, Rio and São Paulo, and the underdevelopment of most of the rest of the country is startling. Brazil is another textbook case for dependency theorists. Its entire economic history is one of booms and busts in response to world capitalist markets: gold, diamonds, sugar, rubber, coffee—all were produced for an outside market and supplied at a staggering human cost. Brazilian slavery lasted longest in the Western Hemisphere (until 1888) and was frighteningly lethal, especially in the gold and diamond mines.

Northeast Brazil today is clearly an impoverished shell left behind by the collapse of the sugar economy. The descendants of the slaves live in a land ravaged by capitalist predation. The lavish colonial cities like Bahia and Recife, with their church interiors literally covered in gold leaf, have a beautiful look of decayed splendor, which can only be enjoyed if one forgets the social conditions that created them. Yet I found the contemporary culture of Brazil, and especially of the Northeast, with its exuberant musical, literary, and artistic creativity, extremely attractive and congenial. The similarities with Nigeria, and especially the Yoruba influence, were glaring. In Bahia, I bought a set of two identically dressed figurines, mounted on a common pedestal; these were statues of São Damiao and São Cosme, I was told. To be sure, they were dressed in Portuguese colonial style, but nowhere else in Catholic iconography have I seen the two saints depicted as twins. This was obviously a New World syncretism with the Yoruba *ibeji* ("twin") cult.

The Amazon Basin is yet another Brazil, untouched by Africa and indeed very much the *tristes tropiques* of Lévi-Strauss. Manaus and its environs are like a vast patch of spreading leprosy in the rain forest. The devastation is especially noticeable from the air. Where the lush green canopy has been destroyed, a barren, eroded, reddish soil quickly appears, a mini-steppe in the making. Manaus itself has all the ugliness of a boomtown that has gone bust. Its pretentious Opera House still stands. There is a garish emporium of duty-free shops to encourage tourism. The hotels are shabbily pretentious and grotesquely overpriced. Much of the town, however, consists of grim wooden shanties housing a sad, unhealthy-looking *caboclo* population, the deculturated remnants of Amazonian Indians, intermixed with the riff-raff of Europe.

The voyage ended on an irritating note, which will make me think twice about ever initiating an international flight from La Paz again. Both in Mexico City and in Seattle, I was subjected to the most thorough luggage search that I ever encountered. The assumption of both Mexican and U.S. Customs was presumably that only a cocaine smuggler would start his trip in La Paz, as my ticket clearly showed. A few weeks later, what was left of our Volkswagen microbus was similarly searched when it arrived by boat in Tacoma. What would have happened, I wondered, if someone had used the vehicle during the many weeks it was in transit to stash a couple of kilos in complete safety?

Four years earlier, I was also concerned about the disappearance of two boxes of quinine capsules from the luggage we were shipping back from Nigeria. I surmised that they had been illegally confiscated, on suspicion of their being illicit drugs, and subjected to chemical analysis. But what protection does the citizen have against being either unwittingly used as a courier by drug dealers or framed by customs agents in search of a bust? None, I concluded. Indeed, the U.S. Treasury Department has powers of search and arrest that rival those of the Gestapo. I am seldom as uncomfortable as when I go through U.S. Customs.

CHAPTER 13

Academic Wanderings

The years 1974 and 1975 were largely spent analyzing and writing up the mass of Peruvian data that we had brought back with us. I was also occupied with playing willing midwife to a cohort of doctoral students. The latter included George Primov, whose dissertation was a direct product of our joint Cuzco research; Gary Hamilton, who was returning from a year in Hong Kong with a fascinating thesis on the role of ethnicity in nineteenth-century Chinese merchant guilds; and Cullen Hayashida, who had just spent a year in Japan investigating the historical origins and contemporary ramifications of what he called Japan's "blood ideology." All three, I am happy to report, had an easy delivery. Writers and dissertations are doing well.

The analysis of our Peruvian data also presented few problems. George and I formed a smoothly cooperative team. Some of George's research had been done semi-independently of the rest of the project and was indeed to have totally unforeseen repercussions a few years later; but at least three-fourths of it was coterminous with my project. This presented somewhat of a problem in terms of publication. His dissertation had to be his own work rather than a collaborative writing with me. Yet its scope and approach so closely overlapped with the monograph I was writing that the publication of either pre-empted the other. The fairest solution, we thought, was that Primov would get junior authorship of the 1977 book *Inequality in the Peruvian Andes*. Although the writing of that book was almost entirely mine, George's contribution to the contents was large enough to enable him to write, in effect, a parallel monograph of comparable scope.

Those were also the years during which I wrote *Man in Society*, first published in 1975 and revised in 1978. In many ways, it was an unsatisfactory book. Published in 1975, it was made almost instantaneously obsolete by the publication the same year of E. O. Wilson's epochal *Sociobiology, The New Synthesis*. What I wanted to write was a general introductory textbook on human social behavior that took human evolution and biology seriously and that was widely comparative, both cross-specifically and cross-culturally. It would thus cross all conventional disciplinary boundaries between sociology, anthropology, psychology, and biology. I also wanted to avoid the deadly pedantry and pretentious vacuity characteristic of practically all introductory sociology textbooks, and in this, my students told me I succeeded.

The book suffered from two serious shortcomings, however. First, it still relied heavily on the older ethological tradition, which sociobiology was on the verge of superceding. Second, it largely ignored psychology as the bridging discipline between biology and the social sciences proper. In particular, it left out the entire fields of cognitive and developmental psychology and did not deal with problems of ontogeny. In 1978, I yielded to my publisher's desire for a revision, and that was another mistake. I should either have left the book alone or have rewritten it from scratch. Instead, I added a chapter and tinkered with the rest to "update" it, but my thinking had evolved too fast from under me to produce a harmonious result. This, incidentally, was my first attempt at revising a book. Hitherto, I had always resisted publishers' pressures to do so, and this ungainly product only confirmed my inclination against revision. A book is a period piece; it is produced in a certain mood and intellectual climate, which cannot be recaptured later. Revised, it loses its integrity and coherence. Revision is almost an act of falsification you play on yourself, unless, of course, your thinking is totally static—in which case you had better stop writing!

The most significant single event of the period in the development of my thinking on human biology was Wilson's *Sociobiology*. It was not until summer 1976 that I had the leisure to read it from cover to cover and to backtrack to the writings of Richard Alexander, William Hamilton, John Maynard Smith, George C. Williams, Robert Trivers, and others. It was a paper by Hamilton in 1964 that marked, better than any other, the birth of sociobiology, and it is true that Wilson is only one of a dozen or so leading theorists in the field. *Sociobiology* largely synthesizes the ideas of others and integrates them in a masterly compendium of empirical evidence. Wilson himself never claimed anything more.

Indeed, when I met him a couple of years later, I found him to be a gentle, modest, unassuming man who was genuinely hurt, surprised, and puzzled by the vituperative and dishonest ideological attacks to which some of his Harvard colleagues and others subjected him. Few men of his intellectual stature are as totally free of arrogance and as generous in giving credit to others, especially not at Harvard, that hotbed of prima donnas. Ideologically, he is best described as an apolitical liberal, with the kind of charming political innocence that characterizes so many American academics. He was certainly ill-prepared for the savage attacks from Richard Lewontin, Stephen Gould, Jerome Hirsch, and others.

It is also interesting how others who had applied evolutionary biology to humans and who were equally prominent academically, such as Richard Alexander, emerged virtually unscathed from the political brouhaha. In part, the almost exclusive media attention to Wilson was a tribute to Harvard University Press' flair for book distribution. But *Sociobiology* was not simply a media event; it was an epochal book not only for the elegant way in which it integrated many convergent strands of thinking and research into a new paradigm, but also for placing the arcane specialty of behavioral ecology on the center stage of intellectual life in a way accessible to non-specialists. *Sociobiology* clearly went well beyond classical ethology, though, of course, it built on it. True, the last chapter on humans was the weakest in the book. At that time, Wilson had little knowledge of psychology and anthropology, and some of his formulations were a little overly truculent and imperialistic. Indeed, if one follows Wilson's writings on humans from *Sociobiology* (1975), to *On Human Nature* (1978), to his two books co-authored with Charles Lumsden, *Genes, Mind, and Culture* (1981) and *Promethean Fire* (1983), one sees a constant progression in sophistication and appreciation of the complexities of human culture.

It was clear to me—steeped as I was in the anthropological tradition of making a shibboleth of the complexity and emergent properties of human culture—that the new sociobiological paradigm offered a much broader and more promising pathway to understanding human evolution than classical ethology. Furthermore, I saw sociobiology as complementary, not threatening, to the kind of broad comparative social science that I was interested in. In a sense, sociobiology was merely extending the scale of comparison from the cross-cultural to the cross-specific and injecting a much needed temporal dimension into the analysis. Here, at last, was a theory that explained both change and stability, order and conflict, in terms of a single, parsimonious, materialist model of individual behavior premised on simple maximizing assumptions. Like all the other theoretical approaches in social science that had any predictive value and bore a demonstrable relationship to the real world—behaviorism, utilitarianism, classical economics, Marxian class theory, exchange theory, game theory—sociobiology treated sociality as the outcome of interaction between selfish maximizers. The sociobiological model also cut a clean swath through many, if not all, the reifications, obfuscations, and pseudo-problems invented by several generations of social scientists in a never-ending effort to hide their floundering ignorance behind a façade of conceptual turgidity and quantified gibberish.

In 1976–1977, I took a sabbatical, principally devoted to retooling in behavioral ecology. Luckily, several of my colleagues at the University of Washington were on the forefront of that field. I attended a number of graduate seminars and colloquia, and benefitted from interaction with colleagues such as David Barash (with whom I co-authored an article in *American Anthropologist*), Gordon Orians, Joan Lockard, the late Bob Lockard, and a few years later, Paul Harvey. I also began to attract a number of students with an interest in human sociobiology, such as Penelope Greene, Judith Heerwagen, Charles Morgan, and Mary Waterhouse, and to be asked to serve on a number of doctoral committees for Ph.D. candidates in animal behavior. In a sense, this was almost like returning to graduate school myself, something that I think should be a mid-career requirement for tenure renewal. Few academics escape mental obsolescence, if not senility, after age 40 or 45.

Shortly thereafter, in 1978, the University of Washington was to host a memorable meeting of the Animal Behavior Society, which featured four separate plenary sessions and a joint panel discussion by William Hamilton, Robert Trivers, Richard Dawkins, and Richard Alexander. This sociobiological extravaganza almost inevitably drew student pickets. Leaflets were distributed attacking sociobiology as a racist-sexist conspiracy, and Barash and I were singled out as local enemies of "science for the people."

In November and December 1976, I also took the opportunity to visit Israel for the first time in my adult life. (A visit as a baby in 1933 left no memory.) My principal hosts were Sammy Smooha, a UCLA student of Leo Kuper who had been my junior colleague in Seattle in the early 1970s, and Joseph Shepher, then the head of the Sociology and Anthropology Department at the University of Haifa. My visit was doubly fascinating. First, under the inspired guidance of Sammy (who escorted me to numerous places and introduced me to many colleagues in Haifa, Tel Aviv, and Jerusalem), I got an intense overview of the subtle complexities of Israeli ethnic relations. In addition to trips with Sammy, I travelled on my own to Jerusalem, Bethlehem, Nazareth, Hebron, Beersheba, Arad, Nablus, Akko, Safad, Gaza, the Negev, the Sinai, the Golan Heights, Masada and the Dead Sea, and Elat and the Gulf of Aqaba. During these trips, I also visited several kibbutzim, including Joseph Shepher's own kibbutz, Kfar Hahoresh, near Nazareth, and both a new and an older kibbutz in the shadow of the Golan Heights.

The second major bonus of my Israel trip was to establish contact with Shepher, whose work on gender roles and pseudo-incest avoidance in Kibbutzim was already familiar to me, but whom I had not yet met. We enjoyed a close intellectual association until his untimely death in 1984. Joseph's interest in human inbreeding avoidance and on testing empirically the "Westermarck effect" (i.e., the interference of a close early childhood association with the later development of erotic attraction) dovetailed with mine, and our association substantially advanced my own thinking and publications in that area. A joint proposal to the National Science Foundation was turned down, so we never published together, but a perusal of our separate articles and books reveals a dense network of mutual references. I shall certainly miss him.

While in Israel, I lectured, both on human sociobiology and on ethnic relations, at Haifa, Tel Aviv, and Jerusalem. Both topics were "hot," especially my suggestion that the concept of "Herrenvolk democracy" applied to Israel, and helped to highlight uncomfortable parallels and similarities between these last two beleaguered outposts of European colonialism, Israel and South Africa. I was being deliberately provocative in order to elicit intellectual discussion, and I was rewarded with many spirited arguments. Interestingly, the climate of open intellectual discourse in the Israeli universities, combined with the high caliber of both faculty and students made for a much freer discussion of even such burning issues than would be possible in American universities. The relationship between ideology and social science is taken for granted in Israel and is itself the subject of disciplined scrutiny rather than a mere stimulus for emotional catharsis and angry knee jerks as seems to be the pattern in American academia. In any case, I found my thinking very congenial with that of the left-wing of the Israeli social science community and much better understood than in the United States, even among liberal Jews.

Israel is one of these countries that can leave few people unmoved, especially that most extraordinary of cities, Jerusalem. Clearly, the only viable political status for the Old City would be internationalization, perhaps under the protection of a Hindu or Buddhist garrison from a small country like Thailand or Sri Lanka. Perhaps the most troubling aspect of the creation of the State of Israel was that it was imposed on the Middle East by Western powers largely as atonement and "solution" for a European "problem" created by Nazi Germany. The connection between the Holocaust and the creation of the State of Israel is one of the greatest of historical non-sequiturs. It is, as if, say, after World War I, Britain and the United States had carved out of Russia an Armenian state in reparation for the Ottoman massacres of 1915. Instead the ephemeral Armenian Republic was left to die unsupported.

There are several reasons why the legitimacy of the State of Israel is so problematic. It is based on a historical claim to national territory, which is neither more nor less legitimate than the claim of Amerindians to the Americas, the Aborigines to Australia, or the Mbuti ("Pygmies") and San ("Bushmen") to Africa. People do not live in the past, or at least they should not. The rationale for Israel as a Jewish state is based on group membership and rights, which include and exclude on the particularistic and ascriptive basis of descent. If one opposes apartheid in South Africa and affirmative action in the United States because both practices are based on state recognition of membership in descent groups, how can one accept an immigration policy based on the Law of Return for Jews and the exclusion of Palestinians? If one favors a secular state and condemns sectarianism in Iran or Saudi Arabia, how can one condone theocracy in Israel? If one opposes Soviet intervention in Afghanistan, Hungary, or Czechoslovakia and U.S. intervention in Vietnam, El Salvador, and Nicaragua, one can scarcely support foreign intrusion into the Middle East and Israeli aggression against Lebanon.

Clearly, the Jews who now live in Israel have, by their very presence, established the right to be there and to live in safety. So do the Palestinians who have been expelled by force or fear. And, for that matter, white South Africans have a right to live in South Africa. But none of these groups has, in my view, an exclusive right, a right to dominate other groups, or a monopoly of certain privileges. Alas, Lebanon, Ireland, Sri Lanka, Cyprus, Rwanda, and countless other countries have abundantly demonstrated the fragility and vulnerability of multi-national states. A non-sectarian, multi-national state of Jews, Muslims, and Christians in a unitary state along the borders of the old Palestinian mandate is simply not realistic. The practical alternatives are an equitable, mutually agreeable partition or a beleaguered, militarized settler state, surviving in the shadow of the American imperium. Both South Africa and Israel have opted for the garrison state and cooperated with their American suzerain in a grand alliance to contain communism in Africa, the Middle East, and Latin America. While the communist brand of tyranny is, on balance, worse than that which exists in a few advanced capitalist societies in the West, it is certainly no worse than most of the

Third World dictatorships that the West supports. Neither side of the Cold War has much moral rectitude left to stand on. No state, in the last analysis, is legitimate.

In 1988, an invitation to lecture in Tel Aviv from my colleagues Yochanan Peres and Eliezer Ben Rafael gave me a second look at Israel. By then, the Palestinian revolt *(intifadeh)* was in full swing, and Jews were afraid to travel in the occupied territories. Israel was more militarized than ever, but the thrust of the Israeli Defense Forces had been redirected from external aggression against Lebanon to internal repression against the Palestinians in the West Bank and Gaza. The parallels with South Africa had become even more glaring than in 1976, as, indeed, more and more Israeli intellectuals were beginning to see. As the situation continues to polarize, the status quo appears increasingly untenable and unstable to all concerned. Yet the Israeli state, like South Africa, is paralyzed because each represents the exclusive interests of the Herrenvolk that controls it.

Shortly after my sabbatical, in April 1978, my academic cocoon was once more punctured by external political attack. It came in the form of a Golden Fleece Award from Senator William Proxmire for my Cuzco study. (The main monograph, by Primov and myself, had only just been published, in 1977.) Just prior to the award, there had been some belated but ominous requests for an account of certain expenditures on the NIMH grant in question. That line of investigation yielded few fruits. Actually, I refunded an unexpended $1,500 on the grant, and the only questionable item was $300 overspent on the travel budget. The reason was simple: the Arab oil embargo intervened between my departure in 1972 and my return in 1973. Thus, my return ticket had cost $300 more than my flight south. I thought I was off the inquisitorial hook, but the witch-hunt was just beginning.

On April 19, 1978, Proxmire issued a news release awarding a Golden Fleece to NIMH for my Cuzco research under Grant M1119712. The amount of the grant was $97,000 for 18 months of field work. This sum covered salaries for myself, three assistants and a secretary, equipment and supplies including a motor vehicle, and travel expenses. The amount is probably inferior to the cost of a three-day presidential junket to Rancho del Cielo. What made the announcement sensational, however, was that Proxmire had found a sex angle to my project, which he exploited to gain publicity. George Primov had, with my full knowledge and consent, studied the brothel of San Tutis ("San Putis," in local parlance, a Spanish pun on *puta*, or "whore"), near Cuzco. The obscure little cat-house in the high Andes suddenly achieved world-wide notoriety. It "made" the *Wall Street Journal, Time* magazine, the *Sunday Times* of

London, *Le Monde*, the *Washington Post*, *Playboy*, *Penthouse*, the *National Inquirer*, the Phil Donahue and Dick Cavett shows, and many other print and TV media ranging from the sublime to the ridiculous. Imagine Proxmire's glee in supposedly finding the proverbial sociologist who spent $100,000 to find his way to a brothel!

Needless to say, I did not take the attack sitting down. I counterattacked in numerous press interviews and in an article published in *Academe* (the AAUP's organ). Proxmire's allegations ranged from false to misleading. The brothel study was a tangential afterthought to the main study. It was conducted largely on Primov's own time and with only minimal use (perhaps $50) of project resources. It could very properly not have acknowledged NIMH support at all, and, indeed, it was the courtesy acknowledgment that put Proxmire on to it. In our final monograph, the brothel study occupied a half-page paragraph in a 325-page book, which gives an accurate measure of its salience. Besides, I felt I owed no apologies to Proxmire or anyone else for studying whatever I pleased. Certainly, the study of sexual behavior is as proper a topic for social scientists as any. Proxmire's juvenile snickers on the Dick Cavett show may have impressed his Wisconsin voters, but I felt that he emerged from the episode as a prurient buffoon.

Most disappointing was NIMH's reaction. In an attempt to cover themselves, the bureaucrats sought to deflect the "blame" onto me. They apologized to Proxmire for not having adequately supervised me (as if it were the proper function of a granting agency like NIMH to supervise researchers), accused me of imaginary or ludicrous breaches of the terms of the grant, and sent me sermonizing letters: "Your failure to respond in a responsible way to reporting requirements is jeopardizing your own professional reputation, that of the University of Washington, . . . [and] the future support of social science research." Perhaps NIMH bureaucrats do not know it, but scientists report the results of their research not in memos to bureaucrats but in scholarly publications. My reports were for anyone to read, and copies had been sent to the Library of Congress.

Unfortunately, I cannot prove it, but I suspect that the Golden Fleece Award did adversely affect my chances of further funding for research. Three subsequent attempts to return to Cuzco to conduct research on tourism (another "frivolous" topic for the senator, no doubt) were turned down, two of them by NSF and one by Fulbright. The letter of refusal for the Fulbright request came, oddly, from the United States Information Agency, a well-known CIA front. My friends on the right tell me that I ought to be grateful for small mercies. In a "people's democracy," they say, I would have found myself in a psychiatric hospital or a "re-education" camp long ago. No doubt, they are right.

By the late 1970s, it was clear that the affluent and expanding days of American academia were over. The market was being glutted with an oversupply of badly trained Ph.D.s from mediocre universities. The quality of both students and training had been steadily eroded by grade inflation, the pedagogical reforms in response to the "student movement," and the opening of universities to virtually all comers. Professorial salaries were devastated by several years of double-digit inflation unmatched by wage increases. "Stagflation" brought in a broad swath of budget cuts. Increasingly populist demands dictated a reallocation of shrinking resources away from research in the "pure" sciences and the more arcane subjects, and toward teaching and applied, technical pursuits.

Locally, the budget axe felled two thriving programs, the demise of which greatly impoverished the University of Washington and sadly reduced my intellectual engagement in it. One was African Studies and the other the Committee for the Comparative Study of Ethnicity and Nationalism. African Studies had been organized as a committee in the mid-1960s. As a matter of policy, we did not want to give degrees in the field, but a group of a dozen to fifteen faculty members offered a score or more of courses in anthropology, sociology, political science, history, art history, musicology, literature, and a half-dozen African languages. We had a number of graduate students, many of whom won language training fellowships. In addition to our varied curriculum, we organized an active visiting lecturer program, a number of concerts of live African music, several art exhibits from local collections (some with published catalogs), and free public lectures to the community.

All this cost the university some $10,000 a year (out of an operating budget of about $300 million). The courses were either part of our usual teaching or taught on top of our regular load. We hosted visitors in our homes and took them to dinner at private expense to atone for insultingly low honoraria. Yet we needed some minimal level of support to continue operating. When the financial crunch came, we started losing, by attrition, crucial faculty positions in history, political science, and comparative literature. Africa was defined as peripheral. It was normal for a department to have twelve or fifteen specialists on North America; one on Africa was a luxury. Finally, the dean let us know that the disappearance of the African continent from the curriculum map of the University of Washington was a small price to pay for a $10,000 saving.

The story of the Committee for the Comparative Study of Ethnicity and Nationalism was similar. Started in 1972 with seed funds from the National Office on Education, it was also niggardly funded by the university. Intended from the start to be a high-level graduate and faculty study group, the committee was primarily a vehicle to coordinate interdisciplinary doctoral studies in anthropology, history, political science, and sociology, and to organize each spring a lively seminar with a half-dozen or more speakers. Between us, we produced a score of Ph.D.s, and nearly all of our yearly seminars were published as special issues of journals or as edited volumes. We had our own publication series and achieved high international visibility, both individually and collectively. Hardly a year went by without each of us being invited to one or two international symposia on ethnicity. (In my own case, for instance, I was invited to Britain thrice, to the Netherlands twice, and to Italy and Mexico once, not to mention numerous domestic trips.) All these activities were, again, conducted on top of our regular teaching duties and cost the university a mere few thousand dollars a year in part-time secretarial assistance, air fares, supplies, and the like.

A seminar on ethnic tourism co-chaired in 1981 by Charles Keyes and myself, and published as a special issue of the *Annals of Tourism Research,* was our swan song. While our support was being cut back from little to nothing, the university was spending hundreds of thousands of dollars keeping alive moribund "ethnic studies" programs which, in contrast to ours, had a dismal record of academic productivity. By 1987, however, limited funding was restored, and I assumed the chair of the group. Perhaps the worst of penury is over.

In the face of these discouraging developments, I seriously considered relocating in Europe in the late 1970s. At that time, the dollar was weak, and European salaries looked attractive. In 1978, I applied for a chair in anthropology of development at the Free University of Amsterdam and, the following year, for a chair of anthropology at the University of Zürich. Neither application materialized into an offer, but the contrasting interview routines and politics of the two universities were both highly instructive and amusing. In both places, politics interfered with the appointment, but from opposite ends of the spectrum.

In Amsterdam, the university had become radicalized into a system that the Germans call *Drittelparität:* most committees running the university consisted of one-third students, one-third faculty, and one-third non-teaching staff, such as secretaries and janitors. The student union had been taken over by extreme left Trotskyite and Maoist groups, and the non-teaching employees by standard trade union organizations. The recruitment committee for the professorship consisted of six members, of whom only two were academics. The student members wanted to know whether I would allow students to make up reading lists in my courses; a secretary wanted to know whether I would object to secretaries taking their babies to work; a janitor quizzed me on my attitudes toward trade unions.

Later, when I went to visit the bursar to discuss salary, I expressed my concern on how a university could be run along such lines. "Ach, ja," he told me with a twinkle in his eyes, "but I control the purse's strings. The nonsense, you just ignore. And, if you cannot tolerate it, you just go home and draw your salary for life. Nobody can do anything to you once you are appointed." The appointment to this people's university, incidentally, is still by a formal letter signed by the Queen.

By then, I knew, of course, that my candidacy was dead. I still enjoyed my visit to Amsterdam, one of my favorite cities, and went through the motions of giving a seminar and a public lecture, between visits to the Rijksmuseum and the Van Gogh Museum. Both speaking engagements created a wave of intellectual shock when students discovered my interest in sociobiology. I was received in frosty silence rather than open hostility, for the politeness of the Dutch characterizes even student radicals, but the indignant stupefaction plainly visible on so many bright young faces was a joy to contemplate. I succeeded in *épater le prolétaire*.

Zürich, which I visited the following year, could not have been a sharper contrast. While Amsterdam was teeming with a rich fauna of South Moluccan militants, dishevelled student radicals in discarded army uniforms, gaudy prostitutes in their picture windows, hordes of drug addicts and "street people" in the parks, stridently assertive homosexuals, and sundry punks and skin heads from across the Channel, Zürich still presented the staid, respectable, affluent, orderly, immaculate bourgeois façade of a large Teutonic provincial town. Indeed, Zürich, untouched by World War II, was a picture postcard of Wilhelmite Germany. The financial center of Frankfurt is a forest of gleaming glass skyscrapers; the Paradenplatz of Zürich—that laundromat for the world's dirty money—is a low-rise huddle of banks, each a masterpiece of understated, stolid, turn-of-the-century bourgeois architecture.

Yet the first timid tremors of student radicalism were belatedly reaching even Zürich; but, this time, it was the establishment reaction that sank my appointment. My post was to have been a second chair of anthropology, and the discipline had recently come under fire in the Cantonal government (which finances the university). An anthropologist who had followed the radicals with a movie camera was accused of instigating the (very tame) "riots." The prudent plutocracy of Canton Zürich decided that this was not the time to build up such a dangerous discipline. The professorship was not filled, and the post was downgraded to a lectureship.

The late 1970s and early 1980s were marked by the publication of two more of my books, *Human Family Systems* (1979) and *The Ethnic Phenomenon* (1981), which attempted to apply sociobiology to two traditional social science areas, respectively, kinship and marriage in anthropology, and race and ethnicity in sociology. By subsuming both under a sociobiological umbrella, I also suggested a clear linkage between them. *Human Family Systems* was largely an endeavor to rethink the anthropology of kinship and marriage systems. Without seeking to minimize the importance of culture in defining both kin and affinal ties, I tried to show that the idiom of culture represents a fitness-maximizing adaptation of the biology of nepotism to a wide range of ecological, technological, economic, and political conditions.

Cultural codes, both in their observance and in their violation, can be shown to be related, directly or indirectly, to the behavior of individuals who seek to maximize their reproductive success. Nepotism (i.e., preference for kin over non-kin, and for close kin over distant ones) is a common denominator of all kinship systems, but different ecological and social conditions give rise to different solutions. Even within cultures, there is room for much variability. Rules favor individuals who make and enforce them and are violated by those whom they disfavor. Rules exist, not as disembodied, autonomous, deterministic systems, but as a cultural superstructure manipulated by fitness-maximizing actors to yield optimum results, whether in their observance, disregard, or violation. Rules, in the last analysis, are inferences from people's behavior, or rationalizations thereof, and, since most behavior tends to be adaptive, culture is basically an idiom whereby our species adapts its biology to its ever-changing environment.

The Ethnic Phenomenon was an extension of *Human Family Systems*. It treated "race" and ethnicity as extensions of kinship, as kinship writ large. Ethnic and racial groups are defined by common descent, real or putative, and thus ethnic sentiments are diffuse and extended applications of the principle of nepotism. Thus, ethnicity is indeed primordial, but this is not to say that it is unchanging. Ethnicity, like kinship, is a cultural idiom that is constantly manipulated by selfish maximizers.

Frustrated in my endeavors to get field research funded, but unwilling to settle into a deadly teaching routine in a single location, I tried to take at least one extended annual trip abroad during these years. Three extended tours of central and southeastern Mexico, a round in the Caribbean (Puerto Rico, Martinique, and Haiti), a Fulbright in Australia, a term of teaching at the University of Strasbourg, another in Tuebingen, and revisits to Guatemala, Egypt, Morocco, India, and Israel punctuated my residence in Seattle.

Trips to Canada, Mexico, Guatemala, and Europe were largely revisits of already familiar settings. Much as one finds familiar places pleasant and congenial, it is difficult to recapture the excitement and novelty of a first acquaintance. Besides, as with old friends and lovers, changes are rarely for the better. Thus, in Mexico, I had occasion to revisit the setting of my 1959 Chiapas field work and to see the great Maya archeological sites of Uxmal, Chichén Itzá, and Palenque for a second and third time. Each time, the image gets a little fainter; the landscape seems a little more worn and overused; the culture appears a little more polluted by tourism and consumerism. Blue jeans supplant homespun clothes; *perros calientes* displace *tamales;* the air-conditioned bus takes you where only the jeep penetrated before. The anthropologist is demoted to tourist. Cultures and places wear off on one, much as one's clothes and one's body.

Two new acquaintances of these years were Haiti (1980) and Australia (1982). The trip to Haiti was a fairly short one, taken with Eric and Oliver. It revealed the most extraordinarily African country in the Western Hemisphere, a Dahomean peasant society transplanted into the New World. Despite the beauty of the landscape and the artistic richness of the culture (evident in the exuberant production of "primitive" or "naive" paintings), Haiti is depressing because of its combination of abysmal poverty and oppressive tyranny. Ravaged by plantation slavery, exhausted by overpopulation, nearly totally deforested, Haiti ekes out a miserable existence from swidden horticulture. Even marine resources have been devastated by overfishing; Haiti has magnificent beaches, but the coral reefs, which elsewhere teem with life, are virtually stripped of life-forms larger than 10 centimeters. Downtown Port-au-Prince is a pungent, squalid slum, which only becomes livable as one climbs to the delightful heights of Kenscoff where the mulatto elite lives. Cap Haitien, the old French capital, is the decayed shell of a slave society. The most imposing ruin, the massive citadel overlooking Cap Haitien, is a monument to Henri Christophe's tyranny and megalomania, a political tradition perpetuated in the Duvalier dictatorship, *père et fils,* and its military aftermath.

Yet for all its squalor and oppression, Haiti has a vibrant culture, and the island's setting is starkly beautiful. If one learns to ignore the hordes of beggars and unemployed youths that dog one's footsteps and pester one until hired to keep the others at bay, one discovers a dignified, courteous, gentle, cultured people, ground down by three centuries of exploitation and tyranny.

My 1982 trip to Australia was a six-week lecture tour under Fulbright

Field work in Nebaj, Quiché, Guatemala, August, 1987. Contrary to rumors, I am inspecting the old Mauser of a civil patrolman, *not* participating in guerrilla warfare. Photo by David Stoll (whose apocryphal caption reads: "Professor van den Berghe sights Senator William Proxmire coming over the hill").

auspices, with a stay in Sydney (University of New South Wales), briefer visits in Brisbane, Melbourne, and Canberra, and a swing into the "outback," around Alice Springs and Ayers Rock. I found Australia at once more English and more African than I expected. Like many outlying parts of the empire, Australia has a Victorian aura. It is not only British, but British with a time lag. Visually, the impression is created by the ubiquity of the dour old Queen's statue and by the fact that most prominent public buildings date from that period: post offices, town halls, hospitals, army barracks, governor's mansions, prisons, and the like.

But there is more to it than mere architecture: the school uniforms, the sex- and class-segregated pubs, the bowling greens, the cricket, the Cenotaphs to the dead of imperial wars (I even found monuments to the Boer War), the cockney phonetics of the "broad" Australian dialect, the class consciousness (despite a strong ideology of frontier egalitarianism), the private schools, the universities (especially the older and more prestigious ones, like Sydney and Melbourne). Particularly striking is the salience of speech as a criterion of class placement: each utterance becomes a badge of class membership. Even Australian dictionaries recognize three dialects: broad, standard, and educated. "Educated" means BBC English.

At the same time, the sub-tropical setting of most of Australia gives the continent a colonial stamp. Australia is an Afrikaner's dream: a gigantic *veld* with hardly any blacks. Allowing for a few substitutions in fauna and flora (kangaroos for impalas, gums trees for acacias), the ecological setting of the "outback" is much like a sparse African savannah, say like Namibia or Niger.

The great skeleton in the Australian closet is, of course, the Aborigine. There are just enough of them left (a little over 100,000, including the "half-castes," out of a population of some 16 million) to give intellectuals a bad conscience, but not enough to make any political or economic difference. Because they are largely redundant to the economy, their plight is irrelevance rather than exploitation. Lacking the numbers and resources to mount an effective political movement, they can only appeal to the guilty conscience of whites. The outcome is a pernicious blend of paternalism and racism, which perpetuates the Aborigines' complete marginalization from every sector and region of Australian society.

Their plight is perhaps most visible around Alice Springs, that unlikely telegraph station in the middle of nowhere. There, the broken remnants of many small hunting-and-gathering societies camp out on the fringe of the white town, littering the nearby dry river bed with empty liquor bottles. Aboriginal unemployment hovers around 90 percent. People survive on government handouts. Most men, who at one stage were herdsmen on the huge cattle stations, have been superceded by modern technology: now roundups are done by helicopter; drives are in huge lorry trains. The Aborigines' hopeless situation makes that of Amerindians in Canada and the United States look enviable by comparison.

The highlight of my stay was definitely Sydney. With its lush subtropical parks, its hills and beaches, its stunning Opera House, its quaint Victorian neighborhoods, its vibrant downtown area, and, most of all, its vast harbor criss-crossed by sailboats, ferries, cargo ships, and water taxis, Sydney surely ranks, along with Rio, Capetown, Vancouver, and Hong Kong, among the world's most spectacular cities. It is also Australia's intellectual and cultural mecca, although citizens of Melbourne would not agree.

By contrast, the artificial capital of Canberra is like a miniature Washington, D.C.: a set of prettily laid out government buildings, but no

With Irmgard and our sons, Eric, Marc and Oliver, in our weekend retreat, Index, Washington, 1984.

real city. Walking down from the Australian National University campus one evening around 9 P.M., I found myself asking a rare pedestrian for directions to downtown. I was told that I was in the middle of it. The streets were nearly deserted, and I had trouble finding a restaurant that was still open.

For all their professional frustrations, the 1970s and 1980s were happy family times. We decided to have a third child. More accurately, Irmi, at age 44, confronted me with a pregnancy. Given her past history, I thought the risks were too high, but unwilling to face the prospect of an empty nest, Irmi was determined to have another crack at spreading her genes. As usual, she got her way. In this instance, of course, she had a near monopoly of control over the means of production. Our third son, Marc, was born on October 16, 1975, and we have been doting on him ever since, as have his brothers. In effect, we are almost a three-generation family. Eric and Oliver, 14 and 13 years older than Marc, are practically uncles to him, and Irmi and I, grandparents. With our more settled and secure existence, and the confidence of experience, we are able to be much more relaxed parents now than we were with our two older boys. Marc expertly manipulates our indulgence and shamelessly exploits his charm and our weakness.

This was also the period when we had the joy of watching Eric and Oliver survive the metamorphosis of adolescence with a minimum of travails and problems, and emerge into sensible, decent, civilized adults. This was in a period when drugs, trauma, and crises seemed de rigueur in most professional families. Many colleagues predicted that our old-fashioned, no-nonsense approach to child-rearing would backfire and provoke rebelliousness, but I am afraid we disappointed them. We had seen the past, and it worked.

Against the advice of many and the practice of nearly all of my colleagues, Eric and Oliver both stayed at home during their undergraduate studies and attended the University of Washington. They got a first-rate education in the university's selective honors' program, with all the benefits of faculty attention and small classes that the best liberal arts college could have offered. Both Oliver and Eric were strongly marked by their consuming passion for fishing. Eric became a zoologist and is currently finishing a doctoral program in behavioral ichthyology at the University of California in Santa Barbara. Oliver, more of a social scientist by inclination, took an M.A. in Marine Studies at the University of Washington, and is now a doctoral student in political science, specializing in Latin America, at the University of Texas. As smug "K strategists" (i.e., organisms that evolved for heavy parental investment in a small number of high-quality offspring), we feel that we have successfully launched three viable offspring into a highly precarious environment. They should do all right, if only the environment holds up a while longer.

CHAPTER 14

Some Musings on Human Behavior

Both my life experiences and my training as a social scientist have led me to a view of human behavior that the majority of my colleagues, and, indeed, fellow humans, find repugnant. Basically, the likes of me repel all believers. And humans find it very difficult and traumatic not to believe. By belief, I mean possessing a sense of destiny, of purpose.

Evolution (or God, if you prefer) played a dirty trick with us: it gave us the curse of self-consciousness. What an extraordinary by-product of a large brain self-consciousness is! We seem to share some glimmering of it with the great apes, but other animal and plant species seem to have done quite well without it. So why did consciousness evolve in humans? Its liability is obvious enough: the certainty of death, that is, of the inevitable extinction of consciousness. We invent God and immortality (or some secular version of them, such as history and progress) as an escape from existential Angst, but we are too clever to be fooled by our own cheap tricks. So there we are: the unexamined life may not be worth living, but the examined life is unbearable. God, should he exist, is the ultimate practical joker. Without consciousness, we are not human; with it, we strive to escape the inevitable conclusion to which it leads us: that self-consciousness is biodegradable.

Like all other organisms, we are biologically programmed to behave as selfish maximizers. Richard Dawkins put it even better: we play our genes' game of reproducing themselves through their "survival machines"—ourselves. Like all other animals, our behavior evolved by natural selection. Like tens of thousands of other vertebrate species, we evolved complex brains capable of adapting fast to environmental change by learning. Like hundreds of species of warm-blooded vertebrates, we acquired an ability to transmit socially our learned behavior.

But here the human plot suddenly thickened. We became so complexly and precisely attuned to each other that we suddenly (meaning, over a million years or so) loomed much larger in each other's environment. In other words, we began making our own history, as humanists would say. Self-consciousness, I suggest, is an evolutionary by-product of a more and more complex brain attuned to predicting and monitoring the behavior of other hominids. And the best way of predicting the behavior of others is to put ourselves in their place. That, in turn, implies self-consciousness. Intersubjectivity was born. The brain became a mind. The specifically human game was on in earnest. The tools were language and culture.

Unfortunately for the moralists, evolution favors deceit, cheating, and parasitism. Thousands of species blindly evolved seemingly ingenious ways of appearing to be what they are not: angler fish dangle tempting morsels in front of their prospective prey; tasty species mimic toxic ones to deter predators; small animals puff up to seem larger; birds feign injury to attract predators away from nests, and so on. These infinitely varied stratagems excite our admiration, and, as *self-consciously* deceitful animals, we frequently inject purpose into these marvels of natural selection.

Yet, with the possible exception of the great apes, we seem to have a monopoly of *conscious deceit*. Robert Trivers has even suggested that the evolution of deceit in reciprocity systems was one of the important factors in the hominid "brain race." If reciprocity is to work, deceit has to be controlled by detection. Growing brains invented more and more cunning forms of deceit, which, in turn, called for more and more sophisticated detection. We have, for instance, subtle behavioral clues to unmask insincerity. Artful lying is a difficult skill. The ultimate form of deceit is, of course, self-deceit. The best liar is the honest liar. Much of the ideological superstructure of culture—religion, values, political creeds, belief systems—consists of elaborate attempts to disguise motives and interests from oneself and from others.

A materialist view of human behavior that focuses on the individual actor as a wittingly or unwittingly selfish maximizer is thus powerfully *demystifying*. It strips away the ideological superstructures that hide much of the structure of human society. Practically all approaches to social science that bear resemblance to the real world and have some predictability make the same basic reductionist assumptions.

1. The basis of human society is material (and thus biological).
2. Society has no existence beyond its interacting individuals.
3. People selfishly maximize their utilities, as economists would say, or their fitness, in biological language. Overwhelmingly, the best predictor of cooperation and conflict is overlap or divergence of interests between individuals.

This extremely simple, parsimonious theory of sociality has taken many incarnations and assumed many labels. It underlies utilitarianism, classical and neo-classical economics, Marxian class theory, game theory, behaviorism, exchange theory, rational choice theory, and, of course, in modern biology, behavioral ecology. There simply is no other competing model of comparable scope and predictive and explanatory power. Far from threatening much of conventional social science, evolutionary theory *complements* it. A single unified model of culture *in* nature is gradually emerging. The model does not seek to deny or minimize the emergent properties of human culture. Rather it seeks to understand and explain these properties in relation to the biological base from which culture emerged and with which culture continues to interact.

The contributions of modern evolutionary biology to the social sciences are multiple, so much so that future development clearly lies in imbedding the social sciences in a firm biological matrix. Specifically, sociobiology has made at least two important addenda to conventional social sciences.

1. It reminds social scientists that, ultimately, culture is "carried" by individuals subject, like other diploid organisms, to the vagaries of sexual reproduction. Human sociality, like other forms of animal sociality, evolved in the last analysis, as a successful solution to raising babies. Most social scientists seem to have forgotten the "facts of life."
2. It provides us with a simple formula for analyzing nepotism, based on degrees of biological relatedness, as *one* of the mechanisms of human (and animal) sociality.

Nepotism—based on proportion of genes shared by common descent—defines a structure of overlap in genetic interests between individuals. Sociobiology does not predict that relatives always stick together. It predicts that, holding other relationships and interests constant, both conflict and cooperation between individuals are predictable from their degree of kin relationship and the cost-benefit ratio of their transactions. That ratio has to be lower than the coefficient of relationship (e.g., 0.5 between full siblings; 0.25 between half siblings; 0.125 between cousins, etc.) for nepotistic beneficence to take place.

The other two mechanisms underlying human sociality are reciprocity and coercion, both the object of considerable attention in conventional social science. In the absence of both nepotism or coercion, cooperation between two or more individuals is contingent on a net benefit to all parties. Many reciprocity systems are fragile because they are frequently parasitized by cheats and freeloaders, meaning all of us if given a chance. Stable systems of reciprocity, therefore, have to be policed: they must exclude and penalize parasites. This is relatively easy in small, stable groups of up to a few hundred individuals, where ostracism and informal pressures are quite sufficient to control cheating. In large and unstable groups, the problems of policing reciprocity quickly escalate, and coercion starts looming larger.

Coercion is, in effect, a special case of reciprocity. It consists in the use or the threat of force to maintain unequal relationships. Those at the losing end of the relationship are now trying to minimize losses rather than maximize gains, since they are forced to act in ways that conflict with their best interests. Although it exists in most human relationships (even within the family where it is based largely on sex and age differences), coercion quickly escalates with the rise of the state, that template for the systematic use of organized violence, both externally against other societies and internally against its own citizens. The state is, first and foremost, organized for external predation and internal parasitism. A mafia gang is a good prototype of a small, incipient state. Modern governments are big, complex, specialized, bureaucratic mafias.

Coercion and ideology go hand in hand. Because coercion is generally organized for the benefit of the few against the best interests of the many, those in power have an interest in making the powerless believe that they are being parasitized in their own best interest. This is what religious and secular ideologies are all about. Coercion is almost invariably disguised as either nepotism (e.g., paternalism in most pre-industrial states) or reciprocity (e.g., in both capitalist and socialist so-called democracies). Modern states try to make us believe that our taxes are merely a management or service fee we pay to our elected representatives and to our civil servants. Why is it, then, that the "servants" are so overwhelmingly better off than their so-called masters? In some states, for example, Zaïre, and in some international agencies, for example, UNESCO, nearly all of the budget supports the bureaucracy in a life-style many times above that of its constituents. And if the United States sanctimoniously got out of UNESCO, it was not because it would not be a party to such parasitism, but rather because the U.S. ruling mafia was consistently outvoted and outmaneuvered by Third World mafias.

Scratch an ideology, and watch an interest bleed. It follows from the above analysis that no ideological pronouncement can be accepted, except as a smokescreen for an underlying structure of interests. This is not to say that ideology is unimportant. Our capacity for self-deceit can give ideology a life of its own. But ideology is a superstructure derivative of a social structure, which, in turn, evolves out of a biological infrastructure. Social reality is the complex product of the interaction between biological infrastructure, social structure, and cultural superstructure.

It is hardly surprising that such a view of human behavior should be resisted and rejected. This is so primarily, I think, because it is demystifying. Our lives are constantly enmeshed in a web of social lies by which we hide our motivations and interests from ourselves and each other. Lucidity is intolerable. A social science that strips the social structure of its protective myths is profoundly subversive of all established order. But it is also profoundly disturbing of individual existence. Imagine, for example, a courtship constantly exposed to the participants as a fitness maximizing game wherein males and females pursue different strategies based on their different reproductive roles and in which each tries to cheat the other. The female deceives the male about her age; the male pretends to care more than he does, and so on. Scarcely a relationship would survive such an onslaught of honesty. No wonder sociobiology is under attack from all ideological quarters.

If there is a central theme to this account of my life, it is the problem of human inequality. These pages have been a running account of my encounters with tyranny and my attempts both to deal with it and to understand it. In the most intimate and continuous manner, my life experiences and my outlook as a social scientist have evolved in unison. My vocation as a social scientist came out of my rebellion against authority. Like most children, I became a rebel at age 2 or 3. The first whiff of rebellion comes with self-consciousness. What greater frustration than the sudden realization of the 2-year-old that he is being manipulated by his parents, his older siblings, and all those big people who overwhelm him in size and number? However, early childhood rebellion is quickly beaten out of us. We become "socialized," "civilized," "enculturated," tamed, really, for we are the only self-domesticating species. As Desmond Morris put it in *The Human Zoo,* we live in zoos of our own creation.

For me, the reawakening of self-conscious rebellion came around age 12, when I was a student of the Jesuits. In the double context of school and church, the Jesuits confronted me in early adolescence with a worthy target for my rebelliousness. A Jesuit college is a fine-tuned and complex machinery of thought-training and thought-control, honed through centuries of experience and buttressed by a sophisticated intellectual edifice of casuistry. In their historical mission of training an intellectual elite of defenders of the Faith, the Jesuits often produced an ironic outcome in their charges. As their world view is self-contained and provides an answer for everything, any serious engagement with it leaves little room between total acceptance and total rejection. Hence, the Jesuits have been unable to fetter many of the minds they so skillfully trained.

Later, I was to encounter other organized systems and ideologies designed to fetter the human mind and to thwart freedom and autonomy: the Nazi regime, the military, apartheid, and, generally, all state and private bureaucracies. None of them was as challenging and as formative as the Jesuits, because none of them was as intelligent.

Little by little, my attempts to come to terms with asymmetries of power led to the development of both a line of conduct and a world view. The line of conduct was that rules were to be evaded or manipulated to one's advantage. Given great disparities of power, it was unwise to attack the system frontally; instead, it was best to subvert it from within, to twist it in one's favor, to test its limits, to seek its loopholes, to exploit the weaknesses, absurdities, and internal contradictions of its ideology in order to undermine its legitimacy.

The world view I developed was the one that led to the theory of human behavior sketched above. My focus on inequality was especially fortunate because there is no better catalyst than the resentment growing out of inequality to call into the question of legitimacy of the social order and especially the ideological superstructure that seeks to justify existing relations of power and of production. To study inequality is to question the status quo. To understand the material base of society and the social relations that grow from control of, and competition for, resources is to understand how inequality emerges. To see ideology as self-serving justification helps explain how inequality is maintained. All these ideas were fundamental insights not only of Marx, but also of political theorists usually associated with the right, such as Gaetano Mosca, Vilfredo Pareto, and Robert Michels.

The second bit of serendipity, in my development as a social scientist, was my focus on the seemingly most irrational and ascriptive form of inequality, namely that based on "race" and ethnicity. The challenge of ethnicity and "race" as principles of social organization is that they seemed to be outside the purview of the rational, utilitarian modes of analysis that so successfully dealt with *class* relations (notably, classical economics, Marxism, and various forms of exchange theory). Ethnicity and race appeared to vary independently of class and, indeed, to have an atavistic, primordial character not readily explainable through simple, straightforward, rational instrumentalism as manifested in class relations.

The third element of good fortune in my choice of professional interests was my long-standing concern for kinship and marriage. For a long time, I accepted the artificial distinction between micro- and macro-level analysis of social phenomena. I believed there was a qualitative difference between scales of social organization that called for different methodological and theoretical approaches. Kinship was micro, while ethnicity was macro. Any resemblance between them, I long thought, was fortuitous.

More than anything, it was my Nigerian experience that made me realize the continuity between kinship and ethnicity. The outer rings of extended kinship around ego merged seamlessly into the wider rings of ethnicity. Ethnicity was a multi-level concept involving a scale of *nested* identities with ego at the core; the nuclear family next; then the extended family, the lineage, and the clan; and finally, several levels of ethnic membership based on increasingly broad and inclusive categories. Obviously, I was not alone in noting that ethnicity and "race" were based on notions of common descent and, thus, of extended kinship, nor in treating ethnicity as a layered concept expressing itself through principles of "fission and fusion." E. E. Evans-Pritchard, M. Fortes, E. K. Francis, C. F. Keyes, and many others have recognized the continuity of kinship and ethnicity. The interesting thing, however, is how little they made of it.

The missing link in the analysis was an *explanation* of why people tend to behave nepotistically, both in a narrow sense, toward kinsmen and, in a broad way, toward fellow ethnics. The sociobiological paradigm of maximization of inclusive fitness provided a promising hypothesis covering both kinship and ethnicity. It also parsimoniously solved many problems that had plagued social science in both of these areas. More generally, it provided a new way of looking at culture. Instead of treating culture as an almost infinitely plastic and arbitrary system of rules and values shaping the behavior of individuals through "enculturation," culture, in evolutionary perspective, is a flexible but non-random mechanism whereby we adapt quickly to a wide range of environmental changes (including those of our own creation). Culture is the specifically human way of adapting fast. It determines behavior in a direct, proximate way, but it is itself determined, within broad limits, by genetic constraints. Genes and culture *co-evolve,* in short, to produce human adaptation.

During the nearly three decades that have elapsed since I got my Ph.D., we have witnessed the beginning of an important paradigm shift in our approach to human behavior. In the 1960s, environmental determinism and cultural relativism were virtually unchallenged. American anthropology was at the forefront of the great ideological revulsion against social Darwinism and racism. From the 1920s, the Boasian battle-axe of cultural relativism was wielded triumphantly over the intellectual scene, and, by the 1940s and 1950s, Ruth Benedict and Margaret Mead had spread the gospel of anti-reductionism to the four winds of scholarly and lay discourse.

Parallel currents swept other disciplines. For example, behaviorism also threw the biological baby away with the racist hogwash. It attempted to explain behavior on the basis of an environmentalist ontogeny bereft of phylogeny. In common with psychoanalysis, it sought to explain away voluntarism and free will, but it also recoiled from biological determinism. At the very least, it left the biological foundation of behavior unexamined. Biology was a Pandora's box, left deliberately shut, in fear of what might come out of it. In sociology, the Durkheimian and Spencerian reification of a superorganic entity disembodied from its members and obeying laws divorced from individual behavior reigned supreme. Durkheimian structural determinism soon metastasized into British structural anthropology and American structure-functionalism. Our behavior was determined, to be sure, but by those structures that mysteriously emanated from individual interaction, not, perish the thought, by the constraints of the human animal.

That most successful of social sciences, economics, even though it shares both its intellectual ancestry and much of its conceptual apparatus with evolutionary biology, also managed to debiologize man and to produce deterministic models emanating from human interaction. The same became true of the Marxist tradition where modes and relations of production were treated as if they had developed in a biological vacuum. Engels, of course, knew better; in the preface to *The Origins of the Family, Private Property and the State* (1884) he reminded us that the material base of society is twofold: the social production of goods and services and the biological reproduction of human beings. Contemporary Marxists, however, would have us believe that we reproduce in order to produce, rather than vice versa.

SOME MUSINGS ON HUMAN BEHAVIOR

The social sciences are not alone to be blamed for the protracted dominance of this rampant behavioral Lysenkoism until the 1960s. Biologists were also slow in systematically applying the neo-Darwinism synthesis to behavior. Behavioral biology is still the soft underbelly of the discipline; the best brains are generally attracted by the more reductionist chemical and physical frontiers of the field. Consequently, the first thirty years or so of ethology were characterized by a descriptive natural history approach marred by group selectionism and only very loosely anchored in evolutionary theory and genetics. To be sure, the contributions of ethology constituted a valuable accumulation of raw data and, in their often crude popularized versions, served to convince an increasing number of people, and even some social scientists, that behavior as well as anatomy evolved by natural selection. However, the very crudity of human ethology (caricatured as the study of humans as if they did not talk) also created a vociferous environmentalist reaction.

The intellectual breakthrough of the mid-1960s, associated with the names of W. D. Hamilton, John Maynard Smith, George C. Williams, and others, had to await E. O. Wilson's book, *Sociobiology*. Sociology, as usual, is missing the boat, but anthropology and psychology are being profoundly transformed. Scarcely anyone in those fields doubts any more that behavior evolves genetically; that behavior is always the product of a complex interaction between genotype and environment; that the more complex an animal's brain, the more flexibly and rapidly it can adapt to its environment.

When we deal with humans, the discussion is still very heated; but in the past ten years discussions have been marked by a gradual shift in attitudes toward human sociobiology. Specifically, in anthropology, I have seen many of my colleagues move from outraged dismissal, to prudent skepticism, to polite interest, to qualified acceptance. In another decade, I expect, everyone will wonder what the fuss was all about. By then, both the quality and the quantity of the evidence in favor of gene-culture co-evolution will have increased considerably.

The main thrust of that evidence, I am convinced, is not going to reduce the crucial evolutionary importance of all the things that are specifically human: symbolic language, self-consciousness, culture, and so on. Rather, it is going to show that all these species-specific traits evolved by natural selection and continue to co-evolve with genes to produce our uniquely human adaptive trajectory. Our growing ability to modify our environment and to accelerate the pace of our adaptation does not nullify our genetic endowment. It makes an adequate understanding of gene-culture co-evolution all the more urgent. The consequences of our actions have become so drastic and so immediate that the price of biological self-ignorance is steadily mounting. Unless we start seeing ourselves as a biological part and parcel of a fragile planetary eco-system and controlling the devastating effect of our behavior on the biological system out of which we grew, and of which we are an integral part, we do not have much of a future.

B O O K S by Pierre L. van den Berghe

Caneville, The Social Structure of a South African Town. Middletown, Conn., Wesleyan University Press, 1964, 276 pp.

South Africa, A Study in Conflict. Middletown, Conn., Wesleyan University Press, 1965, 371 pp. Second edition in paperback by University of California Press, 1967.

Africa, Social Problems of Change and Conflict (editor, co-author, and translator). San Francisco, Chandler, 1965, 549 pp.

Race and Racism, A Comparative Perspective. New York, John Wiley, 1967, 169 pp. Paperback edition, 1969. Second edition with new Introduction, 1978, 203 pp. Spanish edition: *Problemas Raciales.* México, Fondo de Cultura Económica, 1971, 257 pp.

Ixil Country, A Plural Society in Highland Guatemala (with Benjamin N. Colby). Berkeley, University of California Press, 1969, 210 pp. Spanish edition: *Ixiles y Ladinos.* Guatemala, Seminario de Integración Social Guatemalteca, 1977.

Race and Ethnicity, Essays in Comparative Sociology. New York, Basic Books, 1970, 312 pp.

Academic Gamesmanship. New York, Abelard-Schuman, 1970, 116 pp.

Intergroup Relations, Sociological Perspectives (editor and co-author). New York, Basic Books, 1972, 327 pp.

Power and Privilege at an African University. Cambridge, Mass., Schenkman, 1973, and London, Routledge and Kegan Paul, 1973, 273 pp.

Age and Sex in Human Societies, A Bio-Social Perspective. Belmont, Calif., Wadsworth, 1973, 134 pp.

Class and Ethnicity in Peru (editor and co-author). Leiden, Brill, 1974, 94 pp.

Race and Ethnicity in Africa (editor and co-author). Nairobi, East African Publishing House, 1975, 357 pp.

Man in Society: A Biosocial View. New York, Elsevier, 1975, 300 pp. Second revised edition, 1978, 349 pp. Spanish edition: *El Hombre en Sociedad.* México, Fondo de Cultura Económica, 1984, 320 pp.

Ethnicity and Nationalism in World Perspective (with Paul R. Brass, co-editor). Special issue of *Ethnicity,* v. 3, n. 3, 1976.

Inequality in the Peruvian Andes: Class and Ethnicity in Cuzco (with George P. Primov). Columbia, Mo., University of Missouri Press, 1977, 324 pp.

Human Family Systems: An Evolutionary View. New York, Elsevier, 1979, 254 pp. Spanish edition: *Sistemas de la Familia Humana.* México, Fondo de Cultura Económica, 1983, 313 pp.

The Liberal Dilemma in South Africa (editor and co-author). London, Croom Helm, and New York, St. Martin's Press, 1979, 164 pp.

The Ethnic Phenomenon. New York, Elsevier, 1981, 303 pp. Second edition in paperback by Praeger, New York, 1987.

Tourism and Ethnicity (with Charles F. Keyes, co-editor). Special issue of *Annals of Tourism Research,* v. 11, n. 3, 1984, 198 pp.